THE CARETAKERS

War Graves Gardeners and the Secret Battle
to Rescue Allied Airmen in World War II

CAITLIN GALANTE DEANGELIS

 Prometheus Books

Essex, Connecticut

 Prometheus Books

An imprint of The Rowman & Littlefield Publishing Group, Inc.
4501 Forbes Boulevard, Suite 200, Lanham, Maryland 20706
www.rowman.com

Distributed by NATIONAL BOOK NETWORK

British Library Cataloguing in Publication Information Available

Library of Congress Cataloging-in-Publication Data Available

ISBN 9781633888999 (cloth : alk. paper) | ISBN 9781633889002 (epub)

∞™ The paper used in this publication meets the minimum requirements of
American National Standard for Information Sciences—Permanence of Paper for
Printed Library Materials, ANSI/NISO Z39.48-1992.

For

Staff Sergeant Pasquale J. Galante
27th Troop Carrier Squadron
U.S.A.A.F
Air Medal
Purple Heart
Distinguished Flying Cross

and

Dorothy Champagne Galante
Waterbury, Connecticut
Inspector of Parachute Cord
Heminway & Bartlett

CONTENTS

Northern France and Belgium

English Channel

BELGIUM

Dunkirk

Calais

Ypres

Wimereux

Saint-Omer

NORD

Boulogne

Lille

Montreuil

PAS-DE-CALAIS

Valenciennes

Scheldt

Arras

See Beaumont-Hamel Area map for detail

Cambrai

Abbeville

Bapaume

Somme

SOMME

Albert

Amiens

0   30

Miles

N

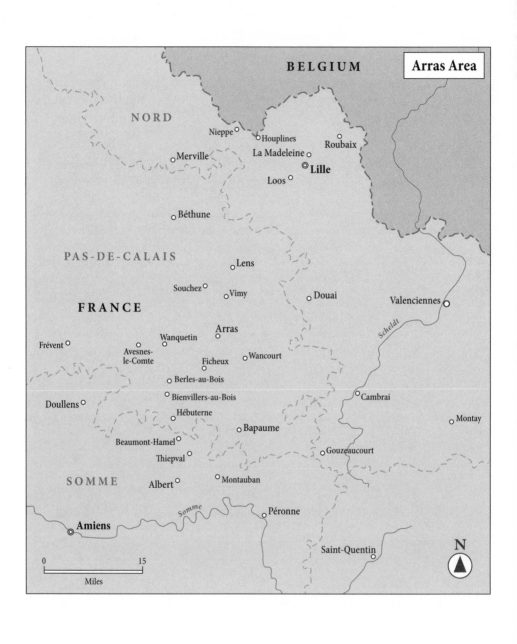

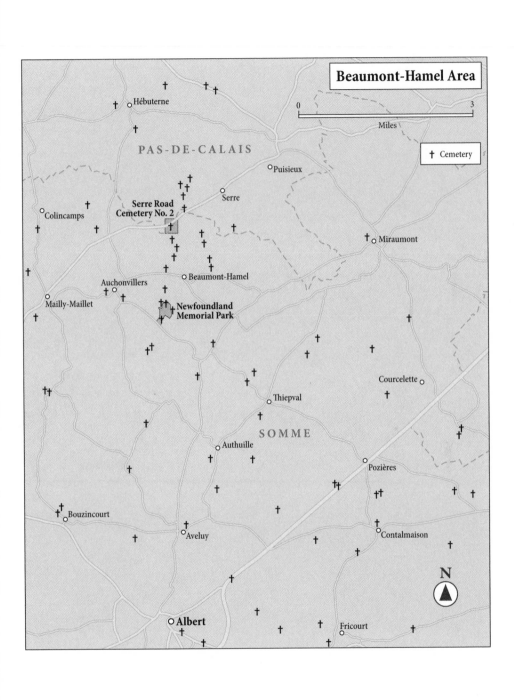

Beaumont-Hamel Area

0   3

Miles

† Cemetery

Hébuterne

PAS-DE-CALAIS

Puisieux

Serre

**Serre Road
Cemetery No. 2**

Colincamps

Miraumont

Beaumont-Hamel

Auchonvillers

Mailly-Maillet

**Newfoundland
Memorial Park**

Courcelette

Thiepval

SOMME

Authuille

Pozières

Bouzincourt

Contalmaison

Aveluy

Albert

Fricourt

N

PROLOGUE

S erre Road Cemetery No. 2 is the largest British military cemetery on
the battlefields of the Somme. Its thousands of brilliant white headstones stand stark against a long, emerald slope about a mile north of
Beaumont-Hamel, a tiny French village that never fully recovered from
the devastating battles of 1916. Nearly 70 percent of those stones bear the
famous epitaph composed by Rudyard Kipling, himself the father of a
missing son: "A Soldier of the Great War, Known Unto God."[1]

Every year, thousands of people visit Serre Road No. 2. Some are
pilgrims who come to leave a quiet offering on one special grave. Others
are tourists who come to contemplate the battles that churned the blood-
soaked fields for miles around. Others are schoolchildren who come because a trip to the Western Front is a part of their history curriculum and
Serre Road No. 2 has a parking area large enough to accommodate a pair
of coach buses.

Serre Road Cemetery No. 2. *Photo by author*

Serre Road Cemetery No. 2. *Photo by author*

But, of all these visitors, very few come to Serre Road No. 2 specifically to see its toolhouse.[2]

On the day I visited, northern France was in the midst of a drought. The grass was not as perfectly, lushly green as it usually is in the cemeteries maintained by the Commonwealth War Graves Commission, but the graves were still adorned with cheerful hollyhocks and a few brave roses. Tufts of sweet william evoked a cozy cottage garden despite the solemn grandeur of the cemetery's neoclassical architecture.

This is a central tension in British military cemeteries. The individual graves are intimate, sometimes heartbreakingly so. But the cemeteries, at least the large ones like Serre Road No. 2, are self-consciously grand. The once-blighted landscape is transformed into a stately oasis of monumental altars and pseudo-Roman temples. All the hideously mutilated bodies are buried under gleaming headstones; the infamous mud is carpeted over with velvety grass; the makeshift meanness of the trenches is replaced with graceful arches and columns. At the front of Serre Road No. 2, a bombastic neoclassical entryway looms over the quiet country road, all white stone majesty across from an indifferent beet field.

As I climbed the gentle slope from the road toward the towering Cross of Sacrifice at the back of the cemetery, I passed dozens of offerings left by earlier visitors. One grave was decorated with a wooden silhouette of a soldier resting on reverse arms. Another had a bright red poppy wreath left by a school group from Lancashire. Everywhere, stocky little British Legion crosses bore Sharpie inscriptions—"Lest We Forget," "Forever in Our Hearts," "For our tomorrow they gave their today"—often accompanied by a photograph of a doomed young man in khaki.

I had photograph as well. Mine showed a squat, square building with deep-set windows and knobbly cobblestone walls, tucked behind one of the elegant stone chapels. On the back, written in the careful, looping hand I had come to know very well in archives on both sides of the Atlantic, was a note:

To Major G. B. Simler in remembrance of his staying as guest? At Serre Rd No 2 Beaumont Hamel
Somme France
1944
B. M. Leech

Benjamin Morris Leech was a cemetery gardener who worked for the Imperial War Graves Commission. A veteran of World War I, he stayed in France to care for the dead rather than returning home to Manchester.

Photograph of Serre Road No.
2 toolhouse. *Sent to George
B. Simler by Benjamin Morris
Leech, courtesy of Mike Simler*

When the Germans invaded again in 1940, the War Graves Commission pulled out of France, but Ben remained in Beaumont-Hamel. All through the Nazi occupation, he continued to care for the graves at Serre Road No. 2 and, occasionally, offered his toolhouse to Allied airmen like 23-year-old Major George B. Simler of Pennsylvania.

I first came across Ben Leech in Martin Middlebrook's landmark book *The First Day on the Somme* (1971). In a brief aside, Middlebrook notes that Ben "helped twenty-seven Allied airmen to escape" by hiding them "in the cemetery toolshed." Middlebrook probably heard the story from Ben's youngest son, Arthur, who also worked as a War Graves gardener in Beaumont-Hamel.

But was it true?

I was intrigued both as a historian of cemeteries and as the grandchild of a U.S. Army Air Forces veteran. My grandfather, Staff Sergeant Pasquale J. Galante, was a radio operator with the 27th Troop Carrier Squadron, which flew C-47s over the Himalayas from India to support America's Chinese allies. As a child, I attended many of his reunions along with my siblings and cousins. We all listened to the stories that he chose to tell us, met his air force buddies, and knew the names of men who did not grow old with them.

Still, I was not sure whether my interest justified writing an entire book. At least, not until I read a letter from Ben Leech's son, Maurice, which was very kindly shared with me by historian Sherri Ottis. Maurice Leech was proud of the work his family did to save Allied airmen, but he—and his father—felt snubbed by the Americans.

"Our greatest disappointment was never to have received acknowledgment from the Air Force (only a diploma in 1945)," he wrote. "But later nothing else."

If anyone knows about repaying unpayable debts with years of mundane work, it is a cemetery gardener. I barely know a rose from a rhododendron, but I do know about the slow, quiet work of piecing together a story from old receipts and medical records, scribbled notes and self-interested reports, telegrams and photographs. The debt can never be repaid, but it can be remembered.

~

The Imperial War Graves Commission was chartered in 1917 with a royal mandate to "strengthen the bonds of union" within the British Empire by commemorating its war dead. More than a century later, the renamed Commonwealth War Graves Commission has shifted its emphasis away from the imperial part, foregrounding its commitment to memorializing each and every person within its remit. "We commemorate almost 1.7 million individuals," explains the Commission's website, "ensuring that all the Commonwealth men and women who died during both world wars are commemorated in a manner befitting their sacrifice."[3]

"All" is an ever-expanding concept. In its early years, the War Graves Commission decided that "all" would include the missing whose bodies were never identified as well as soldiers who were executed. After World War II, "all" grew to encompass civilians who died by enemy action, their names displayed on a special Roll of Honour in Westminster Abbey. More recently, work by Dr. Michèle Barrett and member of Parliament David Lammy has pushed the Commission to reevaluate earlier definitions of "all" that excluded as many as 350,000 "native" porters who died serving with the British in East Africa as well as between 45,000 and 54,000 Indian, Egyptian, Somali, and West African service members who were commemorated collectively rather than individually. In 2021, the War Graves Commission issued a Non-Commemoration Report that promised further research, consultation with descendant communities, and self-scrutiny. "These men were deprived of the equality in death that the IWGC had promised," the report states. "The unfinished work of the 1920s needs to be put right where possible."[4]

Efforts to make the category of "war dead" more inclusive will no doubt continue through the War Graves Commission's second century and beyond. New claims will be presented, new evidence will come to light, new forms of commemoration will take shape. Every expansion, large or small, will convey official, public respect for specific individuals and, by extension, for their families and communities. The Commission will remember them.

There is, however, a limit to the War Graves Commission's duty to remember. Its task is to provide equal commemoration for the war dead, not for survivors, even when those survivors were its own employees.

Over the past century, a gap has opened in the Commission's telling of its own history. The contributions of leaders like Sir Fabian Ware, advisers like Rudyard Kipling, and architects like Sir Edward Lutyens have been documented and celebrated, but much less attention has been paid to the ordinary employees—particularly the wage-earning gardeners, craftsmen, and mechanics—who performed the daily, unending, hands-in-the-dirt work of commemoration.[5] This goes double for "casual" laborers and people the Commission referred to as "local native gardeners," especially those who worked outside Europe, whose names were not systematically recorded.

In most cases, the only individual employee records preserved in the Commission's archives are "staff cards," index cards with brief notations about hiring dates and wages. At one time, each of the first-generation gardeners had a much more extensive personnel file, but the Commission destroyed all but a handful of them in the 1980s and 1990s. This was not done out of malice. Every archive weeds its collection, and the wage staff files—each of them stuffed with hundreds of pages of correspondence, employment records, personal information, and photographs—were considered workaday documents of little interest or historical value. Many of the officers' personnel files were preserved but, of the approximately 500 files belonging to gardeners who were employed by the Commission in 1940, more than 96 percent were destroyed.

There are other sorts of records, though. There are family stories and the memories of surviving children. There are cherished letters and photographs preserved by nieces and nephews. There are also the stories passed down in the families of the airmen that the gardeners helped save, scattered in little bits across the globe. The photograph I brought to Serre Road

Cemetery No. 2 was lovingly preserved by the family of George Simler, who kept a scrap of Ben Leech's dry humor tucked away with their family treasures and generously shared it with a stranger who e-mailed them out of the blue.

Researching the War Graves gardeners has meant digging through the files of American military intelligence (MIS-X), the British Special Operations Executive (SOE), and the French Ministry of Defense's Resistance dossiers, along with the records of Nazi prisons and courts. It has involved archival work in half a dozen countries and, when I have been very lucky, interviews with the children of gardeners. It also meant going back to cemeteries like Serre Road No. 2 with new eyes. I hope that more people will notice the toolhouse.

In 1940, the War Graves community in France and Belgium comprised 526 full-time employees, more than 1,000 wives and children of employees, and several hundred ex-employees and temporary laborers. This book will include glimpses of many of their stories, but it focuses on three.

Benjamin Morris Leech. *CWGC Archives*

Benjamin Morris Leech was a stubborn, cantankerous gardener-caretaker from Manchester. During World War I, he served as a corporal in the 18th Battalion Manchester Regiment, one of the famous "Pals" battalions that was decimated during the Somme Offensive in 1916. Ben joined the Imperial War Graves Commission as a blacksmith in 1920 but later became a gardener in Beaumont-Hamel. In 1940, he lived there with his French wife, Marie, and their four children, looking after a group of cemeteries that included Serre Road No. 2.

Robert "Bob" Armstrong was a gregarious, affable head gardener from County Longford in Ireland. He served as a sergeant in the 1st Irish Guards and was seriously wounded by a bursting shell in 1917. A professional gardener before the war, Bob took a post as a War Graves gardener rather than going home during the chaotic Irish War of Independence. In 1940, he lived in Valenciennes, a small French city near the Belgian border. Bob's Irish citizenship meant that he was a neutral, not an "enemy alien," under the Nazi occupation and probably could have stayed out of trouble if he had not fought back.

Robert Armstrong. *CWGC Archives*

Rosine Thérier Witton. *Courtesy of the Musée de la Résistance, Bondues*

Rosine Léontine Zoé Thérier Witton owned a *café-tabac* in Ronville, a working-class neighborhood in the northern French city of Arras. She was child refugee during World War I, fleeing with her family to the relative safety of Paris. After the Armistice, Rosine's family rebuilt their lives in Ronville, which soon became the heart of the War Graves community in France. In 1932, Rosine married Bert Witton, a gardener-caretaker who had served in the Royal Air Force. When Bert was arrested and interned in 1940, Rosine devoted herself to the Resistance. She counted many other French women from the War Graves community among her comrades.

Ben Leech, Bob Armstrong, and Rosine Witton were part of a community of ordinary people who dedicated their lives to commemorating the dead of World War I, only to be swept up in World War II. When the Imperial War Graves Commission ordered them to "stand to their posts," even in the teeth of the Nazi invasion, they were left behind in France. In the years that followed, they took on a new mission. They honored their commitment to the dead by caring for the living.

THE SOMME

1

Ben Leech was a stubborn man. His friends might have called him dependable. Trustworthy. Determined. Others were not so kind. More than one of Ben's colleagues at the Imperial War Graves Commission thought he was an inflexible, self-righteous pedant who once caused an international diplomatic incident over a few measly trees.

Whether they liked him or not, everyone could agree that Ben Leech was slow to commit himself to action—and implacable once he did.

"He is an honest type," conceded one exasperated War Graves officer, "although a nuisance at times with his demands for his 'rights.'"[1]

The summer of 1940 was no different. On May 10, the day Hitler's army invaded western Europe, Ben Leech received a direct order from his bosses. All gardener-caretakers in France, including Ben, had to remain at work in their cemeteries unless the local civil authorities explicitly ordered them to evacuate. If they abandoned their posts, they would lose their jobs and their pensions.

Ben noted the "last order of the I.W.G.C." in his daily gardening log: "stand fast until told to go by the mayor of the village."[2]

Within a week, the Germans advanced through Belgium and into France. They punched through a weak spot in the heavily forested Ardennes region and stormed across the border, stunning the Allied defenders. While the French and British rushed to counter the attack, seven German Panzer divisions swept across the old battlefields of the Somme, cutting a swath all the way to the English Channel. Their advance split the French army in two and trapped the bulk of the British army against the sea. Shocked, Allied troops fell back to the beach town of Dunkirk in hopes of rescue. Meanwhile, millions of civilians across Belgium and northern France fled their homes in a desperate bid to outrun the Germans.

Even in a crisis, Ben Leech was slow to act. His neighbors joined the throng of refugees clotting the country roads, but Ben carried on with his work. Overloaded farm carts and trucks full of soldiers clattered past the cemeteries, but Ben immersed himself in the whirr of his mowing machine. Back and forth between the rows of white headstones, he cut the early summer grass to a smooth, even height. Then he watered the roses. The War Graves Commission had instructed him to stand his ground unless he was explicitly ordered to retreat. No order came, so he did not leave.

The fighting drew nearer. On roads north and east of Ben Leech's home in Beaumont-Hamel, Luftwaffe dive-bombers dropped out of the clear sky, sirens screaming, to strafe the panicked crowds of refugees. Afterward, the roads were littered with abandoned luggage and burned-out cars. The dead—civilians and soldiers alike—lay unburied in the sun.

German tanks arrived in Beaumont-Hamel on May 20, just ten days after the beginning of the invasion. Ben watched the armored column roll past, but he struggled to realize what was happening. The disaster was too great, too sudden. He could only do what he had done thousands of times before.

"Tanks passed through Beaumont at 12:15," he wrote in his gardening log. "Went to cemetry and watered cutting."

The early days of the occupation were tense and unpredictable. Someone ransacked the Leech family's home. Ben's eighteen-year-old son, Maurice, was briefly arrested. In early June, ten Wehrmacht soldiers were billeted on the Leech family, crowding in with Ben, Marie, and their four children.

In the midst of the upheaval, Ben Leech focused resolutely on his work.

"Cemetries all correct," he reported on May 29, the day after his son was arrested.

All through the summer of 1940, Ben carried on. Some days, he pedaled his green, army-surplus bicycle up and down the swales of the Somme to check on graves near the towering Thiepval Memorial or retrieve tools from vandalized tool sheds in Pozières or Courcelette. Other days, he worked at Serre Road Cemetery No. 2, trimming its endless acres with a twelve-inch hand mower because he had no fuel for the larger motor mower.

The job was far too big. Soon, yarrow flowered in white clouds over the tops of the headstones, and moles frolicked in the once-smooth lawn.

"Grass has beaten me," Ben admitted in August.

That summer, a few other British gardeners remained in nearby villages, but most of them were arrested by German military police by the time the weather turned. They would spend the next four years freezing and starving in Nazi internment camps. Some never returned home.

By an obscure twist of fate, Ben Leech was never arrested. He packed a suitcase, fully expecting his turn to come, but it never did.[3]

Through it all, Ben Leech continued to tend the cemeteries. He had signed a contract to maintain the graves of his fallen comrades to the highest possible standards no matter the circumstances.

"They're my friends," he told his youngest son, Arthur. "They're still alive to me."[4]

What Ben Leech did not know was that the Imperial War Graves Commission no longer considered him an employee.

In London, Commission officials had consulted their lawyers. In light of the Nazi invasion, all the gardeners' contracts had been "terminated by the force of events."[5]

Ben Leech was on his own.

~

Benjamin Morris Leech was born on November 3, 1889, in Hayfield, an ancient village on the edge of the Peak District in Derbyshire. His mother's family kept the local pub, the Bull's Head Inn. At seventeen, Ann Brown married a railway engine driver named Robert Leech. Ben was the fourth of their twelve children and the eldest of eight sons.

When Ben was a toddler, Ann and Robert Leech moved their growing family away from sleepy Hayfield to the raucous, industrial city of Manchester. They settled their children on Railway Street in Openshaw, an eastern suburb recently gobbled up by the expanding city. Ben spent his childhood beside the tracks amid the clatter of trains and the perpetual coal-dust haze.

Ben Leech was a small, slight child with blue eyes and hair that a whimsical officer of the Manchester Regiment would one day describe as "golden" instead of the more usual "fair."[6] If he had been born a few decades earlier, Ben might have spent his early years scurrying under a loom in one of Manchester's thundering mills or wriggling through the narrow passages of a coal mine rather than learning to read. Instead, Ben and his siblings stayed in the classroom until they were thirteen or fourteen.[7]

This adequate education showed in Ben's letters, which were always composed in a careful, looping hand with decent spelling, except for the word "cemetery," which he rarely spelled the same way twice. His dry humor infused even the most routine correspondence. "My name is Benjamin Morris Leech," he once wrote in reference to a clerical error on an insurance policy. "Would you please correct this error . . . I do not wish to cause any trouble when I am dead, having caused enough in my lifetime."[8]

The Leech family were not the desperate poor whose plight had led socialist Friedrich Engels to call Manchester a "Hell upon Earth," but they were poor enough. Robert Leech earned a steady wage working for the Great Central Railway, but it was hardly enough to support such a large family. As soon as the children left school, they worked. Hetty sewed. William went into a textile factory. Roland joined their father on the railway as an engine fitter's apprentice.

Ben followed a different path. By the time he was twenty-one, he had returned to Hayfield and the Bull's Head Inn. He worked at the pub with his aunt and uncle for a while, then returned to Manchester and took a job as a barman at the Marsland Hotel in Ardwick.[9]

In August 1914, the outbreak of World War I jolted Manchester into a frenzy. Factories rushed to convert to war production. Newspapers trumpeted breathless accounts of early battles. The city's factory workers, students, and clerks clamored for their chance to fight. Many of these eager volunteers were funneled into the Manchester Regiment's "Pals" battalions, units made up of men from a single profession or neighborhood. By the end of the year, eight battalions of Manchester Pals—each a thousand strong—were drilling in the city's parks and parading through its streets.[10]

Ben Leech was not among them. He was an ideal recruit: twenty-four years old, able-bodied, and not employed in an essential job. But Ben, ever deliberate, did not volunteer. Instead, he stayed behind his bar, watching the Manchester Pals march off to war.

In fact, none of the Leech brothers was keen to get into khaki. Roland and William were old enough to serve, but they did not volunteer. Neither did seventeen-year-old Harry, who was officially too young but could have fibbed his way into the army like thousands of other boys. Instead, Ben Leech's brothers followed his lead and stayed home.

Over the next year, the giddy excitement of 1914 waned. Early hopes for a quick victory evaporated as the Allies suffered setbacks on every front in 1915. The first wave of enthusiastic volunteers had long since subsided, but the army was still hungry for healthy young men. When patriotic speeches and white feathers did not persuade enough of them to enlist, the British government passed conscription laws. The first draft was set for January 1916.

Before then, men like Ben Leech were given one last chance to "volunteer." The Earl of Derby, who had pioneered the Pals battalions early in the war, came up with an idea called the Derby Scheme. Under this plan, canvassers armed with the names of eligible men would hunt down "slackers" and badger them into making public promises to enlist. Refusal meant disgrace. Agreement often meant being forced to sign attestation papers—an official promise to serve—at once.[11]

Given this meager choice between volunteering under duress and being conscripted, Ben Leech finally signed his attestation papers on November 2, 1915.[12]

His younger brothers felt the pressure as well. Roland was exempt from the draft because of his essential job on the railway, but William and Harry were not. William enlisted a few weeks after Ben, signing his papers just three days before the Derby Scheme's final deadline. Harry did not volunteer. He was eventually conscripted.[13]

Ben Leech was called up in February 1916. His first experience as a soldier was being poked and prodded by a medical officer who translated his living body into data on a form: height: 5'3"; weight: 119 pounds; pulse: a bit too fast.

Ben's chest circumference fell well short of the girth required for ordinary infantry soldiers, but the doctor passed him anyway. The Manchester Regiment needed every man it could get.[14]

The original Manchester Pals had trained for more than a year before shipping out to France, but Ben Leech was hustled through a truncated four-month training course before being sent to the 18th Battalion as a replacement. The 18th had spent a dismal winter in the trenches in France but had not seen much hard fighting yet. That was about to change. Summer was upon them, and with it one of the most catastrophic days in British military history.

~

The British army's main goal in the summer of 1916 was to divert German resources from the massive, ongoing offensive against the French at Verdun. The plan called for a joint French–British offensive in the Somme department, about ninety miles north of Paris. After a weeklong artillery barrage, massed British infantry would attack along a twelve-mile front from the village of Serre in the north to Montauban in the south. The French would advance simultaneously farther south. If they could threaten to break through, the Germans would be forced to divert men and guns from Verdun to stop them.[15]

Ben Leech reached the 18th Manchesters' camp on June 21, 1916, a week before the planned attack.[16] His new comrades were already deep in their preparations for the great offensive. Their brigade was tasked with capturing Montauban, a village at the southern end of the British line. The 16th and 17th Manchesters would lead the attack, supported by the 18th Manchesters and the 2nd Battalion Royal Scots Fusiliers. For weeks beforehand, they practiced on a life-sized replica of the battlefield laid out with flags and dummy trenches in a farmer's field. Over and over again, the men practiced taking Montauban.

"They know every house," wrote 2nd Lieutenant Kenneth Callan Macardle of the 17th Manchesters. "They know every yard. Where every man is to go."[17]

On Ben Leech's fourth day with the battalion, June 24, the opening salvos of the artillery barrage split the sky. The 18th Manchesters were still miles behind the front line, but it was impossible to escape the constant, rolling roar of the guns. The Germans hid in their bunkers, unable to bring in food or water, unable to sleep as the ground shuddered above their heads. Ben and the rest of the Manchester Pals continued running their drills, hoping that the artillery would clear their path to victory.

Unfortunately, the artillery barrage was more spectacular than it was effective. Many of the British shells were too small to damage the German bunkers. Even powerful mines packed into tunnels beneath the German fortifications did not fully destroy them. At Hawthorn Ridge, near Beaumont-Hamel, British engineers detonated an eighteen-ton charge under a German redoubt minutes before the infantry attack, rocking the earth for miles around and sending a fountain of debris hundreds of feet into the air. The awe-inspiring explosion created one of the enduring images of the Great War, but it did not dislodge the Germans from Beaumont-Hamel.

When British infantry went "over the top" on the morning of July 1, they stepped into a murderous field of fire. German machine guns covered the ground from every angle, firing so ferociously that the water used to cool their barrels boiled away. Advancing British battalions were scythed like grain. Some of the worst casualties were concentrated around Beaumont-Hamel. The Royal Newfoundland Regiment, which attacked near the fresh crater on Hawthorn Ridge, lost nearly 90 percent of its men. Few of them got anywhere near the German trenches.[18]

Farther south, the attack on Montauban was more successful. The 16th and 17th Manchesters suffered horrific casualties but reached the pulverized remains of the village—"a monstrous garbage heap stinking of dead men and high explosive"—and held on.[19]

Ben Leech and his comrades in the 18th Manchesters spent the day running back and forth, retrieving the wounded, taking custody of prisoners, and delivering ammunition and water.

"All carrying parties had casualties on the way up caused by machine gun fire and shells," reported Lieutenant Colonel William Smith, the 18th Manchesters' commanding officer. "The loads were found to be very heavy, especially in view of the heat and most men arrived in an exhausted condition." The work was debilitating for a small man like Ben Leech. Nevertheless, it had to be done. "All parties went back for more loads and no time was lost."[20]

At the end of the day, the British held Montauban, one of their few toeholds in the German line.

Although the 18th Manchesters played a supporting role, more than 20 percent of the battalion's men were killed, wounded, or missing on July 1.[21] These casualties could only be called "light" in comparison with the calamities elsewhere along the British line.

During the next four days, Ben Leech had his first experience caring for the war dead. The 18th Manchesters sent out "burying parties from all co[mpan]ys for clearing the battlefield." Ben and his comrades carried corpses, gathered scattered remains, and dug graves.[22]

The date July 1, 1916, is infamous, but for Ben Leech and the 18th Manchesters, it was only the first day of a gruesome month.

On July 9, they took part in the assault on Trônes Wood, a thick patch of forest near Delville Wood. Ben Leech and his comrades had barely taken up their position before they were hit with an earth-shattering artillery bombardment. They hunkered down in shallow ditches while the trees exploded overhead. All along the line, men were obliterated by shell fire, pierced by lethal splinters, and crushed by falling trunks. In short order, the 18th Manchesters lost 266 men and eleven officers, including Lieutenant Colonel Smith, who was fatally wounded.

Worse was yet to come. At the end of July, the battalion participated in a fruitless dawn assault on the village of Guillemont that left 470 men and fourteen officers dead, wounded, or captured. The few survivors staggered back across an open field, where they were picked off one by one by German riflemen.[23]

By the end of July—Ben Leech's first full month in France—the 18th Manchesters had suffered 1,035 casualties, about 125 percent of the battalion's original strength.[24]

Somehow, Ben Leech survived the month without physical wounds. Over the next two and a half years, he lived through many major battles, including the Battle of Arras in the spring of 1917 and the Passchendaele campaign the following summer. Old pals and new replacements fell by the hundreds, but Ben—a corporal now—remained. His only physical injury came in 1917, when he scalded his hand. It was serious enough to mention in his service record but not serious enough to require hospital care.

Despite three years in a frontline infantry battalion, Ben Leech was counted as a battle casualty only once. He was reported missing on March 21, 1918, the first day of the German spring offensive. "Missing" sometimes meant that a soldier was captured, but it often meant that he had been blown to bits or sucked down into bottomless mud or killed in some other way that made his body unrecoverable or unrecognizable. For Ben, "missing" merely meant that he was temporarily separated from his battalion. He rejoined them a week later.[25]

Ben's younger brothers were not so fortunate. William was killed in action near Kut, in modern-day Iraq, on January 9, 1917. Harry, the youngest of the three, arrived in France on March 29, 1918. He was dead within a month.[26]

After the Armistice, Ben Leech could have gone home to Manchester. England did not have much to offer its war-weary veterans, but he could have asked for his old job at the Marsland Hotel or returned to the Bull's Head Inn. But going home meant leaving William and Harry and all the others behind. Ben did not speak of it often, but when he did, he acknowledged that the dead were never wholly dead to him. He had obligations.

There were obligations waiting for him in Manchester as well. In September 1916, about eight months after Ben was called up, a woman named Agnes Groves—a barmaid at the Marsland Hotel—gave birth to a baby boy. She named him Benjamin Leech Groves. Ben never formally acknowledged the baby, nor did he allot any of his pay to Agnes, but she applied for a dependent's pension when he was reported missing.[27] Her application was nullified when Ben turned up alive.

It was all too much. Ben had not been eager to go to France, but neither was he eager to leave. When he was demobilized in January 1920, Ben decided not to return to Manchester. A new organization, the Imperial War Graves Commission, was recruiting craftsmen, mechanics, and gardeners to build a vast archipelago of cemeteries and monuments. Ben applied for a position as a blacksmith's laborer. He would stay in France with the dead.[28]

~

When World War I began, the British army did not have a comprehensive plan for burying its dead.[29] In previous wars, the bodies of officers were sometimes brought home by wealthy families, but ordinary soldiers were usually consigned to anonymous mass graves. After the Battle of Waterloo in 1815, looters picked over soldiers' corpses for anything of value, including their bones, which were dug up by local civilians and used as a filtering agent in the production of beet sugar.[30] During the Crimean War (1853–1856) and the Boer War (1899–1902), some British soldiers were buried in cemeteries, but the government did not pay to maintain their graves. Volunteer organizations did what they could, but without reliable funding, most soldiers' graves soon returned to dust.

Across the Atlantic, a different form of official, government-funded commemoration was taking shape. Between 1861 and 1865, the U.S. government mobilized 2 million citizen-soldiers, most of them volunteers, to fight in the American Civil War. One in six died.[31]

The Civil War was a cataclysm that remade both civil society and the state. It shattered expectations about who should die and how their bodies should be treated. The confluence of many long-term trends—the idea of the "good death," new technologies for transportation and embalming, more efficient postal services, the rise of popular fiction, the colonial myth of inexhaustible resources, public rhetoric about democracy—all led soldiers and their families to expect that their lives should end with meaningful, emotionally satisfying, well-commemorated deaths. At the same time, the U.S. government was asking its citizens to die so that the nation might live. Together, they created a new, mutual obligation: citizens would die for the country, and their government would treat the war dead as precious individuals, not as cogs in the machinery of war. Public funds would turn the space that fallen soldiers filled in the national imagination into permanent, tangible landscapes. In 1862, Congress authorized the creation of the first national military cemeteries, vowing to commemorate all those who had given "the last full measure of devotion."

This was an unprecedented undertaking. Edmund Burke Whitman, the first superintendent of National Cemeteries, observed that "such a consecration of a nation's power and resources to a sentiment, the world has never witnessed." The National Cemeteries were part of the massive growth of the bureaucratic state in the years after the Civil War. Their universal rhetoric—every body recoverable, every name knowable, every grave eternal—expressed a fantastical optimism about data, logistics, and administrative capacity. By 1871, the first seventy-four national military cemeteries contained more than 300,000 graves. Soon after, the program expanded to offer small, white government-issue headstones to all Union veterans. Ordinary citizen-soldiers would be named and honored as precious pieces in the mosaic of the modern democratic state.[32]

The national cemeteries were also symbols of the federal government's power. Many were built on disputed land in the South and West, where flying the U.S. flag over the bodies of its soldiers was a clear—and often unwelcome—declaration of government authority. The most famous of these contentious sites was Arlington National Cemetery, built in 1864 on a liberated plantation owned by the family of Confederate general Robert E. Lee. Like the other national cemeteries, Arlington became a place to honor individual soldiers as well as a promise that the reunified nation would endure as long as its monuments: forever.

People in the United Kingdom experienced many of the same religious, cultural, and technological trends as Americans during the nineteenth century, but the public's relationship to the army was not the same.[33] Unlike the mass citizen armies of the American Civil War, the British army of the late nineteenth century was a small, professional force whose main task was to police Britain's global empire. Officers were drawn from the upper classes, but, as a group, ordinary soldiers did not have limitless claims on public sympathy—or funds.

World War I changed that. British leaders explicitly framed the war as a battle "for the very existence" of the empire. They urged every person in the United Kingdom to "do their bit" in a crusade to save civilization itself. This mass mobilization touched every family. Once the beloved sons of every town, every sect, and every class were in khaki, their deaths became a matter of tremendous political consequence. No one would be grinding their bones to make sugar.[34]

Still, there was no centralized plan to bury them, let alone commemorate each and every one. Early on, a patchwork of individual military units, hospitals, and the Red Cross kept haphazard burial records, but there was no unified system. A few comprehensive policies did emerge, notably a 1915 ban on repatriating the bodies of those who died overseas. Recovering, packing, and shipping human remains in the middle of a war was a logistical nightmare. It was also a political minefield. Would only the wealthy be able to bring their boys home? What about men whose bodies had been obliterated? What would an endless funeral procession wending through every town and village do to the nation's morale?

The man most responsible for creating a comprehensive burial and commemoration plan for British and dominion forces was the founder of the Imperial War Graves Commission, Major General Sir Fabian Ware.[35]

When the war began, Ware was neither a general nor a sir. He emerged from the ranks of tireless middle-class civil servants whose energetic faith in English "civilization" kept the merciless wheel of empire turning. Ware cut his teeth in Lord Milner's proto-apartheid administration in South Africa and believed that the British Empire was the pinnacle of human achievement. In 1912, he published a book, *The Worker and His Country*, which argued that the eternal tension between "individualism" and "collectivism" was perfected in the British Empire, which was "a unity composed of unities." Patriotism in service of the empire was, to Ware, the "supreme virtue of the human order," for which "no renunciation and no sacrifice will ever be thought too great."[36]

Ware was too old to fight in World War I, so he volunteered for a Red Cross ambulance unit in France. When he observed the army's disjointed approach to war graves, he deputized himself to devise a better plan. In 1916, the army formalized his work by giving him command of the newly created Directorate of Graves Registration and Enquiries. In 1917, he was named the founding vice-chairman of the Imperial War Graves Commission.

The War Graves Commission's mission was to commemorate the British Empire's million war dead in perpetuity. It was an impossible task. No one, no matter how boundless their resources or how noble their intentions, could achieve perfect, eternal commemoration. There were too many dead, too many missing, too many grieving families with their own religious beliefs, emotional needs, and political commitments.

The logistical problems alone were overwhelming. How to design and build thousands of permanent cemetery plots across multiple continents, often in places where the war had obliterated basic infrastructure? How to remember the missing and those buried at sea? How to collate and correct a colossal morass of data? How to recover and, when possible, identify hundreds of thousands of bodies?

Sir Fabian Ware's own guiding star was, as ever, the empire. He saw the commemoration of the war dead as an opportunity to bind the increasingly independent-minded dominions together with a shared commitment that would last forever. Soldiers from the dominions would be honored with meaningful symbols on their headstones—maple leaves for Canadians, silver ferns for New Zealanders, caribou for Newfoundlanders—but the main goal was to foster imperial unity.[37]

Sir Fabian's vision of imperial cohesion shaped the War Graves Commission's organizational structure as well as its cemeteries. The dominions of Canada, Australia, New Zealand, South Africa, and Newfoundland were all allowed to appoint a commissioner who would sit equal among the others. India and the other colonies were not. They were nominally represented by the English politicians who held the posts of secretary of state for India and secretary of state for the colonies. Each participating government contributed to the budget in proportion to its graves, from the United Kingdom's 81 percent to tiny Newfoundland's 0.14 percent. By working—and paying—together to honor the "common sacrifice" of the empire's war dead, the Commission aimed to "promote a feeling of common citizenship and of loyalty and devotion to [the Crown] and to the Empire of which they are subjects."[38]

From the beginning, the Imperial War Graves Commission was a paradox. It was technically an independent corporation, but its money came from public funds. Its president was the Prince of Wales, and the British secretaries of state for war—including Winston Churchill—served as its chairman. The Commission was also nominally civilian, but it had a "semi-military nature."[39] Its officers were not active-duty soldiers, but they held honorary military ranks; its gardeners were Crown servants who lived abroad, but they were not part of the foreign service. These slippages—private versus public, civilian versus military, domestic versus foreign—would cause widespread, ongoing confusion at every possible opportunity.

One guiding principle that would evolve over the decades was the Commission's commitment to "equality of treatment." In the 1920s, this term referred to the policy of making no distinctions of rank or class in Commission cemeteries. A private and a general, a railway worker's son and a lord, might lie side by side, their headstones indistinguishable except for the inscriptions.

This "equality of treatment" did not apply to hundreds of thousands of service personnel outside of Europe. Some Indian and Egyptian soldiers were commemorated unequally on monuments inscribed with overall numbers rather individual names. In East Africa, the Commission decided not to individually commemorate as many as 350,000 "native" porters and laborers who died serving with the British army. Even in cases where reliable records of these burials existed, British officials argued that preserving the individual graves of laborers from Kenya, Tanzania, and Uganda would be a "waste of public money." They decided that the graves should be "allowed to revert to nature as soon as possible."[40]

The white British public did not raise a fuss about the non-commemorations in East Africa in the 1920s, but they did have plenty of other complaints about the War Graves Commission. Leftists decried the millions of pounds spent honoring the dead while living veterans starved and went homeless. "DON'T FORGET THE UNKNOWN WARRIORS LIVING," read a handbill distributed at the Cenotaph in London on Armistice Day 1921. Meanwhile, aristocrats attacked the Commission from the right, calling its equal treatment policy "National Socialism" and declaring that "the conscription of bodies is worthy of Lenin."[41]

One of the Commission's most controversial policies was the repatriation ban. The war dead would be revered "for evermore," but they would not be returned to their families. Instead, they would rest among their comrades in foreign fields. Their bodies would become the building blocks of a monument that spanned the globe, preserving the names of individuals within a grand display of imperial unity.

Grieving families had reconciled themselves to overseas burials during the war, but many assumed that they would be able to bring their beloved dead home once the fighting stopped. When mourners learned that the repatriation ban was permanent, they responded with a wail of despair.

"Is it not enough to have our boys dragged from us & butchered, (& not allowed to say 'nay') without being deprived of their poor remains?" one mother wrote in an anguished letter to the War Graves Commission. Thousands more signed petitions begging for the repatriation policy to be overturned. In the House of Commons, a member of Parliament thundered, "You have no right to take the precious remains of bereaved widows, parents and orphans and build them into a monument which is distasteful and hateful to those relatives, as it in many cases is." One resolute Canadian mother traveled to France and bribed someone to open her son's grave. After cutting through the zinc lining of his coffin, she scooped out his remains and carried him home to Toronto in a suitcase. Other parents accepted that their sons' bodies would never come home but arranged for their own ashes to be taken to France and scattered on their graves.[42]

The Commission's cemeteries and monuments held tremendous personal and patriotic meaning for civilians and ex-servicemen alike. Many families who had no grave to visit found comfort in the idea that their loved ones might lie under the Commission's iconic "Known Unto God" stones. They could also visit the Menin Gate or one of the other memorials to the missing, where their beloved's name was carved in stone.

Others hated the monuments. The poet Siegfried Sassoon was famously disgusted by the Menin Gate, abhorring the way it sanitized and glorified the fundamental obscenity of the war. "Who shall absolve the foulness of their fate,— / Those doomed, conscripted, unvictorious ones?" Sassoon asked in his poem "On Passing the New Menin Gate" (1927):

> Here was the world's worst wound. And here with pride
> "Their name liveth for ever," the Gateway claims.
> Was ever an immolation so belied
> As these intolerably nameless names?
> Well might the Dead who struggled in the slime
> Rise and deride this sepulcher of crime.

Sassoon's fury burned bright, but so did the grief of millions with more conventional taste. The War Graves Commission took just as much criticism from "heartbroken parents, wives, brothers, and sisters" who were offended that the sturdy headstones were only engraved with crosses rather than shaped like crosses. Thousands signed petitions demanding cross-marked graves that would allow Christian mourners to "carry on the life from which all the sunshine seems to have gone." In a sop to these petitioners, the Commission amended its designs so that every cemetery with more than forty graves would contain a large Cross of Sacrifice.[43]

Menin Gate. *Photo by author*

While the Commission weighed these various decisions, Graves Concentration Units scoured the shell-blasted countryside of the Western Front for isolated graves. Some were easy to find because they were marked by temporary white crosses. Many were not. The searchers combed the battlefields in grids, looking for sunken ground or patches of unusually bright vegetation that might mark a shallow grave. Sometimes, they found remains because rats brought small bones to the surface. When they found a likely spot, they dug.[44]

One of the men they found was Ben Leech's younger brother Harry.

Harry Leech was twenty years old when he was killed on April 24, 1918, during the German attack on Villers-Bretonneux.[45] The battle is famous for being the first tank-to-tank battle and for the role of Australian troops, who helped retake the town on April 25, the anniversary of the Gallipoli landings.

Harry Leech was not part of those well-known stories. No one knows whether he was killed in the predawn artillery barrage, by the advance of the German tanks, or by the gas attack that accompanied it. When his battalion retreated to a fallback position after being flanked by the tanks, only thirty men were capable of shouldering their rifles. Harry was left behind on the field, missing, presumed dead.[46]

Two years later, a Graves Concentration Unit found Harry Leech's remains. They sifted his bones and the shreds of his uniform until they found some legible object that allowed him to keep his name. Then they carried him to Crucifix Corner Cemetery and buried him between a Canadian lieutenant and a member of the Royal Flying Corps in a row of men brought in from lonely graves in the nearby fields. The army sent Ann Leech twelve shillings in back pay and a £6 war gratuity, but the War Graves Commission kept Harry's body.[47]

Ann Leech was a poor widow. Even though her eldest son lived only twenty miles from Villers-Bretonneux, there is no record of her ever visiting Harry's grave, let alone William's in Iraq. She may not have had the money or the health for such a journey. Still, like so many others, Ann Leech carried her grief to her own grave. When she died in 1930, her family added William's and Harry's names to the headstone she shared with her husband, along with a simple epitaph: RE-UNITED.[48]

~

Kings sign charters and architects draw plans, but nothing is built without labor. The leaders of the Imperial War Graves Commission imagined a global necropolis "greater than that of the Pharaohs," but workers like Ben Leech made it real.[49]

At its peak in 1922, the War Graves Commission employed more than 2,600 workers, most of them in France and Belgium. They also relied heavily on "casual" labor, especially in cemeteries outside of Europe. Local contractors were wholly responsible for construction and gardening in Egypt, Palestine, Iraq, Turkey, and a dozen other countries and colonies where the Commission employed only a handful of full-time white British supervisors.[50]

Ben Leech was employed directly by the Commission in France. He started as a blacksmith's laborer in 1920, then earned his qualification and became one of the Commission's nine principal blacksmiths.

As a blacksmith, Ben Leech's most important task was keeping the endless parade of gardening tools in good repair, but he also contributed directly to the fabric of the cemeteries. The huge bronze crusaders' swords affixed to the Crosses of Sacrifice were forged by contractors, but Ben and his fellow blacksmiths installed them on-site. They also made weatherproof boxes to hold each cemetery's register and guest book and fabricated custom-designed gates.[51] By 1929, Ben and his fellow workers had completed 883 freestanding cemeteries in France and Belgium, along with many hundreds of smaller plots in French civil cemeteries. They erected 541,136 headstones and inscribed another 185,400 names on the memorials to the missing.[52]

Working for the War Graves Commission meant settling permanently in the borderlands between the living and the dead. Many employees found this comforting. The quasi-military structure of the Commission offered a gentler transition to civilian life than the abrupt "demobbing" that most ex-servicemen experienced at the end of the war. The work was grueling, but it was also constructive. Plants grew. Beautiful gates took shape under their hands. Every hammerblow and clip of the pruning shears was imbued with purpose and meaning, a tiny service to the comrades who would never grow old with them.

War graves work had spiritual and psychological dimensions, but most of Ben's fellow workers also had practical reasons for seeking a job with the Commission. French Canadian gardener Arthur Kirouac initially returned home to Northampton, Massachusetts, with his young French wife, Leonora, but she was so homesick that they soon packed up their infant son and returned to the bombed-out ruins of the Somme. Albert Douglas Chapman could have returned to Canada, but he was in love with Bertha Tally, the daughter of an egg-and-chip shop owner in Poperinghe. Henry Hayler, a professional gardener before the war, returned to England and took a job on a rich man's estate near Hastings. One day, the lady of the house asked Hayler to drive her into town for some shopping. When they returned, Hayler's drunken employer accused the gardener of taking liberties and threw a punch. Hayler hit back, then quickly packed his bags. France was probably safer.[53]

Like Ben Leech, many War Graves gardeners had brothers buried in the Commission's cemeteries. Among them was Robert "Bob" Armstrong, an Irish gardener who had been a lance sergeant in the 1st Battalion Irish Guards. His younger brother, Private James Henry Armstrong of the 2nd Battalion Irish Guards, was mortally wounded at the Battle of Loos in 1915. He died alongside Rudyard Kipling's son, John, who was a junior officer in the same battalion. Both boys were eighteen.

Both Bob Armstrong and Rudyard Kipling dedicated the rest of their lives to remembrance work. Kipling served as the Imperial War Graves Commission's literary adviser, composing epitaphs and choosing appropriate quotations for memorials while simultaneously writing a two-volume regimental history of the Irish Guards. He also wrote a short story, "The Gardener" (1925), in which an all-knowing, all-loving being appears to a bereft mother in the form of a cemetery gardener. Bob Armstrong was not a divine incarnation, but he guided many mourners to the graves he cared for year in and year out. His commemoration work was no less than Kipling's.

Ben Leech had as many reasons for staying in France as anyone. There were his obligations to the dead, of course, along with the grim prospect of finding a job in Britain's anemic postwar economy. Then there was Agnes Groves. Ben was not eager to face her and baby Ben, especially after he began a new relationship with a French woman named Marie Caron.

Marie Berthe Caron was a resourceful, hardworking woman who had lived a difficult life even before the war devastated her country. She was seventeen and a servant in a rich man's house when she gave birth to her first daughter, Yvonne. Marie refused to name the baby's father. When her own father died a few years later, Marie left Yvonne with her widowed mother and went in search of work. She cooked and cleaned and ended up in Saint-Omer, a small city about twenty-five miles from Calais that became a hub for British troops. Marie was in her early thirties and working in a cabaret when she met Ben Leech.[54]

The first official record of Ben and Marie's relationship is an entry in the Saint-Omer birth registry for their son, Maurice Leech, who was born on June 16, 1921. Ben and Marie were not legally married, but both of their names are on the birth record, and Maurice was given a French version of Ben's middle name, Morris. The couple married a year later, solemnizing their marriage at the Saint-Omer town hall with two munici-pal employees as witnesses.[55]

Shortly after the wedding, Ben, Marie, and baby Maurice moved to Ronville, a working-class neighborhood just south of Arras. The War Graves Commission had a depot there—Ronville Camp—which included a workshop, a garage, a plant nursery, a storehouse, and temporary hous-ing for single men. Since Ben and Marie were married, they lodged with another War Graves family on Route de Bapaume, the main commercial street in Ronville. Their next two children were born there: Beatrice in 1924 and Roland in 1925.

As the 1920s waned, so did the pace of construction. Between 1920 and 1924, the Commission completed 515 cemeteries on the old Western Front; between 1924 and 1928, they built 212. There were still a few projects in progress, notably the Thiepval Memorial on the Somme, but most of the cemeteries were finished. It was time to start thinking about the future.[56]

Unfortunately for the employees, long-term maintenance was much less labor intensive than active building. By early 1928, the Commission had reduced its staff by two-thirds, intending to keep a permanent staff of only 550. A handful of craftsmen would stay on, but the Commission no longer needed nine blacksmiths.

When Ben Leech learned that there was no place for him on the per-manent staff, he protested. He had been away from Manchester for twelve years, and his job prospects there were bleak. Besides, he worried that Marie and the children would not adapt well to life in England. With his termination date approaching in the spring of 1928, Ben pled his case.

"He asked me whether it would not be possible for him to be em-ployed on the Horticultural Staff," an officer wrote to the Commission's head office in London.

The Commission weighed Ben Leech's petition. On the one hand, he was thirty-eight years old and had no experience in any job remotely resembling gardening. On the other, he was a "sober and industrious employee." The Commission decided to grant him a trial as a gardener's laborer.

Ben seized his chance. "He appears to be quick in grasping the work," his new supervisor reported. "With further tuition [he] should make a use-ful employee in the cemetery."

Becoming a gardener's laborer meant starting back on the bottom rung. As a blacksmith, Ben had earned a yearly salary of £182, or £3.10.0 per week. As a gardener's laborer, he would make £104, or £2 per week. It was a 43 percent pay cut. Even after a year of training and a promotion from laborer to the standard position of "gardener-caretaker," Ben would make only £3 a week.[57]

In addition to the financial hit, Ben's new job meant moving to Beaumont-Hamel, seventeen miles south of Arras. This was no small matter. Moving to a new area was expensive, and Beaumont-Hamel was not a desirable location. Ronville was still a work in progress, but it was part of a city with functioning infrastructure, schools, shops, and a concentrated community of English speakers. Beaumont-Hamel was not. It was a village of 222 people still clawing its way back into existence after the battles of 1916 reduced it to little more than a smear on aerial reconnaissance photos.[58]

Beaumont-Hamel was part of the Zone Rouge (Red Zone), the area so badly damaged by the war and littered with unexploded ordnance that the French government considered it unfit for farming or human habitation. Efforts to fill in trenches, clear barbed wire, and recover corpses had made substantial progress, but the area around Beaumont-Hamel was still bleak. A decade after the Armistice, the village still lacked basic necessities like clean drinking water. Gardeners in rural areas typically spent two shillings a week—5 percent of Ben Leech's new wage—on bottled mineral water to avoid the arsenic and cyanide that contaminated local wells.[59]

Still, Ben wanted the job. He and Marie rented a newly constructed house near the gaping Hawthorn Ridge crater, where weeds and wildflowers had begun to soften the edges of the blast. Marie planted carrots and cabbages in the very ground that so many British soldiers had died to capture. To the south was the Newfoundland Memorial Park, seventy-four acres of preserved trenches presided over by a bellowing bronze caribou. To the north, across the fields, was Serre Road Cemetery No. 2, where the War Graves Commission held Friday burial services for newly discovered remains.

Ben Leech had been a barman, a soldier, and a blacksmith. Now he would be a gardener.

His new contract required Ben to devote his "whole time and services" to War Graves work and to "obey and comply with all orders and directions issued by the Commission."[60]

Ben signed. His term of service began on July 1, 1928, exactly twelve years since the first day of the battle of the Somme.

ROUTE DE BAPAUME 2

I f anyone had asked the War Graves community to predict who among them would emerge from the next global war laden with medals from grateful nations, few would have chosen Rosine Thérier Witton.

Certainly, Rosine would not have chosen herself. She was a "modest type of person" who spent her later years deflecting questions about her heroism.

"You were very brave," Rosine wrote to one of the airmen she protected from the Nazis. "I admire you and all the airmen of the R.A.F. also the Canadians + Americans; we in France have only done our duty to help you and to shelter you; the Heros are you and all your friends."[1]

The governments of France, the United Kingdom, and the United States begged to differ. Between them, they awarded Rosine so many decorations that she once lost her British Empire Medal during a ceremony and did not even realize it was missing.[2]

Everyone in Ronville knew Rosine Witton. She ran the *café-tabac*—part newsstand, part tobacconist, part bar—on Route de Bapaume, across from the Cinema Rex. Anyone walking between Ronville Camp and the Arras War Graves office might stop in to buy cigarettes or sweets from the small, spritely woman, barely five feet tall, who wore her dark hair in a curly pompadour.[3] Rosine's French customers remembered her as the plucky girl who helped her mother resurrect their shop from the ashes of the Great War; her British customers knew her as a friendly, bilingual businesswoman and, after 1932, the adored wife of gardener Bert Witton.

Under Rosine's *café-tabac*, the ground was hollow. In 1916, tunnelers from New Zealand had burrowed deep under Ronville, connecting a series of abandoned medieval quarries with a vast warren of subterranean passages. After six months of excavation, the caverns were large enough to conceal 20,000 men. In April 1917, these hidden British troops sprang out of camouflaged exits near the German lines and helped win the Battle of Arras.[4]

Rosine's shop perched on a precarious strip of solid earth between two of the largest caverns: Carrière Wellington and Carrière Christchurch. The empty spaces yawned beneath the everyday bustle on the surface.

~

Arras was the center of the British War Graves community in France in the 1930s. In the early days, the Imperial War Graves Commission had run its operations out of a slapdash camp near Saint-Omer, but they built a permanent headquarters in Arras in 1929. The trim, red-brick building across from the Arras train station was frugal and tidy, with a simplified Flemish gable that paid homage to the city's historic architecture.

Arras was a sensible choice for the Commission's headquarters. If a mapmaker stuck a pin through the Arras office and drew a circle with a radius of sixty miles, it would encompass nearly all the British military

Former Imperial War Graves Commission office, 7 Place du Maréchal Foch, Arras. *Photo by author*

cemeteries in France and Belgium, from Ypres in the north to Saint-Quentin in the south, from the English Channel coast in the west to Mons in the east. This made Arras a convenient home base for War Graves staff and mourners alike. A host of businesses catering to battlefield visitors clustered around the War Graves office. Cafés advertised Guinness, hotels welcomed English-speaking patrons, and tour companies promised "CARS FOR HIRE, BRITISH DRIVERS." A few doors down, the Arras British Legion office kept huge battlefield maps and ledgers full of the names, ready to assist visitors searching for their beloved dead.

If the new office was the head of the War Graves Commission in France, Route de Bapaume was its spine. The busy commercial street began near the station and ran south over the train tracks, past Rosine's *café-tabac* and Ronville Camp, and on toward the battlefields of the Somme.

The Commission's officers lived in more prosperous neighborhoods, but dozens of gardeners, craftsmen, clerks, and mechanics settled in Ronville. Ben and Marie Leech lived at 160 Route de Bapaume, just a few blocks south of Rosine's shop, before they moved to Beaumont-Hamel. Ronville was home to many families like theirs: a British husband, a French or Belgian wife, and their children. Together, they formed a vibrant, multinational, working-class community devoted to the perpetual remembrance of the war dead.

Postcard showing businesses catering to English-speaking visitors in the Place de la Gare, Arras, 1920s–1930s. The Imperial War Graves Commission office is just out of frame to the right. *Collection of the author*

The French and Belgian women who married War Graves gardeners were survivors of World War I in their own right. They were refugees and displaced persons, laundresses and sex workers, farm women without farms, and city-dwellers whose cities lay in ruins. For many, the roofs they shared on Route de Bapaume were their first stable housing since 1914. Some were widows whose French husbands never returned from the front. Others, like Marie Leech, were unmarried mothers who never named their children's fathers. War Graves families frequently included stepchildren, orphaned nieces and nephews, and babies legitimized by their parents' marriages.

Unlike the other War Graves wives in Ronville, Rosine Thérier did not move to the neighborhood because of her husband's job. She met Bert Witton because she was already there.

∼

Rosine Zoé Léontine Thérier was born on Route de Bapaume on November 23, 1906. Her father, Auguste Thérier, was a carpenter, and her mother, Léontine Bécourt, was a shopkeeper. Rosine and her older brother, Auguste, were born into a life of steady work and modest comfort.[5]

Rosine was seven years old in 1914, when the Great War came to Arras. German troops attacked the city during the early battles of the "Race to the Sea" but were repulsed by the French. In retaliation, the Germans turned their artillery on Arras. Young Rosine was one of the 26,000 civilians who cowered in cellars as the German guns brought the city down around their ears. Homes and shops crumbled. Landmarks, including the sixteenth-century Hôtel de Ville, were gutted. "ARRAS IN RUINS," blared an international press not yet accustomed to seeing European cities reduced to rubble.[6]

Nearly everyone fled. At first, Rosine's family sought refuge in a suburb, but it was not far enough. The Germans had settled on the high ground along Vimy Ridge, north of the city, and the entire area was overrun with troops—first French, later British—and military infrastructure. After a year of hovering nearby, the Thériers accepted that they would not be able to return home to Route de Bapaume anytime soon. Rosine's father went to Paris and secured a hovel under the stone arches of a railway bridge in Joinville-le-Pont, just south of the Bois de Vincennes. It was not comfortable, but at least it was not being shelled.

In the second week of February 1916, an entry in the periodical *Refugies de Pas de Calais* notes that "Thérier, Rosine, 8 ans" arrived in Paris with her mother and fourteen-year-old brother.[7] That same week, Ben

Leech was called up by the British army in far-off Manchester, preparing to be sent to the front that young Rosine had just escaped.

Rosine's family were refugees, but they were safer than many of their relatives. Léontine Bécourt's family hailed from the villages east of Arras, where the German army used French civilians as forced labor and destroyed every useful orchard, well, and field when they withdrew. Rosine's father was too old to join the French army and her brother too young, but several of her cousins donned the blue uniform of the *poilus*. One of them, twenty-two-year-old Gaston Bécourt, was killed fighting on the Somme in 1916.[8]

Rosine was eleven when the Armistice was signed in November 1918. When her family returned home to Ronville, they found a desolate ruin. Route de Bapaume was still discernible as a straight line through the piles of dusty brick and splintered rafters, but the neighborhood was gone. A War Graves officer who supervised the construction of Ronville Camp in the spring of 1919 called the site "a piece of shell torn wasteland" where "the few inhabitants lived in the ruins of buildings." Rosine's neighbors agreed. One compared the task of rebuilding Ronville to the labors of Hercules, dubbing a particularly stubborn heap of debris "little Vesuvius."[9]

Officially, Ronville was part of the Zone Jaune—Yellow Zone—an area that had been heavily damaged but required less extensive rehabilitation than the Zone Rouge. Residents were free to return and rebuild if they dared. Reconstruction began at once, but progress was slow. In the mid-1920s, years after running water and electricity were restored to wealthier neighborhoods, Ronville was still drawing its drinking water from communal cisterns.[10]

For some residents, the prospect of rebuilding Ronville was too overwhelming. Up and down Route de Bapaume, Rosine's neighbors put their property up for sale. The owners of Number 43 advertised their former home as "a house in ruins . . . with a garden, all in the sun." The sale included all rights to any future claim for war damages. Over the next decade, speculators who snapped up ruined properties from refugees made a killing in government compensation.[11]

Life in the wreckage of northern France was chaotic, unsanitary, and violent. Thousands of acres of fertile topsoil were buried under chalk and clay churned up by the relentless shelling. Stagnant pools in the pitted ground bred insects and rats. Civilians squatted in cellars and surplus army huts, while the men clearing the battlefields often lived in temporary labor camps on the outskirts of ruined towns. The boomtown conditions led one French official to call the area "a new Klondike."[12]

Clean water was scarce, but alcohol was plentiful. Estaminets and caba-rets flourished, catering to workers who drank heavily after spending their days clearing rubble, exhuming human remains, and defusing unexploded shells. In 1921, the town of Albert on the Somme had 2,999 residents and fifty-two bars and cafés. Robbery, rape, and murder were common. So were accidental death and maiming. Anyone could walk into the wreckage and pick up as many unstable grenades as they pleased. Salvaged firearms, bayonets, and trench knives were everywhere. Among local children, a favorite game involved pouring lines of cordite from unfired bullets and setting them alight like firecrackers.[13]

War Graves families shared these hardships with their neighbors. In the early years, some gardeners lived in Commission housing in Saint-Omer and Ronville, but others lived in huts or dugouts in the Zone Rouge.

It was "a rough way to live," remembered gardener Albert Roberts, who recalled families living in "wartime conditions" for years after the Armistice. "Two men with their families occupied one single artillery dug-out at Le Touret M[ilitary] C[emetery]," he remembered. "Two children were in fact born in the dugout."

Margaret Grinham, the wife of War Graves officer Frank Grinham, spent the winter of 1921 in a freezing Nissen hut with her toddler daugh-ter, Philippa, dipping their silverware into hot water so it would not stick to their fingers. The following spring, the whole family went out together to search for isolated graves.

"Philippa very often spotted them before we did," Margaret wrote, "she'd say, ''ere's one, Daddy.'"[14]

Growing up on the old battlefields could be dangerous. At least one War Graves child, nine-year-old Leslie Rolfe, lost several fingers when an explosive detonated in his hand.[15]

Other War Graves children were haunted by their battlefield play-ground. Joseph Hillier, son of gardener W. J. C. Hillier, frequently played in the abandoned trenches and shell holes around Ronville. Once, when he was no older than ten, he fell through a shallow grave in Achicourt Wood and landed in the rotting remains of a corpse.

"I have had many a fright," Joseph testified in 1940, when he appeared before the Lancashire Tribunal for Conscientious Objectors to argue that growing up in a "vast graveyard" made it impossible for him to take up arms.

"I have seen too much to allow myself to kill," Joseph told the tribunal. Some of his memories were so gruesome that he refused to recount them in open court. After the tribunal heard Joseph's testimony behind closed doors, they immediately granted his request for noncombatant status.[16]

Rosine Thérier was several years older than Joseph Hillier. She may have played in the pestilential trenches as a twelve-year-old in 1919, but her family's pressing needs probably kept her busy as she grew older.

The Thérier family did their part to rebuild Ronville. Rosine's father was a carpenter whose skills were in the highest possible demand, and her brother followed in his footsteps. Both of them worked for the French government ministry in charge of restoring devastated towns and infrastructure. They spent their days undoing the destruction of the war one home and shop at a time.[17]

French construction workers led the rebuilding effort, but some of the earliest work in Ronville was done by Chinese laborers. In 1919, the War Graves Commission commandeered a company of the Chinese Labour Corps to build the foundations of Ronville Camp. The workers spent the spring and summer of 1919 "salvaging abandoned Nissen huts" that became barracks and workshops for the War Graves gardeners and craftsmen. They also reclaimed thousands of discarded railway ties, which they used to build a sturdy access road. This was the beginning of the Commission's permanent presence in Ronville.[18]

While Rosine's father and brother helped resurrect Arras and the Chinese laborers built Ronville Camp, Rosine's mother, Léontine, reestablished her shop. Instead of a café, Léontine opened an *épicerie*, a grocery store. It was exactly the sort of business the neighborhood needed to encourage refugees to return. Young, single men could live in army-style barracks and drink more than they ate, but Ronville could not sustain a stable civilian population without bakeries, butcher shops, and greengrocers. Léontine's *épicerie* was one of the quotidian businesses that helped restore the rhythms of peacetime life. Over time, as the emergency subsided, her shop evolved into a *café-tabac*. Rosine learned the business at her mother's side.

Nail by nail and onion by onion, the Thérier family helped rebuild Ronville. When Rosine was a teenager, they moved out of temporary housing and into a new home at Number 6 Route de Bapaume. It was a modest, low-slung brick terrace without indoor plumbing or other modern conveniences. Still, it was a permanent house, not a makeshift shelter. Rosine hung white lace curtains in the front parlor and kept hens in a coop near the outhouse.[19]

∼

Number 6 Route de Bapaume, 2022. *Photo by author*

By 1926, when Rosine turned twenty, Arras had surpassed its prewar population of 26,000. Many of the residents were returnees like the Thériers, but there were also plenty of newcomers. The English-speaking War Graves employees living on Route de Bapaume were part of a larger, polyglot community of immigrants and expatriates who made their homes in northern France.

In the wake of World War I, France needed workers to replace the millions of French men who had been killed or disabled. Northern France was particularly desperate because tens of thousands of civilians had either died or chosen not to return. Immigrants filled crucial jobs in mining and agriculture and helped rehabilitate the Zone Rouge.

In addition to the immediate labor shortage, postwar France faced the alarming prospect of slower population growth. Leaders worried that France would be at a long-term disadvantage against Germany, which was still growing fast. To head off this demographic disaster, they adopted policies that encouraged European workers to settle permanently in France. Changes to French immigration law in 1927 made it easier to become a naturalized French citizen and abolished a long-standing policy that stripped French women of their nationality if they married foreign-born men. Women like Marie Caron, who married Ben Leech in 1922, had forfeited their French nationality, but Rosine Thérier, who married Bert Witton in 1932, remained French in the eyes of the law.[20]

These policies shaped the demographics of devastated areas. Before the war, foreign-born *étrangers* were vanishingly rare in small villages like Beaumont-Hamel, Thiepval, and Montauban, but that changed dramatically in the postwar years. By the early 1930s, these villages typically had foreign-born populations of 20 to 30 percent, with some, like Thiepval, approaching 50 percent. Italian masons helped build the Imperial War Graves Commission's towering Thiepval Memorial; Polish agricultural laborers worked in its shadow.[21]

The War Graves Commission employees were a small part of this larger foreign-born population. Unlike the gardeners in Belgium, who were concentrated around Ypres, the gardeners in France were scattered widely across the Nord, Pas-de-Calais, and Somme departments, with a few farther afield. There were clusters in places like Beaumont-Hamel, where the cemeteries were most numerous, but most gardeners in France lived in villages with only one or two English-speaking families.

Gardeners who wanted to socialize with their fellow expatriates often traveled to Arras. There were whist drives and holiday parties and an annual Sports Meet on Bastille Day organized by the British Legion. These gatherings nurtured lifelong friendships among the Anglo-French community, which included many British people beyond the War Graves families. Among Rosine Witton's friends were Berthe Fraser, a French woman who ran a perfume shop with her bespectacled, London-born husband, John, and Arthur Richards, the vice-chairman of the local British Legion chapter. One day, they would be Resistance comrades as well as friends.[22]

While many of the gardeners preferred to spend time with their fellow English speakers, others integrated more fully into their adopted communities. Bob Armstrong, the Irish gardener who had lost a brother at Loos, was a gregarious man with a wide circle of French friends. His home in Valenciennes was on the eastern outskirts of the Commission's turf, relatively far from both Arras and Ypres, which may explain why Bob became much more fluent in French than some of his colleagues. Even Ben Leech and Bert Witton, whose families spoke French at home, were never fully comfortable with the language. "Please excuse my writing in English," Ben once apologized in a letter, "but my French would be too awful."[23] Bob Armstrong, by contrast, threw himself wholeheartedly into the life of his adopted home.

Questions of language and nationality were as important to the War Graves Commission as they were to the gardeners. The Commission purposefully hired men to create what Sir Fabian Ware called a "balanced staff," that is, a staff that embodied Sir Fabian's vision of imperial cooperation. The dominions were represented at every level—by gardeners and mechanics as well as by architects and administrators—with positions explicitly reserved for Canadians, Australians, New Zealanders, and South Africans "in proportion to their contributions to Commission funds."[24]

The Commission was explicit about hiring candidates to fill national quotas. Sir Frederick Kenyon, one of the Commission's chief architects, was doubtful about hiring a young Canadian veteran named Frank Higginson because he was "not of the same standing from the point of view of architectural experience" as the other junior architects. "But if Canada has no one better qualified to offer, I think we might give Lieut. Higginson a trial," Kenyon wrote. Frank Higginson went on to design the much-admired Cabaret Rouge Cemetery near Vimy Ridge, but he was hired for the maple leaf on his cap, not for his architecture portfolio.[25]

The Commission's staff was supposed to represent the empire but within very narrow boundaries. Members of the permanent staff were required to be white, male British subjects who had served in the armed forces and spoke fluent English. These criteria were far more important than previous experience. The Commission was happy to train complete novices like Ben Leech and Bert Witton who met the demographic qualifications. Skilled workers who did not fit these narrow parameters of race, gender, and nationality were not eligible for positions on the permanent staff.

A few small deviations proved the rule. John Boucher, a veteran of the Guernsey Light Infantry, had moved to the Channel Islands from France when he was three weeks old. Boucher was already working as a cemetery gardener when the Commission discovered that he was not, technically, a British subject. They granted him a dispensation to join the permanent staff but noted that, unlike the other gardeners, "his service on the Commission's staff was not regarded as the service of the Crown."[26]

The Commission's narrow hiring criteria sometimes meant replacing proficient workers with newcomers. Before the War Graves Commission took over from the army in 1921, dozens of women from Queen Mary's Army Auxiliary Corps worked as gardeners in British cemeteries in France. They planted flowers, kept the cemeteries tidy, and even dug graves, but the War Graves Commission did not offer them permanent positions.[27] The Commission did hire women for clerical roles, as temporary drivers in the very earliest days, and as medical personnel but not as horticultural staff.[28]

The Commission also lost essential skilled labor by hiring only white workers to its permanent staff. In 1919 and 1920, Chinese craftsmen carved thousands of headstones for their comrades in the Chinese Labour Corps, a job that the Commission considered "a work of love and not one of finance."[29] Since both Britain and France were keen to prevent Chinese men from settling down after the war, nearly all the Chinese workers were transported back to China in 1920. Many of them were surely eager to go home, but others had formed romantic relationships with French women and might have been interested in staying if they had been given the opportunity. They were not.[30]

The Commission did intervene to keep sixty-three Chinese workers in France in 1920—going so far as to have them "taken off the train as they were leaving"—but only for the few months necessary to complete the carving work. In later years, when headstones with Chinese text needed routine replacing, the Commission's craftsmen lacked the expertise to carve the names of the dead. Unable to replicate the original text, they made replacement headstones that commemorated members of the Chinese Labour Corps by their service numbers.[31]

These choices ensured that the War Graves Commission's cemeteries were far more homogeneous above ground than they were below. White Canadians and white South Africans tended the graves of their comrades at Cabaret Rouge and Delville Wood, but there were no Indian gardeners at Neuve Chapelle and no Chinese gardeners at Noyelles-sur-Mer.

The War Graves Commission did, in fact, employ gardeners who were not white British men but only as "casual" laborers. In 1936, the Commission paid 127 "Local Native Gardeners" in addition to the permanent staff of 596. Some of these "native" gardeners were French, Belgian, Italian, Polish, and Turkish men who worked in British cemeteries in their home countries and were excluded from the permanent staff because they were not British subjects. Others were British colonial subjects who worked in cemeteries in Asia and Africa. They were ineligible for the permanent staff because they were "natives," not white settlers. Some of these gardeners worked in Commission cemeteries for decades, but they were still classified as temporary workers. They were paid lower wages and were not eligible for benefits. The Commission did not even keep systematic records of their names.[32]

One of the casual workers whose name does not appear anywhere in the Commission's archives was a French woman named Julia Dauvergne. She was the cleaner who kept the Arras headquarters tidy. Like so many other War Graves employees, Madame Dauvergne found it convenient to live near her workplace. She rented a room just a few minutes' walk from the office, at Number 6 Route de Bapaume, where she lived with Rosine Thérier and her parents.[33]

~

By the early 1930s, Rosine Thérier lived in the midst of a well-established War Graves community. Each day, when Madame Dauvergne walked up Route de Bapaume from the Thérier house to the War Graves office, she followed the same route as Superintendent Pay Clerk Charles Cheeseman, who lived at Number 10, and the Commission's nurse, Sister Betty Stuart, who lived in an apartment on the next block. Rosine was friendly with sweet, hospitable Marie Medlicott, who lived across the street with her husband, Harold, and their children, and with Suzanne Legg, who was only two years older than Rosine but was already married to gardener Wilfred Legg and mother to Freddy, Harry, and baby Gladys. Around the corner, Hélène Allen and her gardener husband, Thomas, named their daughters Poppy and Marguerite after the British and Belgian remembrance flowers.[34]

It is not clear how Rosine met Bert Witton, but she had plenty of opportunities. He may have been a customer at the *café-tabac*, or they may have been introduced by one of their many mutual acquaintances. However they met, the blond, sober-faced gardener caught Rosine's eye. They married in 1932, when Rosine was twenty-five and Bert was thirty-four.[35]

Sidney Albert Witton, "Bert" to his friends, was one of the younger War Graves gardeners. He was born on June 6, 1898, in the East London docklands, one of eight surviving children in a family that buried five others. As a teenager, Bert worked alongside many of his relatives at a factory in Silvertown, a sliver of industrial grime floating between the Royal Victoria Dock and the Thames. Bert made telegraph cables. It was essential work, especially during the war, when vital communication infrastructure needed constant repairs.

Perhaps Bert would have stayed in Silvertown if not for the explosion. On January 19, 1917, fifty tons of TNT stored at a munitions factory detonated. The blast killed seventy-three people, injured hundreds more, and leveled the entire neighborhood. None of Bert's immediate family were killed, but Silvertown resembled Ronville. Newly unemployed, Bert enlisted in the Royal Flying Corps (RFC).[36]

The RFC sent Bert to France as a laborer. When he was discharged in 1920, he took a similar job with the War Graves Commission. It was grim work. Bert and the other laborers scoured the battlefields for bodies, dug graves, and lay the horticultural groundwork for the new cemeteries. Bert had never worked with plants before, but he discovered a knack and was promoted to gardener-caretaker in 1921. As a young, single man, he was probably assigned to one of the Commission's mobile horticultural units that roamed the ravaged countryside in tall, green lorries marked "Travelling Gardening Party."

Bert was laid off during the staff reductions of the late 1920s but rehired a few years later once the Commission realized their cuts had bitten too deep. In the meantime, he married Rosine and moved into her parents' house.

Rosine and Bert were better off financially than most other gardeners' families. Some War Graves wives took in lodgers or sold homemade meals to make ends meet, but few had reliable independent incomes like Rosine's. The *café-tabac* meant that the Wittons did not depend wholly on Bert's wages. Other gardeners took on debt to survive from one payday to the next, but Bert and Rosine built up modest savings. When Rosine's parents died, she was able to buy out her brother's share in Number 6 and own the house outright. That made the Wittons unusual among War Graves gardeners in France, most of whom rented or lived in lodgings.

It was not easy to survive on a War Graves gardener's wage.[37] Despite the Commission's initial plans to pay gardener-caretakers an annual wage of £175 (£3.7.4 per week), the Treasury approved a substantially lower rate of £156 (£3 per week). Unlike the salaried officers and clerical staff, who had regular raises built into their pay scales, the gardeners' wages were stagnant. The only way for a gardener to make more money in his thirtieth year than in his first was to be promoted to head gardener, a rare feat in a workforce where nearly everyone was of a similar age and seniority.

The gardeners' low wages made life difficult in postwar France, where the basic necessities of life were ruinously expensive. At first, the Commission provided barracks and rations, but those supports ended as they transitioned from the construction phase to permanent maintenance. The housing shortage meant that many gardeners shared houses or rented "mere shells" that had to be fitted out with heating stoves and basic furnishings at exorbitant rates.

Food was another vexing problem. Gardeners paid high prices for thin milk and bacon that was "rank and harsh." Tea, a specialty item in France, was beyond their reach. By 1929, fluctuations in the exchange rate removed even the smallest luxuries from their tables. Every eggless, jamless, tealess morning gave the gardeners occasion to grumble that they were "accustomed to English breakfasts before proceeding to their days' work and could not have them."

Even as they struggled to eat like Englishmen, the gardeners were expected to act as "representatives of the British Empire." They assisted mourners who came to their cemeteries, attended local ceremonies, and entertained village dignitaries in their homes. The results could be humiliating. Gardeners were embarrassed when they were forced to appear in public looking shabby. "Even if they were poor," they argued, "they should not look poor." Unfortunately, their paltry wages were "insufficient to maintain their prestige in a foreign country, to look respectable or live decently as British working men are accustomed to live."

The gardeners were semiofficial British representatives, but they were cut off from many of the social programs available to working people in the United Kingdom. Both France and the United Kingdom were experimenting with national insurance schemes to provide medical and dental care to their citizens, but the gardeners were ineligible for both. They were also unable to claim disability pensions because they did not reside in the United Kingdom. The War Graves Commission offered a contributory superannuation scheme designed to provide small payments to retirees over the age of sixty, but the policies did not cover younger employees who became physically or mentally incapacitated.

This exclusion from government benefits was particularly galling because the gardeners considered themselves to be "British subjects working on a task that was peculiarly British." They were Crown servants and felt that "they should not be cut off from the privileges and rights of their fellow countrymen at home."

In addition to worries about their own citizenship, the gardeners and their wives fretted about the legal status of their children. Some pregnant women traveled from France to Belgium to give birth because children born to British parents in Belgium automatically acquired British nationality.[38] If the children were born in France, their citizenship was much more ambiguous. Technically, children born to foreign-born parents in France were dual nationals, but they were frequently treated as foreigners by both countries. To have their British nationality fully recognized, gardeners' children had to affirmatively renounce their French citizenship during a six-month window before their twenty-first birthdays. This meant that the early War Graves babies born in France in 1919 were scheduled to claim their British nationality in 1939 and 1940.

The births themselves were disconcerting for British gardeners. They were often appalled by local doctors' insistence that "the husband should be present during a confinement." The gardeners' wives were also ineligible for government programs that provided pre- and postnatal care to French women. In 1929, the gardeners petitioned the Commission to hire "a good British midwife" who would attend their wives and not expect men to be present in the birthing room.

As their children grew, the gardeners saw how fragile their British identity was. Many of the children spoke very little English. Others were bilingual or even trilingual, though their parents worried that their Flemish was "practically useless outside of Belgium." They knew that children who grew up fluent in French or Flemish were more likely to build their own lives in Flanders, not in the United Kingdom. One gardener with young daughters reported that he "dreaded the possibility of their marrying Frenchmen" but did not see how it could be avoided.

In 1929, a special delegation of Commission officials traveled to Ypres and Arras to investigate the gardeners' living conditions. They were surprised and dismayed by the realities on the ground. The officers "had not realised how much these men were losing in the way of social and welfare amenities such as clinics, welfare centers, and dental treatment for their children." One Commissioner, Lieutenant General Sir George Macdonogh, said that it "came as a shock to him" to realize that gardeners who became disabled would be left without support.

A review of gardeners' wages also revealed unpleasant truths. Between 1924 and 1929, exchange rates and cost-of-living increases effectively slashed the wages of a gardener-caretaker in France by 33 percent, which the Commission conceded was "an enormous drop." Gardeners could no longer afford modest pleasures like the IWGC Ypres football club, which shut down "owing to their not being able to afford the expense."

At the same time, the staff reductions meant that the workload was heavier than ever. "Three years ago there were more men and higher wages . . . now there are fewer men to cover the same ground and less wages, and their responsibilities were increased."

Gardener William T. Cox summed it up. Cox was an Old Contemptible, a professional soldier in Britain's small prewar army who was among the first to land in France in 1914. In 1929, when his fellow gardeners elected him as a representative to present their grievances to the delegation, Cox was living in housing "built expressly for the poor of the village." Appearing before the officers, Cox told them that he was "not alone" in feeling betrayed by the Commission. "If I could get a good job at Home," Cox told Sir Fabian, "I would not stay in Belgium."

These meetings were a wakeup call for the Commission. Sir Fabian expressed "serious anxiety" over "symptoms of what might be called organized discontent among the gardeners in France and Belgium" and fretted that their troubles might become public. J. J. Lawson, a Labour member of Parliament who sat on the Commission's Staff Committee, agreed that public opinion could turn against the Commission if they did not pay the gardeners fairly. In 1933, when the Commission was considering a wage cut in the midst of the Great Depression, Lawson noted that "the Commission would be liable to criticism if they lowered wages at the present time, when the world seemed to be agreed that salvation lay rather in an increase in wages."

In response to the gardeners' complaints, the Commission made several changes. In 1930, they hired Dr. Muriel Rippin and Sister Betty Stuart, who made free house calls to gardeners and their families. The Commission also instituted special allowances of ten or fifteen shillings per week when exchange rates were particularly unfavorable and paid for two annual train and ferry tickets so that gardeners and their wives could visit family in the United Kingdom. Gardeners from the dominions were allowed to save up leave and travel vouchers over a number of years to make longer trips to Australia or Canada.

Another new benefit were two English-language schools for the children of Commission gardeners. The British Memorial School in Ypres opened in 1929. It was founded by Eton alumni as a memorial to their fallen classmates but was supported with substantial funding from the Commission. A similar school opened in Arras the next year, wholly at the Commission's expense.[39]

Both schools offered a pointedly patriotic British curriculum designed to educate War Graves children in "their native tongue." The Ypres school thrived in part because nearly all of the Commission families in Belgium lived within cycling distance of Ypres. This was not the case in France. Even Beaumont-Hamel was too far for Ben Leech's children to attend school in Arras every day. The Arras school lasted only three years, closing in 1933. To acknowledge this difference in access, the Commission offered modest education grants to families in France who wished to send their children to school in the United Kingdom.

Sir Fabian and the Commissioners were willing to listen to the gardeners' grievances, but they were dead set against any formal labor organizing. Their greatest weapon against unionization was a sense, shared by many of the gardeners, that their work was more than a mere job. Caring for the dead, they said, was a vocation that could not be governed by the same sordid concerns as spinning cotton or driving a bus.[40]

In 1926, when workers across the United Kingdom organized a general strike in support of striking coal miners, Sir Fabian felt "a little anxious" that the gardeners might join in. To prevent any shows of solidarity, he sent a circular that explicitly defined War Graves work as wholly separate from mundane labor.

"Our work is of a kind that should be outside and above industrial and constitutional disputes," Sir Fabian wrote. "We hope that during the present crisis all members of the Commission's staff in France and Belgium will continue as usual to carry on their sacred task with the same efficiency and devotion as in the past."[41]

It was true that many gardeners regarded their work as a hallowed duty, inextricably entangled with their obligations to fallen comrades. Still, they needed to eat.

By the mid-1930s, attrition among the gardening staff forced the Commission to rehire several laid-off gardeners, including Bert Witton. They also hired a class of teenage "pupil gardeners," most of them the sons of current gardeners. The Commission was unwilling to hire these boys to permanent positions unless they spoke enough English to "converse with the visitors to the cemeteries," but they saw the long-term value in hiring workers who thought of the job as a duty handed down from father to son.[42]

The Commission also hired nine young reservists in 1936. These were men who served in the regular army after World War I and were still liable to be called up in an emergency. One of them was Peter Moir, a twenty-four-year-old Gordon Highlander from rural Aberdeenshire who was posted to Beaumont-Hamel as a pupil gardener in 1936.[43]

From the Commission's perspective, these new hires were a bargain. Bert Witton had been a gardener-caretaker in the 1920s, but he was rehired as a gardener's laborer, a lower position at a lower wage. The pupil gardeners were also cheap during their training period, though the prospect of hiring them to the permanent staff raised some hackles at the Treasury.

"I saw some of these youngsters when I was in France," wrote one Treasury official. "There is no doubt that many of them are far more Belgian or French than ever they are English. Particularly in Belgium, many of them look Belgian." Given the pupil gardeners' general Belgianness, he considered it "quite monstrous to pay them at the rates fixed" for British workers but did not see "how we can get round the difficulty."[44]

The gardeners were thinking about the future as well. They had wrung some concessions out of the Commission, but their wages were still too low. At the same time, the French labor movement was winning substantial new protections, such as a forty-hour workweek and the right to unionize, that were adopted by France's Popular Front government in 1936. That same year, the War Graves gardeners formally organized themselves into a union, the Wage Staff Association (France and Belgium), under the umbrella of the British Transport and General Workers' Union.

The union's first major action was to bring a complaint against the Imperial War Graves Commission in Britain's Industrial Court. The gardeners demanded higher base wages paid in sterling, modest yearly raises of 2s 6d per week, and an extra shilling per week for every year over ten years' service. Under this scheme, the maximum weekly wage would be £4 10s.

The War Graves Commission fought back. They argued that the gardeners' wages were comparable to the wages of gardeners in the United Kingdom and that all extenuating circumstances had already been "taken into account."

The Industrial Court sided with the gardeners. In a legally binding ruling, the court set a lower maximum wage than the union had requested—£4 instead of £4.10.0—but ordered the Commission to raise the base wage for an experienced gardener to £3.10.0, paid in sterling, and to provide annual increases of 2s 6d per week.

The 1938 decision "astonished not only the Commission and the Treasury but also the men."[45]

For Sir Fabian and the Commissioners, the surprise was not a pleasant one. They thought of themselves as generous employers, not as people who needed to be forced into fairness. The Industrial Court's judgment stung their pride as well as their budget.

In order to cover the wage increase, the Commission needed to economize. They did not cut the salaries of top officers—Sir Fabian's yearly salary was £2,500, sixteen times a gardener-caretaker's wage—but they did consider reducing the gardening staff by half. Unfortunately, it would be impossible to maintain the cemeteries with 250 gardeners when 500 were already stretched thin. Colonel Frank Higginson, who had risen to the role of chief administrative officer in France (salary £1,200), suggested that they might be able to make it work if they adopted "the American system" of "neatly kept lawns" without flower borders around the headstones.

"This changes the cemeteries from English Gardens to nothing more than well-cared for military burying grounds," Higginson warned.

Captain Reginald Haworth, the chief accountant in France (salary £900), agreed that reducing labor costs was the "major economy possible." If they stopped replacing gardeners who retired or quit, perhaps they could plug the gaps with local, seasonal labor. In the meantime, Haworth pledged to stay alert for "unnecessary expenditures" and to keep tabs on "the mileage of the cars."[46]

To cut costs, the Commission closed branch offices in Béthune and Abbeville. They also moved the headquarters from Arras to Wimereux, on the coast near Bolougne, reducing travel expenses. It would also make communications easier if, as many were beginning to fear, another war was on the way. The 1938 reorganization left the Commission with four offices on the Western Front: the new head office at Wimereux and branch offices in Arras, Albert, and Ypres.[47]

Perhaps it was time for a change anyway. Sir Fabian was sixty-nine years old, and the overhaul gave him an opportunity to move Colonel Frank Higginson to London to groom him for command. In his place, Sir Fabian could hire a new chief administrative officer for Europe at a lower salary.[48] He spent the first several months of 1938 on the prowl for a suitable Canadian to replace Higginson, preserving the all-important "balance" of the staff.

For the War Graves community in Ronville, the Industrial Court award was a triumph. Most of the officers moved from Arras to Wimereux, but the brick office across from the train station still functioned as a branch office, and Ronville Camp was as active as ever. A weakening franc meant that the gardeners' sterling wages were worth more, even at a time of high inflation. Bert Witton's weekly wage jumped 27 percent when the new mandatory minimum of £3.10.0 went into effect.[49] The money was welcome, but so was the knowledge that the Wage Staff Association had won a victory by standing together.

The moment was short lived. The War Graves community was about to meet their new boss, Brigadier John Mervyn Prower, who would hold their lives in his hands during the disaster gathering on the horizon.

"RUNNING SHOES" 3

I f Brigadier John Mervyn Prower had served the War Graves Commission in peacetime, his personal and professional failings might never have hurt anyone. He could have done the work he excelled at—organizing wreath-laying ceremonies, liaising with French dignitaries over bottles of fine wine, chumming around with British officers—and never made a life-or-death decision.

Unfortunately, Brigadier Prower started his new job as the Commission's chief administrative officer for France and Belgium on September 1, 1938, just as Europe blustered toward the brink of war. By the time the Commission fobbed him off on the army less than two years later, the damage was done. Ben Leech, Rosine Witton, Bob Armstrong, and the rest of the War Graves community in France lived the rest of their lives in the aftermath of Prower's brief tenure.

On paper, Prower was perfect. He was "tall, distinguished looking and well educated" and spoke French "with complete fluency." Born in Quebec in 1885, to a family of striving imperial functionaries, Prower was sent to England to attend Bedales, a progressive boarding school. After graduating, he served as a lieutenant in the Hampshire Regiment and had an impressive rose-and-tiger tattoo on his forearm to prove it. Prower left the army in 1912 to try his hand as a gentleman rancher in British Columbia, but rushed back into the service when World War I erupted. He was part of the First Contingent of the Canadian Expeditionary Force, which crossed the Atlantic in October 1914.[1]

Prower's record in World War I was exemplary. He served as a brigade staff officer before taking command of a frontline Canadian infantry battalion in August 1916. Under Prower's leadership, the 8th Battalion

Canadian Infantry (90th Winnipeg Rifles) proved its mettle in battles like Mouquet Farm and Vimy Ridge. Prower himself was awarded the Distinguished Service Order twice and was mentioned in dispatches several times. In 1918, he was given command of the Canadian Corps Infantry School, in charge of infantry training for the entire Canadian Expeditionary Force.[2]

On the surface, Prower's war record was unassailable. Yet there were hints of the stories he liked to tell himself and others. In 1918, Prower was injured in a mundane road accident. He was riding in the sidecar of a motorcycle that was run off the road by a Royal Air Force (RAF) vehicle, leaving Prower with a broken jaw and four fewer teeth. Doctors in England heard a much more heroic tale. "Blown out of a motor car by bomb from a Hun plane," one wrote in Prower's medical records. "Wounded by a fragment from an Enemy aeroplane Bomb," noted another.[3]

After the war, Prower attended the British Army Staff College at Camberley. There, he crossed paths with many of the officers who would lead the British Expeditionary Force (BEF) in World War II, including its commander, Lord Gort, and his adjutant, Sir Douglas Brownrigg. They would all meet again in France in 1939. In the interim, Prower served in India and Canada, retiring from the Canadian army as a brigadier general in 1938.

Just as Prower was stepping down from his military career, the War Graves Commission was in need of a Canadian for its top job in France. Prower came highly recommended.

"Brigadier Prower will fill the post most admirably," Canadian Prime Minister Mackenzie King assured the War Graves Commission.[4]

Brigadier Prower faced a major challenge. The War Graves staff in France had lived and worked together for two decades, and any new leader would have struggled to gain their trust. Prower did not try.

Instead, Prower antagonized his new colleagues from the start. He complained. He wrote sarcastic memos. He bestowed unwanted nicknames. Rather than living in frugal housing close to the new head office in Wimereux, Prower installed his wife, daughter, and three maids in a grand château in Montreuil-sur-Mer, nearly thirty miles away. There was no practical reason for him to live in Montreuil, but Prower enjoyed living in a stately home that had once been part of Sir Douglas Haig's headquarters. He made the daily forty-five-minute commute to Wimereux in a Commission-owned Delage driven by a chauffeur.

It was a bad fit all around. Prower's fellow War Graves officers had internalized the Commission's commitments to moderation, economy, and service. Particularly in the wake of the 1938 labor dispute, the officers were keenly aware of the need to justify every franc and every drop of petrol. Prower's attitude—that a little light War Graves work enlivened his retirement in the French countryside—was fundamentally at odds with their values.

Still, Prower's colleagues might have forgiven his self-indulgence if he had not openly disparaged the Commission's work. Prower criticized the design of cemeteries, whined about the gardeners' attitudes, and told visiting dignitaries that the Thiepval Memorial was "certain to tumble down." Some of these criticisms were warranted but tactless. Prower never quite grasped the ethos that led Sir Fabian to speak of the Menin Gate as if it were his child and sign off letters with "Keep the cemeteries blooming."[5]

When Prower's complaints filtered back to London, Sir Fabian grumbled that he was a "new broom" who imagined that "he could have done the work in the past better than we did."

"He has got a queer social superiority complex which is essentially out-of-date as far as this democratic country is concerned," Sir Fabian complained in a private letter. "But I have already written too much about this, which indicates that I am irritated."[6]

The part of the job that Prower liked was its tendency to place him in proximity to power. He was happiest when visiting government officials—the more senior, the better. After the BEF arrived in France in September 1939, he spent much of his time at its headquarters in Arras, socializing with Lord Gort's staff, "all of whom are old friends of mine." Prower never missed an opportunity to brag. On trips to England during the winter of 1939–1940, he shared details of the BEF's position in France so indiscreetly that Sir Fabian was forced to reprimand him in writing.[7]

"My dear Prower, Do, I beg of you, exercise the utmost discretion while you are in England," Sir Fabian wrote in February 1940. "Quite a number of people, not only members of the Commission, have repeated to me such information which I had been careful not to give them (even when I knew it myself) telling me you had mentioned it in conversation."

Prower was much less interested in the day-to-day work of the cemeteries. To gardeners in the outlying areas, he was more a rumor than a supervisor.

"I hear criticisms of you rather on the absentee landlord line," Sir Fabian wrote after receiving complaints from gardeners in Cambrai and Reims that they had neither seen nor heard from Prower in months.

Prower dismissed these grievances. "I have never come across a Commission gardener who suffers in silence," he scoffed.[8]

Of all Prower's strained relationships, none would have more serious consequences for Ben Leech, Rosine Witton, and Bob Armstrong than his clashes with his second-in-command, Captain Reginald Haworth.

Haworth was Prower's temperamental opposite. A lifelong accountant from Liverpool, Haworth had a permanent frown line above the bridge of his spectacles. During World War I, he served in the Royal Army Service Corps, managing logistics in Belgium. That won him no medals, but his superiors praised his "able and methodical administration," undertaken with "care and exactitude . . . at a time of great stress and under circumstances of considerable personal risk and strain."[9]

After the war, Haworth became the Commission's chief accountant in France. He lived in a middle-class neighborhood in Arras rather than in Ronville but was still intimately involved with the lives of the staff. Haworth oversaw their payroll, issued their travel vouchers, and approved reimbursements for their medical fees as well as dealing with the nitty-gritty details of construction contracts and maintenance budgets.

He also took an unofficial interest in the gardeners' happiness. In 1930, a Liverpool golf club sent a parcel of used golf equipment "at the request of Mr. Reginald Haworth . . . for the use of the British gardeners who were permanently stationed in France, being employed in looking after the graves at Arras."[10]

Given Haworth's thorough understanding of the Commission's operations and his commitment to the well-being of the staff, Sir Fabian believed that he would be an invaluable helpmeet to Brigadier Prower. Accordingly, he promoted Haworth from chief accountant to deputy chief administrative officer during the 1938 reorganization, moving him from Arras to the new headquarters in Wimereux.

This was a good idea in theory, but it disintegrated on first contact with the mutual animosity between Haworth and Prower. Haworth was rigid and fretful; Prower was cavalier and heedless. They butted heads over everything.

Their most consequential disagreement concerned the Commission's responsibility to its staff in the event of a German invasion. The Commission withdrew its few permanent employees from Germany in August 1939, but the prospect of a wider war loomed. After the Nazi conquest of Poland in September, Haworth wanted to create a robust plan to evacuate the gardeners and their families in case a similar fate befell France and Belgium. Prower disagreed. He thought that Haworth was a hysteric who conjured nightmare scenarios that would never come to pass. It might,

Prower conceded, be necessary to pull back from a few cemeteries near the Maginot Line, but those withdrawals would be local and limited.

Sir Fabian Ware tended to agree with Brigadier Prower. He was much more interested in preparing the gardeners to carry on in an active military zone than in planning for worst-case scenarios. After France declared war on September 3, 1939, it restricted the movement of foreign nationals within its borders. No *étranger* could legally travel more than five kilometers from home. Since the Commission's work required routine travel for gardeners and officers alike, this order would have brought routine maintenance to a standstill. Sir Fabian sent Prower to petition the French government for special movement passes for the War Graves staff.

Prower, in his element, acquired the passes. Still, he favored a different solution. Rather than maintaining their civilian status, he proposed drafting the entire War Graves staff into the Royal Engineers. Ordinary gardener-caretakers would become sappers, head gardeners would be noncommissioned officers, and the salaried office staff would be commissioned officers.[11]

Sir Fabian agreed that the plan had promise but eventually concluded that it would not work. For one thing, it was not possible for any British military personnel to work in neutral Belgium, not even as cemetery gardeners. For another, Sir Fabian suspected that the dominions, especially Australia, might object to having their citizens unceremoniously conscripted.

"In the past, we have found that great embarrassment is caused to a Dominion Government by anything of this kind," Sir Fabian warned.[12]

In the end, they compromised. The salaried staff in France became general list officers in December 1939 but continued to be paid by the Commission rather than the army. The wage staff—and all staff in Belgium—remained civilians. Officers in France were permitted to wear military uniforms, while the gardeners were issued green-and-gold brassards and military-style caps with brass badges "similar to that worn by War Office messengers." The Commission also provided each gardener with a gas mask.[13]

These preparations aligned with Allied expectations during the "Phoney War," the eight-month period between the declaration of war in September 1939 and the German invasion of western Europe in May 1940. The Allies were prepared to fight a defensive war but did not believe that the Germans could conquer France as they had Poland. After all, the French army was strong, and its defenses were the best in the world. The Maginot Line, a series of fortifications along the Franco-German border, could not be beaten, at least not quickly. Defenses along France's border with Belgium were weaker, but the Allies reasoned that the Germans would not attack through the dense Ardennes Forest, which was not suited to a swift armored advance. Most likely, the Germans would come through central Belgium, where the flat roads were better for tanks.[14]

This posed a problem. Belgium was staunchly neutral. It was counting on the Allies to help fend off an invasion, but it would not allow their armies to enter its territory to prepare defensive positions. Instead, French and British troops spent the winter of 1939–1940 massed on the French side of the border, ready to dash into Belgium the moment the Germans attacked. Their plan was to rush forward to the River Dyle. With the help of the Belgian and Dutch armies, they would stop the Wehrmacht before they reached Brussels.

Privately, some British officials had reservations about this plan. It would not be easy to move an army over seventy-five miles of unfamiliar ground and set up a strong defensive position in a matter of days. Lord Gort himself had doubts, but he did not air them in public.

Brigadier Prower absorbed this outward confidence from his pals at headquarters. When he explicitly asked Lord Gort's staff whether a general civilian evacuation would ever be necessary in France, they replied that "such an evacuation appeared so unlikely that no decision had been taken as to whether the road control in those areas would be under the British or the French armies." In any case, "not much difficulty need be anticipated."[15]

French civil authorities made their own tepid preparations. Officials in the Pas-de-Calais department devised a plan of "rural dispersal." In the event of an attack, the populations of cities like Arras would scatter into the surrounding countryside, much as the children of London were sent out of the city center. This plan envisioned aerial bombardments of French cities, not tanks in the streets. A wholesale evacuation from Pas-de-Calais was "neither contemplated nor provided for."[16]

In the Nord department, which hugged the Belgian border from Dunkirk to the Ardennes, civil authorities were more pessimistic. If the Germans penetrated far enough into Belgium, their artillery could shell cities like Lille and Valenciennes. If that happened, civilians would be transported by rail to safe areas farther west. When Brigadier Prower asked for specifics, Nord department officials assured him that the War Graves staff would be treated just like the rest of the civilian population.

Both Brigadier Prower and Sir Fabian accepted the assurances of British generals and French civil authorities, but Captain Haworth did not.

He believed in planning for rain while the sun shone. Even if the Allies' plan worked perfectly, there was likely to be some upheaval, especially in Belgium. Haworth, who had extensive experience running logistics in wartime Flanders, knew what havoc could be caused by clogged roads and disabled trains. He also feared that France would close its borders against a flood of Belgian refugees. What would the Commission do if a quarter of its employees were trapped in Belgium with the Wehrmacht bearing down on them?

In order to alleviate both Haworth's anxiety and the simmering hostility in the Wimereux office, Sir Fabian decided to transfer Haworth to Belgium. With infinite tact, he used the declaration of war as an excuse to promote Haworth to the hastily invented post of deputy controller (Belgium area) in Ypres. In this new role, Haworth would report directly to Sir Fabian in London, bypassing Prower altogether. He could start at once.

Prower crowed over Haworth's departure. "The whole morale has risen here and it is a pleasure to come into the office," he assured Sir Fabian. When Haworth's wife left Wimereux to join her husband in Ypres, Prower asked her to deliver a message:

> Be sure to tell your husband not to be in any great hurry to send his Refugees here, we don't want them. Tell him there are many kilometers between the frontier and Ypres, he need not put his running shoes on the first moment the Germans enter Belgium. When I last saw him he gave me the impression he was going to evacuate his people there the first moment after that happened. Be sure and tell him there is no hurry for that.[17]

When he received this note, Haworth was incandescent. He had endured Prower's sneers for a year, but this too much. The refugees Prower did not want were the men Haworth had worked with for twenty years. He saw it as his responsibility to ensure their safety.

During the next eight months, Haworth channeled his anger into his work. Free from Prower's oversight, he had headroom to craft a meticulous evacuation plan for the 133 War Graves employees in Belgium and their families. He charted routes. He prepared vehicle requisitions. He assigned every Belgian War Graves family to a color-coded evacuation group. At every turn, he kept the staff apprised of their roles and responsibilities.[18]

Haworth also encouraged the gardeners to send their families to safety while it was still possible. Over the border into France was good; back to the United Kingdom was better.

"It may be dangerous for women and children to remain here—and difficult to get away," Haworth explained in a plainspoken letter in

February 1940. Many of the families took his advice. Haworth updated his evacuation lists whenever someone departed or arrived. He drew careful red lines through the names of Kathleen Knock and her six children— James (eleven), Thomas (nine), Arthur (eight), Ellen (five), Frederick (four), and Mary (three)—when they left for England, leaving gardener Frederick Knock to carry on alone in Passchendaele. Conversely, when the Boucher family of Poperinghe welcomed a new baby on March 7, 1940, Haworth celebrated by adding the newborn to the roster for evacuation group G (Violet).[19]

Haworth was a rare Cassandra among British officials. Soon after arriving in Belgium, he visited Sir Robert Clive, the British ambassador in Brussels, to ask what help Clive could offer in an emergency. Baffled, Clive assured Haworth that the War Graves staff had nothing to worry about. After all, they "would be on the right side of the fighting line."

When Haworth left, Ambassador Clive wrote to Sir Fabian to express his alarm over Haworth's morbid imaginings. Sir Fabian thanked Clive for giving Haworth "calming advice" and expressed his hope that Haworth was "the sort of man who would keep his head . . . in a real emergency."[20]

To Haworth himself, Sir Fabian offered a gentle warning. "I had a very nice letter from the Ambassador about your visit," he wrote, sandwiching a reprimand between morsels of praise. Without agreeing with Haworth, Sir Fabian offered a compromise. If Haworth exercised a bit more restraint, Sir Fabian would direct Brigadier Prower to make a formal transportation plan for any Belgian staff who crossed the border into France.

"I like the way you have taken the men into your confidence," Sir Fabian soothed. "Get round as much as you can and keep them working with a good heart."

Sir Fabian did prod Brigadier Prower into drafting a perfunctory evacuation plan for the staff in France, but it was nothing like Haworth's detailed instructions. Instead, Prower composed a blunt, eighty-two-word circular informing the gardeners in France that they were expected to remain at work unless the civil authorities in their villages gave explicit orders for them to evacuate. If that happened, the gardeners "should carry them out in the same way as the French Civil population." In other words, they should expect no help from the Commission.[21]

Even if they evacuated from their homes, the gardeners were ordered to stay in France. Anyone who left the country would lose his job. "If men of the Permanent Maintenance Staff leave France," Prower wrote to Sir Fabian, "it may be considered by the Commission that they have failed to keep their contract which may be terminated."[22]

Quietly, some of the gardeners in France began making their own preparations. All winter, Henry Hayler, the gardener at Aubers Ridge, spent his Sundays ferrying off-duty British soldiers to the battlefields at Vimy Ridge and Fromelles in his four-seater Peugeot. They paid him in petrol. Between trips, Hayler's best friend, gardener Bill Squires, would come around to share a pipe and chew over the latest gossip while their children played soldiers nearby, marching back and forth in German helmets they had picked up on the Aubers battlefields.[23] Where would they strike this time? Squires agreed that Hayler should hoard every spare drop of fuel.

Some of the gardeners were not at home with their families. Peter Moir and the other young reservists hired in 1936 were recalled to their regiments in September 1939. Peter left his heavily pregnant wife, Suzanne, and their one-year-old son, Angus, in Authuille, a village between Beaumont-Hamel and Albert. He and George Hignett, a gardener stationed in Longueval, traveled to Scotland to rejoin the Gordon Highlanders. They trained for a few weeks, then returned to France as part of the BEF. Peter spent the winter of 1939–1940 near Lille, two steps from the Belgian border. His 4th Battalion was among those poised to race forward to the River Dyle to stop the Germans.[24]

Before a shot was fired in France, British soldiers had already begun to die. The War Graves Commission commemorates 526 personnel who died in France between September 3, 1939, and May 9, 1940, some in training accidents or plane crashes, others of ordinary illnesses or mishaps.

Among the first to die was nineteen-year-old dispatch rider Lance Corporal John Hignett, who was killed in a motorcycle accident on October 5, 1939. He was the younger brother of George Hignett, the Gordon Highlander who worked in Longueval. John Hignett was buried in Marieux Communal Cemetery, one of the first World War II soldiers buried on the Somme.

In preparation for death on a much larger scale, the army called Sir Fabian back into service. This meant that he was simultaneously an active-duty major general in charge of Graves Registration and Enquiries and the vice-chairman of the ambiguously civilian War Graves Commission. In theory, the two jobs were distinct; in practice, they blurred into a perpetual state of uncertainty.

In an effort to draw a clearer line between his military and civilian roles, Sir Fabian appointed Major C. Keith Phillips, the Commission's legal adviser, to oversee new burials in France. Phillips commanded two small burial units, each consisting of two junior officers and about thirty men detailed from infantry battalions as gravediggers. Otherwise, he was mostly on his own. He had no car, no batman, and no clear place in the structure of the BEF. When a single private was sent to assist him, Phillips discovered that his new "clerk" was nothing of the sort.

"He is 19 years of age," Phillips moaned, "has 9 months service, cannot write shorthand, & has only just begun to typewrite."[25]

To make matters worse, no one knew who was supposed to pay Phillips. The question devolved into "an unseemly and rather squalid tangle" that created tension between Phillips and Lord Gort's staff. "He is over-sensitive and has worked himself into a state of real unhappiness and thinks that your staff don't love him etc. etc.!" Sir Fabian wrote to General Brownrigg. To smooth things over, Sir Fabian promised to place the Commission's resources at Phillips's disposal so that he could perform his duties with minimal demands on the BEF.[26]

Now it was Brigadier Prower's turn to feel slighted. Why should such a plum military post go to Major Phillips when he, Prower, had much more recent and high-ranking military experience and was so well connected at BEF headquarters?

Sir Fabian saw Brigadier Prower and Major Phillips as his right and left hands in France, but Prower felt that he had been sidelined. He began a vicious campaign to undermine Phillips at every opportunity.

"Brig. Prower was in his Hotel + stated that he could not let me have an IWGC car," Phillips wrote on November 8, 1939, days before the annual Armistice Day ceremonies. With no car, Phillips could not attend ceremonies with his fellow dignitaries.

"Armistice Day," he noted in his war diary. "IWGC car no longer available for me."[27]

Later, when General Brownrigg confided to Brigadier Prower that no one at BEF headquarters was quite sure who was in charge of current burials, Prower misrepresented himself as the man in charge. This led to several minor but nettlesome misunderstandings that metastasized into a headache for Sir Fabian. He found Prower's meddling "embarrassing" and "erratic" and sent his sincere apologies to Phillips.

"Prower does make things difficult for you, and this I fully realise and have all along realised," Sir Fabian assured him.[28]

Yet Sir Fabian struggled to rein Prower in.

"MAKE CONTACT WITH PROWER," he directed a Commission official via telegram, "AND EXPLAIN AGAIN TO HIM THAT HE MUST CONFINE HIMSELF TO COMMISSION WORK."

Sir Fabian also expressed his exasperation to Prower directly. "I cannot be happy if I feel that the man in France does not consider—as do the War Office, every soldier I know and all the Governments—that the care of the war cemeteries and memorials at the present time is a matter of the very first importance," Sir Fabian scolded. "If, on the other hand, you feel that the control of the Commission's work is of secondary importance at the present time then say so plainly and I will try to hasten your military appointment."

Affronted, Prower fired back at Sir Fabian.

"Please get it out of your head that I am dying to start soldiering again," he wrote. Prower bristled at the accusation that he was neglecting his War Graves work but conceded that he wanted to take a more active role in the current war.

"Quite frankly I do feel that 34 years military training is being wasted," he sulked. "Unless the Army suddenly realises what a goldmine of knowledge + experience they are leaving incarcerated in Wimereux, I see no reason to ever hope to soldier this war."[29]

Brigadier Prower's personal frustrations during the long, dull months of the Phoney War left him inattentive to his staff and unimaginative about the possible scope of the disaster they faced. He believed—on good authority—that the Allies would stop Hitler's army long before a single German toe touched French soil. After all, the French army was formidable, and his friends on Lord Gort's staff did not seem worried. Prower was not wrong to trust them. Defeat was neither inevitable nor particularly likely. But Prower's attitude—hope for the best, plan for the best—would have dire consequences for the War Graves families in France.

A wholesale civilian evacuation may have been unlikely, but it was not unimaginable. Captain Haworth imagined it in detail. He spent months sounding the alarm and making all possible arrangements within his small sphere of influence. In doing so, he set up a natural experiment. Two nearly identical groups—War Graves families in Belgium and their colleagues in France—faced a common crisis with a measurable outcome. How many of Haworth's people would be trapped in Nazi-occupied Europe? How many of Prower's?

On May 10, 1940, the news crackled from radios around the globe: the Nazi invasion of western Europe had begun. By the end of the day, the Germans had conquered Luxembourg, bombed the Netherlands, and penetrated miles into Belgium. French and British forces surged over the border, still confident that they could stop the German advance.

In France, War Graves officers at the Wimereux, Arras, and Albert offices opened their filing cabinets and took out 393 pre-addressed copies of Brigadier Prower's orders.[30]

One copy was addressed to Ben Leech in Beaumont-Hamel. May 10 was a Friday, so Ben was working in the cemeteries, shepherding the flowers through their transition from spring to summer. Perhaps the dispatch rider from the Albert office left his letter at the house with Marie, or perhaps he went out to the cemeteries to hand Prower's orders directly to the gardeners.

A whole stack of orders went to Ronville. Perhaps the messenger started at the top of the street with Bert Witton at Number 6 or at the other end with Wilfred Legg at Number 281. In between, there were letters for Herbert Dickens and Lionel Burge and for Henry Bull and William Medlicott, who lived in adjoining houses. Sister Betty Stuart may have gotten her letter at her apartment on Route de Bapaume, or the messenger may have stumbled across her on a house call at another War Graves home.

Most of the letters went to gardeners in the Pas-de-Calais and Somme departments, but some went farther afield. Bob Armstrong and the two gardeners under his supervision were in Valenciennes, an hour's drive east of Arras, near the Belgian border. There weren't many British gardeners so far east. There also weren't many strong defenses. The Maginot Line ended ninety miles short on the other side of the Ardennes Forest.

Ben, Bert, Bob, and the other gardeners slit open their envelopes and read Brigadier Prower's terse message:

SPECIAL CIRCULAR
TO ALL MEMBERS OF THE STAFF

> Should the Authorities of the Commune in which you are resident publish any instructions in regard to EVACUATION, you and your family, if any, should carry them out in the same way as the French Civil population.
>
> If you are evacuated you should, on arrival at the destination, immediately complete and detach the form at the foot of this circular and post it in the accompanying addressed envelope. You should have a 90 centimes stamp with you to put on the envelope.

J.M. Prower
Chief Administrative Officer
Imperial War Graves Commission

The change of address form at the bottom of Prower's letter was formatted for a French address. No gardener should leave the country.

When Captain Haworth issued his own orders to the gardeners in Belgium, he struck an entirely different tone.

"It is quite useless to get excited," began the first item in a list with nine bullets. "Remain calm under all circumstances."

Instead of advising his men to provide their own stamps, Haworth quoted the famous "Once more unto the breach, dear friends" speech from Shakespeare's *Henry V*: "Every British ex-serviceman attached to the Imperial War Graves Commission is now expected to shew the metal [*sic*] of his pastures." The remaining seven items explained where to go, what to bring, and where to meet if anyone got separated.[31]

Thus, the fortunes of the War Graves staff in France and Belgium diverged along tracks set down by their leaders. In Belgium, they would stick together. In France, all employees would have to decide what to do for themselves.

"MEN MUST STAND TO THEIR POSTS"   4

B ob Armstrong lurched into the War Graves Commission garage in Arras on his Commission-owned motorcycle. He was sweat-stained and haggard after the forty-mile ride from Valenciennes, but there was not a moment to lose. It was Thursday, May 16, 1940, just six days after Hitler launched his invasion of western Europe. Valenciennes was in flames. The Nazis were coming.[1]

For hours, Bob had nudged his way through the crowds of refugees who choked the road from Valenciennes to Arras. Desperate parents pushed children in prams. Elderly people rode in horse-drawn carts piled high with mattresses and chairs. Farmers prodded their plodding cows. Here and there, an automobile trundled along at wheelbarrow pace. Military vehicles found themselves hopelessly snarled in the sea of wretched humanity streaming west and south, trying to outrun the Germans. No one was directing traffic.

The going was slow, but Bob was determined to reach Arras. He had received the same orders as all the other gardeners in France on May 10—stand your ground unless explicitly ordered to evacuate by the local civil authorities—but it was hard to believe that those orders were still in force. There were no German ground forces in Valenciennes, but the Luftwaffe was bombing the city. Perhaps Brigadier Prower and the other War Graves officers did not yet understand what was happening.

Bob would make them listen.

Like many of the civilians on the road, Bob had faced the Germans in the last war. In 1917, he had been a young lance sergeant in the 1st Irish Guards when a bursting shell shattered his hip, leaving his right leg an inch shorter than the left. The injury still pained him, but it didn't stop Bob from becoming a War Graves gardener. In fact, the six-foot Irishman was so good at his job that the Commission promoted him to head gardener in charge of twenty-two cemeteries in the Valenciennes area. Still, the leg was never as strong as it had been, and Bob sometimes dreamed of leaving the cemeteries to become a florist.[2]

Bob had many friends in Valenciennes. His short-lived, childless marriage to a Belgian woman ended in divorce in 1932, but Bob was cheerful and gregarious. He was so popular with his French neighbors that the civil authorities once awarded him a medal for his "helpful and courteous" service to the city. When one of his cronies was asked to name Bob's closest friends, the man despaired, "one could name all Valenciennes."[3]

Now Bob's friends were fleeing for their lives. He could not save them, but he had a duty to protect the two gardeners under his supervision. He could not give them official permission to retreat, but he could plead their case to the officers.

When he arrived in Arras, Bob went straight to the War Graves garage on Rue de Grigny. The low-slung building near the railway tracks housed several Commission-owned cars and lorries, all well maintained and fully fueled. Bob parked his motorcycle beside the little fleet.

As soon as he dismounted, a clerk named Jack Day pressed him for news. Were the rumors true? Had the Germans really broken through? How bad was it?

Like everyone else in Arras, Day was unsure what to believe. Telephone lines were down, and the radio news was vague to the point of uselessness. The only thing Day knew firsthand was that Arras had suffered an air raid a few nights earlier that killed several British officers and left two unexploded bombs in Faubourg d'Amiens Cemetery.

The German ground forces had not reached Arras yet, but there were alarming portents. The sidings at the train station were crammed with overcrowded refugee trains and boxcars full of nervous horses. British soldiers were laying anti-tank mines and blocking off the major approaches to the city. A massive barricade—disabled vehicles, stray timber, shipping crates—spanned Route de Bapaume in front of Rosine Witton's *café-tabac*.

Bob Armstrong assured Jack Day that the situation to the east really was dangerous. Then he hurried off in search of Captain Alfred Melles, the officer in charge of the Arras office. Melles reported directly to Brigadier Prower. If the orders had changed, he would know.

Bob wasn't the only supervisor from the Commission's eastern outposts speeding toward Arras on Thursday, May 16. Traveling Superintendent Gardener Robert Bird was on his way from Cambrai, a town between

Arras and Valenciennes. At noon that day, five of the gardener-caretakers in Bird's district had walked off the job and converged on Bird's house to ask for official permission to leave Cambrai without jeopardizing their jobs. Failing that, they asked for vehicles to evacuate their wives and children before the Germans overran the town.

Bird could not countermand Brigadier Prower's order, but he promised to bring the matter to Arras. Around the time Bob Armstrong was parking his motorcycle, Bird was beseeching Captain Melles to lend him a few of the idle cars from the Rue de Grigny garage. With just three cars, Bird argued, he could ferry the Cambrai families to safety. It would take only a few hours.

Melles was sympathetic but unwilling to act without orders. He telephoned Brigadier Prower's office in Wimereux to "raise the question of evacuation," but was rebuffed by the new second-in-command, Major George Greensill. Melles tried to convince Greensill that the situation was dire, telling him that "it appeared to be a general evacuation, quite uncontrolled" and that gardeners from the eastern cemeteries were reporting that "official control had gone by the board."

Greensill understood, but there was nothing he could do. Brigadier Prower was not in the office, and no one had any luck raising his Montreuil château on the telephone. Until Greensill heard otherwise, Prower's order was still in force. Furthermore, no Commission cars could be used to evacuate women and children. "No transport was available for this purpose," Melles informed Bird.

When Bob Armstrong reached the office a little while after Bird, he received the same answer. Captain Melles acknowledged that "various members of the staff suffered unpleasant experiences owing to heavy bombing raids" but argued that, as far as he knew, none of them had actually been injured. Instead of providing material aid, Melles offered vague assurances that he would "try to assist any distress cases, if they arose."

Bob Armstrong was already in considerable distress. He stalked back to the garage, where he told Jack Day that he had been ordered to return to Valenciennes. Day was stunned. He immediately telephoned Melles and begged him to reconsider. When Melles refused, Day tried to reason with him. Perhaps they could let Bob work in the Ronville Camp nursery until things calmed down. After all, it would be a shame to send him away with a Commission motorcycle, "as we were very short of motor cycles."

Melles stood firm. "[He] said that his orders were that men must stand to their posts," Day reported. "He insisted that Armstrong should retain his motorcycle and proceed to Valenciennes."

No account survives of Bob Armstrong's journey back to Valenciennes. If it was anything like Robert Bird's trip back to Cambrai, it was as terrifying as the battles of their youth.

As Bird approached Cambrai, his car became mired in the flood of frightened refugees. Babies wailed. Cart wheels creaked. Parents coaxed their footsore children to walk another mile.

Over the din, Bird heard a droning sound. He looked up. Out of the brilliant blue, a swarm of Stuka dive-bombers swooped down toward the crowd on the road. Bird counted twenty-two planes.

He dove for cover. The planes dipped low, terror sirens screaming as they dropped their bombs at ten-yard intervals. Some refugees flung themselves into the ditches on either side of the road, but many were caught in the open. Deep, concussive blasts tore through the crowd. Wagons and automobiles exploded. People were torn to bits.

Before anyone had a chance to recover, the Stukas turned in a huge arc. On their second pass, they flew lower over the road, machine guns blazing. They could not miss.

Robert Bird had seen the carnage of the Somme and Passchendaele when he was a young soldier, but the massacre on the Cambrai road left him aghast. "The scene was indescribable," Bird wrote in his official report.[4]

～

All along the northern half of the old Western Front, the Nazi advance rolled on. Once the Germans punched through the French defenses at Sedan, they found that the hard shell hid a soft interior. Tanks and infantry swept in an arc from the Ardennes to the coast, taking ground so quickly that they outran their own communication and supply lines. Between Thursday, May 16, and Thursday, May 23, 1940, the Germans captured more French territory in a single week than their fathers had in four years.

It was a critical week for the War Graves gardeners in France. On May 16, nearly every gardener was still working in his cemetery. By May 23, half had escaped to the United Kingdom, and half were trapped in occupied France. Their lives turned on the choices they made and the chances they took during that week.

When Bob Armstrong rode to Arras on May 16, gardeners could still seek guidance from their leaders at the four War Graves offices. That became much more difficult the next day, May 17, when two of the offices—Albert and Ypres—shut down.

The Albert office, which oversaw cemeteries on the Somme, was directly in the path of the German advance. The mayor of Albert issued an official evacuation notice to Albert's 9,000 residents at about three o'clock on May 17. This was exactly the circumstance Brigadier Prower had imagined. In accordance with his order, the Albert office staff packed their most precious documents and called Wimereux to inform Prower that they were retreating south toward Paris. They departed before sundown.[5]

Farther north, in Ypres, Captain Haworth did not wait for orders from local authorities. After months of careful planning, it was time to put his evacuation scheme into action. On May 17, Haworth sent a notice to all 133 employees in Belgium, instructing them to be ready to move the next morning.

No plan survives first contact with the enemy, and Haworth's was no different. His party of 250 civilians endured hardships at every turn. Brigadier Prower did not provide the transportation he had promised, so the Ypres group did their best with a handful of cars and a fleet of bicycles. After a confused journey to the French border that included much back-and-forth to ferry the youngest, oldest, and sickest refugees in their few available cars, Haworth's group made an unsuccessful attempt to board an overcrowded refugee train. This seemed like a setback at first until they witnessed the aftermath of a Luftwaffe attack on a packed train farther down the road. "All I could see was blood, blood, blood," remembered fifteen-year-old Yvonne Lane.[6]

The fifty-mile journey from Ypres to Calais turned into a "six days' nightmare, when each day seemed like a period of 10 years." Haworth's civilians were strafed by the Luftwaffe in the daytime and bitten by rats when they bedded down in barns at night. They ran out of food and walked until their feet were bloody. One gardener who went ahead of the main group was briefly arrested by British military personnel as a spy. Haworth himself was treated with suspicion and put under armed guard when he "ran up against the liver of a youngish but angry [British] Major" in Calais. When the group finally boarded the ship *City of Christchurch* in Calais on the morning of May 23, the Belgian staff and their families were battered and exhausted, but nearly all of them were safe.[7]

The situation was entirely different in France. On May 17, the same day the offices in Albert and Ypres closed, Brigadier Prower held a meeting at the head office in Wimereux. Despite the branch office evacuations and the worrying telephone calls from Captain Melles in Arras, Prower saw no reason to amend his orders. Instead, he reaffirmed them.

"Any male members of the staff evacuating other than under official orders should be told to return to his post," wrote Major Greensill, recording the meeting's decision. "If he failed to do so would be deemed to have abandoned his employ."[8]

This was not an idle threat. Later that afternoon, two gardeners, Lawrence Dawson and Harry Wilkins, arrived in Wimereux with their families. Both were from Belgium, but they had not waited for Haworth's group. Prower chastised Dawson and Wilkins and ordered them back to their cemeteries. The gardeners protested. They could not possibly take their wives, children, and an elderly mother-in-law back through the crush of refugees. Prower would not budge.

After some shouting, Dawson and Wilkins agreed to return on the condition that Prower take personal responsibility for delivering their families to safety. Prower gave his word. That evening, as the two gardeners fought their way back toward the border, Prower brought their families to his château and set them up in the servants' quarters.[9]

Prower still intended to enforce his orders, but the gardeners in France were starting to worry less about their jobs and more about their lives. The officers in Wimereux were stubborn, the officers in Arras were deferential, and the officers in Albert were gone. Every family had to make their own decision.

In Aubers, the Hayler family chose to flee. On the morning of Saturday, May 18, instead of going to work, Henry Hayler cycled to a nearby British battery to ask the soldiers what was happening. Their answer frightened him. He raced home to his wife, Sarah, and their sons, thirteen-year-old Ernest and eleven-year-old Marcel.

Sarah was worried too. She had sent Marcel to the village on an errand, and he returned to report that the street was deserted and the shopkeeper was packing her inventory into the cellar. "I would have thought you would have gone by now," the shopkeeper told Marcel.

The Haylers loaded their car with food, important documents, and the petrol Henry had saved over the winter. The boys wanted to bring their toys, but there was not enough room. As Henry Hayler tied suitcases to the bumper, Marcel and Ernest set their pet rabbits free in the long grass behind their house.

On the way to the coast, the Haylers stopped in nearby Laventie to pick up Bill Squires, his wife Doris, and their thirteen-year-old daughter, Iris. It was a tight squeeze with seven people in the Peugeot, but they were lucky to have a car when most gardeners had only bicycles. Henry Hayler steered his little evacuation party toward Dunkirk, hoping it was not too late.

Farther south, Bertha Chapman and her family also took to the road. This was not Bertha's first experience as a refugee. She had spent World War I in exile in Switzerland while her mother and older brother stayed behind in Poperinghe to run an egg-and-chip shop. When Bertha returned to Poperinghe, she met and married Canadian gardener Albert Douglas Chapman. They raised their sons in Heilly, a village on the Somme. The oldest, Alfred, was at school in England, but thirteen-year-old Cyril and eight-year-old Harold were still at home.[10]

Like the Haylers, the Chapmans were among the fortunate few who owned a car. They packed their treasures and their dog, Bella, and joined the throng of civilians streaming toward Rouen, a port on the Seine.

By now, the traffic was even more confused. French troops and ambulances jockeyed for passage through the woebegone throng of refugees. Fresh shell holes made some roads impassable. Everywhere, dead civilians lay crumpled on the side of the road or slumped in the seats of abandoned cars.

Then from the sky came the unmistakable wailing of sirens. Bertha and Albert Chapman flung their sons out of the car and into a ditch, crouching over them as the German machine guns rattled. An antiaircraft battery in an adjacent field returned fire. Soon, the ditch was full of cordite fumes. The boys coughed and choked, so Bertha tore strips from her dress and soaked them in the ditchwater to make rudimentary gas masks. The children clutched the cloths to their faces to keep their eyes from burning.

When the shooting stopped, the Chapmans dusted themselves off. On the road, people shrieked in agony and grief, while the dead lay in silent, bloodstained heaps.

The Chapman family continued toward Rouen. The planes returned, so they hid again. The car ran out of fuel, so they walked. Decades later, Cyril Chapman would remember the dead with awful clarity. One in particular haunted him: a man who died at the top of a ladder and stayed there, "with all his inner parts hanging down to ground level."[11]

Despite several more air raids, the Chapmans reached Rouen safely. Others were not so lucky.

The first War Graves gardener to die in the evacuation was Leopold George Shreeve, who was killed by German soldiers around noon on Sunday, May 19. Shreeve was riding in a car driven by another gardener, W. Price. When they found the road blocked by German tanks, Price reversed direction and sped off. Five German soldiers opened fire, riddling the car with bullets.

At first, Price thought he had made a clean getaway. Then Shreeve murmured, "I think I'm hit." Horrified, Price examined his friend, who was bleeding from wounds in his stomach and back. Price rushed to a French military aid station, but it was too late. Shreeve died in the car.[12]

Only seventy-two hours earlier, Captain Melles had rebuffed Bob Armstrong and Robert Bird, in part because none of the gardeners had been hurt. Now Shreeve was dead, and the Luftwaffe was headed for Arras.

At 3:20 p.m. on May 19, a few hours after George Shreeve's death, the Arras office staff heard "a series of terrific crashes" along the railway tracks. The explosions came closer and closer, growing louder as they approached the crowded station.

Officers and clerks dashed for the cellar. Just as they reached it, a blast ripped through the building. Windows shattered. Doors flew off their hinges. Shards of office equipment embedded themselves in the walls like shrapnel.

Huddled in the dark cellar, the War Graves office staff waited in horrified anticipation as German bombs exploded all over the south side of Arras. Houses along Route de Bapaume collapsed from direct hits. Bombs ripped through Ronville Camp. War Graves families and their neighbors ran past Rosine Witton's café, streaming toward the entrance to the *abri*, the air raid shelter in the old New Zealand caverns.

Back at the station plaza, wounded people staggered into the War Graves basement with broken bones and shrapnel wounds. Sister Betty Stuart patched them up with calm efficiency, working by flashlight.

When the bombing finally stopped, the War Graves staff crawled out into the light. The office was a ruin of splintered furniture and scattered papers, but it was nothing compared to the carnage outside.

The train station was an inferno. Corridors full of hay where French soldiers had bedded down the previous night were blazing. So were the freight cars on the tracks. Trapped horses shrieked in panicked agony. One railway employee lay in a clinker pit with his leg torn off, bleeding to death. French soldiers lay sprawled in the street, killed by machine-gun fire. Nearby, a woman's corpse was crushed under fallen masonry.

Worst of all were the refugee trains. At least twenty cars packed with civilian families had been parked outside the Arras station, waiting for engines to tow them to safety. Now they were smashed and smoldering, with bodies burning in the wreckage. A man stumbled past, clutching the headless body of a small child. Nearly a hundred civilians were already dead; hundreds more were wounded or dying.

"I spent three and a half years [in France] during the last war, two years on the Somme," wrote Joseph Gothwaite, the Commission's inspector of stones and material, "and never saw anything even approaching this bombardment."[13]

Sister Stuart did not stand around gawking. She rolled up her sleeves and waded in, working side by side with the French doctors already on the scene. All afternoon and into the evening, she bandaged wounds and splinted limbs, impressing her colleagues with her "extreme bravery." Late that night, exhausted and filthy, Stuart stumbled home to her apartment on Route de Bapaume, only to find that a stray bomb had leveled the building.

It was clear now that the Germans would reach Arras within a day or two. British tanks were mustering near Vimy Ridge, north of the city, while General Erwin Rommel's 7th Panzer Division advanced from the east. The local government had still not issued a formal evacuation order, but Captain Melles decided he could not wait. It was time to leave Arras, orders or no.

Unfortunately, it was far too late for Captain Melles to reach all the employees in Ronville. After the bombing, he spent two hours driving through the debris-strewn streets, hoping to order employees to fall back to an assembly point in Bienvillers-au-Bois, twelve miles to the southwest. His efforts were mostly futile. Some gardeners had tacked notes to their doors saying they had gone to the underground shelters or into the countryside. Others had simply vanished.

Rosine and Bert Witton did not wait for Captain Melles's permission to leave Arras. They fled on foot with their neighbors, joining the tide of refugees straggling westward. "We walked about 30 miles," Rosine wrote later. She and Bert had put their money into their house, not a car. That was a perfectly reasonable choice in the prewar years, but it was not much help for getting to Calais. After days of tramping the roads, Rosine and Bert found themselves "surrounded from all parts" and "push[ed] away" from the coast. Exhausted, the Wittons returned to Arras.

Captain Melles did find a few employees in Ronville. In a report to the Commission, he mentioned speaking to future internees Harold Medlicott, Henry Bull, John Preston, and Herbert Dickens, all of whom were planning to take their families down into Carrière Wellington for the night. Melles told the men that he had already sent the office staff to the rendezvous point and that all remaining War Graves employees should convene there as soon as possible.

The men asked if the Commission could provide vehicles to carry children and the wounded. Melles, who had earlier vowed to help "distress cases" if they arose, hesitated. He did dispatch one Commission car to transport the Newman family, whose house had been bombed, but only one. Melles promised Jack Day that he would return the next morning, Monday, May 20, to unlock the garage and release the rest of the cars. Then he drove off with the keys, leaving the others behind.

Despite his promise, Captain Melles did not return to Arras. By the morning of May 20, "the situation was grave," and "German mechanized units were not far distant." Jack Day waited for Melles at the garage for more than three hours, even when the Luftwaffe returned for another raid. When a Welsh Guards officer finally shouted at Day to get out of Arras (or at least off the street), Day pedaled away on a bicycle. There were still at least three roadworthy cars locked uselessly in the Commission's garage.[14]

The Arras office was the last of the Commission's three branch offices to fall. By Monday, May 20, only Brigadier Prower's head office in Wimereux was still open.

Frantic gardeners and their families began pouring into Wimereux, clamoring for help. Some were injured, others were angry. All were frightened. Soon, there were more than a hundred people at the War Graves office.

Prower remained resolute. He issued "personal instructions to the men to return to duty," but these were "largely ignored."[15]

"We maintained our policy of sticking at work and only moving with the civil authorities," Major Greensill noted, but "gardeners in nearly every case reported that every body had gone from their villages when they themselves left."

Prower was not ready to contemplate retreat, but the other officers prepared anyway. When Major Greensill began packing important papers, a thrill of panic went through the refugees. People began to mutter that the officers were planning to save themselves and leave the gardeners and their families to their fate. They had reason to worry. Several officers had already sent their own families to the ports, some in Commission-owned cars.

Major Greensill sensed the refugees' mood souring. "Some of the men were getting awkward," he noted. In an effort to keep the gardeners from overhearing "one-sided telephone conversations" and becoming even more alarmed than they already were, Greensill banished them from the office.

There was nowhere to send them. Wimereux was filling up with refugees and Allied soldiers preparing to defend nearby Boulogne. One hapless soldier who did find a berth was Major Phillips, the Graves Registration officer who had endured Prower's torments all winter. Phillips had lost contact with his own men in the pandemonium and resolved to assist his old War Graves friends instead. He "installed his office" at Major Greensill's house and began searching for a ship.

On Monday, May 20, Wimereux was still able to receive occasional telephone calls from the Commission's home office in England. These were not particularly helpful. The situation on the ground was deteriorating far too quickly for anyone to make useful decisions from afar.

Sir Fabian Ware simply did not understand what was happening. On May 20, he issued an emergency order reiterating his firm expectation that all Commission staff would, "under whatever circumstances, remain in France." They could send women and children to England, but no Commission employee should step foot on a boat. If they were forced to leave Wimereux, they should fall back to a new position somewhere in France, though Sir Fabian's order did not specify exactly where.

"The above makes it clear the we expect the Commission staff to stick it," he scrawled across the bottom.[16]

This order was not compatible with reality. As Monday, May 20, became Tuesday, May 21, the bombing of Wimereux intensified. Major Greensill and Major Phillips threw all their efforts into finding a ship—any ship—that could transport the women and children to England. They had clear orders from Sir Fabian to prevent the men from leaving but were not sure whether they could stop them.

Greensill and Phillips should have been able to turn to Brigadier Prower for guidance in this moment of crisis. Unfortunately, Prower had disappeared.

The last time anyone had seen their commanding officer was the afternoon of Monday, May 20, when he left the Wimereux office with 100,000 francs and a Commission-owned car. Prower's plan was to return home to Montreuil, where he had arranged for a Red Cross ambulance to drive his wife and daughter to Le Havre. Then he planned to drive around the countryside searching for the displaced staff of the Albert office in order to give them emergency cash. It was a job for a junior officer, but Prower claimed it for himself. He left the Wimereux headquarters at three o'clock on May 20 and never returned.

The twenty-five-mile drive from Wimereux to Prower's château usually took about forty-five minutes, but with the main roads impassable, he was lucky that it only took three hours. The Dawson and Wilkins families were still in the servants' quarters, but no one offered them a seat in the ambulance. Prower made vague noises about returning the next day to help them, though anyone who had seen the roads knew that was a fantasy. Prower's wife, Ella, and eighteen-year-old daughter, Lorna, reached England safely. Blanche Dawson, Lily Wilkins, and their daughters did not.[17]

Ironically, both Lawrence Dawson and Harry Wilkins escaped. After Brigadier Prower sent them back to work, they met Captain Haworth's evacuation group on the road. They had a terrible journey, especially Dawson, who lost his left hand during an air raid. Still, they escaped with the rest of Haworth's group. Dawson and Wilkins did not discover Prower's betrayal until they arrived in England and found that he had saved his own family and left theirs behind.

After seeing his own family off to safety, Brigadier Prower drove inland. He had not gone far before he was mired in the refugee traffic. He persevered, creeping along toward the Albert staff's last known location.

"To change my plans or cancel my mission never so much as entered my head," Prower would later explain to a horrified Sir Fabian.

It was an appalling time for the War Graves staff to be leaderless. Captain Haworth's group was inching toward Calais, Major Greensill was pleading with any ship's captain who would speak to him, and Brigadier Prower was wandering around Picardy with no way to contact or be contacted by anyone. In the words of one junior officer, the underlings "were left to hold the baby, and a large baby at that!"[18]

At least Prower could not do much additional harm from the road. If he had remained in Wimereux, he might have enforced Sir Fabian's order to keep the gardeners in France. As late as Tuesday, May 21, Prower was still arguing that the Albert and Arras officers should have remained at their posts despite the evacuation order in Albert and the bombing in Arras.

"A precipitant retirement of these H[ead]q[uarte]rs should be nipped in the bud," Prower wrote, "such a retirement setting a not very good example to the gardening staff."[19]

While Prower was deluding himself about nipping a retreat that had already gone to seed, Allied forces struck back against the invaders. On May 21, eighty-three British tanks supported by the Durham Light Infantry swung along the south side of Arras, delivering a sharp counterpunch to Rommel's overextended division. They fought all afternoon, attacking across Route de Bapaume barely a mile south of Rosine Witton's *café-tabac*.

The British tanks fought well, but they were too few and lacked adequate air support to sustain their momentum. Many of the tanks broke down or ran out of fuel. At the end of the day, the British withdrew toward Vimy Ridge, where the Durham Light Infantry occupied the preserved trenches around the Canadian National Memorial visitor's center, protected by the concrete replica sandbags.[20]

The Battle of Arras (1940) was a success for the Allies, but it was a delay, not a victory. The counterattack made the Germans wary of outrunning their strength, which bought crucial time for Allied forces to retreat toward Dunkirk. They could not stop the invasion, but if they could delay the Germans, they might survive to fight another day.[21]

As Hitler's forces closed in on the English Channel ports, Major Greensill was near despair. British soldiers were taking up fighting positions in the streets of Wimereux and wiring the bridges for demolition. The War Graves civilians assembled at the Wimereux office were "getting very restless and giving vent to caustic criticisms."

Then a miracle. After a strong appeal from Major Phillips, the hospital ship *St. Julien*, which was loading wounded soldiers at Boulogne, agreed to take the War Graves women and children. Major Greensill mobilized every available axle to shuttle them to the quay.

The Hayler and Squires families were among the refugees who boarded *St. Julien* on May 21. They had been through an ordeal of their own, hiding in ditches when the road was strafed and watching as soldiers at a checkpoint shot a man point-blank. They were turned away from Dunkirk, so they drove along the coast to Calais and then Boulogne, just in time to join the *St. Julien* party. The War Graves officers ordered Henry Hayler and Bill Squires to stay behind with the rest of the men.

Everyone got a shock several hours later when Ernest Hayler, who had been exploring the ship, reported that he had seen Bill Squires on board.

"Dad must be with him," Sarah told her son. "Go and find him."

Ernest scoured the ship until he found his father and Bill Squires sharing a bowl of rice pudding in the galley. *St. Julien*'s departure had been delayed to wait for more wounded, and the captain had allowed the War Graves men to board at the last minute. Henry and Bill had not realized that it was the same ship. They believed that their families were already halfway to England. Their reunion was a happy one, but it was also an exception to the many tragedies playing out behind them.[22]

The decision to let 120 War Graves evacuees, including men, board *St. Julien* caused outrage on the quay at Boulogne, where thousands of French civilians were begging to be saved as well. Despite the emergency, most ships that left the English Channel ports in the last days insisted that refugees show British passports in order to board.

Officials in the United Kingdom agreed that passport controls had to be enforced. One War Graves gardener, Ernest MacFarlane, smuggled his son's French fiancée, Odette Dupuis, onto a ship by claiming she was his daughter. He was later prosecuted and found guilty of helping an undocumented person enter the United Kingdom illegally. He was fined, as was another gardener, Charles Posford, who gave Dupuis shelter.[23]

Shortly after *St. Julien* departed, civil authorities in Wimereux finally ordered an evacuation. The last remaining War Graves officers pinned a notice to the head office door saying that it was "temporarily closed" and directed all further enquiries to Brigadier Prower's distant château. Then they scattered to save themselves.

With the closure of the Wimereux office, any War Graves gardeners left in France were completely on their own.

Bertha Chapman's family reached Rouen mere hours before it fell to the Germans. They begged the captain of a Norwegian coal boat, *Ringhorn*, to take eleven-year-old Cyril and eight-year-old Harold, but he refused. The English Channel was mined, and, besides, *Ringhorn* wasn't equipped for passengers.

That night, Norwegian sailors smuggled the Chapman family into the pitch-black hold. They crouched in the dark, holding their breath while Germans tromped across the deck, inspecting the ship before departure. Luckily, the search was cursory. *Ringhorn* left the next morning with the Chapman family hidden below.

Once they were under way, the Chapmans were taken to see the captain, who seemed unsurprised to see them. After a horrendous week at sea, they lumbered into the port of Barry in Wales. Cyril, who still winced every time an airplane passed overhead, was bewildered by the sight of holidaymakers "enjoying themselves on the beach with what appeared having not a care in the world while so much was going on in Northern France."[24]

Other Commission families escaped via Dunkirk. The main evacuation of the British Expeditionary Force—Operation Dynamo—did not start until May 26, but a few ships began evacuating the wounded and other "useless mouths" several days earlier.

On Wednesday, May 22, a party of eighteen War Graves civilians slipped past the military barricade around Dunkirk and into the burning city. The youngest was eight-year-old Maggie Egan. The gardeners climbed onto a barge along the quay and waited for the moment when *St. Julien*'s twin hospital ship, *St. Helier*, moved in close enough to touch. In a mad dash, about 650 soldiers, airmen, and civilians swarmed the ship, many of them "jumping from the quay to the boat rails." All the War Graves civilians, including Maggie Egan, made it aboard.

A few days later, seventeen-year-old Elaine Madden made an even more harrowing escape. Elaine's Australian father, Larry Madden, had been a War Graves clerk in Ypres, but he left in 1932 after Elaine's mother died of a septic miscarriage. Elaine remained in Poperinghe with her grandparents, growing up trilingual in English, French, and Flemish. She attended the British Memorial School in Ypres with the other War Graves children, but her father was not a current employee, so Elaine was not on Captain Haworth's evacuation list.

As the Germans drew closer, Elaine's grandparents feared for her. They remembered the last German invasion of Belgium and knew that a girl with British papers might be doubly vulnerable to rape and internment. Together with her teenage aunt, Elaine set out on foot, following the retreating British to Dunkirk. Sympathetic soldiers disguised the girls in overcoats and helmets and smuggled them onto the beach, where they waited for rescue with the bedraggled, beaten army. They broke cover only once they were aboard ship. Four years later, the multilingual Elaine would return to Belgium by parachute as a trained Special Operations Executive agent.[25]

Not until Saturday, May 25—four days after *St. Julien* left Boulogne, three days after *St. Helier* left Dunkirk, and two days after *City of Christchurch* left Calais—did Brigadier Prower finally advise Sir Fabian Ware that ordering the War Graves staff to remain in France was "unsound." It would be better to send the men to England, Prower wrote, where they would no longer be "in the way."[26]

Sir Fabian agreed that Prower could send excess staff back to England but encouraged him to retain a small group to carry on in unoccupied areas. On May 29, a week after most of the War Graves refugees departed, Sir Fabian instructed Prower to "continue work at any cemeteries still accessible." Prower was still ordering gardeners to work as late as June 5, when he asked R. MacDougall to "get back sometime with a scythe" to "straighten up" the Commission plot in Oulchy-le-Chateau Churchyard, which was "a veritable hayfield."

"It is essential that we should so to speak keep the Commission flag flying in France," Sir Fabian wrote to Prower on June 5. "Even if the worst happens, some small administrative staff should be in constant touch with the appropriate French authorities."[27]

Boulogne fell. Calais fell. British and French troops protected Dunkirk long enough for the navy to evacuate more than 338,000 soldiers, far more than expected. Fighting continued, but the dam had been breached. On

June 10, the French government abandoned Paris. On June 22, they surrendered.

In the final days, a few more War Graves personnel escaped via ports farther west. Brigadier Prower arranged for a message to be broadcast over French radio directing any remaining War Graves staff to join him at a temporary headquarters he established in Brittany. This advice was not very useful, as there was an active battle zone in between, but a few displaced gardeners did manage to link up with Prower in Fougères. Others sent pathetic letters saying that they were doing everything possible to reach him.[28]

When it became undeniable that France would fall, Prower sent most of the remaining employees to the port of Cherbourg, keeping twenty staff—including Sister Stuart—with him. After a series of retreats that sent them hundreds of miles south, this final group of War Graves personnel squeezed aboard a Dutch ship that departed Bordeaux on June 20 as part of Operation Aerial, the evacuation of the French Atlantic coast.

The Imperial War Graves Commission had been driven out of France.

∿

While the dust was still settling, the leaders of the War Graves Commission in London congratulated themselves on the success of their evacuation. Using testimony from returning officers, they produced a report that concluded that the Commission's officials had done an admirable job in the midst of an "inferno of indescribable confusion."

Sir Fabian expressed his admiration for the officers who "doggedly devoted themselves, hour by hour, to those for whom they were responsible."

"As we look back," he wrote, "it seems marvelous that they succeeded in mercifully extricating so many of our staff and their families and bringing them back in safety to England."

Sir Fabian sent the report to Minister of Information Duff Cooper on June 10. He hoped that an extract could be published in the press as an answer to the deluge of inquiries the Commission was receiving from relatives of the last war's dead. Sir Fabian did offer one caution. "I do not think any allusion should be made to Brigadier Prower's adventures on the top of Page 5," he wrote. "They might be misunderstood."[29]

Cooper acknowledged the report but was not impressed. The mourning public might well be worried about the cemeteries, but Cooper saw "nothing in the report that would be calculated to calm their anxiety."[30] Besides, the nation was "so deeply concerned about the fate of those who are actually engaged in fighting" that they were "hardly in the mood" for a story about the War Graves gardeners.

The report found a more receptive audience among the commissioners. Major General Sir John Kennedy called it "a story of determination, endurance, and courage which will form a chapter in the history of the War Graves Commission of which we shall all be very proud." Another reader called the evacuation report "an epic not less impressive than the Dunkirk affair" and congratulated Sir Fabian "for having picked such good officers."[31]

These plaudits were based on a selective reading of the facts. Of the 526 employees stationed in France and Belgium, 309 (59 percent) reached the United Kingdom, 206 (39 percent) were stranded, and eleven (2 percent) were either dead or unaccounted for.

The overall numbers were bad enough, but they masked the awful difference between gardeners in Belgium and their colleagues in France. Of the 133 men in Belgium, only sixteen failed to reach England. Most of these sixteen either declined to join the group or were unavoidably separated during the journey. Captain Haworth had endured months of mockery and condescension for sweating the details of his evacuation plan, but he kept his people safe.

Brigadier Prower did not. At every turn, he ordered men to stand to their posts. When the final roll was called, only 47 percent of the 393 employees in France escaped. Slightly more than 50 percent were stranded. The rest were killed or missing.

In truth, no one knew exactly how many War Graves civilians died during the evacuation. There were witnesses to George Shreeve's death, but other men disappeared into the chaos and never reemerged.

One was Walter Edgar Coller, a former Welsh Guardsman and gardener in Merville. On May 22, a bomb narrowly missed Coller's house, shattering windows and leaving "a large bomb crater" near the front door. Coller and his wife, Elodie, headed for the Belgian port of Ostend, where a witness saw them board a ship with a "boy aged 7 or 8." The ship left Ostend on May 26, but it never landed anywhere.[32]

Another gardener who vanished during the pandemonium was Michael Flood, who was one of Captain Haworth's evacuees from Belgium. Flood had sent his wife, Grace, and son, Louis, to England months earlier but stayed behind in Ypres. He departed with Haworth's group on May 18 and was riding with a group of gardeners on bicycles when they ran into trouble. Accounts differ. Perhaps they were caught in an air raid; perhaps they were confronted by German soldiers. In any case, Michael Flood "went off his head."

Like his fellow gardeners, Flood was a veteran. He spent four full years on the Western Front in World War I, enduring nerve-rattling bombardments and gas attacks. Now it was all happening again. The other gardeners tried to stop him, but Flood rode away from the group and vanished. Years later, the Red Cross confirmed that Michael Flood died in a state-run asylum in Luxembourg in 1943. The three years between his disappearance and death remained a mystery.[33]

The chaotic evacuation caused death through physical illness as well. Gardener Maynard Pursglove, formerly of the Royal Sussex Regiment, reached England safely but died on June 8, 1940, of pneumonia aggravated by multiple sclerosis. Pursglove's chronic illness had remained under control for years while he lived the quiet life of a gardener but flared up lethally under the stress of the evacuation.[34]

The circumstances of gardener J. Foolkes's death were even more obscure. A note in a Commission file says only that the Wiltshire Regiment veteran died on September 13, 1940, "as a result of unsuccessful attempt to evacuate."[35]

After the disaster, the Commission investigated the gardeners' fates, but it never collected comprehensive information about their families. A few hints survive in scattered records—gardener John Harris's fifteen-year-old daughter Violette was killed in an air raid, gardener William Paull's teenage daughter was admitted to a hospital in Southampton as soon as their ship docked, and gardener Charles M. Baker's wife Gaby "narrowly missed being killed" by a bomb—but there was no comprehensive list. One document compiled in June 1940 noted that eleven gardeners' wives were "lost" during the evacuation, though it did not elaborate. The next line, "Children," had only a question mark.[36]

Not everyone who escaped was willing to praise the Commission's performance. Robert Bird, the supervisor from Cambrai who had visited Arras on the same day as Bob Armstrong, used his official report as an opportunity to vent his frustration with the leadership in France.

"Had full use been made earlier of the Commission cars stationed at Arras, many more of the staff could have been moved," he wrote. "I feel very bitter over the fact that on Thursday, [May] 16th, I was refused transport to enable me to get my staff out of the vicinity of Cambrai while there was still time."[37]

Behind closed doors, some of the Commission's senior leaders admitted that mistakes had been made. Sir Fabian asked Brigadier Prower to provide "full facts" about his movements to "meet uninformed criticism," but his answers were hardly reassuring. One commissioner commended the officers in general but singled out Prower for disapproval: "All the members of the staff seem to have carried out their work in a most praise worthy manner, with the exception of the one man from whom I should have expected most."[38]

Sir Fabian tried to soften criticisms of Prower. He argued that Prower "simply made the mistake, not uncommon on the part of energetic Commanding Officers, of undertaking a subordinate officer's work and thus cutting himself off from his Command." But even Sir Fabian could not deny the truth. "The fact remains that during the more very critical hours [Prower] was not in command at Wimereux as he should have been."[39]

Sir Fabian knew that Brigadier Prower had to go. He had been a problem for months, but Sir Fabian had kept him in a position of authority anyway. The staff and their families had borne—and were still bearing—the consequences.

In order to bring Prower's employment to a tactful conclusion, Sir Fabian encouraged the army to take him back into active service.

By the end of the summer, Prower had command of his own brigade.

～

Bob Armstrong did not escape from France. The last anyone on the Commission's staff saw him, he was riding back to Valenciennes on his motorcycle.[40]

On Friday, May 24, a week and a day after Bob's visit to Arras, his sister, Augusta Lindsay, wrote to the War Graves Commission to ask for news of her brother.

"I am very upset as we have not heard from him this past 3 or 4 weeks," she wrote. Could the Commission please tell her where Bob was and how she could reach him?

Augusta received only empty assurances. "I am sorry to say that we have not yet heard of Mr. R. Armstrong," wrote a commission official, "but have no reason to believe that he is not in a place of safety."[41]

"PANIC?"   5

O n Friday, May 17, 1940, the day after Bob Armstrong was turned away from the Arras office, Ben Leech opened his daily entry in his gardening log with a question: "Panic?"[1]

Ben was not the panicking sort. He was a man who wrote lists and kept receipts and never rushed into anything. It was hard to believe that the invasion was real, especially since there were no Germans in Beaumont-Hamel yet. Still, it was difficult to ignore the unending stream of refugees trudging past, muttering about horrors farther east.

Ben Leech watched them with a sense of detachment. Panic might be afoot, but he had orders, which he reiterated in his gardening log: "Last order of the I.W.G.C. for us to stand fast until told to go by the mayor of village."

Since the mayor of Beaumont-Hamel had not ordered him to evacuate, Ben treated May 17 as an ordinary workday. In the morning, he hitched a lawnmower to his bicycle and rode out to Sucrerie Military Cemetery, about two miles northwest of Beaumont-Hamel. He spent the day mowing.

Among the bedraggled civilians who plodded past Sucrerie Cemetery as Ben trimmed the grass were Head Gardener Fred Martin; his wife, Clarisse; and their nine-year-old niece, Ginette. They lived in Bucquoy, five miles north of Beaumont-Hamel, and had decided not to wait for evacuation orders.

"There were thousands on the road," Martin wrote in a letter to his mother in Cornwall. "[The road] was black with people & jerry kept his eye on them, they are devils to machine-gun the refugees." The Luftwaffe attacks were "especially terrible for the children," Martin noted. "Ginette had her cry."

The adults were just as bewildered. "After twenty years, I never thought we should be refugees in France," Martin wrote. "It's not War but Destruction."[2]

While the refugees fled south, British and French troops rushed north and east, struggling against the chaotic traffic. One battalion that rode directly past Sucrerie Cemetery on May 17 was the 1st Tyneside Scottish (the Black Watch). They were part of a half-trained labor division, not experienced infantrymen, but they were planning to hurl themselves into the path of the advancing Germans. The sight of so many pathetic refugees stiffened their resolve.

"Poor little Kiddies on top of Farm carts," Company Sergeant Major Charles H. Baggs wrote in his journal. "By God, waite untill we meet the German ——, we shall do our best to give him all we have got."[3]

As he watched the hurrying troops and ceaseless stream of refugees pass by, hour after hour, Ben Leech became increasingly uneasy. Like Bob Armstrong, he began to question whether Brigadier Prower's order was still in force.

At the end of the workday, Ben left his mower at Sucrerie and slipped in among the refugees on his bicycle. He pedaled six miles south to Aveluy, a village near Albert, in search of Traveling Superintendent Gardener Edward Goad. Goad held the same rank as Robert Bird, the lowest of the salaried officers, just above the head gardeners. Ben hoped he would know the latest news.

Ben found Goad at home, packing suitcases into his private car. He had just come from Albert, where the mayor had issued an evacuation order. At that very moment, Captain Samuel Burkey and the rest of the War Graves office staff in Albert were busy loading five Commission-owned cars with critical documents and "the most valuable stores."[4]

Edward Goad planned to join the Albert office's retreat as soon as he could convince his wife, Louise, to leave Aveluy. So far, he hadn't had much luck. Louise Goad was Aveluy's schoolteacher and the mayor's secretary. Earlier in the day, the mayor had deserted the village without notice, leaving 500 frightened civilians to fend for themselves. In his absence, Louise Goad took over the administration of Aveluy. She gave directions to her neighbors, assisted a British officer in finding billets for his men, and invited several French officers to stay in her home. She was far too busy to evacuate.[5]

Ben Leech explained to Edward Goad that there was no official evacuation order in Beaumont-Hamel. Strictly speaking, the same was true in

Aveluy, but Goad did not care. He planned to leave as soon as he could drag Louise away from her duties and urged Ben to leave as well. In fact, when Ben pedaled away that evening, Goad was under the impression that he was only going home to fetch Marie and the children.

"I quite expected to see him again the following day," Goad recalled.

In fact, Edward Goad did not see Ben Leech again for more than four years.

Goad spent the next day, Saturday, May 18, in the deserted Albert office, assisting gardeners and making a mostly futile effort to maintain contact with Brigadier Prower's office in Wimereux. By the time he finally convinced Louise to leave Aveluy at dawn on Sunday, May 19, their retreat was accompanied by the rattle of gunfire. Pressed for time and fuel, they did not drive through the villages in search of stranded gardeners. Instead, they fled for the coast with their teenage daughter, Phyllis.

"There was a panic," Goad wrote in an apologetic report to Sir Fabian Ware. "I did all that was possible under the circumstances."[6]

Edward Goad did all he could, but no individual could fix the fundamental flaws in the Commission's evacuation plan. Ben Leech ran up against one its central paradoxes when he returned to Beaumont-Hamel after his meeting with Goad. There, he found that "all the chiefs of administration of Beaumont evacuated without giving us warning." With no remaining civil authorities, there could be no evacuation orders.

By the evening of May 17, many of Ben Leech's colleagues were long past caring. Ben's direct supervisor, Head Gardener Frank Ray, joined a group of gardeners and their wives who spent that night behind the ersatz castle walls of the Ulster Memorial in Thiepval. The next day, they bribed a farmer to drive the women to the coast while the men followed behind on bicycles. Robert Mullenger, one of the five gardener–caretakers in Ben's gardening group, hopped on a farm cart with his wife and went wherever it was going. Another man in the group, Thomas Haley, went south, ending up in Carcassonne, near the Spanish border. Both Mullenger and Haley managed to outrun the German advance, but they were still stuck in France. Of the six men in Ben's gardening group, only the head gardener, Frank Ray, reached England.[7]

Even if they wanted to evacuate, families like the Leeches lacked transportation. Unlike the officers, very few gardener-caretakers owned private cars. Ben Leech had his bicycle, and Maurice may have had another, but they certainly did not have enough for the whole family. If they were going to make a dash for the coast, it would be on foot.

Many War Graves families had the same problem. Gardeners with large families or young children were especially likely to be left behind, along with anyone who was seriously ill or disabled. Unlike Captain Haworth's party in Belgium, which used the few available cars to transport the most vulnerable members of the community, the every-man-for-himself plan in France meant that the people with the most resources and the fewest obstacles were most likely to reach safety.

A few of the gardeners—like Henry Hayler and Alfred Douglas Chapman—did have cars that allowed their families to escape. Others used their private vehicles to help their neighbors. In Beugny, near Bapaume, Head Gardener Arthur Clark used his car as an ambulance.

"There were many casualties in the village and Mr. Clarke was using his car to evacuate the wounded to Bapaume hospital," reported letter cutter Michael O'Neill, who passed through Beugny on May 17. Clark's decision to delay his evacuation to help his neighbors cost him his freedom and, ultimately, his life. He died in an internment camp in 1944.[8]

Of all the 393 War Graves employees in France, the group that evacuated most successfully were the officers. In addition to their private cars, the officers also controlled most of the Commission-owned vehicles. These critical transportation resources ensured that every single War Graves officer arrived safely in England along with all but one member of the permanent salaried staff. The one left behind was John Preston, a low-level clerk who lived in Ronville. Two temporary salaried employees were also stranded: letter cutter Bernard Parsons and the newly appointed transport superintendent, Stanley Hawkins, who refused to leave his home in Achicourt "on account of wife's family and dogs." Apart from Preston, Parsons, and Hawkins, every stranded War Graves employee was a wage-earning gardener, craftsman, mechanic, or laborer.[9]

The situation in Albert was typical. The salaried office staff used five Commission-owned vehicles and Captain Burkey's private car to evacuate on May 17. Unlike the Hayler family, who fit seven passengers into their Peugeot, each of the six cars in Burkey's convoy carried four or five people. The group included only three children under the age of eighteen and no family with more than one child.[10]

Before they left, the Albert office staff made no effort to contact gardeners in the outlying villages. Brigadier Prower had not ordered the officers to take responsibility for the men in their areas, and Captain Burkey made no extemporaneous effort. Beaumont-Hamel was only seven miles from Albert, but Burkey never sent a bicycle messenger to alert the gardeners that he was leaving, let alone a car.

Among the people left behind was twenty-two-year-old Suzanne Moir, whose husband, Peter, was fighting with the Gordon Highlanders in Belgium. Suzanne was at home in Authuille, sick with pneumonia. Alone and ill, with two children under the age of two, there was no way she could evacuate without help. Suzanne Moir's house in Authuille was only three miles from the Albert office, but she was not included in Captain Burkey's convoy. As the fighting drew closer, Suzanne packed her infants into a pram and set out on foot. She did not get very far.[11]

Panic took many forms. As the catastrophe unfolded, some members of the War Graves community saved their own skins. Others threw themselves into helping others.

Ben Leech went to the cemetery.

"Went to work as usual," he reported on Saturday, May 18, the morning after he visited Edward Goad.

A few other gardeners turned up for work that morning but only to give notice that they were leaving. Ben must have told them that he intended to stay in Beaumont-Hamel because one of the departing gardeners entrusted him with a note and some money for Head Gardener Ray. Ben cycled to Ray's house in Pozières the next day but could not find his supervisor. He had no idea that Ray had already left with the Ulster Tower party.

After a fruitless search, Ben pedaled back across the battlefields to Serre Road Cemetery No. 2. It was a Sunday, not a usual workday, but he put in a few hours anyway. He seemed unable to do anything else.[12]

Finally, on Sunday evening, something changed for the Leech family. Perhaps they heard the approaching guns. Perhaps Ben realized that everyone else was gone. Whatever finally spurred them to action, they spent the evening of May 19 "prepar[ing] to leave, packing up necessarys."

It was too late. The Leeches left their home at 8:30 on the morning of Monday, May 20, but were overtaken by German tanks before they had gone five miles. Discouraged, they turned back. Ben was home by 11:30, in time to watch elements of the 2nd Panzer Division sweep through the village.

"Tanks passed through Beaumont-Hamel at 12:15 noon," he wrote in his gardening log.

Ben Leech did not panic in a burst of frantic activity. Instead, as the tanks lumbered past, he withdrew from everything happening around him. Marie and the children were trudging homeward after their aborted evacuation, but Ben did not walk with them. Three British soldiers lay dead on the Serre Road, but Ben did not bury them. Someone broke into the Leech family home and ransacked it, but Ben was not there to stop them.[13]

Instead, he spent the first afternoon of the Nazi occupation at Serre Road Cemetery No. 2, watering the roses.

∽

The dead were everywhere. Across northern France, corpses sprawled in roadside ditches, smoldered in the ruins of bombed out cars, and bobbed silently in rivers. In villages near Arras, hundreds of civilian dead lay heaped in quarries and farmyards where they were executed by the Germans in retaliation for token resistance. In Arras itself, dozens of bodies lay under the rubble of the train station until the end of July.[14]

It is impossible to say exactly how many people were killed during the Nazi invasion of France. Modern historians estimate that 100,000 French civilians died, along with around 90,000 French soldiers and 12,000 British. Another 1.8 million French and 40,000 British soldiers were captured.[15]

As the active fighting moved farther south, refugees in the north returned home to the grim aftermath of German victories. In Bas-Warneton, a tiny Belgian village on the French border, civilians recovered the remains of fifty-three British soldiers. Many of them were found in pulverized houses along the Ypres-Comines canal, which the British had used as machine-gun emplacements until they were overrun.

Among the dead in Bas-Warneton was Peter Moir, the young gardener from Beaumont-Hamel. Moir's headstone says that he was killed on May 24, but that is probably not accurate. The 4th Gordon Highlanders were still near Lille on the 24th, spending a "quiet day" waiting for attacks that never came. On the night of May 25/26, the battalion moved north to Bas-Warneton to defend the Ypres-Comines canal. The 4th Gordon Highlanders was a specialist machine-gun battalion, so its men were parceled out in small groups attached to the 13th and 143rd infantry brigades. Their job was to hold the line at all costs.[16]

The German attack came on May 27.

"Infantry driven back by enemy leaving our guns to cover B[ri]g[ad]e fronts," noted the 4th Gordons' war diarist. The machine gunners were "under heavy mortar fire" all day, but they held the Germans back until the British infantry mounted a counterattack that night.

It was a small success but a crucial one. If the Germans had broken through the British line south of Ypres on May 27, they would have severed the main route that Allied troops were using to retreat to Dunkirk. Tens of thousands of soldiers passed through that corridor on the night of May 27, thanks in part to the machine gunners of the 4th Gordon Highlanders who died to keep it open. Local civilians laid Peter Moir to rest in the village cemetery.

Fifty miles south, on the southern outskirts of Arras, civilians in Ficheux were facing an even more gruesome scene.

On May 20, three days after they drove past Sucrerie Cemetery, the 1st Tyneside Scottish made a plucky stand near Ficheux. They confronted the Germans on a farm owned by the Pronier family, but they were no match for tanks.

"I could see the Boys fighting like Hell with Tanks all around them simply going over the men, and what a terrible sight," wrote Company Sergeant Major Charles Baggs. The Germans "simply blasted us out of the Embankment."

Baggs and the other survivors were quickly captured. As they were driven into Ficheux, they passed the Pronier family's barn, which was "blazing like hell, and some our boys inside, burnt to death."

"We saw at least two bodies, half in and half out of the barn door, burnt black," Baggs reported. "God what a sight!"[17]

Several days after the battle, the Proniers returned home.

"It was a horrible, unbearable spectacle," recalled Monsieur Pronier. "There were corpses everywhere."

In the fields, dead men from the Tyneside Scottish and the Durham Light Infantry were swollen and teeming with flies. In the barn, "cadavers were mixed together with bodies that were completely burnt . . . it was a shapeless mass giving off a pestilential odor." Even worse was the carnage in the farmyard. Pigs, freed from their pens in the confusion, had gorged themselves on the dead, spattering the farmyard with blood, hair, and dismembered fragments: "Here a skull, there a foot." [18]

With handkerchiefs wrapped tightly around their faces, the residents of Ficheux dug a pit across the road from the Pronier farm and dragged dozens of corpses into it with a long hook.

"As soon as the bodies were in the pit, we quickly threw on earth and planted a dozen recovered rifles, on which we placed British helmets," remembered one of the gravediggers, Anatole Lefebvre.

Despite this hasty burial, Lefebvre collected as many identity tags and papers as he could. They would prove essential a year later, when the mass grave was opened and the British dead were reburied at Bucquoy Road Cemetery. Of the 136 bodies, Lefebvre and his comrades identified seventy-one. Another twenty-six were wholly unidentified. The remaining thirty-nine were definitely buried in the cemetery, but it was impossible to match a specific name to a specific grave.[19]

All across northern France, the dead of 1940 were buried beside the World War I graves.

Among them was Flight Officer David H. S. Bury, a Royal Air Force (RAF) pilot whose father was killed in action near Armentières in 1915. Twenty-five years later, Bury was flying over Arras, protecting the city from the Luftwaffe. Dipping too low (or perhaps already wounded), he hit a transmission tower and crashed 100 yards from Chili Trench Cemetery.

Bury was not killed instantly. Instead, he survived long enough to drag himself out of the wreckage and crawl toward the Cross of Sacrifice so that he could die among friends. When War Graves gardener James Peet discovered Bury's body sprawled among the headstones at Chili Trench, he buried him where he lay.[20]

Many of the stranded War Graves gardeners dug graves in the aftermath of the invasion. In Festubert, Head Gardener Albert Roberts buried British and German soldiers alike, "planting an inverted bottle on the graves containing any records I found." When he was not digging graves, Roberts attempted to clean up Gorre British and Indian Cemetery, which had been damaged by British troops who "dug trenches in many parts" and by German artillery. Most of the cemetery wall was destroyed, along with a "large portion" of the headstones and the toolhouse, which "had a direct hit from a bomb or shell."[21]

Farther north, near Merville, gardener William Hogan intervened when he noticed that many bodies were being buried without being identified.

"I carried out the services of identification of these bodies," Hogan reported, "collecting their personal effects in the presence of witnesses. A record was made by me. My wife made small bags for each body or soldier and these effects were then enclosed and labelled and handed to [a member of the municipal council] for safe custody."[22]

Stephen Grady, the fifteen-year-old son of gardener Stephen Grady Sr., was busy in the cemeteries as well, but he had a different purpose.

"We are not digging graves. No, it is guns, not bones, that we need to bury underground."

After the Allied retreat, Stephen and his friend Marcel Lombard scoured the woods and fields around their home in Nieppe for abandoned weapons. They quickly amassed an impressive cache of rifles, pistols, ammunition, grenades, flares, and a fully functional machine gun. With nowhere safe to hide their loot, the two boys dug a chamber behind the Cross of Sacrifice in Pont d'Achelles Cemetery.

As he dug, Stephen worried—but not about the Germans.

"I am more concerned about the bones we keep turning up; not from bodies buried in any grave, but those in need of one," he wrote. "If we find dog tags or a skull, I shall have to tell my father."[23]

Stephen Grady had no specific plans for his arsenal. Not yet.

~

On June 2, 1940, two weeks after the Luftwaffe bombed the War Graves office, Adolf Hitler arrived in Arras.

After touring the city's main squares, Hitler rode through the debris-narrowed streets in an open-topped Mercedes flanked by SS guards. Under the gap-toothed facade of the ruined train station, the convoy passed a knot of French women who pulled their children away even as their heads swiveled toward the cars. A dozen German soldiers rushed across the plaza, straining toward Hitler with outstretched arms. Behind them, the abandoned, windowless War Graves office stood empty. Hitler drove past without stopping.[24]

This was a victory lap, though the fighting was not over. On June 2, there were still thousands of Allied soldiers on the beaches at Dunkirk, and French troops were still battling to keep the Germans out of Paris. Nevertheless, the outcome was certain. France would fall.

In his moment of triumph, Hitler's top priority was not a visit to the active battlefront. Instead, he insisted on taking a leisurely tour of World War I monuments along the old Western Front.

The trip began in Belgium on June 1. In Ypres, Hitler strolled through the Menin Gate, gazing up at the endless names. British troops had demolished the causeway in a futile effort to slow the German advance, but the monument itself had sustained only superficial damage. Afterward, the convoy moved on to Langemarck German Cemetery, where Hitler paid tribute to the much-mythologized dead of 1914. When he left, hundreds of jubilant Wehrmacht soldiers colonnaded his path with Nazi salutes.[25]

Hitler did not make this trip alone. His entourage included senior officers like Field Marshal Wilhelm Keitel and Alfred Jodl. Other generals— Günther von Kluge, Viktor von Schwedler, and Erwin Rommel—joined them along the way. These field commanders were in the midst of a major offensive, but Hitler demanded that they accompany him to the French cemetery at Notre Dame de Lorette and the Canadian National Memorial at Vimy Ridge. The past was very much on his mind.

To Hitler, the conquest of France undid the humiliating defeat of his youth. He believed the myth that Germany had lost World War I not because its army was defeated but because its stalwart soldiers were betrayed by traitors at home, particularly Jews and leftists. Hitler rose to power by promising to restore German greatness, in part by rewriting history.

To make the point explicit, Hitler forced the French to sign the 1940 surrender in the same railway carriage where the 1918 Armistice had been signed. The carriage had been preserved in a museum, so Hitler had the walls torn open and the carriage dragged back into place in the "Glade of the Armistice." He also ordered the destruction of the monuments that ringed the site, all except a bust of Marchal Ferdinand Foch, which was left as a symbolic witness. The railway carriage was sent on a tour of Germany so that ordinary people could touch a relic of the redemption.[26]

Hitler used his Western Front tour to portray himself as moderate and reverential. This played well in Germany, but it also had another purpose: to undermine the American public's faith in the British press.

As the disaster unfolded in France, British and Canadian newspapers ran lurid reports—purportedly from eyewitnesses—alleging that the Luftwaffe had purposefully destroyed the Canadian monument at Vimy Ridge. "GERMANS BOMB VIMY MEMORIAL," screamed the *Daily Mirror*. The *Liverpool Echo* went with "VIMY MEMORIAL SHATTERED . . . NAZIS BOMB GRAVES."

The Canadian papers ran one breathless condemnation after another. "In an act of shocking, cold-blooded vandalism, the invading Nazi hordes have deliberately destroyed Canada's war memorial at Vimy Ridge," declared the front page of the *Edmonton Journal*. Many newspapers quoted the monument's sculptor, Walter Allward, who despaired, "The Huns have gone quite mad." On Prince Edward Island, the *Guardian* (Charlottetown) published a lugubrious description of the "'hallowed acres' around Arras" that ended with an apocalyptic flourish: "Known unto God, too, are the unspeakable deeds of Nazi shame at this hour. Vengeance is mine, I will repay, Saith the Lord."

There was one problem with the story: it wasn't true. Nazi propagandists circulated a photo of Hitler's visit to the undamaged memorial as "proof that the British report was untrue." Within days, the image appeared in the *New York Times* and other leading American newspapers. If the British press was telling hysterical lies about Vimy Ridge, the photo asked, what other reports of Nazi atrocities might be untrue?[27]

The Nazis did destroy some World War I monuments in France, but they did so selectively. Unlike their campaign of cultural annihilation in Poland, the Nazis intended to preserve many French cultural sites for the pleasure of German holidaymakers. As long as the war memorials did not overtly insult Germans, they were acceptable—even admirable—as places of historical interest that testified to Germany's ultimate triumph.[28]

Adolf Hitler at Vimy Ridge, June 2, 1940. *Photo by Heinrich Hoffmann, 242HLB FH1 5034 7005, courtesy of the National Archives and Records Administration (United States)*

Hitler himself modeled this type of recreation. Later in June 1940, he made a second trip to Flanders accompanied by two of his old army comrades. Together, they visited sites that loomed large in their personal memories. At one point, they drove directly past Aubers Ridge Cemetery, where the flowers that Henry Hayler had planted were still bright among the headstones.

Tens of thousands of off-duty German soldiers followed Hitler's example. During the occupation of France, visiting World War I monuments and cemeteries was an approved leisure activity, often organized by officers for the benefit of their young soldiers. German soldiers sent home photos of happy, sunlit outings to Ypres, Vimy Ridge, and Thiepval, where they smoked, smiled, and lounged among the British and French graves.

In order to make this memorial landscape more palatable to Germans, Hitler ordered the removal of what he called "Haßdenkmäler," or "hate monuments." In August 1940, Field Marshal Wilhelm Keitel issued instructions that gave many examples of these "hate monuments," including captured German arms, stones that marked the limit of German advances, and "small museums and old German battery positions" that "keep feelings of hostility against Germany alive."[29]

"At the command of the Führer," Keitel's order read, "it is ordered that such monuments of hatred are to be removed in the interests of German reputation." It instructed all German units in occupied western Europe to photograph any offensive objects in their vicinity before November 1, 1940. If the monuments were movable, they should be packed up and shipped to the Zeughaus, the German military museum in Berlin. If not, they should be destroyed.[30]

The Haßdenkmäler order also made reference to "individual instructions that have already been issued," suggesting that specific monuments were marked for destruction earlier in the summer. Indeed, the Nazis demolished several monuments in the early weeks of the occupation. These included a marker at the site of the first German gas attack near Ypres; a memorial commemorating the civilian victims of a 1914 massacre in Dinant, Belgium; and a monument to Edith Cavell, the English nurse executed in 1915 for assisting British, French, and Belgian soldiers behind German lines. In Lille, German soldiers knocked the heads off a memorial to five local heroes who were executed as spies in 1915, leaving the effigies in a threatening, half-destroyed state.[31]

Monuments that challenged German racial supremacy were particularly targeted for early destruction. In Reims, the Nazis demolished a memorial honoring Senegalese and Malian soldiers who successfully defended the city from German attacks in 1918. In Paris, they destroyed a statue of French general Charles Mangin, who commanded Senegalese troops during the occupation of the Rhineland. The Nazis considered the presence of Black soldiers on German soil a particular outrage. They dynamited Mangin's monument within a week of capturing Paris.[32]

One of the first British cultural custodians to witness this targeted destruction was Ben Leech.

On Sunday, July 14, 1940, Bastille Day, Ben and two other gardeners—George Walker of Mailly-Maillet and Arthur Page of Varennes—went on an inspection tour of cemeteries and memorials. They cycled from Albert to Péronne, a thirty-mile round trip, stopping at "all cemeteries en route."

In his gardening log, Ben reported that the South African Memorial at Delville Wood was untouched, but the same could not be said of the Australian monument at Mont Saint-Quentin. The sculpture, which depicted a slouch-hatted Australian bayonetting a prone German eagle, had been pulled to pieces.

"Aussie at Mont St. Quentin broken off at ankle and lying on ground," Ben wrote. "All plaques pulled off."[33]

The Australian monument was not erected by the Imperial War Graves Commission, which strove never to build any memorial that could be considered offensive to the enemy. Their mission was to commemorate the dead, not the victory.

Indeed, during the interwar years, British leaders had expressed a sentimental hope that the Commission's work might actually prevent future wars. The idea was encapsulated by King George V on a visit to the Western Front cemeteries in 1922: "In the course of my pilgrimage, I have many times asked myself whether there can be more potent advocates of peace upon earth through the years to come than this massed multitude of silent witnesses to the dead?"

Sir Fabian Ware agreed. Some critics at home accused the Commission's cemeteries of celebrating "rigid militarism," but Sir Fabian saw the "silent cities" as an eloquent bulwark against future aggression. Between 1936 and 1939, he appealed to his counterparts in Germany, Italy, and France, believing that war graves work provided a back channel for promoting peace. In the words of the Commission's official historian, Sir Fabian envisioned "a sort of minor League of Nations" based on a shared commitment to commemoration.

"The common remembrance of the dead," Sir Fabian assured his international colleagues in a 1938 speech, was "the only thing that would draw together all nations in amity."[34]

Adolf Hitler was not hostile to the Commission's work. In fact, he found very little to dislike about the British military cemeteries. They were not the same as German military cemeteries, which featured mass "comrades' graves" and shady trees that evoked forests rather than gardens, but Hitler did not object to the neoclassical architecture, the grandeur, or the eternal commitment to honoring the dead of a war that shaped his life and his politics.

Where Hitler differed from King George V and Sir Fabian was in his understanding of what the war graves meant. To Hitler, they did not represent the terrible cost of war. Instead, he saw them as a reproach to a nation that had betrayed its glorious dead.

In the end, the important thing about the silent dead was that they were silent. Leaders could invoke their moral weight to justify war as easily as peace. The Imperial War Graves Commission's purpose was to unite the empire with a cohesive, eternal memorial that commemorated individual sacrifice within a greater whole. That sort of monument could be understood in many ways. But it could not stop a war.

"ENEMY ALIENS" 6

The arrests began on July 13.

Early that morning, when Rosine Witton's hens were beginning to stir, a truck rumbled down Route de Bapaume. It stopped outside Number 6, where armed men assembled in front of the house. If Rosine peeked out from behind her white lace curtains, she would have recognized them by their field-gray uniforms and the oversized metal gorgets dangling from thick chains around their necks. These were the Feldgendarmes, the German military police.

They had come for Bert.

In the wake of the Nazi invasion, civil authorities gave the Germans lists of every British man and boy over the age of sixteen living in the Nord and Pas-de-Calais departments. Three days after the collaborationist Vichy government took power on July 10, Rosine Witton's neighbors were roused by pounding fists and curt commands.

Commission mechanic William Medlicott and gardener Harry Bull were arrested in their adjoining houses across the street from the Wittons. So were garage workers Wilfred Legg and Herbert Dickens. Legg's fifteen-year-old son, Harry, was below the age cutoff, but Dickens's seventeen-year-old son, Richard, was arrested with the others.

Age was a guideline, but it was no guarantee. The youngest member of the Ronville War Graves community captured by the Nazis in July 1940 was probably nine-year-old Francis Burge, who lived just around the corner from Rosine and Bert. Francis and his mother, Berthe, were released before the end of the month, but his father, gardener Lionel Burge, would spend more than four years in captivity with his colleagues.[1]

Some of the War Graves prisoners were given a few minutes to gather personal items, but others were hauled off without delay. "We were not allowed to take any clothes with us," testified Albert Grounds, one of the gardeners who had begged Robert Bird for permission to leave Cambrai. Those who were allowed to bring a bag packed clothing, medicine, and food, along with tobacco, playing cards, and novels. Few realized that they would also need basic items like cups, spoons, and bowls. In the coming weeks, some prisoners would resort to using tin cans and gas mask canisters to collect their daily rations of thin, greasy soup.[2]

A few of the prisoners were pessimistic enough to be practical. Despite the July heat, Bernard Parsons, the letter carver from Étaples, packed "a couple of army haversacks" and "an old overcoat . . . rolled in a blanket in true military style." Parsons's overcoat was a prescient choice. Many of his fellow prisoners spent the winter of 1940–1941 shivering in the light summer clothing they happened to be wearing on a Saturday morning in July.[3]

Bert Witton was lucky enough to have a valise. He brought his pipe and tobacco and a fresh shirt. With the Felgendarmes standing watch, Bert bid Rosine a brief farewell before being led out of Number 6 and into the waiting truck. He would never see the house again.

The Ronville prisoners bumped along Arras's cobbled streets to Saint-Nicaise Prison on the west side of the city. There, they were deposited in a single fetid cell along with other British men from Arras. John Fraser, the husband of Rosine Witton's friend Berthe, was there. So was Arthur Richards, the vice-chairman of the local British Legion chapter.

"The conditions were filthy," Richards remembered. Saint-Nicaise had no running water, and many of the men were "devoid of any clothing or necessaries apart from which we stood up in." Canadian gardener Lewis Fulton Bonnell of Wanquetin remembered the shock of their treatment at Saint-Nicaise. "We thought at the time [it] was very poor," he said. "Actually, it was excellent in comparison to what we would receive later."[4]

Meanwhile, Feldgendarmes fanned out across the Nord and Pas-de-Calais departments. They descended on large towns and small villages, arresting War Graves gardeners at home and at work.

Gardener Reginald George Covey was cutting a neighbor's hair in Bienvillers-au-Bois when the Germans arrived. He asked for permission to stop at the village school so that he could say good-bye to his two young sons, who were in Saturday morning classes. "After hugging us, he said, 'see you soon,'" remembered Leslie Covey, who was nine years old in 1940.[5]

Another gardener, Charles Maurice Baker, was arrested at work in Merville Communal Cemetery. In his pocket, he had a list of the varieties of roses he had planted along each row of headstones. The list was returned to his wife, Gaby, when Baker died in Nazi custody two years later.[6]

The gardeners had very little information about what was happening to them. Some, like William Glennon and his pupil-gardener son, Joe, were told that they were being press-ganged as gravediggers. The Glennons hoped that William, who was born in Ireland, might be released as a citizen of a neutral country, but he did not have an Irish passport. The Germans interned him along with his British colleagues.

On the morning of the second day of the roundup—July 14, Bastille Day—the Feldgendarmes arrived at the home of French Canadian gardener Omer Briere in Souchez, near Vimy Ridge.

Briere's thirteen-year-old son, Jean, was still in bed when he heard the tramp of feet outside. "My mother called from the bottom of the stairs, 'Jean, get up quick!'" he recalled.

Jean pulled on a bathrobe and flew to the window, where he saw a long line of soldiers coming toward the house. With them was Bill Toomer, a gardener who worked with Briere at Cabaret Rouge Cemetery and was now being frog-marched along under guard.

The Germans allowed Briere a moment to say good-bye to his distraught wife and children. At the last moment, Jean slipped the rosary his father had carried during World War I into his pocket.

"I told him it would protect him again this time."[7]

Omer Briere, Bill Toomer, and the other gardeners arrested in the countryside were brought to Saint-Nicaise. The cells were filling up, but there were dozens more arrests to come.

On the third day, July 15, the Germans reached Hébuterne, a village on the southern edge of the Pas-de-Calais department. The location was significant. Administratively, the Nazis had carved the two northernmost departments away from the rest of France, placing the Nord and Pas-de-Calais under the jurisdiction of the military administration headquartered in Brussels. Immediately south of Pas-de-Calais, the Somme department was divided in half. The land north of the river Somme was part of a special buffer—the Zone Interdité, or "forbidden zone"—while the southern half of the department was part of the ordinary occupied zone. The river itself formed part of the "north-east line," an internal border that ran all the way to Switzerland.

These divisions created a bureaucratic barrier between Hébuterne and its neighbor to the south, Beaumont-Hamel, which was in the Somme department and the Zone Interdité.

In day-to-day life, the differences between Hébuterne and Beaumont-Hamel were slight. Both were agricultural villages so small that they shared a single baker, whose mixing machine was currently running on petrol given to him by Ben Leech.[8] Serre Road Cemetery No. 2 was so large that it straddled the line between the villages. Its front gate was in Hébuterne, and its toolhouses were in Beaumont-Hamel.

Under the Nazi occupation, the line between Hébuterne and Beaumont-Hamel meant the difference between immediate arrest and an uneasy, fragile freedom. On July 15, Ben Leech was safe at home in Beaumont-Hamel, but all three War Graves gardeners in Hébuterne—Albert Haines, John Hamilton, and Charles Henry Holton—were arrested.

Charles Henry Holton was a former sapper from Buckinghamshire who learned to garden so that he could stay in France with Maria Agathe Sauty. They had six children, including twins Noël and Noëlla, who were born on Christmas Day 1920.[9] In 1940, nineteen-year-old Noël was arrested along with the other War Graves men. His twin, Noëlla, decided to follow them to Arras on her bicycle.

It was fourteen miles to Arras, a long, hot ride on a midsummer day, but Noëlla Holton was determined to bear witness. She followed the truck north through the ripening fields, through Ronville, past Rosine Witton's *café-tabac*, and toward the Arras train station.

In the Place de la Gare, Noëlla Holton watched, helpless, as dozens of bedraggled British prisoners were unloaded in front of the War Graves office. There was nothing she could do except watch as the Germans ordered her father and brother into waiting cattle cars. When they did not move fast enough, the guards hurried them along with "violent blows with their rifle butts."[10]

Other War Graves families followed their men to Arras as well. Jean Briere and his mother, Rosaline, packed a sack with provisions for Omer Briere. They arrived at Saint-Nicaise just in time to see the prisoners being loaded into trucks. Jean could not find his father in the crowd, but he did spot their neighbor, Bill Toomer. Toomer shouted that Briere had already gone to the station with an earlier group.

"I thought my mother was going to lose consciousness," Jean recalled, "but she broke into long sobs." Jean tried to dart between the guards, but one of them raised his rifle. Desperate, Jean tossed the bag of food to Bill Toomer, hoping that he would pass it along to his father. Then Jean and Rosalie returned to Souchez, "dead on our feet with fatigue and crushed by disappointment and immense grief."[11]

Rosine Witton may have watched Bert herded into the cattle cars with the other War Graves men. Perhaps she packed a bag like the Brieres, hoping to toss it to Bert as he shuffled past. Perhaps she only watched in silent terror like Noëlla Holton. Perhaps one of her customers told her what was happening and she ran up the street to the station just in time to watch the train roll away north, toward Lille.

The internees' first stop was Caserne Négrier, a fortress in Lille where the Nazis were assembling British captives from across the region. Of the 600 prisoners, around 100 were War Graves employees or their children.

At the end of July, a few of these prisoners were released due to their age. Technically, the Germans were not supposed to intern civilians over the age of sixty, but this policy was erratically enforced. In 1943, a Red Cross inspection of the camp where most of the gardeners were interned found that one-tenth of the internees were over age sixty. There were also two thirteen-year-olds at the main camp and two boys, ages nine and twelve, at a sub-camp.[12]

A few of the gardeners' teenage sons, including Noël Holton, were also released at the end of July, but there were no hard-and-fast rules. Maurice Hill, whose father was one of Bob Armstrong's gardeners in Valenciennes, was six months younger than Noël Holton but remained interned for the duration of the war.

Some War Graves men were set free due to illness or injury. Jack Wood, a War Graves gardener from Houplines who had been forced to retire in 1938 due to ill health, was deemed unsuitable for internment because he had recently had a major operation. His neighbor, Henry William Hollingdale, who had worked for the Commission in the 1920s, was also released, though he was not quite sixty. In the coming years, Jack, Henry, and their wives, Marthe Wood and Lucy Hollingdale, would all join the Resistance.[13]

Another soon-to-be-*résistant* released from Caserne Négrier on account of his age was Arthur Richards, the sixty-two-year-old typographer and British Legion vice-chairman from Arras. Richards was set free with nothing but his release papers and the clothes he had worn continuously since his arrest. Since he had no money for a train ticket, Richards walked the thirty miles from Lille back to Arras, plotting against the Nazis with every step.

Bert Witton had no hope of being released on a technicality. He had turned forty-two on June 6 and was in excellent health. Instead of going home to Rosine, he was loaded into an unventilated cattle car with the other prisoners and shipped over the border into Belgium. Lest anyone contemplate escape during the journey, the Nazis threatened retribution against their families.[14]

After a tedious, uncomfortable journey that included a brief sojourn at a military barracks in Liège, the prisoners arrived at the Citadel, a Napoleonic fortress overlooking the city of Huy. Many of the gardeners would remember the next five weeks as "the worst period of our internment."[15]

The Citadel was supposed to be a temporary holding place, so the Germans had not bothered outfitting it with niceties like bedding or food. The prisoners slept twenty men to a cell with only a thin layer of dusty straw separating them from the stone floors. One gardener, William Greenwood of Armentières, suffered a serious injury when he was "kicked in the small of my back by a German soldier and fell down a flight of stone steps."[16] Greenwood was injured badly enough that he was released on September 8, 1940, rather than being transported to the next camp.

At Huy—"the famine camp"—the men were short of everything. Without soap, they were soon reeking in the August heat. During the day, they sifted the kitchen garbage for potato peelings, which they boiled into an intestine-twisting gruel, and carrot tops, which they dried and smoked in lieu of tobacco. Some scrounged for dandelion leaves on the tiny parade ground. Sometimes, the Germans allowed a small delegation to go into town to purchase food with the prisoners' own money, but it was not enough to keep the flesh on their bones. All the internees sloughed off alarming amounts of weight.

"I think a month or two more at Huy would have killed me," Bernard Parsons wrote. Lewis Fulton Bonnell agreed. "The rations were so bad that during parade the last week, it became common to see a man collapse from weakness. Had we remained there for the winter on the same rations, very few, if any, would have come through alive."[17]

In starvation conditions, the War Graves men cared for one another by sharing food whenever they could. One day at Huy, Bernard Parsons was "obsessed with thoughts of food" to the point that he cracked open several poisonous plum pits and ate them, not caring that their natural cyanide could be fatal. Gardener Reginald Covey noticed that Parsons was struggling. Quietly, Covey told Parsons that he had a lead on a stolen potato and offered to share it in exchange for a bit of the mustard Parsons had been given by a sympathetic Belgian. Parsons agreed. "We cut [the potato] in two and having spread a good layer of mustard on it ate it quite eagerly raw," Parsons wrote in his diary.

The most famous prisoner at Huy, author P. G. Wodehouse, also recalled a memorable meal during the journey into Belgium. Wodehouse, the world-famous author of the comic Bertie and Jeeves novels, had been arrested at his villa in the seaside resort of Le Touquet. He packed his bag with books rather than food, which made the voyage a hungry one. Wodehouse was rescued by War Graves gardener Bert Haskins, who "suddenly appeared at my side with a half a loaf of bread, butter, radishes, a bottle of wine and a slap of potted meat." Wodehouse was touched by Haskins's generosity. "He didn't know me, but out of sheer goodness of heart he came and gave me the stuff." The two men formed a fast friendship that outlasted their internment. After the war, Wodehouse dedicated an edition of the novel he drafted in captivity, *Money in the Bank*, to Haskins.

"I had the most tremendous liking and admiration for the War Graves Commission men," Wodehouse wrote in 1945. "They really are the salt of the earth."[18]

~

While the War Graves men from Nord and Pas-de-Calais were starving in Belgium, many of their colleagues farther south were stuck in limbo. Instead of a coordinated roundup, Nazi officials in the Somme department arrested War Graves gardeners in a slipshod campaign that straggled on for many months.

Some gardeners in the Zone Interdité were arrested in late July, including Ben Leech's friends George Walker and Arthur Page, who had visited the dismembered Australian monument at Mont Saint Quentin on Bastille Day. Ben fully expected that the Germans would come for him next. "Packing suitcase in readiness of arrest," he wrote on July 29. Four days later, it was, "Continue packing ready to go to camp but nothing as yet come." The mayor of Beaumont-Hamel, home again after his short exile, visited Ben and told him that the Nazis had ordered him to "give particulars of foreigners residing in Beaumont Hamel" and that Ben "must be prepared."[19]

Ben waited patiently, but the Feldgendarmes never knocked on his door.

"To Albert about reporting," Ben wrote in his gardening log, "but was told I could not report there." Confused, he went home.

Most of the War Graves gardeners living in the "forbidden zone" were eventually arrested, but there was no obvious geographical or chronological pattern. Arthur Page, who lived in Varennes, was captured in July 1940, but Henry Ellis was not taken from neighboring Warloy-Baillon until September 18, 1941. Alfred Benham was arrested in Pozières on

November 13, 1940, but Amos Poole was free in nearby Fricourt until February 1941.[20]

A very small number of gardeners went into hiding to avoid arrest. These included Stephen Grady Sr. in Nieppe and Sidney Wray, who hid for more than four years in Chaulnes, south of the Somme. He was protected by Marcelle Lattreux Clement, a widow with five children. Madame Clement was once "questioned 7 hrs by the Gestapo while Wray was there," but the Germans did not find Wray. They did keep the house under close surveillance, sending three police officers to stop by "for lunch every day" and forcing Clement to feed them "at her own expense." Despite this nerve-jangling arrangement, the Nazis never caught Sidney Wray.[21]

Some War Graves gardeners avoided arrest simply because they were not at home when the occupiers turned their fickle attention toward a particular town. Gardener George Horn fled to Paris in May 1940 and stayed there for a full year, so he was not at home in Albert when several of his neighbors were arrested in July 1940. The ban on travel to the Zone Interdité kept him from returning to Albert until July 1941. The Germans required Horn to register with local authorities and warned him not to travel more than five kilometers from Albert, but they did not intern him. When they finally did arrest Horn in July 1942, it was for his active Resistance work, not his nationality.[22]

The three gardeners living in Beaumont-Hamel—Ben Leech, Robert Mullenger, and S. C. Humphreys—were never arrested at all.[23] Ben never really knew why. Decades later, his son Maurice floated a theory that a French interpreter in Albert "was of great help to us and saved a lot of resistants," but he could not remember the man's name.[24] The Imperial War Graves Commission investigated Ben's case in 1944, but they were unable to nail down specific details. "Apparently owes his being left at liberty to good offices of Mayor & to lenient German Kommandatur," a Commission official shrugged.[25]

It is certainly possible that Ben Leech's paperwork was deliberately lost by a sympathetic clerk or that the mayor of Beaumont-Hamel protected him. That might explain why Mullenger and Humphreys remained free as well.

It is also possible that it was a mistake. The Nazi occupation was brutal, but its administration was chaotic, with redundant, overlapping jurisdictions and law enforcement systems. Some things slipped between the cracks. The haphazard arrests of War Graves gardeners in the northern Somme department suggest that the local administration was disorderly or at least that no one treated the arrest of middle-aged foreigners living in rural villages as a very high priority.

Gardeners from the Somme were not sent north to join their colleagues from the Pas-de-Calais and Nord departments. Instead, most of them were sent to Saint-Denis, an internment camp near Paris. At Saint-Denis, internees generally had better access to food than their northern counterparts and benefited from a milder climate, but it was no rest cure. Of approximately forty War Graves gardeners interned at Saint-Denis, three died there. Among them was Ben Leech's friend George Walker, who was fifty-two years old when he died of heart disease aggravated by the stress of internment on August 8, 1943.[26]

Many women and children from the War Graves community were also interned. Those at the highest risk were British-born women like Lily Wilkins, who spent three years interned at Liebenau, a camp in Germany, after Brigadier Prower abandoned her and her daughters during the evacuation. Lily's daughters, sixteen-year-old Lillian and eleven-year-old Joyce, were left alone in Ypres to fend for themselves.[27]

French-born War Graves wives were also interned, though not as frequently as British-born women. Gaby Baker, whose husband Charles died in 1941, was interned with her ten-year-old-son, Charles, from April 1943 until May 1945. More commonly, French women married to British men were held for a few weeks or months and then paroled, allowing them to live at home as long as they registered with local authorities.[28] Several War Graves women, including Noëlla Holton and her mother, Maria, were imprisoned in a small camp in Avesnes-sur-Helpe but returned home before the end of the war. Others were interned at Vittel and Besançon, camps in eastern France. At least one gardener's daughter, twenty-two-year-old Mary Weller, and one gardener's wife, Virginie Roberts, died in internment camps.[29]

～

The practice of interning "enemy aliens" was not unique to the Nazis. During World War II, both the Allies and the Axis nations detained civilians who were citizens of enemy nations.[30]

Civilian internees were different from other types of prisoners. They were not prisoners of war, captured while serving in the armed forces. Neither were they criminals, under the jurisdiction of civilian courts. Most important, they were not among the millions of people sent to concentration camps as part of the broader persecution of religious, ethnic, or ability groups. The word "internment" has been widely and erroneously used to refer to the incarceration of 100,000 American and Canadian citizens of Japanese ancestry, but civilian internees were people detained by an enemy power, not those who were persecuted by their own governments.[31]

Bert Witton and his fellow War Graves gardeners were the mirror image of German citizens interned by the United Kingdom. Beginning in 1939, the British government interned thousands of German and Italian nationals. Tribunals were supposed to ensure that only dangerous people with fascist sympathies would be detained, but the system was far from infallible. Some detainees were ordinary immigrants with no particular allegiance to Hitler or Mussolini. Others were Jewish refugees who had fled to the United Kingdom for safety. Some German Jews found themselves imprisoned in camps with Nazi sympathizers, where they endured daily abuse. Some even went on hunger strikes in an effort to pressure the British government to set them free to "do something to help in the defeat of the murderers of our families."[32]

Although British authorities generally provided civilian internees with adequate food, shelter, and heat, hundreds died in British custody. The most lethal single incident occurred on July 2, 1940, when the British ship *Arandora Star* was torpedoed by a U-boat while transporting German and Italian internees to Newfoundland. More than 800 people were killed, most of them Italian and German civilians of the same generation as the War Graves gardeners. A German torpedo sunk *Arandora Star,* but the British policy of shipping internees across the Atlantic or to Australia on unescorted, unmarked ships with fewer lifeboats than *Titanic* placed the internees in extreme danger. Their bodies washed up on the Irish coast all through the summer of 1940.

∿

When the starving internees at Huy finally received orders to board a train on September 8, 1940, there was much speculation about their destination. Perhaps they were "going back to dear old France." Perhaps to Germany. Anywhere had to be better than the Citadel.

Before he boarded the train, Bert Witton was issued traveling rations: a fifth of a loaf of bread, a third of a sausage, and a pat of margarine. It was more food than he had seen in weeks.

"A real banquet," declared Bernard Parsons. "How big that piece of sausage seemed—I felt that I could go to the end of the earth with such a plentious supply."

Even better, the train waiting at the station was a real passenger train with seats and windows, not like the cattle cars that brought them to

Belgium. Bert crowded into a compartment with seven other men. If the train went west, he might be back in Arras in a day or two.

Instead, the train went east. "There was no longer any doubt where we were going," Bernard Parsons wrote in his diary. "My heart felt very low and a Jewish boy opposite me sobbed in the now completely dark corner of the compartment and I tried to squeeze a tear but my heart had become like a stone."

For three days and three nights, Bert and the other War Graves men watched the German countryside slip by. They were locked in their compartments with nowhere to lie down and nowhere to relieve themselves. A few times, the train stopped so the Germans could distribute coffee or soup, but the journey continued. By the third day, the prisoners were unkempt and reeking, their legs so swollen that their ankles resembled "a freshly served rolly polly pudding with the marks of the tying string still in evidence."[33]

On the afternoon of the fourth day, the train stopped in Tost (now Toszek, Poland), a small town in the German part of Upper Silesia, about fifteen miles from the Polish border. They were marched from the train to a gloomy, four-story brick building ringed with barbed wire. It loomed over a smaller mess hall, an administrative building, sheds, and a walled yard that was large enough for 1,200 internees to assemble for roll call each morning. The main building resembled an abandoned mill, except for the thick metal bars on its windows.

Officially, the camp was called Ilag VIII H. "Ilag" was short for "internierungslager," or internment camp, and the H distinguished it from a smaller satellite camp, Ilag VIII Z, in Kreuzberg (Kluczbork). The internees were a mishmash of British subjects who had been captured at sea or picked up in occupied countries. Among them were the civilian crew of a British troop ship sunk during the Norwegian campaign and a cadre of Canadian missionaries who had been on their way to South Africa when their ship, *Zamzam*, was sunk by a German cruiser off the coast of Brazil. In 1942, ninety miscellaneous Americans joined this motley assemblage.[34]

The first order of business at Ilag VIII was registration. German guards rifled through Bert Witton's valise and stood over him as he shaved and bathed with the other internees, five to a tub. Each new arrival was given a sequential prisoner number that was affixed to his mail but not, as in a concentration camp, to his skin or clothing.

Bert Witton was prisoner #304. That was the number the clerk inked onto his biometric data card, along with his height (1.68 meters, or five feet, six inches) and hair color (dark blond), as well as his thumbprint, his profession (*gärtner*), and his next of kin: *Mme Witton, 6 Rue de Bapaume, Arras, Frankreich*. It was the number someone chalked onto a slate for Bert to hold in front of his chest as the guards snapped a mug shot. In the photo, Bert is freshly shaven, with his hair brushed neatly back from a high forehead. He wears a summer-weight shirt, collar open, still creased from his bag.[35]

The Germans weren't the only ones counting. At Huy, Bernard Parsons had made a list of Commission men that he kept up to date as a few stragglers arrived in later transports. Eventually, there were 112. Acting as the staff's representative, Parsons handed his list over to the camp commander, who promised to forward it to London.[36]

In October, when rumors began to fly that the Ilag VIII prisoners might be sent out to work for the Germans, Parsons met with the commander

Top row (left to right): Sidney Albert Witton (304), Omer Briere (794), Reginald Covey (541), Frederick Fisher (514). Middle row (left to right): Albert Haines (623), George Bailey (1094), Herbert Haskins (690), William Harold Medlicott (431). Bottom row (left to right): Bernard Parsons (815), John Oldman (642), Albert Roberts (526), Archibald Mowat (247). *Original source: WO 416, The National Archives (United Kingdom)*

again. He informed him that War Graves Commission employees could not volunteer for labor because doing so would violate their contracts.

"I explained to the commander that we considered ourselves still under contract to the commission and still paid by them," Parsons wrote in his journal, "and that one of the clauses in our contract is that we should give all our time to the Commission and not take up other paid work."

The German officer understood, though he explained that the men might be forced to work as slave laborers. "Being forced would not affect our contract," Parsons replied.[37]

Facing the possibility that they might be separated, the 100-odd members of the Commission staff held a meeting at Ilag VIII on October 26, 1940. If this was their last chance to meet as a body, they wanted to agree on a few basic points "as a base of our demands when we are liberated."

They agreed on five resolutions:

First, they affirmed that the Imperial War Graves Commission owed them their full wages from May 1940 until the future date when they resumed their work.

Second and third, they wanted to be compensated for their imprisonment and for any loss of property in France.

Fourth, they expected medical care and a "suitable period of rest and recuperation" after their release from the internment camp.

The gardeners' final demand concerned the disastrous failure of the Commission's evacuation plan. While the Nazis were ultimately responsible for their plight, the gardeners agreed that the War Graves Commission bore a share of the blame.

"In view of the fact that every man did as ordered and stuck to his post," they demanded an "enquiry into lack of proper arrangement for our evacuation and into the complete disappearance of all our leaders."[38]

"SEND SOME MONEY IF POSSIBLE" 7

B ob Armstrong's most precious possession was his Irish passport. Before 1940, the little green booklet, #B1208, allowed him to spend Christmases with his family near Balinalee. After 1940, it kept him out of an internment camp.[1]

Unlike the vast majority of War Graves gardeners, Bob Armstrong was not a British national. He was born on October 7, 1894, in Newbliss, County Monaghan, to Protestant parents. The Armstrong family was itinerant for most of Bob's childhood, but they never lived in the northern counties that would become Northern Ireland and remain part of the United Kingdom. After sojourns in King's County (later County Offaly), Tipperary, and Wicklow, Bob's father, James, finally found steady work as the estate manager at Currygrane, a grand country house in County Longford.

At Currygrane, as in every other place he ever lived, Bob Armstrong made friends. Among them was Seán MacEoin, the local blacksmith's son, who would later make a name for himself as a hero of the Irish War of Independence.

Bob did not stay at Currygrane long. Within a year or two, he left his parents and his five siblings to make his own way in the world. After some horticultural apprenticeships, he worked as a gardener at the Royal Hospital Kilmainham in Dublin, where his foreman recommended him as a "hardworking and trustworthy man." In 1915, Bob joined the 1st Irish Guards, following his younger brother, James Henry, who was already a rambunctious private in the 2nd.[2] Both Armstrong brothers were wounded in France, but only Bob survived.

When he was demobilized in 1920, Bob Armstrong faced a dilemma. The war in France had ended, but the war in Ireland was just beginning.

Many of Bob's neighbors at Currygrane took up arms for the cause of Irish independence. Seán MacEoin—the Blacksmith of Balinalee—led an Irish Republican Army (IRA) flying column, a small, mobile force that fought several battles against Crown forces. Another neighbor, Seán Connolly, was killed in action in 1921. Afterward, the Black and Tans burned his family's house, which was adjacent to Currygrane. They destroyed the Connollys' crops and shot all the livestock dead in the fields. Around the same time, two other local men "were shot by the IRA for being spies."[3]

The Armstrong family could not avoid the violence. Currygrane was the family home of Field Marshall Sir Henry Wilson, one of the British army's most senior officers. An ardent and abrasive Unionist, Wilson was fanatically opposed to Irish independence. After leaving the army in early 1922, he was elected to Parliament, where his passionate denunciations of Irish nationalism were considered extreme even among his conservative peers. In June 1922, two IRA members assassinated Wilson in London. When they were hanged two months later, partisans burned Currygrane House to the ground.[4]

Bob Armstrong's parents stayed on the ruined estate, accepting a parcel of sixty acres from the Irish Land Commission. It was more than they had ever owned before, but it was still a "small bad farm" that barely kept them fed.

With the situation so unsettled at home, Bob Armstrong decided to work abroad. He still kept in touch, particularly with his younger sister, Augusta Lindsay, and visited as often as he could. To help them make ends meet, Bob allotted £2 of his monthly wage—about 12 percent—to his mother and then, after her death, to Augusta. He would turn up at Currygrane during the winter months, when the cemeteries were quiet, bursting with good cheer and laden with gifts.[5]

Although Bob worked abroad, Currygrane was still his official residence on December 6, 1922, the day the Irish Free State Constitution came into force. Since he was legally "domiciled" in Ireland and born to Irish parents, Bob automatically became an Irish citizen. This would become extremely important in 1940. Ireland never declared war on Germany, so its citizens were neutrals, not enemy aliens.

When the Nazi occupation began, Irish citizens across France scrambled to prove that they were not British. This was not always easy. Many Irish people living abroad had never bothered to swap their old British passports for Irish ones. Worse, many had French identity cards that identified them imprecisely as *britannique*. In the early months of the occupation,

Irish diplomats issued so many emergency passports that they ran out and had to design an alternative document that could be printed in Paris.[6]

Some Irish-born War Graves gardeners had Irish papers, but others did not. Michael Dempsey, a gardener from County Laois who lived in Arras, stood behind Bert Witton in the registration line at Ilag VIII and received the next prisoner number, 305. William Glennon and his son Joe were assigned #618 and #742. Meanwhile, at least five Irish gardeners remained free.

This "freedom" had strict limits. Irish nationals in occupied France lived under tight movement restrictions as well as the shortages and surveillance that constrained everyone living under Nazi rule.

Still, Bob Armstrong was not interned. Both of the gardeners under his supervision were arrested, but Bob was at liberty to go on tending the graves at Saint-Roch Cemetery in Valenciennes. If he kept his head down and did not make any trouble, he might remain free.[7]

∼

When news of the catastrophe in France reached Ireland, Augusta Lindsay was frantic. She wrote to the War Graves Commission for information about her brother, but they brushed off her inquiries.

Summer turned to autumn. Christmas came and went with no word from Bob. Augusta fretted constantly. She was comforted by the fact that the War Graves Commission continued to send a £2 check each month. As long as they were still paying her an allotment out of Bob's wages, Augusta could believe that he was still safe and working.

Then, on January 24, 1941, a miracle.

A telegram from the Irish Legation in Vichy arrived at the Irish Department of External Affairs in Dublin. It read,

> Armstrong Valenciennes informs father Currygrane Edwardstown [sic] Longford and sister Mrs. Lindsay Cambrian Churchtown Road Dundrum that very well sends love. wishes sister to send some money if possible.[8]

The telegram caused a sensation among Bob's relatives. They had not heard a peep from him in nine months, and now they had his love and assurances that he was "very well." He needed money, but that made sense. It was nearly impossible to get a message to someone in occupied France, let alone a paycheck.

The Irish government proposed a neat solution to this problem. If Bob's family wished to send him money, they could deposit it with the

Department of External Affairs in Dublin, which would instruct the Irish diplomats in Vichy to forward an equal amount to Bob in francs. The Irish government was prepared to transfer up to £100.

No one in the Armstrong family had £100. Bob's father, James, was an elderly man with a poor farm, and Augusta relied on the £2 allotment from Bob's wages to make ends meet. The other siblings, Emmie, Fred, and Edward, may have been able to scrape together a little cash but not £100.

Luckily, the family knew someone who owed Bob money: the Imperial War Graves Commission. After all, the Commission had assured Augusta that they had no reason to believe Bob was not safe. Nine months' wages for a head gardener amounted to £156.

Both James Armstrong and Augusta Lindsay dashed off letters to the Commission, asking them to forward Bob's accumulated wages.

"My brother is alive and well, but requires some money," Augusta wrote, "kindly let me know if you are prepared to advance him some to carry on."

James Armstrong did not refer to the money as an advance. As he understood it, the War Graves Commission owed his son the wages specified in his contract. James asked the Commission "to send on what money is due to him."

"Also," he added, "if you can inform me how he could be got out of France."[9]

The Armstrong family did not know that the Commission considered all staff contracts in occupied France to be "terminated by the force of events." In consultation with their legal advisers, the Commission decided that the contracts were canceled by force majeure, that is, nullified by an extraordinary event that made it impossible for one or both parties to meet their obligations.[10]

This was certainly not the view of the internees at Ilag VIII, who "considered ourselves still under contract to the commission." But the internees did not have lawyers.[11]

The Commission's decision was out of step with most of their peer organizations. For example, the Canadian Department of National Defence did not cancel the contracts of the Vimy Ridge caretakers. They continued paying them even when they were interned, keeping their wages "set aside for them." Similarly, British civil servants caught behind enemy lines and military prisoners of war were not automatically terminated when they were captured. The gardeners were Crown servants, but they were not soldiers or civil servants. Their ambiguous status left them without the protections offered to other Crown servants stationed overseas.[12]

The Commission made their decision in consultation with the Treasury, which agreed that the contracts were void. Treasury officials advised the Commission to "keep their hands free" so that they could "act as a good employer" after the war was over. If they wanted to offer the gardeners emergency assistance, they should do so on a strictly ex gratia basis, that is, as a gift, not in fulfillment of a contractual obligation. That way, they could "give the men either more or less than what would have been legally due, according to the merits and circumstances of each case."[13]

The Commission canceled the gardeners' contracts, but they were still keen to maintain goodwill. To that end, they offered gardeners who returned to the United Kingdom an immediate £10 loan to help replace basic clothing and household items. The Commission also assisted the staff in finding new jobs. There was plenty of work in wartime Britain, and if the gardeners' new positions paid less than their previous wages, the Commission offered to pay the difference for a period of six months.[14]

This aid was welcome, though some gardeners felt that it was too little and ended too soon.

"I do not agree with your point that we have had the necessary time or money to adapt ourselves to conditions in this country," wrote gardener Hugh Gabriel when the concession pay ended in 1941. "If we had been able to bring our homes and cloths with us yes, but when one has had to buy everything all over again for self & family I fail to see your point."[15]

Head Gardener Sidney Stock was less polite. He saw the Commission's limited assistance as an outrageous betrayal after his decades of loyal service. "You have made me very embittered and I would like personally to meet those responsible," Stock declared. He pointed out that he was fifty-two years old and could not easily "take up an apprenticeship" in a new profession. Moreover, Stock believed the Commission owed him much more after "what I went through in France (oh no not alone)" and "what I have lost personally serving under the Crown from 1914 until 1941." The aid he received was only "a pin prick to what the real Concessions you should carry out."

"I wish no favours give me my deserts," Stock wrote. "I do not wish to be rude just to impress you you are doing the wrong thing . . . I hope above all you will be absolutely embarrassed with letters, and that it will really personally worry you & those concerned."[16]

Angry gardeners in the United Kingdom were one thing, but gardeners who were stranded in Europe were another matter entirely. The

Commission was adamant that their contracts were no longer valid, but a September 1940 meeting of the Finance Committee shows that they were still working through the implications of that decision. What were their obligations in cases like Bob Armstrong's, where a gardener was still working in his cemetery in compliance with Brigadier Prower's orders?

Without conceding any contractual obligations, the Finance Committee recommended that "where a man is found to be actually at work in his cemetery," the Commission should credit him with "full pay." If the Commission could find an "authorized channel" that would allow them to send this money to the gardener, they should forward "so much of it as may be desirable."

It was, of course, difficult for the Commission to determine whether a gardener was still working. The Finance Committee suggested that it might be useful to ask diplomats from neutral countries for information. Their final resolution read, in part,

> Members of the Commission's horticultural staff who may be stated by the United States (or other neutral authorities charged with the interests of British subjects in France or Belgium) to be still carrying out their work in British war cemeteries be regarded as still on the Commission's staff and entitled to receive their full rates of pay in accordance, where applicable, with the award of the Industrial Court.

This resolution was unhelpfully vague as to whether "still on the Commission's staff" meant that a working gardener's original contract was still valid, but that was a problem for another day. The full Commission adopted the resolution at their meeting on January 8, 1941.[17]

Right away, the Commission used this new policy to respond to inquiries from gardeners' families. Just five days after the resolution passed, an official wrote to Alex Chapman, who had asked about pay for his interned brother, Samuel.

"We regard the contracts of all the men who are not working in their cemeteries as terminated by force mageure [sic] in May or June 1940," the official explained. "We are therefore under no legal obligation to pay them."[18]

Bob Armstrong's telegram arrived in Ireland on January 24, just two weeks after the Commission's "full pay" policy was adopted. If Bob was still working and could be contacted via neutral authorities, the policy dictated that the Commission should send him his money.

That did not happen.

James and Augusta's pleas landed on the desk of Colonel Henry Francis Chettle, the Commission's deputy controller. The relevant question should have been whether Bob was still working, but Chettle did not try to find out. Instead, he focused on Bob's Irish citizenship.

The Commission's policy did not explicitly state that Irish gardeners should be treated differently from British gardeners, but Colonel Chettle disagreed. Irish nationals, he reasoned, were not truly trapped in France. Therefore, the Commission's emergency measures did not apply to them.

Before offering a final decision, Chettle wrote to the Foreign Office for clarification. "I should be grateful for advice—not necessarily in writing," he wrote. Over the telephone, a Foreign Office official agreed with Chettle. Irish citizens in France were "free to move about or come home."[19]

This was a serious misunderstanding of Bob Armstrong's circumstances. Despite the Foreign Office's blithe assurance, Irish citizens were certainly not free to move within France, let alone leave it. Getting permission to exit the country was an arduous, expensive process that even wealthy and well-connected people found extraordinarily difficult. In addition to special exit permits, travelers needed visas to enter Spain and Portugal and were generally required to pay all travel expenses in advance. If they did manage to reach Lisbon, they had to pay airfare of about £35—two months' wages for Bob and 10 days' salary for Colonel Chettle—for a flight to England.[20]

After nine months without wages, Bob Armstrong was penniless. Even if he got permission to leave France legally, he could not have afforded to pay for visas and trains and airplanes.

Armed with misinformation, Chettle decided that Bob Armstrong was not entitled to his full pay. Since he was an Irish citizen, he was not "subject to the conditions imposed on members of the Commission's staff holding British passports." In Chettle's words, the Commission's emergency financial arrangements simply "do not apply to Eire citizens."

Colonel Chettle wrote a condescending reply to Augusta Lindsay, informing her that the Commission would not send Bob's wages. Throughout the letter, Chettle argued that Bob was "no doubt free to move about or come home." He used phrases like "if he decides to stay in France" and "if he prefers to come home," implying that Bob's presence in France was entirely a matter of choice. "His position is different from that of other Commission employees detained against their will," Chettle told Augusta.[21]

Nowhere did Chettle mention the direct orders from Brigadier Prower and Captain Melles that sent Bob back to Valenciennes in the teeth of the German advance. The Commission's official position was that Bob

Armstrong had remained in France—and continued to remain there—voluntarily.

The Commission's refusal was a terrible blow to the Armstrong family, but it was not the only one. In writing for help, Augusta Lindsay had attracted Colonel Chettle's attention to the fact that she was still receiving her £2 monthly allotment. If Eire citizens were not eligible for pay, they were not eligible for allotments.

"The Commission further regret," Chettle told Augusta, "that in the circumstances they are unable to continue the payment of £2 a month."

Augusta Lindsay had gone to the Commission to beg for help for her brother. Instead, she lost even the pittance Bob had set aside to provide for her.

It was clear that neither Bob nor his family would get any help from the Commission, so Augusta did what she could on her own. For the next three years, while her children went ragged and she struggled to feed them, Augusta scrounged for pennies to send to Bob in France.[22]

∼

The Armstrongs were not the only family frustrated by their interactions with the War Graves Commission. The few surviving personnel files document many families' anguish and anger.

"The present plight of these men lies with the W[ar] G[raves] C[ommission] London Office, in spite of whatever excuse they may bring forward," wrote Alex Chapman, brother of interned gardener Samuel Chapman.

Like the gardeners themselves, Alex Chapman was appalled by the botched evacuation. "How is it that the foreman is home and not the men under him?" he demanded. In another sharp letter, Chapman objected to the cancellation of his brother's contract. "A grave injustice is being practiced . . . I am far from satisfied with the efforts of the Commission to do all in their power to relieve the hardship of these men, their employees."

Alex and Samuel's mother, Florence Chapman, minced no words: "Their plight is your responsibility."[23]

Commission officials regarded the Chapman family's letters as "ill-tempered attacks," but they were hardly the only gardener's family complaining.

A particular point of frustration was the Commission's failure to keep the families informed about their loved ones' whereabouts. "Very frankly, I think there is something radically wrong with the organisation of the I.W.G.C.," wrote Edwin Hinbest, brother of interned gardener Charles

Hinbest. "They are unable to trace their employees, who are incarcerated in normal civilian internment camps, before the relatives are able to do so."[24]

Hinbest's mother, Alice, wrote to the Commission repeatedly to ask for information about her son and his family. After months without a reply, she received a notice informing her that her £2 monthly allotment was being discontinued so that the Commission could reimburse the U.S. government for relief payments to Hinbest's wife and children. Alice was relieved to learn that her grandchildren were alive but exasperated that the Commission had not told her as soon as they knew.

"Previous application to you requesting information as to the whereabouts of my son and/or his family has been fruitless," she wrote. "Might I ask you for some enlightenment in this matter?"[25]

The cancellation of allotments was also a contentious issue. Most of the gardeners' allotments were small—between £1 and £3 each month—but they were often critically important to elderly parents, disabled siblings, or children who were attending school in the United Kingdom. The Commission did not recognize any legal responsibility to pay these allotments after the contracts were terminated, but they left open the possibility of continuing the payments ex gratia. In early 1941, they began reviewing cases. If the reviewers deemed the recipient sufficiently needy, they could choose to continue the payments, which would be recouped from the gardener's wages after the war. If the recipient was not in dire need, the allotment would stop.

One of the dependents whose allotment was canceled was Irene Kirkwood, the sixteen-year-old daughter of gardener Arthur Kirkwood. Before the war, Irene's parents sent her to live with an aunt and uncle near Durham so that she could attend an English secondary school. Her father allotted £2.10.0 every month for her expenses. In 1940, both of Irene's parents were interned: Arthur Kirkwood at Ilag VIII and Jessie Kirkwood at Vittel. When the Commission contacted Irene's uncle regarding her remittance, he informed them that Irene was securely housed and fed. Since she was not destitute, the Commission canceled her allotment.[26]

Other cases were thornier. When Arthur Wilson, a gardener from Poix-du-Nord, was interned at Ilag VIII, the Commission continued to send a monthly payment of £1 to his elderly mother, Rose. Then, in March 1942, the Commission decided to change its criteria, unilaterally cutting off any allotment that did not support a wife or minor child.

"There is as you know no legal obligation on the Commission to make these payments," the Commission explained in a letter to Rose Wilson.

A friend of the Wilsons wrote back to plead their case. In fact, all of the letters from Rose Wilson were penned by this friend, suggesting that Mrs. Wilson may not have been able to write. The friend argued that Rose and her disabled daughter relied on the tiny sum for basic necessities and that Arthur himself had recently "expressed in a letter from a German prison camp a hope that she is still getting it." "It is obvious he still desires her to have it," the friend begged.

In response, the Commission made a "special concession," agreeing to continue Mrs. Wilson's payments for three months and to continue to review her case on a regular basis thereafter.[27]

Some gardeners were appalled to learn that the Commission had cut off their dependents in their hour of need. Edward Dines, an interned gardener from Abbeville, protested when the Commission stopped the small allotment for his son, Jack, who was an inmate of the Newbury Union Workhouse. "There may be a complaint as to cessation of allocation," the Commission noted, though the details were lost when the War Graves Commission destroyed Edward Dines's personnel file.[28]

Over and over, the Commission denied families' requests for modest financial help. In one case, Emily Wells, the mother of gardener Alfred Wells, asked for help sending parcels to her interned son. "Mrs. Wells has nothing beyond her Old Age Pension and therefore cannot afford to send quarterly parcels," a friend wrote on her behalf. "Is there a fund from which you send parcels to your gardeners or from which you could make a grant to help us send quarterly?"

There was not. An internal memo noted that the Commission had refused several similar requests from other families. "I suppose that the reply is the same?" the anonymous memo writer asked.[29]

Even when financial assistance was directly related to travel costs for released internees, the Commission was reluctant to help. Gardener Hubert Luck was released from Ilag VIII in late 1942, possibly because he was ill. When the British consulate in Portugal asked the Commission to accept a £35 charge for Luck's airfare to London, the Commission hesitated. Luck was "not traveling on instructions from I.W.G.C. but as an ordinary refugee," they replied.[30]

The answer was the same for gardener Alfred Layland, who escaped from the Nord department and spent two years working in a Commission cemetery in Marseilles. In 1942, American diplomats advised Layland to flee before the Nazis took full control of the Free Zone. Men under the age of forty-nine were not allowed to leave Vichy France, so the forty-six-year-old Layland altered his passport to read "1892" instead of "1895" and escaped to Lisbon. When Layland's brother Walter asked the Commission to advance his brother's airfare, they refused.

"We had not given instructions for your brother to return from Marseilles where, as you know, he had settled down to look after the British cemetery," a Commission official wrote. "We can only assume that he is traveling as an ordinary refugee. It does not therefore directly concern the Commission how he travels to England."[31]

Both Luck and Layland eventually found their way to the United Kingdom by sea.[32]

To be sure, the War Graves Commission's finances were a delicate matter. Its leadership had always been acutely conscious that their budget came from public funds and that every penny had to be spent with public scrutiny in mind. Another complication was the 1939 Trading with the Enemy Act. This law severely limited financial transactions with any "enemy," which it defined as any individual living in a territory controlled by a power at war with the United Kingdom.

"It seems clear that our men are technically enemies within the meaning of the Act," one Commission official wrote.[33]

The Commission was constrained in many ways, but it was not actually short of cash. The Nazi invasion had interrupted War Graves work in Europe, but that work did not generate any revenue. There were no customers to lose, no ticketed events to cancel. At the time of the invasion, the Commission had already received its normal operating funds for the 1940–1941 fiscal year. On April 10, 1940, a month before the invasion, the commissioners approved the routine release of salary funds for the upcoming year. When the Commission stopped paying its gardeners, that money sat on its books as surplus. After much discussion, the Commission decided to lend its wartime surpluses back to the British government as zero-interest loans in support of the war effort. In 1942 alone, this loan totaled £120,000, almost exactly matching the prewar budget for salaries in France and Belgium (£121,413.17.5 in 1939–1940).[34]

The War Graves Commission did use some of its discretionary budget to cheer the interned gardeners. Beginning in 1941, they sent each internee a Christmas parcel containing 200 cigarettes, two pouches of tobacco, and a Christmas card from Sir Fabian. Many of the gardeners wrote back to express their sincere appreciation for these gifts, using the precious extra postcard they were allowed to send at Christmas.[35]

But even these gifts underscored the chasm between what Commission officials were willing to give and the men's actual needs.

"Many thanks for your kind letter," gardener Frederick Martin wrote to Sir Fabian from the Saint-Denis internment camp in 1942. "I have not yet received the Xmas parcel you have so kindly sent me, but I trust it will turn up shortly."

The next year, Martin sent a similar thank-you to Sir Fabian. "It gave me much pleasure to hear from you again," he wrote, but "I am sorry to have to tell you up to time of writing this letter to you, I have never received any parcels."

In a third letter, Martin maintained the same bright tone. "It would have given me great pleasure to have received that parcel from you," he wrote but explained that he had never received a single cigarette. Martin thanked Sir Fabian "for all your trouble" but ended his letter with a request.

"You will excuse me sir if I point out to you that I am in need of under clothing. If you could do anything for me I shall be greatly oblidge to you for doing so, + thank in advance."[36]

~

Bob Armstrong's family was eager to extract him from France, but it is not clear that Bob would have left even if he could. The Irish Legation had advanced him £30 to keep body and soul together, and his friends in Valenciennes would not let him starve. Bob moved into a cramped, gray rowhouse with a family named Penez, "where he was considered a child of the house."[37]

By the fall of 1940, Bob was busy, and not just in the cemeteries. His official French Resistance file, which names him a *sous-lieutenant* of the Forces Françaises Combattantes, dates the beginning of his service to October 1, 1940.[38]

The idea of waging a clandestine war against an occupying power was not a novel concept to Bob. He had not lived at Currygrane during the Irish War of Independence or the Irish Civil War that followed, but he did visit. Family lore suggests that Bob, despite his service in the British army, may have occasionally helped his old friend Seán MacEoin with some of his IRA activities. Another story holds that Bob's father, James, once lied to the Black and Tans to protect MacEoin, who was hiding at Currygrane. MacEoin was later captured and sentenced to death, but his life was saved by the adoption of the Anglo-Irish Treaty in 1921.[39]

Whether or not Bob Armstrong was directly involved in any revolutionary actions in Ireland, he was certainly aware of them. Currygrane was alive with underground activity. Several of the men who lived on the estate or adjacent townlands were part of MacEoin's flying column, including James Killean, one of Currygrane's tenant farmers.

Killean's wife, Catherine, was just as committed to the cause. In 1917, she founded a branch of the Irish Republican women's auxiliary Cumann na mBan and was soon leading more than 300 women from the surrounding area. According to Seán MacEoin, everyone called Catherine Killean "The Boss." She provided critical support to MacEoin's fighters, and the IRA frequently used her house at Currygrane as its local headquarters. It is possible that Bob's father may have helped. Indeed, Catherine Killean testified that she stashed "rifles and ammunition and gelignite" at Currygrane with the help of "an old servant," who could have been James Armstrong.[40]

Even if Bob Armstrong heard about these actions secondhand, he was familiar with the idea of irregular fighters and the steel-nerved civilians who supported them.

The situation in France in 1940 was not the same as in Ireland in 1920, but there were similarities. After the Dunkirk evacuation, northern France teemed with fugitives. Some were escaped prisoners of war. Others were evaders, soldiers who had never been captured. All through the summer and fall of 1940, these desperate men hid in fields and forests, begging civilians for help.

One of the escapers was twenty-six-year-old Corporal George Hignett, the War Graves gardener from Longueval who had been recalled to the Gordon Highlanders with Peter Moir. Hignett's battalion was part of the 51st Highland Division, which stayed to fight alongside the French while the main British strength retreated to Dunkirk. It was a futile effort. Pushed back to Saint-Valery-en-Caux, the Highlanders were trapped by the sea, the high cliffs, and the advancing Germans. On June 12, 1940, all 10,000 of them were captured along with their French comrades.[41]

As George Hignett trudged east with his fellow prisoners, he made a plan. If he could slip away from the column before it left France, he could go back to Longueval and ask his neighbors for help.

About twenty-five miles from Arras, Hignett got his chance. While the guards' attention was elsewhere, Hignett and a comrade "jumped down the road embankment and hid in a culvert." Overhead, thousands of prisoners shuffled past. Hignett and his friend waited until they disappeared down the road. Then they ran.

"I made immediately for Longueval, where, before the war, I had been employed by the Imperial War Graves Commission," Hignett later told an investigator with MI9, the British military intelligence agency in charge of escape and evasion.

Hignett stayed in Longueval for four days, resting, collecting provisions, and planning his next move. He traveled to the coast in an attempt to find a fishing boat but had no luck. Stymied, he traveled back inland to seek help from his War Graves colleagues.

"Ginger Hignett at Hebuterne," Ben Leech wrote in his gardening log on July 10, a month after the 51st Highland Division surrendered and just five days before the Feldgendarmes arrived in Hébuterne to arrest Albert Haines, John Hamilton, and Charlie and Noël Holton. Ben did not elaborate on Hignett's visit. Writing anything was risky.[42]

By the time the German police arrived in Hébuterne on July 15, George Hignett was already gone. He skulked around northern France for more than a month, then made his way south, headed for neutral Spain. He was captured during his first attempt to cross the Pyrenees but was eventually released and successfully crossed the border on the night of December 18–19, 1940.

For this daring escape, George Hignett was mentioned in dispatches. He would return to France as part of the Allied invasion force in June 1944.[43]

Thousands of British soldiers were on the run in northern France, but few of them had local friends like George Hignett. Many found help anyway. While few French people were willing to declare themselves *résistants* in the early days of the occupation, many were willing to feed a bedraggled soldier who turned up on their doorstep or let him sleep in the barn. A few hundred evaders and escapers managed to return to England in 1940, but most were eventually captured.

Near Valenciennes, a trio of evaders—Tom Dainton of the Royal Army Service Corps, Harry Croydon of the Dorsetshire Regiment, and Eric Uden of the King's Royal Rifle Corps—were in desperate need of help. Besides being hungry and lost, one of them was "very ill with disentry." If they did not get material assistance soon, they were done for.[44]

Fortunately, the three men fell into the hands of a newly formed Resistance group—Réseau Saint-Jacques—and one of its earliest agents, Bob Armstrong.

Saint-Jacques was one of the first formal Resistance networks in France. It was founded in August 1940 by Maurice Duclos, a right-wing intelligence agent sent from London by General Charles de Gaulle. While most early Resistance networks were homegrown and took many months to organize themselves, Saint-Jacques was an official arm of de Gaulle's Free French intelligence bureau. It had structure and leadership and was tasked with gathering intelligence, training guerrilla fighters, and assisting evaders.[45]

Saint-Jacques was a small network, but it had more than one Irish connection. Maurice Duclos's family brokerage was headquartered in the same

Paris building as a wine-trading business run by Count Gerald O'Kelly de Gallagh, formerly Ireland's first minister in France. When the Irish Legation was forced to leave Paris for Vichy in 1940, O'Kelly's premises became a semiformal Irish diplomatic office. Meanwhile, Duclos used his family's office as the headquarters of the Saint-Jacques network. This may have been coincidence, but at least one other Irish person besides Bob Armstrong—Janie McCarthy, a teacher from County Kerry—worked with Réseau Saint-Jacques.[46]

Bob Armstrong was a long way from Paris, but he certainly did contact the Irish Legation and may also have contacted someone in Paris in search of help. It is also possible that he was brought into Saint-Jacques via his many Resistance-minded friends in Valenciennes. However he learned of the network, Bob volunteered right away. Of the two dozen agents who worked under Colonel Jean Vérines in the Nord sector, only eight joined before Bob. Initially, the Resistance welcomed Bob, "with the intention to use him as a translator," but they soon found that "all actions suited him." The agent files of the Saint-Jacques network state that Bob Armstrong "volunteered for every dangerous mission (conveying and liaising)."[47]

One of Bob's first missions for Saint-Jacques was sheltering Tom Dainton, Harry Croydon, and Eric Uden. He had no legal obligation to care for three wandering English soldiers—indeed, he broke the law and risked death by doing so—but he did it anyway.

"DEAR BOB," the evaders wrote later, "WE THANK YOU SINCERELY AND HOPE THAT SOME DAY WE SHALL BE ABLE TO REPAY YOUR EXCELLENT KINDNESS." Their message is written in capital letters with odd errors that suggest it may have been transmitted in imperfect Morse: "WE WHERE STARVING AND IN HEED OF GOOD SOLID FOOD WHEN YOU CAMB TO OUR ASSISTANCE."

After he patched them up, Bob Armstrong sent Dainton, Croydon, and Uden on their way, probably with a guide. Unfortunately, the three soldiers were captured later in their journey and sent to a prisoner-of-war camp, Stalag XX-A, for the duration. Still, they appreciated Bob's efforts. "FROM OUR HEARTS WE UNANIMOUSLY SAY WE SHALL NEVRE FORGE YOU MAY WE MERT AGAIN."[48]

These were the first three evaders Bob Armstrong sheltered, but they would not be the last.

RÉSISTANTS OF THE FIRST HOUR   8

One day in August 1940, a few weeks after Bert was arrested, three men walked into Rosine Witton's *café-tabac*. One was a railway worker who lived nearby, the second was a local politician, and the third was a balding, soft-eyed man named Eugène D'Hallendre. He would soon become one of the most important people in Rosine's life.[1]

Eugène D'Hallendre. *Courtesy of the Musée de la Résistance, Bondues*

August 1940 was still early days for the French Resistance, but Eugène D'Hallendre was already an important organizer. A former naval aviator, D'Hallendre was an inspector for the French national railway company. The job required frequent travel and contact with railway workers, who were a key group within the Resistance. D'Hallendre was also a city councillor in his hometown, La Madeleine, a suburb of Lille. Anyone could approach him to discuss town business, and there was nothing suspicious about his hosting frequent, eclectic meetings at his house.[2]

From the earliest days of the occupation, Eugène D'Hallendre threw himself into Resistance work with astonishing energy. Beginning in 1940, he wrote blistering anti-Pétain pamphlets, typing copies one by one with help from his wife, Lucienne, and teenage son, Edgard. He wrote essays for the underground newspaper *La Voix du Nord* and helped with distribution. Later, D'Hallendre became a regional leader of the Organization civile et militaire (OCM), one of the largest Gaullist Resistance networks in France. His wide-ranging, overlapping activities were typical of the early Resistance in the north, where "networks" were often more of an ethos than an actual organization. As late as 1943, Special Operations Executive (SOE) agent F. F. E. Yeo-Thomas reported to London that assigning names to so-called resistance groups gave a false impression of coherence when the reality was "a most confusing hotch-potch of seemingly conflicting currents."[3]

D'Hallendre also helped rescue Allied evaders. He worked with both the Pat O'Leary Line and the Comet Line, two of the largest and most successful escape networks. At the height of his activity, D'Hallendre coordinated four main safe houses. One of them was Number 6 Route de Bapaume, the home of Rosine Witton.[4]

Much of that work was still in the future. During their initial conversations in the summer of 1940, Eugène D'Hallendre did not ask Rosine to shelter evaders. Instead, he presented himself and his associates as representatives of a network still struggling into existence. They had seen Rosine's fierce patriotism and noted that her husband's arrest had left her fizzing with outrage. Was she ready to help them build a real, lasting organization?

It was a crucial question in 1940. In the first year of the occupation, organized Resistance networks like Bob Armstrong's Réseau Saint-Jacques were the exception, not the rule. The clandestine press was still in drafts; Charles de Gaulle was relatively unknown; and French communists generally held back until Hitler attacked the Soviet Union in 1941. It would take several years—and widespread opposition to forced labor orders—before the French Resistance became a mass movement.[5]

Even SOE, the famous British special forces unit that trained agents to sabotage infrastructure and organize Resistance efforts behind enemy lines, was still embryonic in August 1940. Prime Minister Winston Churchill set SOE in motion with his instruction to "set Europe ablaze" on July 22, 1940, but it would be months before they put a boot on the ground in France.[6]

Instead, the French Resistance of 1940 was made up of small, informal groups of civilians acting with little coordination or strategy. These "*résistants* of the first hour" were a minuscule minority. They were outliers and pioneers, isolated candles who kept "the flame of French resistance" from flickering out.

Rosine Witton was one of them.

Even before Eugène D'Hallendre recruited her, Rosine had already begun to act. As early as June 1940, she began visiting British soldiers in local hospitals and prisoner-of-war camps, bringing sweets and cigarettes, and chatting with the prisoners in English. Many members of the War Graves community did similar work, particularly in the weeks before the men were arrested. Gardener Arthur Kirkwood and his wife Jessie salvaged clothing and English-language books from the homes of War Graves gardeners who had fled to the United Kingdom and brought them to the British prisoners.[7]

Rosine's friend Berthe Fraser was particularly active in this relief work. "Each week," she later testified, "I arranged to send about 100 packages containing food, blankets, clothing, soap and other articles, tobacco and cigarettes, which were collected by a small group of helpers." Rosine Witton, who had preexisting relationships with tobacco wholesalers, was probably one of these "helpers." Berthe brought the supplies to a transit camp in Doullens where British captives awaited transport to permanent camps in Germany.[8]

Ministering to British prisoners was not, strictly speaking, an act of resistance. The Germans allowed civilians to provide these small comforts, so the work was not a direct challenge to Nazi authority.

Still, visiting British prisoners was an important act of solidarity. At a time when many French civilians felt humiliated by their country's defeat and infuriated by the British allies who had abandoned them, caring for British prisoners was both a mercy and a demonstration of faith in the Anglo-French alliance. Rosine Witton and her friends were stretching the muscles of their courage.

Then came the July arrests. Rosine watched as the Germans took Bert away, along with Berthe Fraser's husband, John, and dozens of other friends and neighbors.

The catastrophe left many of the War Graves women destitute. The British government would eventually provide relief payments through the American and Swiss embassies, but these did not begin until October 1940. Meanwhile, as British nationals, they were barred from most employment. Charities like the British-American Civilian Emergency Services in Paris tried to help women, children, and elderly people, but their limited funds did not stretch far.

Rosine Witton and Berthe Fraser did what they could to help the struggling families in their community. They provided moral support—and often food—to the War Graves women, both in Ronville and beyond.[9]

"Chum, I am very please[d] to see you are getting out a bit," Bert wrote from Ilag VIII, "and that you have been to see Mrs. Covey + Pallin." Marie Covey and Irma Palin were the wives of interned gardeners who lived in Bienvillers-au-Bois and Berles-au-Bois, villages about halfway between Arras and Beaumont-Hamel. Rosine had to make a special effort to visit them, but it was important to keep the bonds of affection and solidarity strong.[10]

Hating the Germans and helping her neighbors did not make Rosine Witton unusual, but her hostility to the Vichy government and its leader, Marshal Philippe Pétain, did. Rosine and her friends considered the surrender a "shameful capitulation." Their attitude set them apart from most French people, who respected the elderly Pétain for his heroic service in World War I. Many saw his concessions as regrettable but necessary to protect France from the worst excesses of the Nazi regime. Rosine disagreed. At home, listening to her radio, she spat every time she heard Pétain's name.

For many people in France, the first priority was to live as normally as possible under the occupation. Rosine Witton could not pretend. Her husband was gone, the Commission was gone, and the whole Anglo-French community was reeling. Rosine was a provincial shopkeeper, not an inveterate political radical, but she belonged to a community that embodied the Anglo-French alliance in the very marrow of its being. As a postwar investigator noted after interviewing Berthe Fraser, "in her entourage, however bourgeois, almost everyone shared the same opinions and was ready to participate in any activities that could harm the enemy."[11]

The first time Rosine consciously thought of herself as a *résistante* was shortly after Bert's arrest, when Berthe Fraser whispered a secret. She was doing more than delivering parcels to the prisoner-of-war camp in Doullens. With the help of a few committed comrades, she was helping British soldiers escape.

They were a small group: Dr. Emile Poiteau, who smuggled men out the camp; Eliane Meplaux, who sheltered them at her home in Hébuterne; Jules Gosse, who guided them across the Somme into the occupied zone; and Berthe Fraser, who paid for it all. The group cooperated with a wider network of suppliers and hosts that included at least two War Graves gardeners, Lewis Fulton Bonnell in Wanquentin and George Horn in Albert.[12]

All across northern France and Belgium, small groups like Berthe Fraser's were forming to smuggle Allied soldiers to safety. In the coming years, some of these early organizations would grow into durable "escape lines." One was the Pat O'Leary Line, an organization run by the British intelligence agency MI9. The most successful escape line was Réseau Comete—the Comet Line—which guided around 750 people over the Pyrenees. It was founded in 1941 by a young Belgian woman named Andrée de Jongh alias Dédée. The Comet Line accepted funds from MI9 but not direct oversight. De Jongh insisted that her network should remain under the control of civilians, not entangled with British agents or armed resistance that might endanger its core mission.[13]

Rosine Witton would eventually work for both Pat O'Leary and the Comet Line, but she began her work before either existed. In July 1940, there were no escape lines, only scattered dots reaching out along preexisting lines of fellowship. Rosine considered the day Berthe told her about Eliane Meplaux and the others as the day she "began her resistance."[14]

Rosine Witton, Berthe Fraser, and their friends were part of an extraordinarily committed—and extraordinarily early—kernel of the Resistance. Their Anglo-French community tended to be fairly conservative, but they shared a few important characteristics with the left-wing organizations that became such important incubators of the Resistance. They were a cohesive group before the invasion. They trusted one another. They were loyal to a cause.

It was a start.

Rosine and Berthe soon found a comrade in Arthur Clarke Richards, the British Legion vice-chairman who had walked home from Lille after his brief internment. Originally from Birmingham, Arthur Richards served in the Royal Warwickshire Regiment during World War I. After demobilization, he stayed in France rather than returning to his wife, Rose, and their five young children, who grew up believing that their mother was a war widow. In fact, Arthur Richards was alive and well, living in Ronville with a young Belgian woman, Berthe Hequet, and their infant son. He worked at a local printing firm.[15]

After returning to Arras at the end of July 1940, Arthur Richards joined Berthe Fraser's little group of helpers.

"I sent about 50 French patriots into the free zone including a French priest and about 20 British soldiers some of which came in from Belgium," Richards later testified. He did not remember all the evaders' names, as it was "imprudent to keep documents," but he did remember three Gordon Highlanders who spent "a good Xmas" at his home in Ronville in 1940. Richards's most important contribution was his lifelong experience in printing. Working with a French designer, he made false documents for approximately 300 evaders.[16]

With a flair for the dramatic, Richards adopted the alias Coeur de Lion (Richard the Lionheart), after the medieval crusader king who ruled England from abroad. Eventually, the name became associated with the fragile escape network that grew up around the Anglo-French community in Arras.[17]

Coeur de Lion was not a fully functional escape line. It was a loose assemblage of friends and neighbors with no formal structure, no clear hierarchy, and "no aid whatever" in terms of funding from outside sources. Several members of the War Graves community contributed to its mission.[18]

One of Coeur de Lion's early affiliates was Zoé Evans, the widow of a War Graves clerk who had worked in the Arras office until his death in 1937. Like Rosine Witton and Berthe Fraser, Zoé Evans was a shopkeeper in Arras. Her clothing boutique was just a few steps from the Arras Hôtel de Ville, directly under the window of the chamber where the mayor and his council met. Also like Rosine and Berthe, Evans had no dependent children living at home. She did have a twenty-three-year-old son, Henri, but he was off serving with the British forces. In 1940, Evans began working as a guide, conveying evaders over the north-east line.[19]

Many of the French women associated with Coeur de Lion had British loved ones. Berthe Fraser was British by marriage. Eliane Meplaux had two older sisters who had emigrated to England and sometimes sent their British-born children to stay with Eliane's family in France. Aimée Lievre, a French nurse who delivered supplies to evaders and sketched detailed plans of German military installations, was Arthur Richards's new partner. Like Rosine Witton, many of them spoke some English and were already used to thinking of themselves as part of a coherent community that was spread across northern France rather than confined to their own village or neighborhood.

Thus, when Eugène D'Hallendre stepped into Rosine Witton's café in August 1940, she already thought of herself as an active *résistante*. Bert's arrest ignited her spark, the Coeur de Lion community helped it catch, and Eugène D'Hallendre offered her as much fuel as she wanted.

Rosine Witton took on four specific responsibilities as part of Eugène D'Hallendre's Resistance network.

First, D'Hallendre asked her to help supply food for "British soldiers secretly lodged in the region around Lens," north of Arras. Rosine agreed without hesitation.[20]

Her second task was to safeguard information. Rosine's *café-tabac* became a *boîte de lettres* (letterbox), a secure location where Resistance operatives could leave messages for others to retrieve without attracting attention. The *café-tabac* was ideal for this sort of work because anyone could stop in without arousing suspicion. It placed Rosine in a position of enormous trust.

Third, Rosine helped run a morale-building scheme disguised as a fund-raiser.

Behind her counter, she kept a stack of portraits of Charles de Gaulle, the exiled French general who had appointed himself leader of the Free French. These images were similar to images of Marshal Pétain that had flooded France in the months since the Vichy takeover. Everywhere, post offices sold postcards emblazoned with Pétain's image, and schools gave prizes to children who sold the most copies. At five francs each, these images raised money for the Vichy-run aid organization Secours National while papering the entire country with Pétain's face.

Gaullist *résistants* were determined to counter this propaganda. Charles de Gaulle was little more than a tinny voice on the radio, but they hoped to elevate him as an alternate national hero. With the help of a sympathetic printer in Douai, Eugène D'Hallendre reproduced a photograph of de Gaulle in a similar format to the Pétain portraits. Rosine Witton was one of the distributors, selling the portraits for five francs each to her "most loyal and steady regulars."[21]

The portrait scheme was nominally a fund-raiser, but its purpose was not primarily financial. Five francs was enough to purchase a kilo of green beans in Arras in August 1940 but not enough for a tin of sardines, let alone enough to cover the costs of clandestine printing.

The true purpose was to keep the embers of resistance warm at a time when many French people felt disconnected, hopeless, and overwhelmed by the shock of defeat. For those who wanted to believe that the Resistance was real, the portraits of de Gaulle were proof. They were flimsy, cheap, and fragile, but they existed. They showed that someone had the capacity to print and distribute them. Someone was organizing. When one of Rosine's customers purchased a portrait of de Gaulle, they revealed themselves to her and caught a glimpse of the little candles burning all around them.

Rosine's fourth role was the most dangerous, but it was also the one that required her specific skills. Many shopkeepers could have held messages or sold pictures, but Rosine was a fluent English speaker with twenty years' knowledge of Ronville's comings and goings. She played a critical role in recruitment and security.

Recruiting people into the Resistance was always risky. As a lifelong resident of Ronville who spent her days in the local gossip hub, Rosine Witton was in a good position to identify likely candidates and potential problems. She knew her neighbors' backgrounds, families, and financial circumstances and could keep an ear out for rumors about their loyalties.

One of the volunteers who approached Rosine was a gendarme—a local police officer—named Paul Leblond.

"You are married to an Englishman, and I know you are active," Leblond told her. "I want to do something, too."

It might have been a threat or a trap. Gendarmes could make exceptionally useful *résistants*, but they could also be exceptionally dangerous. Rosine had to trust her own judgment.

She decided to give Leblond a chance.

Rosine set up a meeting at the home of Dr. Henri Artisson, an OCM operative who lived near the train station. There, Eugène D'Hallendre and his associates questioned Leblond closely, testing his motivations and their own intuition. In the end, they agreed with Rosine. They could trust Leblond.

After the meeting, a relieved Leblond confided to Rosine that he had come armed, just in case.

"The others were armed, too," she informed him unsentimentally. "If it hadn't worked out, you wouldn't have left alive."[22]

In addition to screening recruits, Rosine Witton was also an interrogator. Northern France was awash in young men claiming to be British soldiers, but it was difficult for the Resistance to tell the difference between a genuine evader and a Nazi infiltrator. Later, some escape networks would verify evaders' identities by contacting London via wireless, but most groups relied on local English speakers to test evaders' stories. They found several willing recruits among the War Graves community.

One interrogator was Stephen Grady, the teenage gardener's son who hid weapons in Pont d'Achelles Cemetery in Nieppe. Stephen was recruited by a local Resistance leader who needed "a native English speaker to quiz any airmen who bail out in our zone, to test whether they are telling the truth." Eager to help, Stephen took the code name "Iroquois" and built up a repertoire of security questions.

The consequences for failing Stephen Grady's test were dire. Once, a man claiming to be a Canadian airman named Eastwood proved to be unfamiliar with Royal Air Force (RAF) slang like "yellow doughnut" (an emergency raft) and "Caterpillar Club" (airmen who had parachuted from a disabled aircraft) and thought that Harvard was only a university, not a common plane used to train pilots in Canadian service flying training schools.

"I am pretty certain that man in there is not a Canadian airman," Stephen told his comrades. Grimly, the adults took over. They sent Stephen back to his cemetery while they shot the imposter and disposed of his body.

"My mind is full of images of Eastwood as I work in the Nieppe cemetery that afternoon, tidying the borders of the War Graves plot," Stephen remembered. "Yet, this man will have no white headstone in a military cemetery, no gracious resting place for his mother to visit."[23]

Another bilingual War Graves *résistante* was Hilda Weller, the sixteen-year-old daughter of Australian gardener Cyril Weller. Both of Hilda's parents were interned, along with her older sister, Mary, who died in 1943. Hilda stayed in Avesnes-le-Comte, a few miles west of Arras, working as an "interpreter and liaison agent." American airmen who met Hilda reported that she "speaks good English and gave active assistance." When a local Resistance leader was asked to name civilians who played crucial roles in helping evaders, he put Hilda Weller's name first on the list.[24]

Rosine Witton was not natively bilingual like Stephen Grady and Hilda Weller, but she was fluent enough to offer a valuable opinion on evaders' authenticity. In one case, she was not convinced by a group of three evaders claiming to be from the RAF.

"They took Madame Witton to interview them," recalled Eugène D'Hallendre's son, Edgard. "Big surprise! They didn't speak English, but a curious sort of French with a drawling accent." The men may have been French Canadians or merely fluent in an unfamiliar dialect of French, but Rosine Witton was not confident enough to vouch for them. Eugéne D'Hallendre trusted her judgment. "They were suspicious," Edgard reported, "so they dropped them."[25]

Edgard's memory that the three men were "dropped" implies that they were merely cut loose to fend for themselves rather than killed. If so, the *résistants* took a tremendous risk. A German infiltrator who had met them face-to-face could give evidence that might condemn them to arrest, prison, or death.

The danger was real. Anyone caught helping British evaders or escapers could be charged with the capital crime of "encouraging a hostile power during a war against the Reich."[26] Men who worked for escape lines could be sentenced to death by firing squad, while women were generally deported to slower deaths in concentration camps. These harsh sentences became much more common after 1942, but *résistants* in northern France were still courting terrible danger in the earlier period.

Despite the threat of arrest, deportation, or death, many members of the War Graves community helped evaders during the first year of the Nazi occupation.

Sometimes, they offered help to evaders who wandered into their vicinity. Around the time George Hignett visited Hébuterne, Ben Leech fixed a bicycle for someone named "Southern" who stayed in Beaumont-Hamel for two days. "Visit cemeteries all O.K.," Ben wrote on July 13, 1940. "Saw Southern off on route." Two days later, on July 15, the gardeners in Hébuterne were arrested. Ben expected to be picked up next, but he still helped two evaders who arrived in Beaumont-Hamel on July 17. "Two R[oyal] A[rtillery] stayed all day repaired their bikes," he noted in that day's gardening log, right beside the news "All gardeners in P[as] D[e] C[alais] taken into custody."[27]

In Nieppe, eighteen-year-old Rosemary Grady set out buckets of water for the thirsty French and British prisoners being marched to Germany. Small actions became larger actions, and soon the Grady family had "three British soldiers hiding in our attic." In October 1940, fifteen-year-old Stephen moved them to the toolshed at Le Grand Beaumart cemetery in nearby Steenwerck.

"This windowless place is dark and airless by day, but should be comfortable enough at night," Stephen later wrote, "if they don't mind the whiff of oil and petrol and grass clippings which is, I think, my favourite smell in the world." The three soldiers stayed for a couple of weeks, then set out on their own.[28]

In Wanquentin, just west of Arras, a Canadian War Graves gardener named Lewis Fulton Bonnell hid a pair of Black Watch evaders. Bonnell's work was cut short by his arrest—as an internee, not a criminal—on July 6, 1940. His wife, Marie, passed the evaders on to a neighbor, Marcel Roussel, who cooperated with the Coeur de Lion network. The evaders posed as laborers on Roussel's farm for several months until he could arrange transportation across the Somme.[29]

Another War Graves gardener who helped evaders was George Horn, from Albert. In 1941, Horn began working with an escape network called

Lord Denys, mostly delivering supplies and identity papers to safe-house keepers like Eliane Meplaux.

"[I] worked with a Madam Melplo who was known as the heroine of the Pas-de-Calais," Horn testified after the war. He also made regular visits to the family of Mackay McLeod, a Scottish-born veteran of the Royal Canadian Regiment who sheltered an escaped Cameron Highlander for an entire year. Horn "used to go and visit them in spite of the Germans as I was not allowed to leave Albert." The evader got away, but both George Horn and Mackay McLeod were arrested and deported to Germany. A Commission investigation found that Horn and his partner, Gabrielle Dherville, were arrested "for listening to English broadcasts," though Horn's Resistance work went beyond mere listening.[30]

Eugène D'Hallendre, Rosine Witton, and the people affiliated with Coeur de Lion were "*résistants* of the first hour." They began their work in the dismal days of 1940 and 1941, when the Resistance was small, scattered, and fumbling. By the end of 1941, many of them had been arrested by the Nazis.

Eliane Meplaux and her husband, Léon, were first denounced in August 1940 but were released when the Germans who searched their house "found nothing." Léon was deported to Germany after a second betrayal in January 1941, but Eliane deployed an effective defense. With the collaboration of Dr. Poiteau, she "imitated lunacy." The Germans were all too willing to believe that a forty-five-year-old woman was mentally ill rather than cunning and sent Eliane Meplaux to an asylum. One night in April 1941, she snuck out and went "to the place where I had hid my two cases of ammunition and dispose of them." Meplaux spent more than a year "continuing to act crazy" before being acquitted by a military tribunal in Brussels.

"As soon as I was back," she testified, "I recommenced my fight with the enemy."[31]

While Eliane Meplaux was in the asylum, the Germans captured Zoé Evans, the War Graves widow who guided evaders. On March 25, 1941, Evans was arrested with three British evaders at the Arras train station. She had dressed them in the blue coveralls of railway workers, but the ruse fell apart under scrutiny from the Germans. More than twenty people were arrested in the incident, which became known locally as "l'affaire du wagon de Madame Evans." Zoé Evans was imprisoned at Loos prison for more than a year before facing a military tribunal in the opulent, oak-paneled council chamber at the Arras Hôtel de Ville, barely twenty yards from her home. According to her family, she was initially sentenced to death, but the sentence was commuted to either ten or thirteen years of hard labor. Zoé Evans was deported to Germany on September 11, 1942.[32]

Zoé Evans was caught red-handed, but the Nazis occupying Arras sometimes arrested suspected *résistants* on speculation and tried to bully them into confessing. In June 1941, three months after Evans was captured, German police stormed Arthur Richards's house in Ronville. They were probably a detachment of the Geheime Feldpolizei (GFP), the secret police of the Abwehr (German military intelligence), who had a regional office near the Arras train station. They searched the premises, then hauled Richards off to the Hôtel de Ville for interrogation.

"I was cross-examined for about 9 hours," Richards later testified. "They accused me of spying, helping the patriots and British soldiers to get into the free zone, also hiding them."[33]

This was all perfectly true, but the Germans did not have enough proof to convict Richards. Since he remained resolutely silent, his captors trumped up a charge. "The gestapo found on my chain a medal of the Pope, but resembling that of Gene[ral] de Gaulle," Richards remembered. It was enough to hold him at Saint-Nicaise prison for several months.

When he was released in October 1941, Arthur Richards was suffering from infections in his eyes and bladder, hemorrhoids, and "general debility" from the unsanitary conditions and lack of food. Still, he resolved to "start at once much stronger the 'political work.'"[34]

Shortly after Richards's release, Rosine Witton invited him over for lunch. She mentioned the visit in a letter to Bert, a censor-proof way of informing him that Richards was alive and free. "Chum, I am please[d] you had Richard have lunch with you," Bert wrote from Ilag VIII on December 7, 1941, the day Pearl Harbor was bombed. "It must be a change to have someone to talk to give him my regards."[35]

There was a lot to talk about. In the four months Arthur Richards had been imprisoned, several members of the Anglo-French community had been arrested, including Richards's partner, Aimée Lievre, who would spend the next three years in prison. Even young Stephen Grady had been hauled off to Loos prison for several months after he was caught writing anti-German graffiti on a downed Messerschmitt: "'VIVENT LES AVIATEURS ANGLAIS QUI ONT ABATTU CE SALE BOCHE.' Which, roughly translated means 'Long live the English airmen who shot down this filthy Kraut.'"[36]

Berthe Fraser was in prison, too. In September 1941, she was entrapped by the GFP, who targeted her specifically because she was "suspected of supporting Englishmen because of her marriage to an Englishman."

The trap was exactly the sort of infiltration that Rosine Witton was working to prevent. Three GFP noncommissioned officers posed as evaders in need of help. After refusing several times, Berthe Fraser eventually agreed to arrange their passage.

On September 8, 1941, Berthe conveyed the men to a café in Dainville, just west of Arras, and handed them over to her colleague, Jules Gosse. Gosse, in turn, entrusted the infiltrators to twenty-three-year-old Marguerite Copin, who drove them to the Somme in her truck.[37]

At the eventual trial, one of the infiltrators, Unteroffizier Hartung, testified that Copin had been "very friendly to the English soldiers." She gave them beer and English cigarettes and "felt compelled to scorn every German soldier she met on the way, in particular to insult him with 'boches' and to do so so loudly that Hartung and the two other unteroffiziere in the back of the vehicle could hear it well."

Berthe Fraser, Jules Gosse, and Marguerite Copin were all arrested the next day. They spent the winter in the comfortless cells at Loos before being brought back to the Arras Hôtel de Ville for trial in June 1942.

Standing before the Nazi military tribunal that was squatting in the council chamber, Berthe Fraser confessed to aiding the three infiltrators but not to any other crimes. She was sentenced to eighteen months in prison for "attempted support of Englishmen." Marguerite Copin got the same sentence plus an additional six months for her "anti-German" statements. Jules Gosse was sentenced to ten years for smuggling fugitives and letters. Marcel Roussel, the neighbor who helped the Bonnell family's evaders, was tried on the same day and sentenced to seven and a half years. The court only "refrained from the death penalty" because they could not substantiate all the claims against him.[38]

In the wake of these arrests, Rosine Witton feared that she would be next. Her café-tabac was busier than ever. It was no secret that she was a friend of Berthe Fraser and married to an English internee. She could feel the Nazis' attention sliding in her direction.[39]

Around the time of her lunch with Arthur Richards, Rosine decided to close her café-tabac. She rented out the premises to Secours National, the Vichy-run relief organization whose ubiquitous posters portrayed Marshal Pétain as a benevolent patriarch protecting his people from Allied aggression. It is not clear whether Rosine sought Secours National as a tenant or whether they made her an offer she could not refuse. Rosine despised Pétain, but she found that renting to an unimpeachable organization like Secours National created "a very useful blind" for her ongoing Resistance work.[40]

Bert Witton did not know why Rosine closed the *café-tabac*, but he heartily approved.

"I hope you got my card telling you to carry on with renting the place + that by now you have it all fixed up," he wrote on December 23, 1941. "You will be able to settle down to a quiter [*sic*] life till I come home which I hope will be soon." Bert expressed no qualms about renting to the Vichy-run Secours National. "I am more than glad this thing as come along," he wrote, "now my darling you must take rest + look after yourself . . . you have enough to live on money is not everything."[41]

Rosine Witton and her friends were not secret agents. Unlike the men and women trained by SOE, they were never vetted by experts, never evaluated by instructors, never trained in security procedures or evasion techniques or self-defense. In fact, Rosine operated in a manner that directly contrasted with SOE training. Agents were under strict orders not to contact former acquaintances or visit places where they might be recognized, but Rosine worked under her own name, at her own shop, in the neighborhood where she was born. Her comrades in arms were longtime friends and neighbors. This made them terribly vulnerable in some ways but extraordinarily resilient in others. SOE agents typically spent only a few weeks or months in the field before being killed, captured, or exfiltrated. Rosine Witton lasted three and a half years.

Even though Rosine Witton was a *résistante* of the first hour, she harbored a lifelong regret that she did not begin her work even earlier. If she had, perhaps she could have sent Bert to safety.

"I got in touch with a resistance movement soon after my husband was arrested in 1940," Rosine wrote, "so you can just imagine how sorry I was not to have known that organization before."[42]

ILAG VIII TOST

9

Rosine Witton believed in eggs. When her backyard hens were laying, she gathered the fresh eggs and packed them carefully into small cardboard boxes along with cakes of gingerbread and pouches of pipe tobacco. Sometimes, there were as many as ten eggs in the parcels Rosine addressed to Bert Witton, prisoner #304, Ilag VIII Tost.

Rosine's parcels were Bert's main source of fresh food in the internment camp. The prisoners got thin cabbage soup in the mess hall and canned goods from the Red Cross, but most of what they ate was powdered, tinned, or revolting. Rosine's parcels were different. She occasionally included a tin of sardines or kippers, but she preferred to send Bert fresh apples, pears, onions, and tomatoes. One Christmas, she got her hands on an unimaginably precious orange. Bert begged Rosine not to send him rationed goods like butter and sugar, but she ignored him. She packed her parcels with bacon and rabbit saucisson, chocolate and cigarettes, and the occasional bottle of eau de cologne or tin of Brilliantine for Bert's hair.

But it was the eggs that really made an impression.

"My Darling I see you are going to send me another parcel with eggs," Bert wrote with trepidation in his third summer at Ilag VIII. "I hope they are not like the last."[1]

By then, Bert had plenty of experience with Rosine's egg parcels. He appreciated her efforts, but no amount of swaddling could protect fresh eggs as they jostled the 800 miles from Arras to Tost. Prisoner mail was a low priority, so shipments often spent weeks stalled in transit, freezing or sweltering. Letters sometimes traveled from Arras to Tost in as little as two weeks, but parcels took at least a month and sometimes much longer. By the time they arrived at Ilag VIII, Rosine's eggs were nothing but rancid slime and bits of shell.

"When you send eggs you should send them by themselves," Bert pleaded. "Then the other stuff does not get spoiled in any case don't send any more."

Rosine did not listen. Time and again, she sent eggs, and time and again, Bert received a putrid parcel.

"You no my love how bad eggs smell," Bert protested after receiving yet another box of biscuits and cake slathered with rotten egg. "I must tell you the truth it broke my heart to see you take all the trouble + when they get here they are bad."

And yet, once in a blue moon, Rosine's eggs did survive the journey.

"Darling, I got your parcel," Bert wrote on one happy occasion. "I got seven good eggs, three were broken."

That was good enough for Rosine. As long as there was any chance, however remote, that Bert would receive even a single good egg, she would not be deterred.

～

Ilag VIII Tost was a civilian internment camp, not a concentration camp. The distinction governed everything about the place, from its legal status to the conditions endured by internees to the compensation claims they would file against the German government decades later. Auschwitz was just fifty miles down the railway line from Tost, but the two camps had very little in common.

Ilag VIII most closely resembled a prisoner-of-war camp for British or American officers, like Stalag Luft III. The conditions were uncomfortable but not purposefully lethal. The Nazis allowed the Red Cross to inspect Ilag VIII and to provide the internees with lifesaving food parcels and warm clothing. The internees also had access to medical care provided by captured British doctors under the supervision of a German physician. Despite early rumors, internees at Ilag VIII were not forced to work outside the camp. A few men did volunteer to work on nearby farms or construction sites in order to earn a little money and get out from behind the barbed wire, but very few gardeners joined them.[2]

Instead, the internees tried to keep themselves busy. They played table tennis and darts and were occasionally escorted to a local football field under armed guard. They published a camp newspaper, *The Tost Times*, and organized pantomimes, church services, and lectures. Albert Roberts, the head gardener from Gorre British and Indian Cemetery, taught horticulture classes and gave lectures on the War Graves Commission's work that were "eagerly listened to" by the internees. They received pocket money via the Swiss government that they could spend at the woefully understocked camp canteen or pay other prisoners to do their laundry.[3]

In the three years the War Graves gardeners spent at Ilag VIII— September 1940 to November 1943—the camp was a dismal prison, but it was not a site of genocide. Horrific crimes against humanity were committed in the building they inhabited, but the worst of them happened before the British internees arrived and after they left.

Before it was an internment camp, Ilag VIII was a psychiatric hospital for disabled and mentally ill patients, who the Nazis considered "lives not worth living." Since Tost was on the German side of the border, some of the patients may have been murdered during Aktion T4, the Nazi genocide of disabled people in Germany and Austria. Others may have been killed after the invasion of Poland, when Herbert Lange, the future commandant of the Chelmno extermination camp, headed a death squad that traveled from hospital to hospital across Poland using experimental gas vans to kill dozens of disabled patients at a time. Some disabled Poles were not murdered right away but transferred to overcrowded hospitals to die of medical neglect. Others were released to starve on the streets. Still others were assembled in hospital courtyards and shot.[4]

At least one of the supervising doctors at the Tost psychiatric hospital was an enthusiastic participant in these killings. Dr. Ernst Buchalik was an early Nazi Party member who left Tost in the autumn of 1939 to take charge of a psychiatric department in Loben (Lubliniec), twenty miles north. There, Buchalik and his colleague, Dr. Elisabeth Hecker, murdered 302 disabled children under the age of seven by starving them and injecting them with lethal poisons. Buchalik and Hecker sent their brains to Warsaw as specimens for study in a neuroscience clinic.[5]

Outside the walls of Ilag VIII, Jewish residents of Tost were also systematically murdered. There had been a small but thriving Jewish community in Tost for a century. It was home to the family of Dr. Ludwig Gutmann, who was born in Tost in 1899 and went on to found the Paralympic Games after finding refuge in London. A few Jewish residents fled Tost after Kristallnacht, but there were still dozens of families living in Tost in 1940. Most of them were transported to an extermination camp— probably Majdanek—in June 1942. Few, if any, survived.[6]

The hospital buildings that housed Ilag VIII Tost were also used for gruesome purposes after the British internees left. In November 1943, the civilian prisoners were transferred to Giromagny, a camp in France, and

Ilag VIII was converted into a hospital for prisoners of war. In 1945, after the Soviets captured Tost on their way to Berlin, the NKVD, the Soviet secret police, turned the hospital into a "Silence Camp" for German prisoners. A place that had been overcrowded with 1,200 prisoners was hellish with 4,500. As many as 3,000 inmates died within six months.[7]

Judged against its immediate past and its immediate future, the three years that Bert Witton and the War Graves gardeners spent at Ilag VIII were a sheltered interlude in the site's history. Between 1940 and 1943, the War Graves men suffered from hunger and cold at Ilag VIII—some even died—but they were not intentionally murdered like so many others who slept under the same roof and traveled over the same railway tracks. They were caught in the eye of genocide, surrounded but not destroyed.

∾

Bert Witton and the other War Graves internees were comparatively safe at Ilag VIII, but they still suffered terribly. Especially during the winter of 1940–1941, before reliable Red Cross assistance reached them, the internees progressed well down the path toward starvation. Some of the men lost so much weight that they were too weak to climb the stairs to their overcrowded barracks. Many still wore their summer clothes. Comforts like heat and hot water were intermittent. The death rate was low, but it was not zero.

"The conditions here would justify retaliation," a British Foreign Office official wrote after reviewing a Red Cross inspection report about Ilag VIII.[8]

Bert Witton had a bunk in one of the old hospital's long, open wards. The best that could be said for the thin straw mattress with its blue-and-white checked blankets was that it was better than the bare stone floor at Huy. Bunks were stacked to maximize floor space, but the room was still packed. At first, sixty men lived in a ward about the size of ten standard parking spaces, but that number rose to ninety as more prisoners arrived.[9]

The rooms were drafty and too dimly lit for the prisoners to read or write at night. There was no privacy, not even in the toilets, which had no doors. The Germans did not provide the prisoners with brooms or other cleaning supplies, so the living quarters were perpetually grimy. Dingy clotheslines hung between the bunks, and the stagnant air reeked of men in various stages of illness and depression.

The food was just as bad. Internees received two meals each day: a bowl of thin fish or cabbage soup at midday and an eight-ounce ration of bread and fat in the evening. The fat was sometimes a piece of cheese or a one-centimeter-thick sausage, but often it was a dollop of synthetic cooking grease. This diet was supplemented with ersatz coffee in the morning and occasional dabs of butter, margarine, or jam.

"They give us enough to keep body and soul together," prisoner George Gregson grumbled in his journal, "but one would not be surprised if one's soul was filled with an irresistible impulse to seek a more congenial and more hospitable domicile at some time."[10]

Each internee was supposed to receive a food parcel from the Red Cross every week, but the first parcels did not reach Ilag VIII until January 1941, four months after the War Graves men arrived. Robert Seeley, the Ronville Camp workshop foreman, remembered that the prisoners were on a "starvation diet until Red Cross parcels arrived about January 10, 1941."[11]

The next Red Cross shipment arrived six weeks later, when the long, hungry winter was nearly over. Even a year later, in the winter of 1941–1942, the internees sometimes went a month or more between Red Cross deliveries. It was not unusual for them to receive Christmas parcels in April or May. Private parcels like Rosine's plugged some of these gaps, but the Red Cross estimated that 30 percent of parcels sent by the internees' families never reached their destination.[12]

The late arrival of Red Cross food aid was especially hard for men who had been badly starved at Huy. They went into the winter of 1940–1941 with no reserves.

"I said men, no, living skeletons, terrible to see," wrote Bernard Parsons, the stone carver from Étaples, after seeing his War Graves colleagues stripped to the waist for their typhus vaccinations in October 1940. "All tummies have disappeared and ribs are very much in prominence . . . one thing is certain unless they skin us we cannot now get any lighter in weight."[13]

Omer Briere, the Quebecois gardener who cared for Cabaret Rouge Cemetery, had a similar experience when he undressed to bathe with his fellow gardeners. "We start to cry when we see the skeletal state we are in."[14]

Extreme weight loss made it harder to bear the cold. Ilag VIII had a coal-burning furnace, but it was used only in short bursts, and fuel grew scarcer as the war dragged on. Prisoners housed in the fifth-floor attic reported that their quarters were "almost unlivable" with winter temperatures that were "rarely above zero." Meanwhile, the gardeners at Ilag VIII invented their own ways of keeping warm. "It is so cold that I ran 30 times around the Parc inside the camp," gardener Alfred Wells wrote during a week when the temperature dipped to −28°C.[15]

The Red Cross parcels saved lives. Each five-kilogram package contained high-protein and high-fat foods like canned meat, powdered milk, and tinned butter or cheese. Shelf-stable biscuits, dried fruit, oatmeal, sugar, chocolate, and jam made the monotonous camp diet more palatable. Tea, soap, and cigarettes kept up morale and improved sanitary conditions.[16]

All parcels, whether they were sent by families or by the Red Cross, had to be opened in the presence of a German guard. In search of contraband, the guards squeezed tobacco pouches and cut open cakes. Even sealed tins had to be opened under their eyes. One particularly assiduous guard "seemed to imagine that he was dealing with the parcels of the most dangerous spies instead of a gang of harmless and very hungry men," wrote Bernard Parsons. "I think if there had been any heads on the sardines, he would have looked into the mouth of each one."[17]

The prisoners established a central depot—a cross between a mail room and a warehouse—where internees could store their parcels rather than being forced to open all their cans at once. With only three worn-out, handheld can openers for 1,200 internees and as many as twenty-four cans in each Red Cross parcel, queuing at the parcel depot soon became one of the main pastimes at Ilag VIII.[18]

"Darling we want nothing thanks to the Red Cross," Bert Witton wrote to Rosine in the fall of 1941. "If I only knew you were getting what we are, I would be happy."

Bert was putting a rosy spin on the food situation at Tost, but he worried as much about Rosine as she did about him. Rosine had her rental income and a modest relief payment from the British government via the Swiss, but she was still living under the privations of the Nazi occupation. Over and over, Bert implored her to keep good food for herself rather than sending it to him.

"My love, no more from you," he pled. "Beleave me we have all we want. I have a nice tin of tea here and other things. I wish I could send them to you in any case I will bring them home."

The second winter was a little better. The Red Cross sent Bert Witton an overcoat to help him withstand the cold, and he assured Rosine that he was in good health. "Don't worry about me," he wrote in November 1941, "[I] have a nice round face + putting on weight hope you are the same."[19]

Bert Witton did not, in fact, have a "nice round face," but it was true that British internees rarely progressed beyond the intermediate stages of starvation. Captain G. B. Leyton of the Royal Army Medical Corps was a prisoner of war who conducted an observational study at Tost in 1944, after the War Graves gardeners had been transferred to Giromagny. He published his findings in *The Lancet* in 1946 under the title "Effects of Slow Starvation." Dr. Leyton's study compared British prisoners, who received Red Cross food aid, to Soviet prisoners, who did not. He calculated that Red Cross parcels provided the recipients with approximately 1,312 calories each day and allowed them to make "small but appetizing meals . . . of sufficient quantity to appease the hunger of most of the British patients from one meal to the next." Leyton's British patients still showed signs of intermediate starvation—weight loss, fatigue, mental confusion, copious urination—but few of them died. His Soviet patients did.[20]

The military prisoners of war in Dr. Leyton's 1944 study were much younger and fitter than the middle-aged War Graves gardeners. At forty-two, Bert Witton was younger than most of his colleagues. The gardeners were active men whose jobs required physical labor, but they were also ex-servicemen with a range of disabilities. Some had old war wounds that plagued them. Others suffered from recurring malaria or diminished lung capacity from being gassed. Percy Johnson was blind in one eye; Sidney Baxter was deaf; Frederick Fisher had a disfiguring facial wound; Henry Sherbourne had one leg.[21] Nearly all of the gardeners suffered from common middle-aged maladies like hernias, angina, and kidney disease.

"Contrarily to a camp of [military] prisoners, there are in this camp many old or elderly people and many men who are not in the best physical condition," the Red Cross noted in 1942. "The internees are certainly more sensitive than the great majority of the prisoners of war."[22]

Death arrived at Ilag VIII before the first Red Cross parcel. Francis H. Rogers, a forty-four-year-old from Antwerp, died on January 2, 1941, less than four months after arriving at Tost.

"Our friend Rogers was considerably changed," Bernard Parsons remarked after viewing the wizened corpse. Head Gardener Albert Roberts took charge of the funeral arrangements, decorating an elaborate bier with evergreens, candlesticks, and a crucifix. Parsons painted a wobbly Union Jack on a bedsheet to drape over the coffin.

"Rogers is the first prisoner we have seen leave this camp," Parsons wrote after the burial. "How many more of us will go out in like manner?"[23]

The first War Graves internee to die was Charlie Holton, Ben Leech's neighbor from Hébuterne. Holton endured the same miseries as his colleagues during the winter of 1940–1941, but by February, it was clear that his stomach pains and diarrhea were more serious than most. After a brief stay at the camp infirmary, he was transferred to a prisoner-of-war hospital in Langenbielau (Bielawa), ninety-five miles away. He died there on April 23, 1941.[24]

Before he died, Holton fretted endlessly about his family back home in Hébuterne. "I have had no news from home for 4 months, so you can guess I feel a bit worried," he wrote to his sister, Annie Twelftree, in Buckinghamshire. In his last weeks, Holton sent increasingly frantic messages to Annie, begging for news.

"It seemed his one cry, where were they," Annie told the War Graves Commission in a letter expressing her "great shock" at her brother's death.[25]

According to the death certificate provided by the Nazis, Charlie Holton died of stomach cancer. That may be true. But if Holton had cancer when he was arrested in July 1940, he wasn't ill enough for anyone to notice. His personnel file in the War Graves Commission archives shows that he had no recent medical claims and had not missed a single day of work for nearly three years before his arrest.[26] After just nine months in Nazi custody, he was dead.

A parcel that Annie Twelftree sent to her brother—chocolate, soap, warm socks—arrived too late. Head Gardener Alfred Haines distributed the contents among Holton's friends. "I am able to inform you that he passed away peacefully," Haines wrote to Annie Twelftree, falsely implying that he had been at Holton's bedside when he died.[27]

Half a dozen other Commission employees died after Holton, some at Tost and some at other camps. Charles Maurice Baker, the gardener from Merville who was arrested with the rose list in his pocket, never fully recovered from the swollen legs that afflicted so many of the men on the trip from Huy. He died on October 22, 1941. Harold Stanley Hawkins, the transport superintendent from Achicourt who would not leave his dogs, died of "increasing heart and circulatory weakness" six weeks later, on December 1, 1941.[28]

One of the dead gardeners, William Meller, was born Wilhelm Moeller, the son of German and Swiss immigrants who settled in London in the 1890s. During World War I, Meller served in a labor battalion of the Middlesex Regiment known as "The Kaiser's Own" because most of its members were the sons of German nationals. He died of unspecified causes on May 13, 1942, imprisoned in his father's homeland as an Englishman.[29]

At Ilag VIII, despair was as dangerous as disease. Some internees woke the wards with their screaming nightmares; others withdrew into silence. Everyone worried about the families and friends they had left behind. By the winter of 1942–1943, the Red Cross was sending increasingly dire warnings to the British government about the state of morale at Ilag VIII.

"Nearly all the internees have lost all their initiative and think only of their food and their personal grievances," they reported. Unless drastic changes were implemented, the prisoners were at high risk of "moral and physical disintegration."[30]

Depression among the internees was a deadly serious problem. In December 1940, just three months after they arrived at Ilag VIII, one of the War Graves men attempted to take his own life.

"A man in the next room—an IWGC gardener from Arras—tried to commit suicide tonight by cutting his throat," George Gregson wrote in his journal. "Such things must be expected here."[31]

The desperate man was Wilfrid Legg, who lived on Route de Bapaume, near Bert and Rosine. Friends reported that Legg had been "cheerful and normal" on the morning of December 21 but spent the afternoon writing a "rambling and rather disjointed" letter, pouring out his worries and complaining of inadequate medical treatment. That night, while many of the other internees were holding a Christmas concert in the chapel, Legg slashed his own throat with a razor. Friends reached him before he bled to death, but he was sent to the infirmary in critical condition.[32]

"I went to the hospital to see Legg," Bernard Parsons wrote a few days later. "He was looking well except that his neck was heavily bandaged. I said very little to him about his attempt on his life—but expressed the hope to him that he would go back home with all his friends and reminded him of the fact that his wife and children still had great need of him."

Wilfred Legg was not the last internee to attempt suicide at Ilag VIII. George Gregson admitted to at least five serious tries and blamed his repeated failures on the poor quality of the available razor blades. In the fall of 1942, another near miss sent the Arras gardeners into a flurry of worry over a man Bert Witton referred to only as "our friend." He sent Rosine several updates assuring her that the Arras contingent was keeping the man under constant, careful surveillance.

"Don't you worry about me doing anything so rash," Bert wrote. "I would have done so a long time ago if I had not had you . . . don't worry I shall come back alright."[33]

Still, Rosine had reason to worry. Bert usually wrote sunny letters that glossed over the grim reality of the camp, but his resolve was not infallible.

"God when is the war going to end soon I hope," he wrote on October 16, 1941, after a little more than a year at Ilag VIII. The next month, Bert was even gloomier. "Darling I feel lonely today," he wrote on November 28. "My heart is crying out for you + while I am writing my eyes + all blurred + that big lump is in my throat."

Three days later, Bert's tone ricocheted dramatically. "My Dearest Darling Rosine," he chirped on December 1, "don't worry your dear little head." In the space of a single page, he called her "Darling" eight times. Bert wrote this frenetically cheerful letter on December 1, the same day Stanley Hawkins died. It was also the day the internees held an auction of Charles Maurice Baker's possessions to raise money for his widow.[34]

Rosine was not deceived. The War Graves wives were her friends, neighbors, and sometimes comrades in arms. They shared news and compared notes, piecing together stories from hints across multiple letters. When a family received a death notice or a parcel of personal effects, it was no secret.

In fact, communication between the Ilag VIII internees and their wives in France was so robust that they were able to operate a small black-market economy. The men were not allowed to send Red Cross food or clothing to their families, but they found other ways to exchange goods. Rosine frequently provided fifty or 100 cigarettes to an internee's wife in Arras, and in exchange, her husband handed over his Red Cross cigarettes to Bert. "Chum I had fifty Cig off Ballinger," Bert wrote in one of several letters arranging these exchanges, "so you must let me know how many you gave her so I can get the rest from him."

Bert's mood frequently depended on how much mail he was receiving. When parcels were abundant, he promised Rosine that he was in the best of health and begged her not to send him a crumb. When parcels failed to arrive on time, he could think of little else.

At least once, Bert lost his temper and wrote something he truly regretted. Rosine did not save the offending postcard, but she did save his apology.

"My dear forgive me for that card," he wrote. "It won't happen again. I cannot think what made me do it, but really my love you must let me know what parcel you sent since Feb you see I did not get any for March + only one for April + now May has finished I don't know what to think."[35]

This outburst came just after Bert received bad news from his brother Horace, a construction worker in East London. Their neighborhood had been flattened in the Blitz and several of the Witton siblings displaced, but the news kept getting worse. Horace sent word that their nephew, twenty-eight-year-old Aircraftman 2nd Class Alec Cook, had died while serving with a Royal Air Force (RAF) barrage balloon unit. Another nephew, twenty-five-year-old Sergeant Arthur Witton, was captured in North Africa and sent to a prisoner-of-war camp in Italy. A third, twenty-two-year-old Private Billy Witton, was missing after the fall of Singapore. The Witton family had no way of knowing that Billy was being forced to build the notorious Burma Railway, a project that killed 23 percent of the British prisoners who worked on it. They would not learn that he was still alive until the summer of 1944.[36]

"I think the Witton family are doing their bit + everybody is fed up," Bert wrote to Rosine after receiving one of Horace's letters. "They are like us fed up to the teeth + hoping it will end soon + that everybody has had enough."[37]

There was very little Rosine could do except send her love in letters and parcels. None of her letters to Bert survive, but his answers show that she generally wrote twice a week. Rosine kept Bert up to date on the comings and goings of their War Graves friends, telling him when she dropped in on Marie Medlicott or recounting Ben Leech's occasional visits to Route de Bapaume. Several times, she wrote something that ran afoul of the German censor.

"Chum I got another black out in your letter," Bert wrote in 1942. "Never mind you will have lots to tell me when we meet again which I hope will be soon."

Whatever their troubles, Bert regularly exhorted Rosine to "keep your chin up" and plan for a bright future.

"Look after your darling self so when we do meet again I will have a lovely little wifey to enjoy the rest of our lives in happiness + praise the good Lord never to Part again."[38]

Bert never really told the whole truth in his letters. But neither did Rosine.

She could never tell her husband that she kept some of the eggs. Not for herself but for the steady parade of young Allied airmen who sat across the kitchen table as she wrote her letters and packed her parcels. They had long, dangerous journeys ahead of them, past Nazi sentries and over treacherous mountains. Rosine believed firmly that they stood a better chance after a hearty breakfast—an English breakfast—of fried eggs.

ONE-MAN EMBASSY 10

On January 14, 1941, Ben Leech helped Suzanne Moir write a letter to the U.S. Embassy in Vichy. The United States had not yet entered the war, and Ben hoped that the neutral Americans might be able to help answer Suzanne's most pressing question: what happened to her husband, Peter?

In the aftermath of the Nazi invasion, all normal communication between the British government and its subjects in occupied France ceased. There were still a few channels where a message could slip through, but they were cumbersome. Ben Leech could occasionally send a twenty-five-word message via the Red Cross or write to interned friends and ask them to pass news to England through the prisoner-of-war mail. To send longer messages, he appealed to American and Swiss officials. The few letters Ben Leech managed to send to the War Graves Commission via diplomatic channels typically took three or four months to reach England.

Suzanne Moir received a much speedier reply. On January 24, eight months after Peter Moir was killed but just ten days after sending the letter to the Americans, Ben Leech wrote in his gardening log, "Mrs. Moir received news of her husband death in action."[1]

Helping Suzanne Moir write to the Americans was just one of the many jobs Ben Leech took on in addition to his gardening duties. With his supervisors gone and most of his colleagues interned, Ben deputized himself the senior representative of the War Graves Commission on the Somme. He liaised with French officials, inspected far-flung cemeteries, and appointed himself guardian of the Commission's abandoned equipment.

Ben also took on a quasi-consular role. When he was not mowing or planting at Serre Road No. 2, he cycled far and wide to check on War

Graves families, help them with paperwork, and register new burials. The United Kingdom might not have an active consulate in northern France anymore, but they did have Ben Leech.

As a self-appointed War Graves official, Ben spent much of his time inspecting the cemeteries and memorials within cycling distance of Beaumont-Hamel. In the first year of the occupation, he recorded visits to thirty-six specific sites, along with more general references to "all cemeteries in group" or "all cemeteries in vicinity." Sometimes, he ventured as far north as Arras or as far south as Péronne, a round trip of forty miles.

At nearly every site, Ben found looted toolsheds, broken windows, and other petty vandalism. His gardening log became a dreary litany of mischief in one cemetery after another:

"Doors of tool-houses at Hunters and Hawthorn broken open."

"Sucrerie doors smashed open all small tools gone."

"Ancre toolhouse again broken open."

"Mill Rd. beyond repair both door smashed completely."

Most of this damage was done by local civilians. Ben's neighbors were short of everything from flour to firewood to bicycle chains and saw little harm in taking what they needed from the abandoned cemeteries. They carried off handheld tools like knives, wrenches, and clippers and disemboweled motor mowers for their engines.

"Saw children at farm with barrow," Ben grumbled after the toolshed at Sucrerie Cemetery was ransacked. On a visit to the Thiepval Memorial in July 1940, he found, "3 doors of Monument smashed open" and tools scattered "all over the lawn." The following spring, when the tools were long gone, someone dismantled the outbuildings for scrap metal. "All corrugated iron shed gone," Ben reported in March 1941.[2]

Even comparatively useless items were looted. Someone stole the mouthpiece from the Last Post bugle at the abandoned Albert office though not, apparently, the bugle itself. The pseudo-military caps Brigadier Prower had ordered for the gardeners during the Phoney War were also pilfered. "Commission caps all over the place," Ben noted. "Seems all the children of Albert have one."

Other damage was more symbolic. "All flags torn to pieces," Ben wrote after a trip to Albert. In early 1941, someone shattered the glass case at the Sheffield Memorial Park in Hébuterne and left the roll of honor lying on the ground. Ben cleaned up the mess and moved the list of the dead and its protective casket to the tiny French memorial chapel near Serre Road No. 2 for safekeeping.

Ben Leech noted these instances of vandalism—major, minor, and minuscule—but there was little he could do to stop them. He used his blacksmithing skills to repair locks and gates, to no effect. Eventually, he "hired [a] cart" and brought as many tools as possible to his house.

In general, Ben's attitude toward his neighbors' use of the cemeteries was one of resignation. "Heroine of the Ruins grazing cows on Monument & cemetry," he noted without rancor after encountering Marie-Louise Duthart on a visit to the Thiepval Memorial. Duthart had been one of the first civilians to return to Thiepval in the aftermath of the Great War, and her image—"Heroine of the Ruins"—was reproduced on postcards as "a symbol of the redoubtable qualities of the Picard peasant."[3] Now, in the wake of another cataclysm, she let her cows crop the grass around the Memorial to the Missing. Ben Leech let her be.

Ben frequently encountered German soldiers in the cemeteries, but he tended to regard them as a nuisance rather than a threat. "They greatly respect cemeteries," he wrote after spending a day chatting with a group of Germans who shared their cigarettes and spoke "fairly good English." This "respect" was highly conditional. The Nazis certainly did not respect Jewish cemeteries or cemeteries in eastern Europe. Ben Leech observed this "respect" in France, where Hitler himself had modeled the touring of World War I memorials as an appropriate leisure activity. Following Hitler's example, the occupying troops in France did not cause much malicious damage to the War Graves cemeteries. Some cemeteries were damaged during the fighting in 1940 or by Allied bombings in 1944, but they were not targeted intentionally. The only time Ben Leech mentioned a German purposefully causing significant damage was in October 1940, when a soldier fired a revolver into the ceiling of the northeastern chapel at Serre Road No. 2, "causing plaster to fall and injuring himself."

Caring for the World War I cemeteries would have kept Ben busy enough, but he felt a duty to the recent dead as well. On Sundays, he pedaled near and far in search of British graves. He interviewed French civilians for information—"sometimes misleading"—about burials and confirmed as many names and locations as possible. When Ben gathered a substantial list, he sent it to Gertrude Hamilton, an American woman who directed the British-American Civilian Emergency Service in Paris. Ben had initially approached Hamilton in hopes that he might be able to receive "the same privileges as my interned workmates from the Red Cross," but this proved impossible. Red Cross parcels were for internees, not free civilians, no matter how desperate their situation. Hamilton could not help

Ben with clothes or food, but she did offer to pass his graves registration lists to the War Graves Commission.[4]

"I have recorded to Mrs. G. Hamilton up to date 122 new British graves, mostly in Communal Cemeteries," Ben noted in one of his periodic reports to the Commission. "She tells me she passes them on to you, through the Swiss Consul."

Ben's largest graves registration task was recording the names of the men who were killed near Ficheux and reburied at Bucquoy Road Cemetery in 1941. "There have been about 140 British new burial[s]," Ben reported, "all have wooden crosses but no names yet." Ben interviewed two of the local men who had been caring for the graves, Anatole Lefebvre and Jean Sergeant. He carefully copied the information they had collected amid the carnage at the Pronier farm and forwarded it to the Commission.[5]

Most of Ben's caretaking work involved the cemeteries, but he also extended a helping hand to the families of his fellow gardeners. Many, like Suzanne Moir, needed assistance translating documents or applying to the Americans and Swiss for relief payments. Ben deciphered paperwork, commiserated over the unending stream of bad news, and helped secure household valuables "on account of the damage taking place." His gardening log is full of references to correspondence that the women of the War Graves community shared with him, from the Red Cross message Leona Thomas received from her husband's relatives in England to the sad letter that reached Berthe Shreeve in Thiepval, informing her that her father-in-law had been shot by the Germans.[6]

From time to time, Ben visited Rosine Witton. He also wrote to Bert, assuring him that Rosine could call on him for help. "Darling I have two letter from Ben Leech," Bert wrote from Ilag VIII. "Thank him for me + tell him all the boys thank him for what he has done."[7]

Ben Leech was a busy man, but he was not getting paid. Within a few months of the evacuation, his meager savings were completely gone. Maurice, age eighteen, brought in thirty-eight francs a day as an agricultural laborer, while sixteen-year-old Beatrice earned twenty, but the family was hard pressed to pay rent. They lived off public aid rations distributed by the town, which Ben earned by running errands for the mayor's office. Town officials frequently sent him pedaling to Hébuterne, Albert, or Bapaume to fetch "provisions for village" and once dispatched him all the way to Ribemont—a ninety-three-mile round trip that took thirteen hours—in a fruitless search for flour. One local official put Ben to work fixing farm machinery, haying his fields, and cutting thistles.[8]

In the summertime, the Leech family was able to supplement their public assistance with the occasional rabbit and vegetables from Marie's garden, but their prospects for winter were grim. In October 1940, after five months without pay, Ben applied to the U.S. Embassy for relief payments of 1,400 francs per month, about half his prewar wages. These loans were administered by the Americans—and later the Swiss—on behalf of the British government, which, in turn, negotiated with the War Graves Commission to guarantee repayment of any relief payments to the Commission's ex-employees. The money wasn't enough to live on, but it was something.

Ben's financial situation took another turn in May 1941, a year after the invasion, when German and French authorities decided that something should be done about the British cemeteries. Instead of letting them grow wild and unsightly in the absence of their keepers, the French veterans' bureau, Anciens Combattants, proposed a solution. Under this new scheme, Anciens Combattants would provide modest funding to French mayors, who would appoint temporary caretakers for the British war graves and monitor their condition.

This ought to have been a happy outcome for Ben Leech. At last, he would have cash in his pocket and help in the cemeteries. Yet everything that Ben wrote about the Anciens Combattants takeover was tinged with gloom.

"By order of the German Graves registration, the French Etat Civil (military section) have now taken over contract of my group of British Cemeteries," he wrote in June 1941. As much as he had struggled during the previous year, Ben did not relish losing control over "my group." When the mayor of Beaumont-Hamel informed him that "the cemeteries were being taken over by French," Ben sulked. "Commence borders at No 2," he wrote, "but interfered through having to instruct French gardeners."

Ben Leech had long aspired to a more responsible role than the humble post of gardener-caretaker. Back in April 1940, before the invasion, he had applied for the vacant post of superintendent of transport despite having little experience with vehicles. The job would have brought Ben back to Ronville and nearly doubled his pay, but the Commission never took his application seriously. Instead, they hired Stanley Hawkins, who was new to the Commission but owned a successful garage in Boulogne. Hawkins moved into his new house in Achicourt on May 17, 1940, the same day Ben Leech was contemplating the meaning of panic. Hawkins was arrested with the other Arras staff in July 1940, interned at Ilag VIII, and died in Nazi custody in 1941.[9]

Ben was an ordinary gardener-caretaker, not even a head gardener. Yet during the occupation, the mayors around Beaumont-Hamel treated him as if he were the senior War Graves official in the region. They informed him of their hiring decisions and asked for his advice on horticultural matters. When the time came to hand over formal control of the cemeteries, Ben managed the transfer.

"On the 4th of May I handed over to the Mayor of Beaumont keys of Ancre and Hamel with list of tools in each toolhouse, to Mayor of Courcellette key of Courcellette, Mayor of Thiepval key of Connaught," Ben noted. In his letters to the Commission, he began adding the title "Deputy charge hand" to his signature.

One cemetery posed a problem: Serre Road No. 2. "This cemetry stands in two communes Beaumont Hamel and Hebuterne, and in two departments Somme and Pas de Calais, making it difficult for me to obtain help from the mayors," Ben explained. "No one wants to adopt it, but me."[10]

For the rest of the occupation, Ben Leech "adopted" Serre Road No. 2 and its 7,000-odd headstones. It was an enormous undertaking. He was forced to let the flower borders in the back half go to seed, but he kept the sixteen plots in front of the Stone of Remembrance fully cultivated. On either side of the stone, Ben created "a small nursery" for sweet william. He also tried to keep the roses in bloom. "I have up to now about 800 [rose] cuttings in," he wrote late in the summer of 1942, but "hope to have by end of month September about 1500."

Ben's most fervent wish was for an eighteen-inch Qualcast hand mower to replace the "badly worn" twelve-inch mower he was using. A single pass over No. 2's expansive lawn "meant walking and pushing machine over 40 kilometers." Ben had cobbled together spare parts to keep the little mower going, but it needed lubricating oil. "I have applied for a ticket to buy some from the Mayor of my village, but I may as well talk to myself for the reply I get." Instead, Ben paid 100 francs for a liter—about a month's supply—on the black market. Sometimes, when he could not get oil even at that exorbitant price, Ben reported, "I am doing my best with a scythe."

Once, in a moment of desperation, he even tried bringing sheep into the cemetery to "keep down grass." This was more trouble than it was worth. "Was a washout," he wrote.[11]

If Ben Leech could appreciate one aspect of the Anciens Combattants scheme, it was the promise of a steady income. Beginning in May 1941, he was supposed to receive 2,734 francs a month, a rate comparable to his prewar wages. The reality was less consistent. In September 1941, four months after the takeover, Ben reported that he was not yet receiving the promised wages. "Still working at Serre, no pay," he wrote in one of his precious Red Cross messages to the Commission. "Could do with financial assistance for clothes and taxes. Remember me to all. Please reply."

Even when the payments did materialize, they were nowhere near enough to keep up with the shocking inflation rate. "I find it very difficult to make ends meet," Ben wrote to Sir Fabian Ware in 1942. Basic goods were selling for ten times their prewar prices. Ben gave the price of boots as an example; a pair that cost thirty-nine francs before the war now cost 400 if you could find them at all. "I have no good working clothes or boots for winter," Ben wrote. "I am at present working in badly worn overalls and boots the uppers of which are all done." He once cycled seven miles in pursuit of new overalls but found that he could not pay the price: 280 francs and a pound of butter.

"This is how trade is done now, so I not being a farmer, no overalls," he explained. "We pay dear to starve."[12]

In spite of everything, Ben Leech still considered himself an employee of the Imperial War Graves Commission. He referred to his wages as "money due to me." On July 24, the annual date specified in the Industrial Court decision of 1938, Ben noted, "[I] should get a rise in wages of 2/6." He habitually signed his letters to the Commission with his name and his contract number, 653, and emphasized his dogged adherence to his contract.

"I assure you that whilst I am at liberty all my service will be placed according to my contract to the work of the I.W.G.C.," Ben wrote. He explained that he had sometimes been forced to work for the town to earn his bread but sent copies of his daily gardening log to prove that his work in the cemeteries never flagged. He was doing everything possible "to fulfill the last instructions of our (Vice) Chairman, which was to carry on until stopped."

The Commission had a different view. They considered Ben's contract void, just like all the others. If they ever informed Ben of this decision, he took no notice. He never stopped referring to himself as a Commission employee and even asked for increased benefits.

"I expect that the men who reached England are now at work," Ben wrote in 1942. "This will have placed them all by now in full benefit of the British National Health Insurance—thus increasing their benefit at retiring age. Could not the same be applied to all us poor wretches out here and we're not so lucky."[13]

Ben Leech was not the only War Graves gardener who kept the cemeteries blooming. A postwar investigation counted at least eighteen Commission gardeners who worked for some period of time between 1941 and

1944, some for a few months, some for several years. A handful worked as long as Ben Leech did, though none worked longer.[14]

Five of these active gardeners, including Bob Armstrong, were Irish nationals. At least seven others were interned briefly but released on the grounds of age or infirmity. The rest either dodged arrest because they were internally displaced in 1940 or were idiosyncratic cases like John Boucher, the Guernsey veteran who was technically a French national.[15]

Some local mayors used the Anciens Combattants funds to hire the wives and children of British gardeners. The mayor of Nieppe knew that the Grady family needed a breadwinner while Stephen Grady Sr. remained in hiding, so he hired Stephen Jr. to fill his father's post. Young Stephen was put in charge of Pont d'Achelles, the cemetery where his weapons cache was hidden, and two War Graves plots in communal cemeteries. "With Pont d'Achelles, I make a special effort," Stephen recalled, "because I know my father can see it from the window of his prison upstairs."[16]

Another teenager, Jeremie Fitzgerald, took over for his father, Head Gardener James Fitzgerald, in Mons. He managed to send a letter to inform the Commission that he was hard at work and "asked I.W.G.C. to employ him after the war."

Wages were certainly welcome, but some of the women and children who took up the gardeners' abandoned mowers did so before there was any prospect of pay. Marie Camier Bonnell, the wife of Canadian gardener Lewis Fulton Bonnell, was working in the British military cemeteries in Wanquentin as early as July 1940, gardening while her one-year-old daughter, Mary Rose, toddled in the grass. Louise-Marie Thomas took charge of Pont-du-Hem Cemetery in La Gorgue after the death of her husband, gardener Charles Thomas, who succumbed to pneumonia on July 15, 1940. Several other wives took over for their interned husbands, including Stephanie Jones in Gouzeaucourt and Olivie Lee in Le Touret.

Daughters answered the call as well. Violet Borrett, age twenty, began tending her father's cemeteries in Wancourt, near Arras, in October 1940, long before the Anciens Combattants program began. Farther south, near Albert, twenty-one-year-old May Moss cared for the graves in Sailly-le-Sec for more than three years. Violet Borrett and May Moss were never considered for full-time jobs after the war like Stephen Grady and Jeremie Fitzgerald, but they tended the cemeteries under the most difficult circumstances.[17]

Two of the gardeners paid by Anciens Combattants were Ben Leech's neighbors in Beaumont-Hamel: Robert Mullenger and S. C. Humphreys. It is not clear whether Humphreys evacuated in May 1940, but Mullenger did. He left Beaumont-Hamel "with friends in [a] farm cart." They made it as far as Brittany, where Mullenger remained until the spring of 1941. Refugees were prohibited from returning to the Zone Interdité, at least early on, so no reasonable person could blame Mullenger for failing to return to Beaumont-Hamel promptly.

Ben Leech was not always a reasonable person. He regarded Mullenger and Humphreys as shirkers for not working during the first year of the occupation, even when no one was paying them and Mullenger was hundreds of miles away. These details did not impress Ben. "Malenger and Humphrey running round," he noted in the clipped, dismissive tone he always used when referring to the pair in his log. Both Mullenger and Humphreys worked in the Beaumont-Hamel cemeteries after May 1941 and occasionally assisted Ben at Serre Road No. 2. Still, when Ben wrote to the Commission in 1942, he swore, "I have had no help of any sort this year or last." It was not true, but it showed what he thought of Mullenger and Humphreys. [18]

Ben Leech was not a man who saw the world in subtle shades of gray. The rigidity of his moral compass—and his adversarial relationship with Mullenger and Humphreys—was on full display in the winter of 1942–1943, when he inflated a dispute over trees into an international diplomatic incident.

The trouble started on November 28, 1942. With the third winter of the occupation looming and Serre Road No. 2 put to bed, Ben went on an inspection tour. He was not expecting to find anything badly amiss. After all, nearly everything of any value had already been stolen, and the mayors were supposed to be keeping watch.

He got a shock when he reached the South African Memorial at Delville Wood. There, he found the residents of Longueval engaged in "the wholesale cutting down of largest trees." The area around the monument was a "quagmire of ruts," with "a great deal of damage caused by carts cutting up the turf." Ben confronted a man and two women who were sawing through ash trees and silver birches, but they told him that they had permission from the mayor to take firewood from the Memorial grounds. Ben stormed off to confront the mayor, threatening that "if the damage and tree-cutting was not stopped, I would notify Monsieur le Préfet de la Somme, through the office of the Swiss Consul."

Ben left the mayor's office appeased, but when he returned to Delville Wood a month later, he found the lawn crisscrossed by "ruts nine inches deep." The cutting continued, with "well over a hundred thousand francs of wood" stolen from the site. Ben reported that some farmers had taken as many as ten cartloads of logs. An enormous stack near the caretaker's cottage was just waiting to be hauled off to the baker in nearby Flers.

"He can buy wood from nearly all the woods around here," Ben seethed.

This was not a charitable response. Like everyone else in occupied France, the people of Longueval were barreling toward another desperate winter without reserves of food, clothing, or money. They were taking trees from Delville Wood to warm their homes and bake their bread. Ben's pronouncement that they could buy wood elsewhere was laughable when the local cost of firewood was 250 francs per cubic meter. At that price, a farmworker like Maurice Leech would have to work for twenty-four days to buy a single cord of wood.

Still, Ben was indignant. He wrote strident letters begging the Commission and the Swiss consul to intervene "before wood is completely stripped." As if the damage to Delville Wood was not enough, Ben added the alarming observation that "there has also been a lot of fir trees cut in Newfoundland Park, Beaumont-Hamel."[19]

Ben's letter did not reach Sir Fabian Ware's desk for several months, but when it did, it triggered an urgent inquiry from the government of South Africa. A flurry of memos in the British Foreign Office culminated in an official request for the Swiss to confront the French government, making the "strongest possible representations to prevent further damage at Delville Wood, Beaumont Hamel or at any other memorial sites or cemeteries which are the concern of the Imperial War Graves Commission."[20]

The Swiss were already making their own inquiries. Even before Ben Leech's complaint reached England, they contacted Beaumont-Hamel mayor Robert Lenglet to demand an investigation into the state of the Newfoundland Memorial Park. Lenglet immediately solicited formal reports from Robert Mullenger and S. C. Humphreys.

Both of Ben's fellow gardeners rolled their eyes at his alarm. Mullenger submitted a two-sentence report agreeing that "about 17 to 20 fir trees" had been cut but exhibited no dismay. Humphreys was more pointed. There was no new damage in the Newfoundland Park, "so the person who made the complaint must have been referring to the fourteen small pine trees" that had been cut nearly a year earlier.

"I was caretaker of the Park cemeteries before the war," Humphreys wrote with palpable exasperation. "I have felt it my duty ever since the invasion to see that everything is respected as far as possible under the circumstances." As far as Humphreys was concerned, his caretaking responsibilities had to be balanced with the realities of the ongoing emergency. He ended his report by noting that he himself had taken some "wood of no value" from the Newfoundland Park to heat his own home "owing to the scarcity of fuel."[21]

Ben Leech's reaction to the cutting of Delville Wood may have seemed peevish, but it was clearly grounded in passion. His letter to the War Graves Commission was a long, fluent screed about the desecration of Delville Wood with a single offhand sentence about the Newfoundland Park tacked onto the end. Seeing that particular place in ruins—its trees felled and its turf torn to shreds—hit Ben hard. He had been there before as a green private thrown into the chaos of nearby Trônes Wood, where the trees exploded overhead until every trunk was a jagged stump and the men of the 18th Manchesters lay dead all around him. Perhaps seeing the new growth cut down was just too much for him to bear.

Throughout the long years of the occupation, Ben spent long, lonely days at Serre Road No. 2, mowing the endless grass and daydreaming about putting the world back together again. His letters to the Commission are full of detailed fantasies about restoring the cemeteries to their pristine prewar state.

"If you could send me some temporary authority in writing French and English (I don't speak French correctly), I may be able to get men placed in some of the cemetries that are not being looked to," he wrote. If the Commission would forward "a reasonable amount of money a month to pay 5 men a decent living wage" via the Swiss, Ben believed he could return ten neglected cemeteries "to prewar standard."

The following year, Ben requested a bicycle or at least money to replace worn-out parts. His graves registration trips "sometimes take me over two hundred kilometers hard riding in one day," he explained, "and not being able to get the spare parts, my activity in getting any more names must come to an end."

The Commission "considered Mr. Leech's request" but decided not to send him money for a bicycle. They appreciated his information, but felt that "it would be better for him to reserve his strength for the work of maintaining cemeteries."

Perhaps the Commission would have decided differently if they had known that Ben's trips were a convenient cover for Resistance work. According to his official Forces Françaises Combattantes identity card, Ben Leech was an active member of Arthur Richards's network from April 1942 until the liberation. Testimony from Allied airmen suggests that Ben may have been acquainted with the clandestine air operations organized by the Bureau d'Opérations Aériennes, which landed many Special Duties flights in the fields around Arras. He certainly served as a courier, delivering information to Arthur Richards and distributing false identity papers to evaders in the countryside.[22]

Like Rosine Witton, Ben Leech could not mention any of his underground activities in his letters. All he could do was make his requests and hope that someone in the Commission office would feel the urgency of his need.

Instead, Ben reiterated his steadfast commitment to his contract. "I am the only I.W.G.C. employee who is not interned that carried out according to your last circular letter to carry on," he wrote in a direct letter to Sir Fabian Ware. "I never left my cemetery for any length of time, and since drawing on British fund have not done any other work for pay. . . . Sir, hoping I am not overstepping my duty in asking too much, and hope for a speedy and favorable reply."

For years, Sir Fabian had told the gardeners that their work was a "sacred task." He urged them to regard it as a duty that was "over and above" worldly concerns and ordered them to remain at their posts when their lives were in danger. But if he ever replied to Ben Leech, there is no record of it in the Commission's files.

"HONNEUR AUX HÉROS" 11

The first airmen Bob Armstrong buried at Saint-Roch Cemetery in Valenciennes were the crew of a Wellington bomber—four New Zealanders and an English gunner—who were shot down in the predawn hours of October 25, 1942.

The Wellington was on its way back to England after participating in a multi-wave terror raid on Milan. This was not a mission aimed at munitions factories or aerodromes. During daylight on October 24, more than seventy Royal Air Force (RAF) Lancasters flew in low over the city center, so low that they could see individual civilians scurrying for cover. Some opened fire with the machine guns meant for warding off Luftwaffe fighters. Later that night, the Royal New Zealand Air Force followed in their wake, dropping their own bombs on Milan about an hour before midnight. Between the daylight raid and the aftershock, the Allies killed at least 170 Italians and destroyed scores of civilian buildings, including schools, hospitals, and homes.[1]

With Milan burning behind them, the bombers turned north for the long journey back to England. Most of them made it, but the Wellington piloted by twenty-one-year-old Sergeant Jim McConnell did not. It crashed near Valenciennes, killing all five members of the crew. People on the ground managed to extract their remains from the wreckage, but the bodies were too badly damaged for individual burials. Bob Armstrong dug two collective graves in a new row he laid out on the south side of the War Graves plot at Saint-Roch.

The deaths of the Wellington bomber crew happened at the beginning of a major transition in the European air war. Earlier that month, on October 9, 1942, the American Eighth Air Force had flown its first raid with more than 100 bombers. The Americans had been flying smaller missions since late summer, but the Lille raid was meant to announce that they had finally joined the European air war in force. Over the coming months, British and American commanders hammered out a strategy for a Combined Bomber Offensive that would make the Milan raid of October 1942 seem quaint.

For now, at least in Valenciennes, the Germans still regarded Allied airmen as worthy enemies who deserved honor in death. Sergeant McConnell and his Wellington crew were buried with full military honors, including "music, wreaths, and prayers." Luftwaffe pallbearers carried them to their graves while throngs of French civilians crowded the cemetery, paying their own tributes with flowers and tears. Bob Armstrong erected five white crosses over the graves.

As one Allied plane after another crashed near Valenciennes, Bob expanded the new plot at Saint-Roch. By the end of the war, it contained one grave for a British soldier killed in May 1940 and thirty-three for British, Canadian, Australian, and New Zealand airmen.

Like Ben Leech and the other War Graves gardeners who continued their cemetery work during the occupation, Bob Armstrong carried out his duties to the best of his ability. He struggled with the same shortages of fuel and oil, the same difficulty maintaining tools, and the same frustration that he could never quite achieve peacetime standards. Bob made the rounds to several cemeteries but concentrated his efforts on Saint-Roch. Occasionally, he had help from Harold Maurice Hill, one of the two gardeners who had worked under his supervision before the war. Hill was interned and released in 1940 and again in 1942, and his teenage son, Maurice, was still at Ilag VIII. When he was at liberty, Hill came to Valenciennes "from time to time" to work with Bob and share the latest news.

Bob kept the War Graves plot neat, but the current war occupied a growing share of his attention. The clandestine work he had begun as an agent of Réseau Saint-Jacques matured along with the Resistance. When the Saint-Jacques network dissolved following a spate of arrests in 1941, Bob made new contacts with Libération Nord and the Bureau des Opérations Aériennes (BOA). Libération Nord was a sprawling Resistance network with a multifaceted mission, but BOA had a more specific job: to arrange the clandestine RAF landings and parachute drops that delivered supplies and agents to France.

The chief of BOA operations in Valenciennes, Captain Gaston Lepine, adored Bob Armstrong. He called Bob "un très charmant camarade"—a very charming comrade—and admired him for "doing the impossible to make himself useful and finding an opportunity to harm the enemy." The two men kept a standing weekly appointment to discuss their Resistance work.

"I was the chief of a parachute zone called LEGAS, responsible for protecting a triangle of transmitters," Lepine explained after the war. "Armstrong knew my activities perfectly. For my part, I did not hide anything from him."[2]

In addition to Gaston Lepine's testimony, another comrade, Marcel Maillard, told the French government that he and Bob participated in missions that included "organising the passage of parachutists, receiving of arms, etc." Charles Deketelaere, a local Resistance leader who worked with both Saint-Jacques and the Organization civile et militaire (OCM), testified that he "employed ARMSTRONG Robert alias 'BOB' for two years, principally as an interpreter for airmen shot down in the area."[3]

Bob was also involved in communications. He often asked his friend Emmanuel Dossche to "take note of certain messages" broadcast over the BBC. Dossche remembered the messages as nonsense—"Valentine, open your umbrella" or "The black cat with a white tail"—but he dutifully followed Bob's instructions, noting the time of the transmission and the number of times the message was repeated as well the content. These cryptic statements were prearranged messages to Special Operations Executive (SOE) agents and Resistance groups. They communicated information such as whether a particular Special Duties landing was on for that night or whether it was time for a specific circuit to strike. Dossche also held documents for Bob. "He entrusted me with various papers to hide, took them back, returned others to me in deposit, until his arrest."[4]

Bob Armstrong's best-documented mission was the rescue of Sergeant Arthur B. Cox, one of the first American evaders in France.

Arthur Bogle Cox was a twenty-three-year-old flight engineer from Tennessee. He was a tall, athletic student whose only job before flying with the Eighth Air Force was working as a lifeguard at the Alcoa municipal swimming pool. On October 9, 1942, his B-24 Liberator, *Big Eagle*, took part in the famous raid on Lille that trumpeted the Eighth Air Force's entry into the air war in Europe.

The plan was to send more than 100 bombers, escorted by American and RAF fighters, to destroy critical railway infrastructure and factories around Lille. Unfortunately, the Americans' faith in "precision bombing" far outstripped their capabilities. Only nine of the 588 bombs dropped on Lille landed within a quarter mile of the aiming points. Instead, high explosives smashed into nearby neighborhoods, killing approximately forty French civilians and wounding ninety others. While some of the railway facilities did suffer minor damage, it was not enough to disrupt them significantly.[5]

Of the 108 American B-17s and B-24s that flew the Lille mission, three were shot down over France, and another ditched in the English Channel. The three planes shot down in France were carrying twenty-eight airmen. Seventeen of them were killed, seven were captured, and four, including Arthur Cox, became the first American airmen on the run in France.[6]

Arthur Cox opened his parachute too early and descended slowly, his canopy horribly visible as he floated toward the ground in full daylight. "The chute carried me over a village in full view of everyone," Cox lamented. As soon as he hit the ground, he started running. For five hours, Cox ran from one patch of woods to the next, taking only "short rests" as he put as many miles as possible between himself and the crash site. He had no idea where he was going other than *away*.[7]

Over the next few days, Cox begged French civilians for food. Eventually, someone fetched an eighteen-year-old farmer's son named Joseph Cornille, who spoke some English. Joseph, whose friends called him Zeph, "said that he knew Org," meaning that he could contact a Resistance organization on Cox's behalf.

In the meantime, Zeph took Cox to Frais-Marais, a neighborhood on the outskirts of Douai. For the next four months, Cox was fed and sheltered by the teachers at the local elementary school, thirty-two-year-old Marie Therese Debrabant and twenty-year-old Victoria Bajeux, and by Victoria's fifty-year-old mother, Marie Bajeux, who was also the school's cook. Victoria's seventy-two-year-old grandmother, Léonie Maton Longatte, "went out every day and picked wild greens along the canal" to help feed Cox. He knew the older woman only as "Mama."[8]

Unfortunately, this little group of helpers had difficulty attracting the attention of the Resistance. "They wrote to Org for 2 months," Cox reported, but "there was no answer." By late November, Cox was beginning to worry. He had an unsettling encounter with a French gendarme while walking with Marie Bajeux to the Debrabant house for dinner, saved only by Madame Bajeux's tissue-thin explanation that Cox was mute and had no identity card. Joseph Cornille continued to bring food and encouragement but no news. Cox "became very impatient and threatened to start out on my own."

Anxious that Cox might really try to leave, Marie Therese Debrabant redoubled her efforts to find help. She may have asked William O'Connor or Thomas Crowley, the two Irish gardeners still living free in Douai, for advice. Someone summoned Bob Armstrong.

"Robt. Armstrong Imperial War Graves Commission . . . came on November 28," Cox reported.

Victoria Bajeux remembered Bob as "un Anglais en civil," suggesting that she may have thought he was an undercover British agent.[9] He was accompanied by a friend whom Cox remembered as "Mr. Lindsay." In fact, this was Bob's comrade Marcel Maillard, a shopkeeper whose nom de guerre may have been a tribute to Bob's beloved sister, Augusta Lindsay.

Bob's arrival was a tremendous relief. Not only was he a fluent English speaker who had direct connections to the Resistance, but he was also very tall. This was not a minor detail. French civilians frequently struggled to find clothing that fit American airmen. The available trousers were often too short, the shoulders of jackets too narrow. When Bob Armstrong met Arthur Cox, he stripped off his own long, broad-shouldered coat and gave it to the young flier.

American evaders were a novelty in 1942, so Bob had to make sure that Cox was genuine. He and Maillard brought a map of the United States and asked Cox to point to his hometown. "I quickly pointed to Knoxville," Cox remembered. "They then turned the map over and asked what states were north, south, east, and west of Tennessee."[10]

Convinced by Cox's geography and his accent, Bob and Maillard took photos to use for false identity papers. These "turned out badly," so the two men returned to retake them.

Bob assured Cox and his protectors that he would set the wheels of a rescue in motion. They should expect a visitor who would give the password "444."[11] It might take a few weeks, but Cox should be ready to depart at any moment.

The man Bob Armstrong summoned was Eugène D'Hallendre. At the end of January 1943, D'Hallendre swooped into Frais-Marais, accompanied by his OCM colleague, Paul Lisfranc. Together, they took Arthur Cox under the wing of the Pat O'Leary Line.[12] "Mr. Dulondure came to Frais-Marais and took me to Douai + by train to Lille," Cox reported.

D'Hallendre brought Arthur Cox to a safe house in La Madeleine run by Valentine Ployart. She was already sheltering another evader, Maurice H. G. Wilson, an RAF fighter pilot who had stayed with Rosine Witton a few days earlier.[13] The two airmen posed for smiling photos with the D'Hallendre family, Valentine Ployart, and her seven-year-old son, Guy. Wilson's gray civilian jacket—which may have belonged to five-foot-six Bert Witton—was noticeably tight and very short in the sleeves. In contrast, Cox's dark, pinstriped jacket fit well in the shoulders and was too large around the middle. Someone had repositioned the buttons all the way over toward the right pocket to pull it snug around Cox's waist.[14]

Arthur Bogle Cox and Maurice H. G. Wilson, 1943. *Photograph by Eugène D'Hallendre, courtesy of the Musée de la Résistance, Bondues*

Arthur Bogle Cox wearing Bob Armstrong's coat, 1943. *Photograph by Eugène D'Hallendre, courtesy of the Musée de la Résistance, Bondues*

Lucienne D'Hallendre, Maurice H. G. Wilson, and Valentine Ployart, 1943. *Photograph by Eugène D'Hallendre, courtesy of the Musée de la Résistance, Bondues*

Arthur Cox left Lille on February 3, 1943, nearly four months after he was shot down for bombing it. A man called "Roger the Legionnaire" escorted both Cox and Maurice Wilson from Lille to Paris to Toulouse, where he turned them over to Pat O'Leary himself. "Pat O'Leary" was really a Belgian army doctor named Albert Guérisse working with MI9. In the last week of February, Guérisse personally conveyed Arthur Cox to Marseilles, where he met Nancy Wake Fiocca, the famous "White Mouse" who would later become one of SOE's most celebrated agents. A few weeks later, Cox crossed the Pyrenees to freedom. He was still wearing Bob Armstrong's coat.[15]

The journey was perilous in more ways than one. Arthur Cox did not know it, but "Roger the Legionnaire" was really an infiltrator named Roger le Neveu. On March 2, just days after le Neveu handed Arthur Cox over to Pat O'Leary, the Gestapo pounced. They arrested Guérisse and nearly all the other operatives in the southern section of the network. Many of them died in Nazi custody. Later, the Pat O'Leary Line would be reconstituted in another form, but Arthur Cox was among the last evaders rescued in the era of Pat O'Leary and Nancy Wake.[16]

Meanwhile, the air war continued to grow in awful power. The raid on Lille that had brought Arthur Cox to France was small potatoes compared to the Combined Bomber Offensive that shook Germany in the summer of 1943. In one eight-day, round-the-clock assault on Hamburg, aptly named Operation Gomorrah, the combined Allied air forces killed as many civilians—around 40,000—as the eight months of the Blitz. They dropped incendiaries along with high explosives, causing horrific firestorms with winds so strong that they sucked people off their feet and into the flames. Victims' bodies were so desiccated by the extreme heat that they shrunk into crisp, contorted mummies, and "the smallest children lay like fried eels on the pavement." It was impossible to get precise casualty figures, in part because thousands of people were incinerated so completely that authorities had to estimate the number of dead by measuring the layers of ash left behind in air raid shelters.[17]

In the wake of this frightful escalation, Germans regarded Allied airmen as murderers rather than honorable enemies. In Valenciennes, the authorities cut back sharply on the honors they afforded airmen buried at Saint-Roch. There would be no more wreaths or music for men who slaughtered German women and children. When an RAF Boston crashed near Valenciennes in August 1943, just two weeks after the immolation of Hamburg, the German authorities posted guards at the cemetery gates and forbid French civilians from attending the burials.

Bob Armstrong and his French neighbors resented this ban. They understood that funerals provided a highly visible opportunity for the community to express support for the Allies. Showing reverence for the dead was obviously political, but it was also a respectable form of public display with broad appeal. Even people who would never dream of cutting a telephone wire or sheltering an evader might be willing to lay a flower on an airman's grave. The funeral ban was a small escalation by the local Nazis, but it was one that a very large number of people were willing to defy.

In Valenciennes, the confrontation came in October 1943, a year after the first airmen were buried at Saint-Roch.

In the wee hours of October 21, 1943, a lone Halifax bomber crashed northeast of Valenciennes, killing everyone aboard. This was no ordinary bomber. It belonged to the RAF's No. 161 Special Duties Squadron, the unit that worked with SOE, MI6, and the BOA to support the Resistance in occupied Europe. The squadron is most often remembered for its matte-black Lysanders—small, single-engine planes that could carry a pilot, two or three passengers, and oblong containers stuffed with arms, explosives, and other critical supplies—but they also flew twin-engine Hudsons to deliver parachuting agents and larger supply drops into the hands of the Resistance.

The Halifax that crashed near Valenciennes on October 21, 1943, was one of 161 Squadron's largest aircraft. Unlike the smaller Lysanders and Hudsons, the Halifax was a four-engine bomber capable of carrying more than seven tons of cargo. It took off from RAF Tempsford just after midnight, carrying a large shipment of supplies for a parachute drop to the Resistance in the Ardennes. Along with munitions, its precious cargo included a much-needed infusion of cash for Zéro, a Belgian intelligence network financed by MI6. The Halifax carried 3 million Belgian francs, U.S.$40,000, and 554 diamonds that Zéro could liquidate on the black market, more than half their funding for the fourth quarter of 1943.[18]

The Special Duties Halifax crashed a stone's throw from the Belgian border, its cargo undelivered. According to official records, seven people—all members of the RAF crew—died in the crash, but Bob Armstrong's friend Emmanuel Dossche reported that he and Bob buried nine bodies.[19]

The timing of the Special Duties crash heightened the emotions around the Valenciennes funeral ban. The seven—or nine—bodies were buried on October 23, 25, and 27, just a few days before November 1, All Saints Day, the traditional day for decorating the graves of the beloved dead. The guards posted at the gates may have kept people out of Saint-Roch while Bob buried the Special Duties crew, but it was harder to keep them out on November 1. Since the British military section of Saint-Roch is adjacent to the civilian cemetery, the Nazis would have had to ban the All Saints observances entirely to keep civilians away from the new graves. Doing so could have provoked widespread discontent. Instead, the Germans let the scene play out.

On November 1, 1943, a throng of mourners descended on Saint-Roch. Hour after hour, Bob Armstrong watched as French civilians heaped flowers on the RAF graves. The first few hundred bouquets covered the fresh-turned earth, but the mourners kept coming, adding tributes "adorned in the allied colors" of red, white, and blue. Soon, the wooden crosses were completely obscured by flowers, wreaths, and seventy-two potted chrysanthemums, a hardy, late-blooming flower that became a popular grave decoration in the aftermath of the Great War. Still, the French civilians did not stop. By the time they were finished, it was impossible to approach the new graves without wading through an ankle-deep flood of flowers.

In case they had not made their point emphatically enough, some of the mourners left marble plaques emblazoned with explicit tributes to the dead airmen:

"Honor to heroes"

"In Loving memory"

"To our brave allies 20 Oct. 1943"

"May all gather before these heroes"

"Your memory will remain immortal"

"Witnesses to your sacrifice, our hearts will not forget"

"Our remembrance will adorn your sacrifice with flowers"

"Those who bravely died for our country deserve to have the people come and pray at their grave"

The Germans did not like these tributes. Eventually, after more airmen died and more bouquets appeared at Saint-Roch, the German commandant intervened.

"They are not heroes," he told Emmanuel Dossche, "they are murderers."

The Nazis posted a new sign outside Saint-Roch: "Following the orders received from the occupying authorities, it is formally forbidden to place on the graves flowers, wreaths, or plaques of any kind."

When people continued to leave offerings on the British graves, German soldiers removed them. They took the plaques to the commandant's office for storage, while wreaths and bouquets were repurposed to adorn the graves of "victims of [Allied] bombings." On at least one occasion,

Decorated graves at Saint-Roch Cemetery, Valenciennes, November 1, 1943. *CWGC Archives*

Germans took flowers from the RAF graves and used them to decorate the grave of one of their Alsatian dogs, "who was killed by French patriots."[20]

Bob Armstrong was not there to see the Germans clear away the plaques and the bouquets. By the end of November 1943, he was locked in a cell at Loos prison, handcuffed and under guard, awaiting trial on capital charges.

THE COMET LINE

12

Joseph Wemheuer woke up in midair. Freezing wind tore at his face as he fell, plastering his flight jacket against his body. He gasped for oxygen, but the air above 20,000 feet was too thin to breathe. Four miles below, the French countryside was a patchwork of tiny fields. Wemheuer was so high up that he could see all the way across the English Channel to the cliffs of Dover, eighty miles away. That was a short trip in an airplane but a long journey without one.[1]

Joseph Wemheuer was a twenty-seven-year-old high school English teacher from Chicago. His father, a German immigrant, played bass for the Chicago Symphony Orchestra, while his mother, a Czech immigrant, cared for lodgers in their home near Lake Michigan. The family spoke German at home. After the Japanese attacked Pearl Harbor in December 1941, Wemheuer volunteered for the U.S. Army Air Forces and became a bombardier.[2]

When Wemheuer began flying missions over Europe in early 1943, the outlook for American bomber crews was bleak. Their fighter escorts did not have the range to accompany them all the way into Germany, allowing the Luftwaffe's experienced fighters to inflict horrific casualties on the bombers. Nearly 60 percent of the men in Joseph Wemheuer's 305th Bomb Group were killed in action between November 1942 and May 1943. Others were killed in accidents or grounded due to wounds or mental breakdowns. Of the men who flew in bombers for the American Eighth Air Force during the winter of 1942–1943, only one in five completed the twenty-five missions that constituted a full tour of duty.[3]

"That was the grimmest time in the war," General Laurence Kuter said of the bomber crew losses in early 1943. "I think that the Charge of the Light Brigade was a Sunday School picnic."[4]

The mission on May 13, 1943, marked an important turning point. Four brand-new bomb groups had just arrived in England to support the exhausted survivors of the earlier four, and some of these new crews were flying their first mission. More than 100 B-17s left England, headed for the Potez aircraft factory in the French town of Méaulte, just south of Albert.[5]

Joseph Wemheuer perched in the clear plexiglass nose of his plane, bombsight between his knees. Just behind him, the navigator, twenty-two-year-old Californian Robert Ramsaur, plotted their course. The pilot and copilot flew the B-17 from a cockpit at the top of the plane, while the radio operator had his own compartment between the wings. The other five men in the crew were gunners who protected the ship from German fighters with machine guns positioned in the tail, waist, top turret, and ball turret. Their combined firepower gave the B-17 its nickname: the Flying Fortress.

As Wemheuer's formation approached Méaulte, the bombers encountered "very light flak." They flew straight and level over the target, a tactic pioneered by the 305th's commander, Colonel Curtis LeMay. Lemay had decided that it was better for his bombers to grit their teeth through the flak rather than take evasive maneuvers that would scatter their bombs miles from the target. That meant flying in a steady, straight line so that the bombardiers could achieve maximum accuracy.

Joseph Wemheuer released his bombs over Méaulte, but he never knew whether he hit the aircraft factory. Before the bombs even reached the ground, his plane was swarmed by German fighters. Bullets ripped through the B-17's thin aluminum skin, pinging off oxygen tanks and severing fuel lines. Within moments, the plane was on fire. A wall of flame erupted just behind the nose, trapping Wemheuer and Ramsaur as the bomber began to fall from the sky.

Wemheuer went to fight the flames, but it was no use. The fire was too fierce. Ramsaur crawled toward the escape hatch with Wemheuer close behind, ready to jump, but it was too late. Something inside the plane exploded. The whole nose of the bomber blew off in a shower of shrapnel. Joseph Wemheuer was flung out into the open air more than 20,000 feet above the ground, unconscious.

"Next I remember, I was out of the ship, floating toward the ground."

The sky was littered with debris from the disintegrating plane. A yellow rubber life raft flapped uselessly in the updrafts while bullets sliced through the air. Wemheuer saw two parachutes amid the chaos, but he wasn't sure they were from his plane.

Still only half conscious, Wemheuer scrabbled at his chest, searching for his ripcord. All bomber crews in the Eighth Air Force were instructed in emergency procedures, but their training did not include any practice jumps. Like nearly all the men who bailed out of a disabled B-17, Wemheuer was using his parachute for the first time.

There were so many ways an emergency jump could go wrong. Sometimes, the airman was wounded or confused from oxygen deprivation. Sometimes, the plane was full of smoke or bucking so hard that the airmen rattled around like pebbles in a tin can. Sometimes, the parachute clips didn't close all the way.

Even if an airman attached his chute correctly, his troubles were not over. Many men were trapped inside spinning planes by rotational forces. Some who jumped were injured when air currents tossed them back against the hull. Even if they cleared the dying bomber, they still had to contend with low oxygen and finger-freezing cold, not to mention a sky full of lethal fire, both from the fighters and from the other B-17s whose gunners were blazing away at the enemy. Once an airman fell below the battle in the sky, an open parachute made him a target for German soldiers on the ground. Sometimes, the parachute failed. If that happened, the airman would have two full minutes to watch the ground rushing toward him before he died.

Joseph Wemheuer was lucky. He remembered to clip on his parachute before he went to fight the fire. The explosion blew him free of the plane's spin. He regained consciousness in time. His fingers worked. The parachute opened.[6]

～

Joseph Wemheuer was one of 137,000 Allied airmen shot down over western Europe during World War II. He was also one of the luckiest. More than 87,000 (64 percent) died when their planes exploded or crashed or their jumps went wrong. Another 45,000 (33 percent) survived the fall but were captured on the ground. Around 5,000 Allied airmen (3 percent) successfully evaded capture.[7]

These evaders were too few to sway the outcome of the war by their numbers alone, but they were invaluable in other ways.[8] Besides their ability to provide up-to-date intelligence about German defenses and conditions behind enemy lines, they were essential to the morale of the Allied air forces. Frightened, battle-weary fliers knew that the odds were against them. As the casualties mounted in the winter of 1942–1943, commanders worried that airmen might refuse to fly. In an effort to boost morale, the Eighth Air Force limited the bomber crews' tours of duty, promising that anyone who survived twenty-five missions could go home. When Joseph Wemheuer was shot down on May 13, only a few individual airmen had succeeded. The first bomber to complete twenty-five missions was *Hell's Angels*, which reached that milestone the next day, May 14, 1943.

Evaders were a pillar in the shaky edifice of bomber morale. "The miracle of their reappearance at Air Force bases and stations in Britain had a marvelous effect, as I was able to witness, on the morale of all who flew against Germany," wrote Airey Neave, an MI9 agent who liaised with the Pat O'Leary and Comet lines.[9]

Successful evaders were sent on tours of air bases to speak about their experiences to rapt audiences of fellow fliers. Ostensibly, the purpose of these talks was to instruct airmen in evasion techniques, but they also soothed their justified terror. Evaders were like lottery winners. They allowed every man to imagine that his own number might come up lucky.

By 1943, American airmen knew that their chances of evading capture depended on receiving help from one of the many escape lines operating in occupied Europe. Unfortunately, when Joseph Wemheuer landed in May 1943, the major escape networks were struggling to recover after several months of relentless Gestapo attacks. The Pat O'Leary Line was decimated by arrests in March 1943, collapsing behind Arthur Cox like a bridge of sand. Meanwhile, the Comet Line was reeling from the arrest of Andrée de Jongh in January 1943. Dozens of other Comet Line operatives had also been caught in the crackdown, including Jean Greindl alias Nemo, head of the organization's Belgian section. De Jongh was interrogated by the Gestapo but not executed. The Nazis were prepared to believe that a young woman could be a helper but not the head of such a vast organization.[10]

These arrests had terrible consequences. At the very moment when the Allies were ramping up the bombing war, both the Pat O'Leary Line and the Comet Line were scattered and leaderless. From Brussels to Bordeaux, volunteers scrambled to reforge broken links and take on new responsibilities. Dédée's father, Frédéric de Jongh alias Paul, stepped into his daughter's shoes, running the Paris section of the Comet Line with the help of Catholic businessman Robert Aylé. Frédéric de Jongh, a fifty-five-year-old former headmaster, was slight and gray haired with thick, round glasses. He could often be found at the Café Curveur near Paris's Gare du Nord, waiting for guides to bring airmen from the north.[11]

One of those guides was Rosine Witton. Her job was to shelter airmen at her home in Arras and ferry them to Paris, where they stayed in safe houses until other guides took them to Bordeaux. In the spring of 1943, Rosine made this dangerous trip about once a week. In addition to her own evaders, Rosine also guided airmen who stayed with Emile and Madeleine Didier, a couple in their fifties who lived just down the street at Number 22 Route de Bapaume.

Rosine Witton and her comrades were new additions to the Comet Line. They had previously formed a tributary of the Pat O'Leary Line, which was decimated by arrests in March 1943. In the aftermath, Eugène D'Hallendre went searching for a new affiliation for their group. Frédéric de Jongh, who was eager for experienced helpers in the wake of the Comet Line's own troubles, welcomed D'Hallendre's network of safe house keepers—Rosine Witton, Valentine Ployart, and the Didiers—to Comète.

There was one snag. Rosine Witton's group was explicitly affiliated with the Organization civile et militaire (OCM), a major armed French Resistance network. D'Hallendre was one of OCM's leaders in the north. Emile Didier was also with OCM, as were nearly all of the outer ring of helpers who funneled evaders toward Rosine's house on Route de Bapaume. Andrée de Jongh had always been wary of affiliating the Comet Line with armed Resistance groups, but the new leaders took the risk. Rosine Witton and her OCM comrades became part of Réseau Comète.

～

The first airman Rosine sheltered at Number 6 Route de Bapaume was Maurice Wilson, the twenty-one-year-old Royal Air Force (RAF) pilot who traveled with Arthur Cox. Wilson arrived in Arras on January 26, 1943, and stayed with Rosine for a day or two until Eugène D'Hallendre transferred him to Valentine Ployart's house.

During his brief stay with Rosine, Maurice Wilson was tickled to find that she spoke English. "Thank you for your brave hospitality," he wrote on February 3, 1943, when he and Arthur Cox were preparing to leave Lille. "I was delighted to meet an Englishwoman . . . [I am] hoping that you will see your husband soon again."

Wilson also mentioned that Rosine had given him an address—possibly for Bert's family in London—and would "remember my promise." Whatever the promise was, Wilson was probably unable to fulfill it. He and Cox were separated later in their journey, and Wilson was captured. He spent the rest of the war as a prisoner at Stalag Luft III. Rosine kept his thank-you note among her most important papers.[12]

In the months after Maurice Wilson's stay, Rosine Witton sheltered airmen from Canada, New Zealand, Northern Ireland, England, and the United States, as well as a Free French commando who was captured during the Dieppe raid in 1942 and escaped from a prisoner-of-war camp.[13] She fed them and provided them with clothing, including woolen berets, which she "made them wear in the style of French laborers."[14]

One of the airmen Rosine cared for was Joseph Wemheuer.

After his miraculous midair recovery, Wemheuer fell to earth and crashed through the boughs of a large tree. He broke four or five branches on the way down, bloodying his legs. Luckily, several French farmworkers spotted him and rushed to his aid. A young woman showed him where to hide, and he gave her his parachute as a gesture of thanks.

"[You can] make dresses out of it," he told her.[15]

Over the next few days, French civilians in the village of Brévillers took care of Joseph Wemheuer. They bandaged his legs and found civilian clothing to fit his six-foot frame. Food was scarce, but they pooled enough cider, eggs, and bread to keep him fed. When German soldiers came hunting for parachutists, they lied.

Most of these helpers were not members of any formal Resistance network. They never received recognition or compensation, but their immediate assistance was critical to Joseph Wemheuer's evasion. The girl who accepted his parachute, the woman who bandaged his legs, and the man who provided him with false identity papers all risked their lives.

The first helper whose name Wemheuer remembered was Dr. Pierre Cuallacci, a socialist Corsican doctor from nearby Frévent, who led a local OCM group. Cuallacci tended Wemheuer's wounds and sent him to Arras to meet Eugène D'Hallendre.

Joseph Wemheuer arrived at the Arras train station with a guide on May 19, 1943. It was the third anniversary of the 1940 bombing that killed so many refugees and blew in the windows of the War Graves Commission office. Now, the War Graves building was a satellite administrative office of OFK 670, the Nazi field command headquartered in Lille. German soldiers patrolled the station platform, checking papers. There were French gendarmes as well, not to mention ordinary civilians who might betray Allied airmen to the authorities in return for a reward of up to 10,000 francs, a year's wages for a farm laborer.[16]

Joseph Wemheuer had false identity papers, but there was no way he could withstand scrutiny. Up to this point, he had communicated with his helpers in "a combination of French and sign language," but the simplest question from a soldier would reveal that he was not French. Wemheuer might have been better off answering in his native German.

Luckily, there was no need. His guide spotted Eugène D'Hallendre waiting nearby and handed Wemheuer into his keeping.

By the time he met Joseph Wemheuer, Eugène D'Hallendre was more focused than ever on helping evaders. Just a few weeks earlier, on April 6, D'Hallendre hosted a crucial meeting between the regional OCM leaders and General de Gaulle's deputy, André Dewavrin alias Colonel Passy. De Gaulle had sent Passy on a tour of France to help unify the fractious Resistance networks by meeting with local organizers. Among the northern Gaullists, that meant Eugène D'Hallendre, Paul Lisfranc, and a handful of their most trusted comrades.

"I went to La Madeleine, to Mr. D'Hallendre's house," Passy wrote in his memoirs. He found D'Hallendre and the others "full of faith and quiet courage" in a way that made Passy self-conscious. "I always felt a little gauche when arriving in an assembly of brave men who were in danger every day . . . especially when you realized that these men looked on you as a kind of messiah because you came from London, you were a close collaborator of General de Gaulle, and you had been parachuted." Passy struggled to convey to the hopeful *résistants* that, in truth, de Gaulle was pinning his own hopes on them.[17]

At the April 6 meeting, the OCM-Nord leaders clarified their organizational structure. They divided themselves into three sections: armed resistance, sabotage, and evasion. Since Eugène D'Hallendre was already involved with the escape lines, he took charge of the evasion sector. After years of splitting his time among many projects, he would focus his energy on moving airmen along the Comet Line.[18]

Joseph Wemheuer did not know anything about these behind-the-scenes machinations. All he knew was that Eugène D'Hallendre was part of the network that American airmen called "the Organization." The young airman followed D'Hallendre out of the Arras train station and across the railroad tracks into Ronville, walking as casually as he could on his battered legs. They passed the Secours National sign on the old *café-tabac* and knocked at Rosine's door.

Joseph Wemheuer stayed with Rosine Witton for six days. She fried eggs for his breakfast and helped him arrange his odd assortment of civilian clothing into an unremarkable outfit. It was always difficult to make Allied airmen blend in among French civilians. They tended to be conspicuously tall, young, and healthy and to have foreign mannerisms. At least Joseph Wemheuer had dark hair. One of Rosine's other charges, Belfast-born navigator Alfie Martin, was notably redheaded. The Resistance dyed his hair black so that he could ride a French train without attracting notice. "My eyebrows and eyelashes were darkened also," Martin remembered, "and, really, I looked a villainous sight."[19]

It was more difficult to disguise injuries. Gordon Crowther, a twenty-year-old Canadian navigator who stayed with Rosine the week before Joseph Wemheuer arrived, broke an ankle during his landing. Dr. Henri Artisson, the doctor who lived near the Arras train station, put on a cast, but Rosine Witton and her friends could not hide the young Canadian long enough for his ankle to heal completely. Just three weeks after Crowther landed, Rosine was forced to take desperate measures. Apologizing profusely, she sawed off the cast so that it would not invite questions on the train to Paris.

Rosine had no choice, but she still fretted about causing Crowther so much pain. "He could hardly walk," she wrote, "and I'm sure he suffered terribly."[20]

For the evaders, hiding from the Nazis was terrifying, but it was also boring. Joseph Wemheuer, who was traveling alone, likely spent his days resting or reading. When Rosine hosted two airmen at the same time, they would play cards and chat. Sometimes, the evaders visited comrades at the Didiers or received a haircut from a neighbor, but they generally had to lie low. In July, when the currants were ripe, a pair of airmen helped Rosine make an enormous batch of jelly "to amuse themselves and pass the time."[21]

Others spent their time drawing pencil sketches of their airplanes. Gordon Crowther drew two sketches of his Wellington bomber, *Wimpy III*, soaring through the clouds above the words "The Scourge of the Reich! Bombs on Germany." He gave one sketch to Rosine Witton and the other to Eugène D'Hallendre. [22]

Sketch of a Halifax bomber by Brian Desmond Barker as a souvenir for Eugène D'Hallendre, March 23, 1943. Barker completed a nearly identical sketch for Rosine Witton, dated March 22, 1943, which is in the collection of the Imperial War Museum, London. *Courtesy of the Musée de la Résistance, Bondues*

Another amateur artist was twenty-one-year-old RAF navigator Brian Desmond Barker, one of several airmen who was aided by multiple members of the War Graves community during his evasion.[23]

When Barker's Halifax was shot down near Valenciennes, he went into a café to ask the owner for help. "She told me she could not help me, but that she knew of someone who might," Barker later told MI9. The café owner went out and returned with Bob Armstrong.

Barker stayed in Valenciennes for ten days. According to the local Libération-Nord chief, Charles Deketelaere, Barker was "taken care of by ARMSTRONG," who helped provide food, clothing, and false papers, and the Singier family, who provided shelter. When the young airman was fed and rested, Eugène D'Hallendre escorted him to Rosine Witton's house. Barker stayed at Number 6 for nearly two weeks. On March 22, he drew a pencil sketch of his boxy Halifax as a souvenir for Rosine. She kept it with Maurice Wilson's note, Gordon Crowther's drawing, and Bert's letters.[24]

Rosine also kept photographs. Many airmen carried small photos of themselves to make forged identity papers, but they were often the wrong size or the wrong pose and had to be retaken. In the last week of May 1943, Eugène D'Hallendre visited Number 6 to take new photos of two of Rosine's charges: redheaded Alfie Martin and Douglas Hoehn, a twenty-five-year-old bombardier from Wisconsin who was shot down during the same May 13 mission as Joseph Wemheuer. Rosine dressed both men

Rosine Witton with Douglas Hoehn and Alfie Martin at Number 6 Route de Bapaume, May 1943. *Photograph by Eugène D'Hallendre, courtesy of the Musée de la Résistance, Bondues*

in ties and crisp, white collars under their ill-fitting jackets. D'Hallendre snapped a series of photographs, not just the formal poses they needed for identity cards. Other photos from the series showed Martin and Hoehn at an open window, framed by white lace curtains, or standing in the door-way while Rosine stood outside, squinting against the bright sun.[25]

At night, the evaders would gather around Rosine's clandestine radio, tuned to the BBC to catch the news broadcast from London. This was an arrestable offense all on its own. French civilians caught listening to "foreign propaganda" could be imprisoned and fined up to 2,000 francs, though millions of French civilians took the chance and tuned in anyway.[26] For Rosine, the most stirring part of the nightly broadcast was the playing of the banned French national anthem, "La Marseillaise."

"She would start marching with the French flag and cheer De Gaulle's picture + spit on Petain," Doug Hoehn remembered. "Oh, I'll never forget her."[27]

Despite the risks, Rosine kept her sense of humor. Around the time Brian Barker arrived at Number 6, Ben Leech also paid a visit. He and Rosine shared a laugh over a mundane kitchen disaster. "Darling, I had a card from Ben Leech," Bert wrote from Ilag VIII. "He told me about the pâté, I had a laugh to myself, I hope it was not burned too much and I hope you told poor old Ben where to step off."[28]

Other stories were only funny in hindsight. Once, returning from the outhouse, Doug Hoehn was startled to find a French gendarme in Ros-ine's kitchen, apparently conducting some unexpected Secours National business.

"He said bonjour monsieur and I only nodded."

Disconcerted, Hoehn hurried into the front bedroom, where Alfie Martin was holding his breath. "Doug must have been dumbfounded," Martin recalled, "but he walked through into the bedroom and closed the door without replying . . . it worried the three of us quite considerably not knowing whether the man suspected or not."[29]

One of Rosine's most important jobs was relaying critical information to her airmen. She "gave them lots of advice" and "explained to them the ups and downs of the journey and told them what not to do."[30] She also passed along news about their crewmates.

Sometimes, the news was very bad. Joseph Wemheuer had been wor-rying about his friends ever since he regained consciousness and tried to count parachutes. During his stay at Rosine's house, someone delivered a list of nine Americans—six of them from Wemheuer's crew and three from Doug Hoehn's—who were killed during the Méaulte raid. According to civilian informants, Wemheuer's comrades bailed out of the plane but were "captured, shot, and buried near Doullens." These observers claimed that the Germans attempted to bury the airmen in unmarked coffins but were thwarted by "a French sister" who "drove nails in the coffins, one for the first name on the list, two for the second, etc." Hundreds of French civilians attended the burial, a show of allegiance that "irritated the Germans."[31]

Doug Hoehn heard a slightly different version of the same story. His civilian helpers reported that the Germans had fired on his crewmates from the ground as they descended. One man was badly wounded in the thigh and died after the Germans refused to allow a French doctor to treat him, while "another fellow was cut almost in two by M[achine] G[un] fire."

Forensic evidence suggests that the version Hoehn heard was probably closer to the truth. Three of Joseph Wemheuer's crewmates—including Robert Ramsaur—were taken prisoner and survived the war. One of the survivors, nineteen-year-old Robert Vertefeuille of Willimantic, Connecticut, had five bullet wounds in his legs, which suggests he may have been shot while descending.[32]

The other six men in Wemheuer's plane probably died when it crashed. After the war, the American Graves Registration Service exhumed the bodies of Wemheuer's and Hoehn's crewmates, who had been buried in the Imperial War Graves Commission plot in Saint-Pierre Cemetery in Amiens. Their graves were marked with names and the words "Engl. Flieger," German for "English airman," suggesting that the Germans did bury them properly. Forensic examinations of the bodies revealed injuries consistent with death in a plane crash, not deliberate execution. The American investigator asked the gardener, Sidney Jeffs, for details, but Jeffs could not supply them. "The caretaker is an English Civilian and was interned by the Germans at the time the remains were buried," the exhumation report notes. "Therefore no information is available."[33]

While Joseph Wemheuer grieved his friends, Rosine Witton reached out to her own comrades for support. Her troubles were mostly secret, but Berthe Fraser and the Didiers could sympathize. "My love, [I] have had a good report from Mrs. Fraser about you," Bert Witton wrote on June 9, 1943, replying to a letter Rosine wrote during Joseph Wemheuer's stay. Berthe could not tell Bert about Rosine's clandestine work, but she could still convey her approval.

Berthe Fraser was busy with her own work. After she was released from Loos prison in December 1942, Arthur Richards brought her up to speed. He was already working for the Bureau des Opérations Aériennes (BOA) and for a Special Operations Executive (SOE) circuit called Sylvestre-Farmer, often known to locals as the "W.O." This network was run by SOE agent Michael Trotobas alias Capitaine Michel and tasked with sabotaging factories, infrastructure, and railway facilities around Lille. Richards introduced Berthe Fraser to Trotobas and his second-in-command, François Reeve alias Lieutenant Olivier.

"At this meeting these two officers asked me to help them," Berthe recalled. "I at once agreed to do so."[34]

Later, SOE's official historian, M. R. D. Foot, would call Berthe Fraser "one of the greatest resistance heroines." She played many roles, "arranging safe-houses, storing explosives, noting German troop movements, escorting escapers, all tasks that came her way were promptly handled." One of Berthe's more harrowing missions involved procuring a hearse, coffin, and flowers to smuggle SOE agent F. F. E. Yeo-Thomas past the Germans so that he—along with two French women and a trove of intelligence documents—could be extracted by a Special Duties Lysander.[35]

Berthe Fraser's indifference to internal SOE politics led her to work with both F-section agents like Trotobas, who answered to the British, and RF-section agents like Yeo-Thomas, who answered to de Gaulle. "She cared nothing for London's careful compartment systems," Foot observed. Instead, "she worked impartially for any French or British organization that needed her." Berthe had several aliases, one of which was *Bleuet*—cornflower—the French counterpart to the British remembrance poppy.

Several members of the War Graves community were connected to Michael Trotobas's Farmer circuit in one way or another. In the Nord department, Jack and Marthe Wood hid guns and explosives, while Stephen Grady cherished a pistol that Trotobas gave him personally. In Ronville, seventeen-year-old Harry Legg sometimes rode shotgun on Berthe's Fraser's more daring stunts. Once, when Trotobas ran short of explosives for his sabotage missions, Berthe arranged to borrow dynamite from BOA and brought Harry along with her to fetch it. "I then went to COIGNEUX (Somme) in a car with Mr. LEGG and brought back some dynamite and arms which had been parachuted on to a ground belonging to the B.O.A.," she wrote in a report to SOE. When Harry Legg wasn't helping Berthe, he was looking for other ways to strike at the Nazis. He was one of the few—perhaps the only—members of the War Graves community who joined the Francs-Tireurs et Partisans (FTP), the armed forces of the underground French Communist Party.[36]

Rosine Witton may or may not have known of her friends' activities. Even if she did not, her own work was enough to keep her on edge.

Ordinarily, Rosine could have confided in Bert but not when all their letters were read by German censors. Still she found ways to tell her husband
that she was worried. Throughout the spring of 1943, Rosine's letters fretted over the cost of food and clothing and made vague complaints about
her "lodgers." She might have meant her Secours National renters. Or not.

Bert offered sympathy from afar. "My love I am please[d] you are quiet
once more, I will be more so if those damn loggers of yours would have
gone but soon I hope," he wrote in response to a letter Rosine had written on March 22, the same day Brian Desmond Barker drew his Halifax
for her.[37]

Rosine must have written about her lodgers often because Bert mentioned them several times. "I do hope you have got rid of that logger,"
he wrote in June 1943. A few weeks later, he followed up with "I hope
by now you have got rid of your loggers + that you are quiet once again,
to be quiet again must be like heaven after what you have put up with."[38]

Bert was supportive, but he was also confused. He knew that life was
hard under the occupation, but Rosine's constant worries about the high
price of food and clothing did not make sense.

"Chum I am supprise," Bert wrote in response to an anxious letter
from Rosine. "You got no children + I have all I want . . . you should be
one of the best dressed around Arras but no its money again."

Bert had no way of knowing that Rosine had spent a staggering 1,900
francs on a complete suit of clothes and underwear for Gordon Crowther
the previous week. When she wrote that particular letter to Bert on May
15, she was hosting RAF gunner John Ayliff David; Joseph Wemheuer
would arrive four days later, on May 19.[39] Rosine relied on forged ration
cards and black-market food in addition to her backyard hens, but money
did not go far with so many young airmen to feed and clothe. She also continued to send parcels of chocolate, tobacco, and ill-fated eggs to Ilag VIII.

Bert was concerned. He assured Rosine that he was thriving on Red
Cross largesse and begged her to feed herself.

"My sweet you say its the bread + yet you send me cake," Bert wrote
in exasperation in July. "Why don't you use the flour for yourself?"[40]

Despite these hardships, Rosine usually refused compensation for
sheltering airmen. The British government reimbursed the Comet Line
for airmen's expenses, but Eugène D'Hallendre's expense reports show
that Rosine routinely declined these payments. The entry for Joseph
Wemheuer notes that D'Hallendre spent 136 francs for one second-class
ticket from Arras to Paris and 272 francs for a round-trip ticket for "Mme
WANTIEZ," one of Rosine's aliases. Below the ticket prices is a note:

"No accommodation costs at Madame Wantiez's house." Rosine did accept reimbursement for unusual expenses like Gordon Crowther's new clothes and a complete shaving kit, but most of D'Hallendre's expense reports note that Rosine Witton "does not wish to be reimbursed for accommodations in Arras."[41]

On the morning of May 24, his sixth day at Number 6, Joseph Wemheuer rose early. He shaved, dressed, and sat down to a hearty breakfast of fresh, fried eggs. Perhaps he was reminded of the special breakfasts served on American air bases before missions, when the airmen ate real eggs instead of powdered for what was, for many, a last meal.

When he was done eating, Wemheuer followed Rosine back up Route de Bapaume to the train station. She warned him to keep his distance as they traveled. They would not sit together on the train, but he must always keep her in sight. Wemheuer tried to look casual, watching how his fellow travelers showed their papers and keeping his mouth firmly shut. He probably spent the three-and-a-half-hour train ride to Paris feigning sleep or hiding behind a newspaper to discourage conversation. Sometimes, Rosine bought copies of the Nazi pictorial magazine *Signal* for her airmen to peruse on the train.

"Propaganda, propaganda," she warned them.[42]

When they arrived at the Gare du Nord in Paris, Rosine and Joseph Wemheuer were met by Robert Aylé, Frédéric de Jongh's right-hand man. They followed Aylé through the bustling station, down a few narrow streets, and into a café where Frédéric de Jongh was holding a table for them.

"The luncheon we had was really quite sumptuous," remembered Alfie Martin, who made the same journey as Wemheuer a week later. "Roast beef, asparagus, potatoes, cherries, and the usual red wine." As they ate, de Jongh asked Wemheuer for his name, home address, and serial number, which he copied into a notebook.[43]

When the meal ended, Joseph Wemheuer left the café with a new guide. He spent the next few days in an apartment near the Eiffel Tower, then took an overnight train to Bordeaux with a small group of evaders. Together, they hiked over the Pyrenees into Spain with the help of Basque mountain guides who knew their way through the narrow gullies and steep slopes. Even in early summer, the crossing was arduous. "Do not attempt to cross Pyrenees unless you are physically fit," Wemheuer told his debriefers. He arrived safely in England on June 17, 1943, thirty-five days after his plane exploded.[44]

Meanwhile, Rosine went home to Arras. She had a single day to rest before Eugène D'Hallendre showed up at her door with another mission. This one was slightly different. Usually, D'Hallendre brought evaders to Rosine's door, but this time, he brought her along to fetch Alfie Martin from an isolated farm. As the new head of OCM's northern escape section, D'Hallendre was training Rosine to take on more responsibility. She did not hesitate. A few hours later, she was jostling down a country road in a horse-drawn cart, bringing another airman one step closer to home.[45]

The relentlessness of Rosine's work took a toll on her health. Sleepless nights and constant travel showed in the lines of her face, and she was plagued by painful boils. In June, she sent a photo of herself to Bert, who was shocked by the change in her appearance.

"My love you look very nice in your frock," Bert wrote, "but my love you look worry + you are a bag of bones, for the love of yourself + me dont worry + look after yourself."[46]

By the time Bert expressed his dismay, Rosine's situation had gone from bad to worse. On May 30, she delivered Alfie Martin and Doug Hoehn to Frédéric de Jongh in Paris, not realizing that it would be the last time she would see the Comet Line chief. A week later, on June 7, an undercover Gestapo agent named Jacques Desoubrie alias Masson sprung a trap. Desoubrie spent months establishing himself as a reliable guide, then asked Frédéric de Jongh to bring extra guides to the Gare du Nord to help with an unusually large group of evaders. When Desoubrie stepped off the train, Gestapo agents swarmed. They arrested Frédéric de Jongh and Robert Aylé, along with several other experienced Comet operatives.[47]

In safe houses across Paris, Comet Line volunteers went to ground again. Some sent their evaders to Bordeaux, while others handed them off to other Resistance networks. One of Rosine's airmen, RAF radio operator Charlie Saville, was shuffled from one dead-end Paris safe house to another for more than a month. His evasion ended in tragedy when his young host, Pierre Marx, was gunned down by French gendarmes in a Paris metro station. Saville was captured and sent to Stalag Luft IVb.[48]

~

The loss of Frédéric de Jongh, Robert Aylé, and so many other operatives in Paris was a terrible blow, but the attack that struck Rosine Witton and the rest of Eugène D'Hallendre's group came from an entirely different direction.

On July 17, 1943, the Arras branch of OCM executed a Nazi double agent who had been working within their ranks. The Gestapo hit back very hard.[49]

At dawn on July 20, Gestapo agents surrounded Eugène D'Hallendre's house in La Madeleine. They were led by SS-Rottenführer Kurt Kohl, the much-feared chief of the Gestapo's Resistance-busting operation in the Lille area. When Kohl pounded on the door, Eugène D'Hallendre told his son, Edgard, to run. It was too late. Soldiers had already gone around the back of the house. Soon, they were inside, manhandling the family and tearing apart the furniture. Kohl slapped Eugène D'Hallendre and slammed him against a wall while Lucienne shouted in protest. Edgard tried to calm his mother "so as not to excite the anger of the police." The whole family was arrested.[50]

The D'Hallendres were far from alone. Across the Pas-de-Calais and Nord departments, the Nazis arrested at least eighty OCM operatives on July 20, 1943. Nearly two dozen of them were in Arras, including Dr. Henri Artisson and Fernand Lobbedez, the city's mayor. Dr. Paul Cuallacci, who had sent Joseph Wemheuer to Arras from Frévent, was arrested, as was Paul Lisfranc, who had helped Eugène D'Hallendre move Arthur Cox to Lille. Within a matter of hours, most of Rosine's close contacts—and quite a few of Bob Armstrong's—were in Gestapo hands.

Rosine heard the terrible news from Madeleine Didier, who came flying up the street to warn her. It was only a matter of time before the Gestapo came for them as well. Unfortunately, the two jelly-making aviators, Canadian Spitfire pilot Kenneth Windsor and English Typhoon pilot Robert Barckley, were still hiding at the Didiers' house. Worse, Rosine was expecting three more airmen who were already on their way to Arras with Henriette Balesi, a fifty-four-year-old nurse who had been part of Edith Cavell's escape network in the previous war. Rosine needed to move them all as soon as possible.

"You don't dare sleep at home tonight," Madeleine Didier told Rosine.[51]

Rosine agreed. She spent a nerve-shattering night with the Didiers, waiting for the early morning train to take Windsor and Barckley to Paris. If Madame Balesi's airmen arrived before it departed, they could come along; if not, Rosine would return for them after Windsor and Barckley were safe.

In the event, there was a mix-up and Madame Balesi was not able to deliver her three evaders to Rosine before the morning train left on July 21. Probably on the advice of Arthur Richards, Balesi brought the airmen to the home of Marie Medlicott, wife of War Graves mechanic Harold

Medlicott, who lived at 195 Route de Bapaume. Marie had never been a safe-house keeper before, but she sheltered the three airmen with help from her daughters, nineteen-year-old Lillian and eleven-year old Evelyn.[52]

"Three soldiers stayed at M. Medlicott (British) . . . while the Germans were searching a house nearly opposite," Richards later testified. "We got them away safely."[53]

After a week with the Medlicotts, Madame Balesi moved the airmen— Henry Brown, Frederick Smooker, and David Macmillan—to the home of War Graves gardener William Bailey in Bapaume. William Bailey was interned, as were his wife, Sylvie Goedgezelschap, and their twenty-one-year-old son, Pupil Gardener George Bailey, but Sylvie's sister, Madeleine Declercq, had keys to their house.

Madeleine Declercq was also a member of the War Graves community. She was not legally married to War Graves gardener Percy Eely, but she and her son lived with him before the war. Some of her evaders knew her as "Madame Eley," while others described her as a "Belgian French lady married to an Englishman—husband in UK." Madeleine Declercq used her sister's house to shelter Brown, Smooker, and Macmillan for three weeks and later housed another dozen evaders there.[54]

While her War Graves neighbors rose to meet the emergency, Rosine Witton wrote one last letter to Bert. It was dated July 21, 1943. Perhaps she wrote it in the predawn hours at the Didiers' house or on the train later that morning or from a café in Paris. The letter does not survive, but Bert's reply does. Rosine must have told him that she was ill, hoping that he would understand that something was badly wrong.

"My love, got yours of the 21st July," Bert wrote. "Very sorry about your illness. All I wish is that I was with you. Don't worry about me my love look after yourself + get well + lets hope it won't be long . . . you are all I have got that counts so my darling don't worry me."[55]

Madeleine Didier accompanied Rosine to Paris on July 21 and returned to Arras the same day, but Rosine took Windsor and Barckley all the way to Bordeaux. The 900-mile round trip took four days. Rosine must have spent much of it wondering whether she should go back to Arras to fetch Madame Balesi's airmen. Despite the obvious danger, she returned.

Rosine returned to Arras on July 24. No sooner had she stepped off the train than three different people hissed warnings to her. The Nazis had arrested Emile and Madeleine Didier earlier that morning.

"Don't go to your house," whispered Huguette Lobbedez, the mayor's daughter, who lived on Route de Bapaume. "The Germans are there."[56]

In Resistance parlance, Rosine Witton was *brulée*: burnt. The Nazis knew who she was and where she lived and would probably have more details very soon.

Rosine slipped through the closing net. She abandoned her home, leaving her hens and the white lace curtains and thirty-three jars of fresh currant jelly. The safest course would have been to take the train directly back to Bordeaux and tag along with a party of evaders going over the Pyrenees. Other escape line operatives had escaped that way.

Instead, Rosine went to Paris. There, she offered her services to Jean-François Nothomb alias Franco, the young Belgian leader who was knitting the Comet Line back together yet again. Nothomb welcomed her, knowing that the frayed network would need experienced guides. Rosine was one of the best still standing.

∽

Rosine took a new name, Rolande, and a new role. For six months, from August 1943 until January 1944, she was a full-time Comet Line operative.[57]

Rosine no longer had a home or a respectable life to use as a cover. Instead, she lived on the trains. Each week—sometimes two or three times—Rosine made the trip from Paris to Bordeaux. She usually escorted two evaders at a time and often supervised a junior guide who was watching over two more. "I always verified convoys with Madame Witton," testified Marcelle Douard, one of the new guides. In Bordeaux, Rosine and Marcelle "passed their clients over to Nothomb and his deputy, Marcel Roger alias Max, who waited for them at the station disguised as Basques."[58]

When she was not shuttling airmen to Bordeaux, Rosine "used to go and fetch air men all round France." Most of her pickups were in the northeast—Corbie, Amiens, Beauvais, Rouen—but she traveled farther afield as well.

She also guided French *résistants* who needed to make a quick getaway. In one case, she had to be very firm with a French man who wanted to be exfiltrated but refused to abide by Comet Line rules. "He could have taken our organization down by his imprudence," Rosine testified in a postwar tribunal. "I myself had to order him to remove this [unauthorized] person who was still with him the day I was to accompany him for departure."[59]

When Rosine did spend a night or two in Paris, she crashed at the Comet Line's new headquarters, an apartment on the fifth floor of 25 rue de Longchamp, just across the Seine from the Eiffel Tower. Nothomb sometimes stayed at the apartment too, as did Jacques Le Grelle alias

Jerome, a British MI9 agent who would later remember Rosine as a guide who worked with "unfailing dedication" in the fall of 1943. Berthe Henocq Roger, the mother of Nothomb's assistant, Max Roger, frequently cooked for the inhabitants of the apartment. When Madame Roger was asked after the war to name the Comet Line operatives whose work she could personally attest, she named five people: Frédéric de Jongh, Jean-François Nothomb, Jacques Le Grelle, Elvire Morelle, and Rosine Witton.[60]

When time allowed, Rosine liked to meet her evaders at a playground on the Seine and treat them to a meal before the twelve-hour train ride to Bordeaux.

"She took us to a little restaurant as you see in Soho," remembered RAF pilot Dennis Hornsey, who recalled the Vienna cutlets, the soup, and Rosine's worries about seeing Bert again someday.[61]

"'He will find me changed,' she said dolefully."

Despite this brief moment of gloom, Hornsey's overall impression of Rosine was one of dauntless aplomb. She smoked placidly with Jacques Le Grelle, navigated a train platform teeming with Nazis, and "contrived to look fresh as a daisy when we arrived, despite the journey, which she did three times a week and never with a holiday break."[62]

Evaders who knew Rosine's name reported it in many variations—Whitman, Wilton, Wheaton—but most of the men she guided in Paris knew her only by sight. Some, like B-17 pilot Frank Claytor, provided enough detail in their reports to identify Rosine: "a lady (35 years old, English husband now P/W, spoke fluent English)." Others offer only fleeting glimpses. Short, dark-haired women bound for Bordeaux flit in and out of their escape and evasion reports, too vague to distinguish definitively between Rosine Witton and Marcelle Douard.[63]

Rosine was doing crucial work, but she could no longer write to Bert. She was a fugitive, and the Nazis might trace the letters. In Ronville, someone—perhaps the Medlicotts or Berthe Fraser—must have continued to collect Rosine's mail because a handful of Bert's increasingly frantic letters survive.

"My love not yet news from you since yours of the 21st July," he wrote on August 25, a month after Rosine fled to Paris. "Pray my love what is the matter tell me my sweet good or bad I dont know what to think."

Rosine's final parcel arrived at Ilag VIII Tost in August 1943, several weeks after she escaped from Route de Bapaume. It contained some rancid chicken, three broken shells, and "seven good eggs."[64]

THE ACCUSED   **13**

Rosine Witton dodged arrest in July 1943, but time was running out for the other War Graves *résistants*. As the disaster of the July crackdown rippled across northern France, members of the War Graves community were swept away with their comrades. At least four of them were arrested between August and November 1943.

For those who survived their ordeal, testifying about it exacted an enormous psychic toll.

"My story would be interesting to you, but I have no wish to relate it more fully," wrote Lucy Hollingdale, a dressmaker from Houplines whose husband, Harry, worked for the War Graves Commission in the 1920s. "It is enough for me to have lived it, and believe me I do not spend a single good night. I always relive those horrors."[1]

Lucy Hollingdale was a longtime member of the Voix du Nord network. She worked mainly as a courier in the region around Armentières. As a British national by virtue of her marriage to Harry, Lucy was not supposed to travel more than five kilometers from home, but the Nazis ordered her to register with authorities in Lille, thirteen kilometers away, every Wednesday. After these mandatory check-ins, Lucy would stop at a local café to meet her Resistance contacts. Together, they would "make arrangement for the parachute to rescue them."[2]

Lucy rarely sheltered evaders in her own home, but she sometimes accompanied them to Arras, where she handed them over to Emile and Madeleine Didier, Rosine Witton's neighbors. More regularly, Lucy used her trusty bicycle to distribute supplies, deliver copies of *La Voix du Nord*,

rds and in conveying...from
'er
HALL
ed r

Mn.
NC
le.
it

enri
lied
e.SE

U

Lucy Hollingdale and the bicycle she
used to deliver supplies and copies of *La
Voix du Nord*. *Courtesy of the National
Archives and Records Administration
(United States), declassification authority
NND 745001*

er

n 1

we have a death certificate, offi
of the

DECLASSIFIED

Authority NND 745001

and collect intelligence that she passed up the chain. Once, Lucy handled "the plan of the German aerodrome of Vitry near Arras and Douai," which was subsequently "report[ed] to England." Whenever she could, she sabotaged infrastructure. "I use to cut all the german telephone communications every where I use to go," Lucy testified in 1946. "If they have know all what I have done they will have cut me to pieces."

On August 22, 1943, a month after the Didiers were arrested, Lucy Hollingdale was helping to care for six evaders. Among them were two Americans: William Middledorf and Francis Harkins. They were staying with Lucy's comrades, the Pouille family, in Armentières, but Lucy agreed to move them to her own home for a few days. Her plan was to make her usual deliveries during the day on August 22, then take the two Americans home with her to Houplines in the evening.[3]

That morning, Lucy pedaled a familiar route to deliver food to some Royal Air Force (RAF) evaders hiding in Verlinghem. She returned home around noon to "get my basket and bag ready" for her afternoon deliveries.

Suddenly, Lucy and Harry were surprised by a knock at the door. It was a German but not one Lucy recognized. He informed her that he was a member of the "secret police," probably the Geheime Feldpoleizei, though Lucy remembered him as "gestapo." The German policeman announced his intention to search the house. Lucy thought of the papers she had hidden so carefully—the names and addresses of dozens of airmen, the photographs she had kept as mementos—but she remained outwardly calm.

"I never lost my head," she remembered. [4]

At first, the policeman searched gingerly, but it did not take him long to notice that the Hollingdales displayed portraits of Winston Churchill and Franklin D. Roosevelt and kept both a Union Jack and an American flag.

"Then the war started."

The policeman confiscated the Hollingdales' identity cards and told them that they had ten minutes to prepare themselves for arrest. Then "he went out to tell the other gestapo who were waiting in the corner of the street."

Lucy knew she had to act quickly. She snatched a packet of incriminating documents from their hiding place and "put everything in the fire." Papers crackled in the stove, curling as the names and addresses of Lucy's airmen went up in smoke.

Moments later, the Germans returned in force. They stomped through the Hollingdales' parlor and emptied the drawers in the bedroom. To her horror, Lucy realized that two photographs had escaped the flames. Without a moment to spare, "I manage to eat them."[5]

The German police searched "every corner every where" but found nothing. The incriminating documents were reduced to ash or dissolving in Lucy's stomach, and the two American airmen were still safe at the Pouille house.

"God was with me all the time," Lucy later wrote to William Middledorf. "The same evening I was expected to take you to my home for a few days with Francis [Harkins] . . . if the gestapo have came in the evening and find you both in my place we will all have been shot."[6]

Frustrated by the lack of hard evidence against the Hollingdales, the Germans turned violent. In a "fearful struggle," two of them seized sixty-one-year-old Harry and began to beat him. Lucy watched in helpless horror as they drove one brutal blow after another into Harry's stomach, but she refused to answer any questions. The beating continued.

"My poor husband being struck down by truncheon blows and kicked and pummeled all over," Lucy remembered.[7]

The last time she saw Harry, he was lying on the floor of their home, unconscious. He died a few months later. It is not clear whether the initial beating did irreversible damage or whether he died from subsequent ill treatment.

Lucy Hollingdale survived to tell the story of her own torture.

"I have been beaten with a stick a poker a chair," she wrote in one wrenching account of her ordeal at a prison in Douai. "They strangle me, drag me by my legs, my head bing to the wall table every were." When Lucy fainted, her torturers would leave her alone until she revived, then stuff her mouth with rags so that she could not cry out. "Broken my tooth, burn my chest with a cigarette put my finger in the door drag me by my hair take my toe nail out . . . from my feet to my head I was all black and blood all over me all days long it was the torture."[8]

In later years, Lucy claimed that she admitted to some of her own minor crimes but did not betray her comrades. "I rather have been kill than to give any information or any soldier or member of the resistance to the German."

This may have been true, but not everyone was able to stay silent under torture. Lucy speculated that the Gestapo may have gotten her name from Madeleine Didier, or from former War Graves gardener and Farmer circuit member Jack Wood, or then again perhaps from a French woman from Douai. With so many *résistants* in Nazi custody, it was impossible to say for sure.[9]

All through September 1943 and into October, Lucy endured torture that scarred her body and preyed on her mind for the rest of her life. "I have been seven weeks in this terrible place," she wrote of the prison in Douai. "It was not better than Belsen."

It was a comparison based on firsthand experience. Lucy was deported to Germany in the spring of 1944 and spent the rest of the war being moved from one prison or concentration camp to another, including Bergen-Belsen. She believed that she was held in more than a dozen places before ending up at Waldheim, a notorious prison for political prisoners near Dresden.

After the war, Lucy shared a few specific memories from her captivity in Germany, like the time she was confined to a "black chamber" with no blanket for four days for breaking her spoon around Christmas 1944. But most of her retellings were meditations on starvation, grief, and her hatred of her captors.

"I should like to be in charge of a prison of all the gestapo," she told William Middledorf. "I certainly have not pity for them, for me they can all starve and died!"

Throughout her imprisonment and for the rest of her life, Lucy Hollingdale maintained a fierce pride in her Resistance work. "I must tell you the truth. I am glad of all what I have done. I know that I have save very many life." Her only regret was for her "poor husband," who "give his life . . . for all the American and British boys."

"I can say I have been very brave," Lucy wrote in testimony submitted to American military intelligence in 1946. "Doesn't matter *who* and *where, no one can have done more than me. Just as much, but not more.*"[10]

~

Eight days after Lucy and Harry Hollingdale were arrested, the Germans came for Irish War Graves gardener William O'Connor. He was arrested "by agents of the Gestapo at his place of work, the cemetery in Douai," on September 1, 1943.

William O'Connor and Lucy Hollingdale had worked together many times. Both of them delivered provisions for evaders and distributed copies of *La Voix du Nord*. After the war, Lucy was one of the people who submitted testimony about William's activities to French government investigators.

"On my honor, I attest that Mr. William O'Connor provided military information about the German troops and procured clothing for allied airmen," she wrote.

William also sabotaged telephone lines and transported revolvers, grenades, and plastic explosives for *La Voix du Nord*, though it is not clear whether he ever hid them in his cemeteries as Stephen Grady did. He may also have worked with Thomas Crowley, another Irish War Graves gardener in Douai, who was a friend of Bob Armstrong and sometimes assisted his colleague, Marcel Maillard, with Resistance work.

"Mr. O'Connor always demonstrated great francophile sentiments, and rendered service with real devotion," wrote Emilie Nisse, a local Resistance organizer in Douai who worked with both William and Lucy. "He always tried to help me and, on several occasions, transported arms and munitions."

William O'Connor was held in the same prison in Douai as Lucy Hollingdale and suffered many of the same tortures.

"Interrogations accompanied by beatings," says a terse note in his official French Resistance file. "Teeth broken."

After standing before a military tribunal in Arras, William O'Connor was given a relatively light sentence—one year plus time served—which suggests that the Germans did not have much hard evidence against him.

Certainly, they had no proof that he had ever handled guns and explosives for the Resistance. If they had, he would have faced a death sentence. Instead, O'Connor was deported to Germany in the last week of 1943.[11]

~

There are two distinct stories about the day Bob Armstrong was arrested.

One was a rumor that circulated among the War Graves internees in the summer of 1944. According to his fellow gardeners, Bob was "arrested 11th Nov. 1943 for striking a German who kicked flowers placed on our graves by French ladies."[12]

A more elaborate version of this tale specified that Bob was "on duty in the Cemetery," when he saw German Feldgendarmes "kicking wreaths from the grave of a recently buried Allied Airman." Seeing this desecration, Bob "promptly knocked down one of the German Police" and was subsequently arrested.[13]

It was an appealing story. The internees could imagine Bob Armstrong still standing at his post, selflessly defending "our graves" from the Nazis on the most sacred day in the War Graves calendar.

The kernel of this story came from Harold Maurice Hill, the released gardener from Le Quesnoy who occasionally went into Valenciennes to work with Bob. Hill wrote about Bob's arrest in a letter to his teenage son, Maurice, who was still interned with the other War Graves men. The tale may have grown in the telling, but that does not mean it was entirely false. November 1943 was the month when the people of Valenciennes defied the commandant's order and carpeted the graves of the Special Duties airmen at Saint-Roch with thousands of tributes. Tempers ran high. Bob Armstrong very well may have punched a Nazi.

The story of Bob Armstrong defending Allied graves may have been true, but it was not the whole truth. More likely, Bob was a late-falling domino in the disaster rippling outward from the arrests of the Organization civile et militaire (OCM) résistants in July 1943.

After the crackdown in July, the Gestapo had innumerable new leads to follow. The investigation was led by SS-Rottenführer Kurt Kohl, the agent who had personally arrested Eugène D'Hallendre. Kohl was a deeply committed Nazi who had a reputation for being both clever and cruel. The residents of coal-rich Lille called him "Charbon," French for "coal," though "kohl" meant "cabbage" in German. Sometimes, it seemed that he was everywhere at once, turning up in plain clothes in cafés to listen, making arrests, and torturing prisoners in the confiscated apartment he used as an office.[14]

In October, Kohl's investigation led him to Valentine Ployart, the safe-house keeper who had sheltered Arthur Cox and so many of Eugène D'Hallendre's other charges. Eugène D'Hallendre had kept many papers and taken many photos of Ployart and her airmen, one of which "was discovered by the Gestapo."[15] Unlike Rosine Witton, Valentine Ployart did not flee when D'Hallendre was arrested, possibly because she could not leave her young son, Guy. Kohl's men arrested her on October 28. Under harsh interrogation, Ployart confessed to assisting eight Allied airmen, including Arthur Cox, as well as various other French and Belgian fugitives.[16]

During the next few weeks, the Gestapo tracked down the other people who had helped Arthur Cox, one by one. On November 3, they arrested the schoolteacher, Marie-Therese Debrabant, in Frais-Marais. Next was Joseph Cornille, the teenage farmworker, who was arrested on November 10. It was only a matter of time before they reached Bob Armstrong. [17]

On November 25, 1943, Emmanuel Dossche, the French caretaker of Saint-Roch cemetery, received a summons from the local German commandant in Valenciennes. He was ordered "to present myself immediately accompanied by the British caretaker." Afraid for Bob's safety, Dossche went alone.

When he arrived at the local German headquarters, Dossche heard an interpreter murmur, "It's not him."

"It's not exactly you that I wanted to see," the German commander said, "but rather the British gardener who takes care of the English cemetery." He explained that the Red Cross had requested information about some of the British war graves and made a show of asking Dossche the particulars. When Dossche replied that he did not know, the officer instructed him "to send Bob to him."

"The trick was too heavy-handed," Dossche testified, "a transparent ploy."[18]

When he was allowed to leave, Dossche went directly to Bob. He had left the Penez family's house and was staying with Marcel Maillard in Wallers, near Douai, possibly because he really had assaulted a German soldier and was lying low. Dossche implored Bob to flee at once. Unfortunately, he did not listen. The next day, November 26, Bob presented himself to the Germans in Valenciennes, "thinking that this way he would be beyond suspicion."

Men working in the yard outside the German headquarters saw Bob go inside. When he emerged some time later, his tall, broad figure was flanked by guards. "He was in handcuffs," the French workmen said, "and his face was bleeding." The talk around Valenciennes was that Bob "resisted arrest and gave several of [the Germans] a very uncomfortable time." A few days later, someone reported seeing Bob loaded into the train bound for Loos, "still in handcuffs, having been beaten again and again, and closely guarded by four Germans."[19]

It was just the beginning of Bob's ordeal at the hands of the Nazis.

Bob was housed at Loos prison, but the Gestapo shuttled him to their headquarters in La Madeleine to be interrogated by Kurt Kohl. Handcuffed in the backseat of a car, Bob was driven to a pair of unremarkable yellow-brick apartment buildings on an ordinary middle-class street. The larger building on the left, Number 20 rue François de Badts, served as living quarters for the Gestapo officers; the smaller building on the right, Number 18, was five floors of modest apartments converted into offices. Between the buildings, a gated porte cochere opened to admit the Gestapo cars into a red-brick courtyard, walled on all sides and hidden from the street.[20]

When the car door slammed behind him, Bob was led down to the cellar of Number 18, ducking his head as he descended the narrow stairs. At the bottom, a warren of tiny, comfortless cells transformed the ordinary basement into a dungeon. Each cubbyhole had been fitted with an iron door, a brick seat, and a dim lamp that made it feel "like a photography lab." The ceiling was too low for Bob to stand. Through the ventilation holes in the door, he could hear other prisoners moaning, praying, sobbing, begging for water.[21]

Treatment at the Gestapo headquarters in La Madeleine varied. Some prisoners were fed to encourage them to talk; others were starved as punishment for silence. Some were ferried back and forth to Loos many times to throw them off balance; others were left in the dark with their dread for days. All were tormented by their fear of what would happen when the lock on their door clicked.

Eventually, the guards hauled Bob Armstrong back into the light. Blinking, he climbed the winding stairs to Kohl's office on the second floor, not knowing exactly what awaited him.

No document tells exactly what happened to Bob Armstrong in Kurt Kohl's office, but survivors who were arrested around the same time described their own experiences.

One of them was Alfred Delporte, the sixty-six-year-old mayor of Montay, who was arrested just three days after Bob. Delporte worked for a Resistance cell run by Eugène D'Hallendre's OCM colleague, Paul Lisfranc. His many duties included gathering intelligence, receiving and storing arms, and recruiting volunteers, but he was arrested for sheltering two airmen. One of them was RAF navigator Henry Brown, who would later be cared for by Madame Balesi, the Medlicott family, and Madeleine Declercq. Like Bob Armstrong, Delporte was interrogated by Kurt Kohl in his La Madeleine office in early December 1943.[22]

In the initial interrogation, Kohl beat Delporte "with club, feet and fist" while demanding a confession. When Delporte denied the accusations, Kohl had him returned to a cell at Loos for the night. The interrogation resumed at Kohl's office the next morning.

"Do you want to confess?" Kohl asked simply. "Yes or no."

"No," Delporte replied.

"Alright, we'll see this afternoon."

Kohl sent Delporte "back to the cell again, in the cellar," and let him sweat for several hours before summoning him again. This time, there was another man in the office: Maurice Thuru, the neighbor who had brought the two airmen to Delporte's house and later handed Henry Brown over to Madame Balesi. Thuru had already endured a terrible beating. At Kohl's prompting, he repeated his story of delivering airmen to Delporte's house.

When Delporte denied it again, Kohl sent both men into an adjoining room where they were "copiously beaten with clubs." Finally, with Thuru "supplicating me to confess," Delporte admitted to sheltering the evaders.

"Monsieur Thuru was martyrized more than I was," Delporte later testified. He did not blame Thuru for speaking "after the tortures he was forced to undergo." "I suffered them," Delporte wrote, "and I know what it means."[23]

Another OCM operative, Roger Vandervelde, testified that he received similar treatment at Kurt Kohl's hands after he was arrested on December 2, a week after Bob Armstrong. Vandevelde remembered that Kohl "beat me with a blackjack, with a baton, with his boot and with his fist." Another Gestapo agent, Hermann Schraeder, also joined in, hitting Vandevelde with "a marble skull that was in his office." Schraeder also "wore a large ring, which was particularly injuring." Still, it was Kohl who "subjected me to the worst tortures." After eight days of interrogation, Vandevelde was rendered "unrecognizable from the blows." When he could resist no longer, Kohl presented him with a written statement and told him to sign.[24]

Bob Armstrong signed a similar document. It was written entirely in German, which he could not read.

Kurt Kohl may have extracted a confession from Bob Armstrong, but the official charges show that Bob revealed precious little information. He was accused of "acting to abet the hostile force in a war against the Reich" by aiding Arthur Cox, but that was all. There was nothing about Libéra-tion Nord, nothing about the Bureau d'Operations Aériennes, nothing about Gaston Lepine's secret transmitters or Emmanuel Dossche's radio messages or any of the many other secrets Bob knew. The fact that Bob was tried only for helping Arthur Cox means that he blocked the flow of damage before it spilled over to his friends in Valenciennes.

In fact, Bob did not even give up Arthur Cox's full name. The trial documents refer to the American airman only as "Arthur," which suggests that the prosecutors were relying on partial information provided by Val-entine Ployart. In her own confession, Valentine referred to her airmen by single names like "Bill" or "Wilson." The Nazis also had a photograph of Cox, probably one of the many taken by Eugène D'Hallendre in which Cox was wearing Bob Armstrong's coat. Given the circumstances, it may have been impossible for Bob to deny that he had helped "Arthur," but he did not volunteer additional information.[25]

Winter came. Bob Armstrong and his comrades spent months in the frigid cells at Loos, nursing their wounds and clutching their resolve. Valentine Ployart and Marie-Therese Debrabant wrote letters to their children. Zeph Cornille made a checkerboard to pass the time with his cellmates and hummed "Au bar de l'escadrille" until he wore out their last nerve.[26] Bob tried to attract the attention of the Irish Legation in Vichy.

The news that filtered through from the outside was almost all bad. The Gestapo had finally broken the Sylvestre-Farmer circuit, which had done such excellent sabotage work around Lille. SOE agent Michael Trotobas was killed in a shootout on November 27, the day after Bob was arrested. Lieutenant Olivier and several close contacts were captured by the Ge-stapo. Information that trickled back to England informed SOE that "a Scotswoman who belonged to the group"—Berthe Fraser—had escaped and was in hiding. SOE ordered that Berthe should "be brought back to this country by any means possible," but they were never able to extract her. She was arrested on February 18, 1944, and sentenced to death.[27]

Trotobas's death and the collapse of the Farmer circuit staggered the Resistance in the north, but it was only one terrible blow among many. On December 27, 1943, the Nazis executed Eugène D'Hallendre. He was shot along with Paul Lisfranc and two others at the Fort de Bondues, just north of Lille. An announcement in local newspapers proclaimed that the men had gathered arms and assisted evaders in "a revolution against the legitimate power in the country." Eugène D'Hallendre, polymath of the northern Resistance and Rosine Witton's dear friend, was buried in the fort's moat with sixty-seven other executed *résistants*.[28]

Over the next few months, many other Comet Line operatives met their own grisly fates. Frédéric de Jongh and Robert Aylé, who had treated Rosine and her airmen to lunch near the Gare du Nord, were shot together at Mont-Valerién, near Paris, on March 28, 1944. Emile and Madeleine Didier were deported on May 4, 1944, as was Dr. Henri Artisson, who had treated Gordon Crowther's broken ankle. All three were designated NN—*Nacht und Nebel*—a special category of prisoners who were condemned to vanish into the concentration camps without a trace. None of them survived.[29]

There was, however, one death that gave the prisoners at Loos hope.

"Sensational news," reported Robert Lefebvre, a priest who shared a cell with Zeph Cornille. "Kohl is dead. . . . This is not a rumor."

On December 29, 1943, a month after Bob Armstrong was arrested and just two days after Eugène D'Hallendre was executed, Kurt Kohl met a sudden and unexpected end.

That evening, he went with two fellow Gestapo agents to arrest a young communist *résistant* at a café in Lille. They were not expecting much trouble.

The Gestapo men made the initial arrest easily enough, but several of the man's comrades were hiding at the café as well. Cornered, one of the young *résistants* pulled a gun and fired. Kohl fell. A short, chaotic fight followed. By the time an ambulance arrived, Kohl was already dead. It hadn't been an organized assassination, just a lucky shot.[30]

When the news of Kohl's death reached Loos a few days later, the prisoners rejoiced. Men with broken fingers and women with broken arms celebrated in their cells along with those who had been hung by their wrists and beaten with Kohl's infamous blackjack or branded with his heated metal spikes.[31]

"I feel as though my chains are falling and I am delivered," wrote Robert Lefebvre. "Zeph joins me in my contentment because Kohl was his interrogator as well."

Kurt Kohl's death did not stop the Lille Gestapo, but it did throw a wrench into the legal cases against his victims. Without Kohl to testify at their trial, Bob Armstrong and his codefendants recanted the statements they had signed under duress.

"The accused . . . maintained their earlier statements only partially," the trial documents note. "A review of their statements was not possible because the interrogator, SS-Rottenführer Kohl, was killed on 29-12-1943 while on active service."[32]

Bob Armstrong's trial was held in a swastika-spangled courtroom in La Madeleine on May 3, 1944. He was tried with four codefendants: the safe-house keeper Valentine Ployart, the schoolteacher Marie Therese Debrabant, nineteen-year-old Joseph "Zeph" Cornille, and Marcel Maillard alias Mr. Lindsay.

Marie and Victoria Bajeux, who had sheltered Arthur Cox in their home for several months, were never arrested or tried. They may have gone into hiding.

Marie and Victoria escaped, but Marie's elderly mother, Léonie Maton Longatte, who had picked greens to feed Cox, played a significant—if passive—role in the defense. Madame Longatte died in April 1943, a few months after Arthur Cox left Douai. Since she was beyond harm, Bob Armstrong and his codefendants made her their scapegoat.[33]

"In the trial process, one had the impression that the accused want to put the blame as far as possible on the deceased Madame Longatte," commented the judge, Dr. Kurt Kalberlah.[34]

Bob Armstrong and his comrades were civilians, but they were tried by a Luftwaffe tribunal. They were allowed to have lawyers, though the judge dismissed most of their arguments.[35]

Still, the codefendants did their best to defend themselves without implicating one another. Valentine Ployart tried to minimize her confessions by testifying that she "acted purely of humane motives in the beginning" and continued her work only because she needed the money she received—1,000 to 2,000 francs per airman—to provide for her son. Marie-Therese Debrabant and Zeph Cornille testified that they did not realize that Arthur Cox was an American. They simply "had not given any thought to the origin and status of the fugitive." Marcel Maillard also played ignorant, saying that he accompanied Bob to meet Arthur Cox, "partially because of the friendship with Armstrong and partially because of curiosity to see the American."

When Bob's turn came, he admitted to a few specific details. He acknowledged that he spoke to Arthur Cox in English and recognized his American accent. Bob also conceded that "he gave 'Arthur' the winter coat that he was wearing." Most damningly, Bob admitted that he was the one who contacted Eugène D'Hallendre. Beyond that, he shielded his friends with silence.

In the end, the defense achieved only one success. Marcel Maillard was able to convince the judge that he was "a simple-minded man" who went along with Bob to gawk at the American but did not actually help him.

Since his codefendants refused to testify against him, Maillard was acquitted "for lack of evidence."

The other four were not so fortunate.

"Even if the accused Debrabant and Cornille acted out of pity and Armstrong out of comradely feelings, this does not justify the view that they can be sentenced to lifelong imprisonment," the judge wrote. "That is also out of the question in the case of the accused Ployart."

All four of them—Valentine Ployart, Marie Therese Debrabant, Joseph Cornille, and Bob Armstrong—were sentenced to death.

KZ-AUßENLAGER HOLLEISCHEN 14

R osine Witton stayed free longer than many of the other War
Graves *résistants*, but she could not outrun the Gestapo forever.
After six months on the Comet Line's Paris–Bordeaux route, the
end came on January 17, 1944.

The Germans had been watching Rosine all autumn. They had excellent intelligence from two different sources: Jacques Desoubrie alias
Masson, the Gestapo infiltrator who orchestrated the arrest of Frédéric
de Jongh in June 1943, and Maurice Grampin alias Henri Crampon, a
genuine Comet Line operative who turned double agent after the Gestapo
threatened his family. Together, the infiltrator and the betrayer provided
the Nazis with enough information to rip the heart out of the Comet Line
yet again.

In the early days of 1944, the head of the Comet Line, Jean-François
Nothomb alias Franco, presented Rosine with a new scheme that would
require her to work particularly closely with Grampin. "At the end of
January, we are going to do a marvelous job of work," he told her. "You
will be able to speak English galore."[1]

Nothomb had been working closely with British intelligence ever since
October 1943, when he traveled to Gibraltar to meet with MI9 agents
Donald Darling and Airey Neave. The civilian leaders of the Comet Line
had always protected their independence, but Nothomb accepted MI9
agent Jacques Le Grelle as a coleader and made other plans to share intelligence and assets with the British. Rosine Witton was one of those assets.

The plan, as Nothomb described it to Rosine, was for her to travel
south with Maurice Grampin to "serve as an interpreter between English
instructors and the maquis." Other English-speaking Comet Line opera-

tives, like the American Virginia d'Albert-Lake, did similar work later in 1944. Rather than sending evaders home, they helped them integrate into the armed Resistance, ready to fight when the D-Day invasion began.

Rosine was wary of any plan that forced her to work with Grampin. The double agent "left a very bad impression on her" to the point where she argued with Nothomb about him.[2] According to Rosine, Grampin was acting secretively and making significant "mistakes" like losing airmen on the Paris metro.

"Rolande, do not be afraid," Nothomb told her.

Rosine was not persuaded. She began siloing information away from Grampin, going so far as to "hide the departure times of the convoys from him."

In mid-January, Grampin traveled south, allegedly to "look for accommodation" for himself and Rosine. Nothomb was also away, in Spain. Rosine was on edge. Nothing felt right.

On January 15, 1944, Rosine was staying in the Comet Line apartment at 25 rue de Longchamp with Berthe Roger. Going out for the day, Rosine descended from the fifth floor, passing several men dressed as utility workers on her way out. Something about them spooked her. Rosine went back upstairs, only to find some of these "workers" fiddling with the electricity meter in the apartment.

"Maman, I forgot my purse," Rosine said to Madame Roger, hoping to excuse her abrupt return.

Eventually, the utility workers left. Rosine was able to convince herself that it was a false alarm. When Grampin returned from his trip the next day, January 16, Rosine did not tell him about the incident because she "could not trust him completely."

The Gestapo struck on January 17. According to Rosine, Grampin was taken first, around two o'clock in the afternoon. She blamed him for the subsequent arrests, telling friends that "he did not, as agreed in such circumstances, hold out for a few hours to allow the others to escape."

That evening, the Gestapo arrested many of the active Comet Line operatives in Paris, including Rosine Witton, her fellow guide Marcelle Douard, and the MI9 agent, Jacques Le Grelle. Jean-François Nothomb was still in Spain, so the Gestapo left an officer to wait for him at the rue de Longchamp apartment. Nothomb arrived home the next day, January 18. Despite "a sharp presentiment of danger," he rang the bell. The Gestapo officer answered.[3]

Rosine Witton never said much about what happened to her in the aftermath of her arrest. When she did describe those awful months, she tended to use the broadest possible strokes.

"I was arrested in Paris at the H.Q. of the Comete Line," Rosine wrote to Alfie Martin, the redheaded Irish navigator who stayed at her home with Doug Hoehn. "I was taken to a prison in Paris at Fresnes and after that sent to a concentration camp in Germany."[4] It is unclear whether Rosine was ever formally sentenced, but during a postwar tribunal in Lille, under oath as a witness, Rosine called herself "a former political deportee, condemned to death by the German Tribunal."[5]

Hundreds of other *résistants* were also sent to Fresnes prison in early 1944. Their experiences varied widely. Rosine may have been among those kept in solitary confinement or crowded into a flea-infested communal cell. She may have received Red Cross packages or not, may have been allowed out for exercise or not. She certainly heard her fellow prisoners singing "La Marseillaise" when their condemned comrades were led to out to be executed.[6]

Like other captured Comet Line operatives, Rosine was interrogated at the Gestapo headquarters on rue de Saussaies. She did not say much about that either, though she did later tell Eugène D'Hallendre's son, Edgard, that the interrogator asked whether Madame Roger was truly her mother. She had been right to suspect the utility workers.[7]

After three months at Fresnes, Rosine Witton was transferred to Romainville, a chilly old fortress on the outskirts of Paris where the Nazis assembled convoys of prisoners for deportation. Rosine was one of 417 women deported to Germany on April 18, 1944. The group included passionate communists and daughters of the French nobility, conscientious Catholics and Jewish saboteurs, teenage couriers and middle-aged civil servants. Some had worked as informants for SOE. Others organized labor strikes or distributed anti-fascist literature. There were at least four Comet Line operatives in the group, including Rosine and her colleague Marcelle Douard.[8]

Rosine and her fellow deportees were loaded into cattle cars at Pantin station in the northeastern suburbs of Paris. At first, the women shouted and pounded their feet every time the train slowed.

"We are going to Germany!" they called to startled onlookers at stations in Épernay and Metz.[9] They sang patriotic songs until they were hoarse and waved bits of cloth through the ventilation slits to let their compatriots know they were there.

"Do you understand?" asked Catherine Roux, a twenty-six-year-old Combat operative from Lyon. "We had to prove to the world that this hermetically sealed train concealed a human presence, hundreds of human beings, and not some anonymous or animal commodity."

Many of the women wrote messages to loved ones and shoved them through the slits "where normally cows put their noses." Yvonne Bridoux, a seventeen-year-old youth organizer arrested for handing out anti-Pétain pamphlets, scribbled a brief note informing her mother that she left France "with good morale." Jacqueline d'Alincourt, a twenty-five-year-old who worked for the Free French intelligence network, BCRA, managed to compose two longer letters. "Terrific morale: everyone all keyed up," she wrote to her family, "I am half out of voice for all the times I sang *La Marseillaise* and the *Chant des adieux*." Railway workers picked the bits of paper off the tracks and mailed them.

The mood dimmed when the train crossed into Germany. For four days and nights, the airless, stinking cars rolled east, then north toward the Baltic Sea. There was no food, no water, no room. "We had tinettes, small barrels to do our business," remembered Andrée Paté, a thirty-year-old communist organizer from Reims. Prisoners dozed against one another but could not really sleep. "I no longer had the slightest notion of time," recalled Jacqueline d'Alincourt, who was "barely conscious" when the train finally rumbled to a stop.

It was the middle of the night. Outside, a pine forest rustled in the pitch dark of a new moon.

"Silence," wrote Catherine Roux. "Sudden stillness. In the distance, a noise. Boots. Keys. Voice. A dancing red light. Clattering, padlocks, the scrape of metal."

"Hell really began when they opened the door," remembered Andrée Paté.

The violence was immediate. Black-clad SS guards armed with sub-machine guns screamed at the prisoners in German. Dogs lunged, "bug-eyed, drooling," barely restrained by their handlers.[10] Some of the French women fell from the train, unable to stand on swollen legs. Guards beat them with rifle butts. Scrambling to avoid the fangs and the blows, the prisoners formed ranks of five. Then they marched through the moonless night to the gates of Ravensbrück.

The French women had heard rumors about "the camps," but few had heard of Ravensbrück. It had opened in 1939 as a labor camp for German communists, Jehovah's Witnesses, sex workers, lesbians, and other women deemed "asocial" or threats to Nazi order. By the time Rosine Witton's transport arrived in April 1944, Ravensbrück had expanded far beyond its original purpose. Now, it housed Polish Resistance fighters, Czech anti-fascists, and women of the Soviet Red Army, along with Romani and Sinti women and political prisoners from across Europe. Jewish women of many nationalities were imprisoned at Ravensbrück, though it was not specifically a camp for Jews.[11]

On the night of their arrival, Rosine Witton and the other French prisoners stood outside the camp gates for hours, "frozen solid," kept in line by the snarling dogs.

"A lead weight fell on our shoulders," recalled Andrée Paté.

At dawn, the shivering women were finally admitted to Ravensbrück. They caught a brief glimpse of the *appellplatz*, where thousands of haggard, starving prisoners were assembled for the morning roll call. These "creatures" were "like nothing we had ever seen before . . . people who astonished us by their facial expression and emaciated state and who looked as if they were from another world."[12] Off to the left, the crematorium chimney towered over low-slung barracks.

The French prisoners were herded into a building where guards ordered them to strip naked. Every scrap of clothing was confiscated. So were the small keepsakes—books, letters, rosaries, wedding rings—that many had saved through their previous travails. "They root out any little souvenir," lamented Jacqueline d'Alincourt, "anything that can link us to our existence as human beings."[13]

Naked and bereft, Rosine Witton and the others shuffled past prisoner-barbers who grabbed them at random and shaved their heads. Not all of the prisoners were shorn, but all were subjected to brutal, public medical examinations that included having their vaginas probed for hidden valuables. When they were finally shoved into the showers, they tried to avert their eyes from one another's nakedness.

Like all the others, Rosine donned the striped blue-and-gray dress of a concentration camp inmate. A red triangle marked her as a political prisoner. Beneath it, her registration number—35297—was stenciled in black. The numbers were sequential, meaning that Rosine was the 35,297th prisoner registered at Ravensbrück.

"We no longer had a name," recalled Jacqueline d'Alincourt. "I became number 35243." Andrée Paté was assigned "the number 35265, which I could never remember in German, another unconscious revolt." Rosine Witton was fifteen places in line behind Catherine Roux, who composed a poem:

After the entrance search
Ravensbrück, 23 April 1944

My God, I no longer have any more clothes upon my back,
I have no more shoes,
I have no more bag, no wallet, no pen.
I have no more name. I've been tagged 35282,
I have no more hair,
I have no more handkerchief,
I have no more the photos of Maman and my nephews,
I have no more the anthology where, each day in my cell at
Fresnes, I was learning a poem,
I have no more anything.
My skull, my body, my hands are bare.

The new arrivals spent the next three weeks in quarantine, where they watched the first of their comrades die from a minor infection. After quarantine, the survivors were integrated into the daily cruelties of Ravensbrück. They stood for hours in the cold at *appell*, slept three to a mattress seething with lice, and ate tiny portions of watery soup.

"You have no soap, you have no towel, you have no menstrual protection," recalled Yvonne Abbas, a twenty-two-year-old communist *résistante* from Pérenchies near Lille. "This was done to humiliate us because we were filthy, completely humiliated."[14] Soon, the malnourished prisoners stopped menstruating. Dysentery took over, transforming their barracks into sewers.

"Everything seemed calculated that the prisoners die without actually being killed,"[15] wrote Virginia d'Albert-Lake, the American Comet Line operative, who arrived at Ravensbrück a few months after Rosine. Every day, women died from exposure, starvation, or diseases like dysentery, typhus, and tuberculosis. Others were murdered more directly. Capricious SS guards punished minor infractions with lethal floggings. In the camp infirmary, Nazi doctors conducted gruesome medical experiments by amputating healthy limbs or injecting prisoners with bacteria to induce gangrene and tetanus. Ailing prisoners were routinely shot, poisoned, or gassed.[16]

Prisoners who were healthy enough to stand were put to work. Many of Ravensbrück's long-term inmates had jobs in the camp's workshops, where they wove cloth, made uniforms, or tended to daily tasks like cooking and carting away the dead. Others worked at a Siemens factory on-site, making electrical components for Nazi weapons. Rosine Witton and the other new arrivals did not have these semipermanent jobs. Instead, each morning, they were forced to stand naked in the "cattle market" to be selected for work details. This often meant hard labor outdoors, shoveling sand, hauling bricks, or pulling a massive stone roller to level the ground.

After a few weeks of this backbreaking labor, Rosine was selected for a different task. One of Ravensbrück's many sub-camps needed a fresh batch of slave laborers to work in a munitions factory. Rosine was among the 146 French prisoners chosen to fill the quota.[17]

Some of the women were glad to get away from the filth and misery of Ravensbrück. Others disagreed, arguing that "manufacturing weapons against our brothers is the worst suffering." A few of the women feigned illness to avoid being selected for munitions work. Jacqueline d'Alincourt simulated scabies by pricking her skin with a needle hundreds of times and rubbing the wounds with dirt. She stayed behind at Ravensbrück when Rosine and the others left on June 4.[18]

This time, the journey was not as cramped. There were fewer prisoners, and the armed guards riding in the cars allowed them to keep the doors partially open for ventilation. Fifty miles south of Ravensbrück, the prisoners gathered at the open doors, marveling as they passed through the bombed-out suburbs of Berlin.

The sight of the destruction left Catherine Roux's "heart blazing with joy."

"Such a vision compensates us for the tiny slices of bread, the watery soup, our plundered parcels, our destroyed letters, our enslavement. Go on, crumble, decay, suffer, cry, rot with gangrene, you accursed people!"[19]

After two days, the train stopped around midnight in a quiet evergreen forest in occupied Czechoslovakia, twenty miles from Plzeň. The Ravensbrück scene repeated—snarling dogs, shouting Germans, painful blows— but the prisoners were less surprised.

The new place was a small town called Holýšov by its Czech residents and Holleischen by the Germans who had annexed it as part of the Sudetenland in 1938. It was home to Metallwerke Holleischen, a munitions factory that supplied the Nazis with antiaircraft shells and ammunition for Luftwaffe fighter planes.

From the Holýšov station, Rosine and her fellow prisoners marched through the fairy-tale forest under a brilliant full moon. After three kilometers, they reached their new home: KZ-Außenlager Holleischen.[20]

The new camp was very different from Ravensbrück. Instead of rows of barracks, it was a square of farm buildings—a sturdy house, barns, a granary—arranged around an enclosed courtyard. The farm had once belonged to a family named Pičman, but they were arrested for opposing the German annexation. The Nazis put bars on the windows and strung electrified wire along the outer walls, transforming the farm into a camp for the French, Soviet, and Polish women who were used as slave labor at Metallwerke Holleischen. Rosine Witton's transport brought their number to 691.

The new arrivals shuffled through the gate, exhausted and apprehensive. Yet, when they climbed to the third floor of the granary, they were pleasantly surprised. The attic had been converted into an orderly refectory furnished with clean tables, earthenware plates, and metal spoons: "a miracle after the filthy bowls of Ravensbrück!" Equally miraculous was the hearty soup of soybeans and congealed fat waiting for them. The soup was no delicacy, but it was the best meal they had eaten since leaving France. For a few brief moments in the predawn gloom, the women rejoiced, their spoons "awakening a little concert of bells in the attic."[21]

It was three o'clock in the morning on June 6, 1944. As Rosine and her comrades ate their soup, American paratroopers were dropping behind German lines in Normandy, 700 miles due west of Holýšov. British soldiers were already standing firm on Pegasus Bridge. At their backs, the largest armada in the history of the world was carrying the Allied invasion force across the English Channel. The liberation of France was under way.[22]

Rosine Witton and the other Holleischen prisoners heard the news of D-Day from Czech civilians at the factory. At first, the French women were cautious. Their hopes had been dashed many times before. Yet, as the days went by and news of the invasion persisted, they allowed themselves to believe. Surely, they thought, they would be free by the time the weather turned cold.

They had no way of knowing that the war would drag on for another year and that their tiny sub-camp, hidden away in the Czech hills, would be among the last to be liberated.

The new French prisoners settled into life at Holleischen. The soup was never as good as it had been on the first night, and they were plagued by lice, but hope for the Allied advance buoyed their spirits. Rosine Witton received a new prisoner number: 50751. As at Ravensbrück, she wore her number under a red triangle on the sleeve of a blue-and-gray striped concentration camp uniform, but there was one addition. The Holleischen commandant, SS Oberscharführer Edmund Schmerze, hated the sight of the women's shaved heads, so he issued them kerchiefs in shades of light blue, yellow, and pink.[23]

Life at Holleischen was dominated by the munitions factory. Prisoners worked in twelve-hour shifts, alternating one week on the day shift

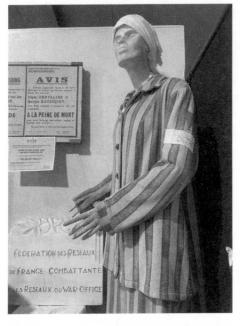

Rosine Witton's uniform from Holleischen, a subcamp of Ravensbrück and Flossenbürg. *Courtesy of Avril Williams*

and one on the night shift. The work was grueling, dangerous, and soul-crushing.

"Imagine the state of our morale in making these instruments to kill our own!" wrote Suzanne Agrapart, a thirty-six-year-old Gaullist *résistante* from Bar-le-Duc.[24]

At first, the prisoners considered refusing to work for the Luftwaffe, but the commandant crushed their mutterings with a simple threat: "There are enough walls at Holleischen to shoot you all."[25]

Instead, the prisoners engaged in small-scale sabotage. Sometimes, they worked slowly, deliberately failing to meet their daily quotas. Other times, they ran their machines on extreme settings so that they would overheat or wear out faster. Prisoners cut the timers in antiaircraft shells to varying lengths so that they would explode too early or too late and bent detonators so that they would not strike true.

When Neus Català, a twenty-nine-year-old Catalan communist, filled cartridges with gunpowder, she adulterated them with "flies, machine oil, and, if not, a good glob of spit." The forty-four-year-old Italian communist Teresa Noce devised a similar tactic, diluting sealant with saliva so that cartridges would not close properly.[26] Jeanne Bouteille, a twenty-three-year-old Alliance operative from the Loire Valley, was responsible for applying lacquer to finished shells. She would pass the same tray through her station multiple times, applying "a layer as thick as possible to use up more." Then she would polish the over-lacquered shells with a cloth soaked in acetone "to make them rust later and render them unfit for service."[27]

There was a test range at Metallwerke Holleischen where male prisoners tested random samples, but they could not catch every faulty shell. If the defects were subtle, they might pass unnoticed.

When a crate of shells did fail inspection, it was rerouted to kommando 119, the group where Rosine Witton worked. Her job was to unscrew the detonators and break the faulty shells into parts so they could be refitted or salvaged for components. A thirty-millimeter shell was about the size of an ear of corn and contained a charge powerful enough to destroy the engine of a B-17.

"It was very dangerous," Rosine later testified with her usual understatement.[28]

Since the shells they worked with were already defective, Rosine's group had to find other ways to resist. They worked as slowly as possible and ruined as many components as they could.

"Gunpowder was stored in crates in our workplace," recalled Marie "Betty" Desbat, a twenty-nine-year-old Alliance operative from Lyon who worked with Rosine in kommando 119. "The wood of the crates was very porous and sucked in water . . . when we cleaned up the workshop at the end of our shift, we poured water as close as possible to the gunpowder crates, and then, from this damp powder, more non-functional cartridges were produced."[29]

Between shifts at the factory, the prisoners kept up their morale by telling one another stories, imagining elaborate meals, and planning fanciful escapes. Some even dreamed of communicating the factory's location to Allied bombers. For a few weeks in the summer, the prisoners sang when they marched to work and back. When singing was forbidden, they whistled.[30]

A Soviet prisoner named Natacha made tiny hammer-and-sickle badges out of scrap metal for her communist comrades to wear under their clothing. When the Gaullist prisoners clamored for their own symbol, Natacha made miniature Crosses of Lorraine.[31] On International Women's Day, Teresa Noce gave a speech in the barracks about "what women around the world had done for freedom and progress." She selected examples that all of her fellow prisoners could be proud of, whatever their differences: Joan of Arc and Dr. Marie Skłodowska–Curie, Emmeline Pankhurst and Rosa Luxemburg, the Jacquerie Peasant's Revolt of 1358, and the Russian Revolution.[32]

Nothing bolstered morale like defiance. On July 14, Bastille Day, the French prisoners organized one of their boldest actions. They made small tricolor cockades out of salvaged cloth or paper scraps daubed with red, white, and blue paint. On July 13, the night-shift workers watched the clock, counting the minutes until midnight. When it struck, the French women stopped working, pinned their cockades to their striped uniforms, and stood to sing "La Marseillaise" in unison.

The German guards had gone to sleep, leaving a Czech foreman in charge overnight. By the time they were roused, the song was finished.[33]

"They lashed out with blows and threatened to use their machine guns," recalled Andreé Paté, but they did not follow through.

A few hours later, the day shift took over. Again, the French prisoners watched the clock, waiting for the stroke of nine. Then they donned their tricolor badges and sang.

This time, the German guards reacted immediately. They screamed and struck with whips and boots, "drunk with hateful fury." When the guards attempted to rip away their colors, some of the French prisoners "put our cockade in our mouth and swallow it." The day shift managed to sing only a few lines, but many of the women remembered it as one of the proudest moments of their lives.

"We, prisoners, unarmed, without help, alienated from our country; bound any day for the noose or the bullet, for the crematorium or the mass grave, with only our little cockades and a few lines of our song, on July 14, we took our Bastille all the same."[34]

A translator convinced the guards not to execute anyone for the Bastille Day protest, but Holleischen prisoners endured many other forms of violence. Beatings, head shavings, and punitively long roll calls were routine. The camp's first commandant, Edmund Schmerze, was a mercurial man who liked to force prisoners to their hands and knees to pick bits of straw from the crushed gravel of the courtyard. Several of the prisoners remembered an SS man they called "Totoche" who would choke prisoners with his bare hands until they lost consciousness. "He was servile toward his superiors and bestial toward the detainees," recalled Neus Català. "His hands and his whole body trembled with pleasure seeing us on the verge of strangulation."[35]

Holleischen had male guards drawn from both the Luftwaffe and the SS, along with female SS auxiliaries. Holleischen was a training facility for SS women, so it had both long-term staff and trainees who were there for a short course in cruelty. When they completed their training, these recruits were sent to oversee slave laborers in other factories and sub-camps.

After the war, several of the female guards at Holleischen were convicted of crimes against humanity and sentenced to prison terms of one to fifteen years.[36]

Nothing infuriated the Nazis as much as an escape. On September 13, 1944, three Polish prisoners—Stanislawa Świergoła, Anna Fabicki, and Irena Colewa—escaped from Holleischen by wriggling out a window. The next day, September 14, the entire camp was assembled in the court-yard. Guards brought out a table and tied down three French women: Noémi Suchet, Hélène Lignier, and Simone Michel-Lévy. Ostensibly, these three were being punished as saboteurs. It was true that their ma-chine had stopped for several hours on a recent night shift, but other prisoners saw little difference between this stoppage and any number of routine mechanical failures. Still, the three French women were punished cruelly. Each of them was beaten methodically with a thick stick, receiving twenty-five blows to the kidneys, while the rest of the camp watched.[37]

The prisoners thought that the punishment was over, but they were wrong. In April 1945, many months after the alleged sabotage, a death sentence came down from higher authorities. Suchet, Lignier, and Michel-Lévy were transferred to Flossenbürg, a nearby concentration camp that had taken over administration of Holleischen from Ravensbrück. They were hanged as saboteurs on April 13, 1945, a few days before Allied troops liberated Flossenbürg.[38]

Despite these horrors, the Holleischen prisoners were spared the grue-some catastrophe unfolding at Ravensbrück. By the autumn of 1944, the main camp was spinning out of control. The pace of arrivals soon out-stripped the camp's ability to feed, clothe, or house the prisoners. When Virginia d'Albert-Lake, the American Comet Line operative, arrived at Ravensbrück on August 22, 1944, she was assigned the number 57631, meaning that more than 22,000 women had been registered at the camp in the four months since Rosine Witton arrived in April. Ten days later, on September 1, Channel Islander Louisa Gould received number 62871, a difference of more than 5,000 prisoners in a week and a half.[39]

Ravensbrück ran out of uniforms, so the SS distributed stolen civilian clothes with large Xs marked on the front and back. It ran out of bunks, so prisoners slept in giant, overcrowded tents. There were not enough latrines, not enough water, not enough food. Eventually, the registration process broke down, meaning that hundreds or thousands of prisoners died without ever appearing on the official rolls. In the camp's final chaotic months, many were gassed or shot just to make room for more arrivals.

While an exact count is impossible, as many as 50,000 of the approximately 125,000 prisoners died.

Among the uncountable dead at Ravensbrück was Madeleine Didier, Rosine's neighbor from Route de Bapaume. According to her mother, ex-prisoners reported seeing Madeleine alive as late as April 1945, when Ravensbrück was disintegrating into a frenzy of pestilence and murder. No one was able to tell her mother exactly how she died.[40]

Holleischen was dismal, but its death rate was nothing like Ravens-brück's. Rosine Witton and her comrades slept indoors and had access to cold running water and functional latrines. They were crawling with lice and blue with cold, but the modest sanitary facilities curtailed the fatal epidemics that blazed through Ravensbrück. Prisoners at Holleischen still suffered from scarlet fever and dysentery, but, officially, there were only eleven deaths. This was certainly an undercount but not wildly far from the truth.[41] Of the 417 women deported from France in Rosine Witton's transport on April 18, 22 percent of those who remained at Ravensbrück died. The 146 women who were transferred to Holleischen all survived.[42]

Rosine Witton came close to being numbered among the dead. One day in October 1944, she was at her workstation, dismantling a case of defective antiaircraft shells. When the inevitable explosion came, the only surprise was that it was not in her own hands.

"A Polish woman working opposite me exploded the shell that she was unscrewing," Rosine explained. "The case of shells in front of her also exploded."

The Polish woman fell to the floor, "torn to pieces" by the shrapnel. Rosine also collapsed. She was hit in the right leg and feared that an artery had been severed. "I was losing blood profusely."[43]

Prisoners rushed to Rosine's aid, applying pressure to her wounds and screaming for help. Others attended the Polish woman. "She was gutted by the explosion of the anti-aircraft shell," recalled Jeanne Bouteille. "For an hour, she was in agony, one eye gouged out, writhing in pain and crying in Polish, 'My God, I won't see my children again!'" By the time someone tried to carry the mortally wounded prisoner to a civilian hospital, it was too late.[44]

Rosine was luckier. She may have been taken to a civilian hospital, but she may have been saved by the Red Army doctors who worked in the Holleischen infirmary. The Soviet prisoners stoutly maintained that they were soldiers, not civilians, and could not be forced to do war work. The SS allowed several of them to run the infirmary. Despite their best efforts, the Soviet doctors had neither equipment nor medicine, only beds lined with paper sheets that "were full of blood stains, pus, and excrement."[45]

Rosine Witton later explained that, after the explosion, "the shrapnel did not come out until three or four months later." She did not elaborate, but her timeline suggests that someone, perhaps the Soviet doctors, removed shell fragments from Rosine's leg in January or February 1945. Somehow, she survived.[46]

Around the time of Rosine's injury, life at Holleischen took a turn for the worse. In the wake of the September escapes, a more belligerent commandant, SS Hauptsturmführer Emil Fügner, was assigned to oversee the camp.[47]

"He was horrible, thin, scrawny, surly, and puffed up with pretentious foolishness," recalled Catherine Roux. The prisoners called him "the Rooster."

Fügner instituted a host of arbitrary rules. When the war news was bad, he flew into rages, forcing prisoners to stand for hours while he harangued them with "patriotic rants." He shaved their heads for minor infractions and screamed that he would transport them all to Auschwitz. Fügner's favorite threat soon became "the leitmotif of our daily life: 'You will be hanged!'"[48]

Winter brought new forms of punishment. In subzero temperatures, Fügner sent prisoners into the forest to dig anti-tank ditches, fell trees, and chip blocks of frigid stone from the ground.

"The stone was so frozen that our pickaxes bounced off the surface," wrote Jeanne Bouteille. "A blow that would have smashed the chest of a buffalo barely detached thin scales of rock." The prisoners stuffed their clogs with straw and wrapped their feet with "bits of paper and strips of wrinkled cloth," but it did little good. Nearly everyone suffered from frostbite.[49]

Despite the cold, some prisoners found comfort in the natural beauty of the woods. "The forest was beautiful and the path comforted me," remembered Andrée Paté, the communist organizer from Reims. Suzanne Agrapart found the ice-glazed forest "splendid and fantastical," even though the frozen ground tormented her feet. Others scoffed. "I refused to admit it," wrote Marie-Marguerite Michelin, a wealthy, fifty-year-old résistante who kept a secret journal. "The trees were poor, the light hard, missing the subtlety and mysterious charm of the Jura mountains." Still, even Michelin admitted that natural beauty lifted the prisoners' spirits. "We enjoyed clouds, sunlight, dawn and dusk. Sky and water, those were two joys the SS could not take from us."[50]

In early March 1945, as the pristine beauty of the winter woods gave way to mud, 402 Jewish women and girls arrived at Holleischen, pushing the camp's population over 1,000. Most of the new prisoners were Hungarian Jews between the ages of fourteen and twenty-five who had been separated from their families at Auschwitz and sent to a Siemens factory in Nuremberg. When the factory was bombed, the prisoners were moved to Holleischen.[51]

"They were walking corpses," Teresa Noce wrote. "There were many young girls among them, but they were so emaciated they were no longer distinguishable from the old."[52]

One of the youngest was Ruth Friedman Cohen, who was fourteen. "I had tuberculosis of the spine," Ruth recalled. "When we left to Holýšov, I started to work for a few weeks, and then I had to stop because I couldn't sit." Ruth Cohen was admitted to the squalid infirmary, but the rest of the Jewish prisoners were housed in a rickety sheep pen across the road from the Pičman farm.[53]

Spring was coming, but conditions at Holleischen were deteriorating fast. The Allied advances were disrupting transportation across Germany, cutting off shipments of components for the factory and basic supplies for the camp. Prisoners' rations were cut again and again.

"We were starving," Suzanne Agrapart wrote. "If this had lasted one month more, we would not have held on." Some prisoners lost forty pounds, others sixty or even eighty. In desperation, they chewed on raw roots, nettles, and dandelion greens. "We found slugs in the forest," recalled Andrée Paté, "which filled our stomachs a little."[54]

When the Jewish prisoners were sent to work in the fields, some tried to smuggle potatoes back to the camp. A pair of sisters were caught by the SS women. "They beat them and beat them, they beat them practically to death," testified Cecilie Klein-Pollack, a nineteen-year-old grocer's daughter. The guards ordered other prisoners to carry the lifeless sisters to Fügner's office. "We never saw them again," Cecilie recalled. "They finished them off." Cecilie had two potatoes concealed in her hood, but she slipped past the guards undetected.[55]

All the prisoners at Holleischen were starving. Many suffered from swollen legs and bleeding gums. Those who worked directly with chemicals at the factory had mottled, pitted skin "in addition to a thinness which for many became alarming." So many women had dysentery that it became impossible to keep the latrines clean.[56]

By April, malnourished prisoners began to die. Marie Lachivert, a thirty-three-year-old from Brittany, died at the end of the month. Officially, her cause of death was recorded as stomach cancer, though her fellow prisoners called it starvation or despair. "Black thoughts attack us," wrote Marie-Marguerite Michelin. "Perhaps if we had a couple of food parcels, a little sugar, or something else to eat, she could have left this place with us."[57]

Another casualty was Marthe Roch, a thirty-eight-year-old OCM operative from the Vosges mountains in eastern France. Marthe was unusual among the French prisoners because she was a Protestant. In order to ensure that she got the proper funeral rites, Marie-Marguerite Michelin asked Rosine Witton and Solange Hartmann to attend her body. "They are both Protestants," Michelin wrote in her journal. "I suggested that I would stay by her body at night, but Solange replied that it was completely unnecessary and not part of their tradition." Instead, Rosine and Solange "said a few simple prayers over Marthe's body, which was wrapped in a blanket and placed on a stretcher."[58] Then the three women read Psalm 130 together: "My soul waiteth for the Lord more than they that watch for the morning: I say, more than they that watch for the morning."

It was April 11, 1945. One hundred and fifty miles north of Holýšov, American troops were liberating Buchenwald. The Red Army was closing on Berlin. The Allied air forces, in total control of the sky, were finally turning their lethal attention toward Metallwerke Holleischen.

The next few weeks would be the most dangerous time in Rosine Witton's war.

"TELL BENNY WE MOST CERTAINLY HAVE NOT FORGOTTEN HIM" 15

D onald Rentschler's day started well. At the morning briefing, the twenty-five-year-old navigator from Indiana learned that today's mission would be a milk run, a short, easy hop into northern France to bomb a V-1 rocket site.

That was good news. For the past month, Rentschler and his crew had been flying long hauls into Germany to bomb heavily defended cities like Berlin and Bremen. They weren't eager for more. Just six days earlier, a mission to Hamburg had left their radio operator badly wounded and their trusty B-17, *Stump Jumper*, riddled with holes. The pilot, Lieutenant Clarence Jamison, had gotten them home to Kimbolton, but everyone was still a little jumpy.[1]

It was June 27, 1944, three weeks since D-Day. Allied ground forces were still fighting in the hedgerows of Normandy, where the Germans were making them pay dearly for every inch of ground.

At least the skies were relatively clear. The much-diminished Luftwaffe had pulled back most of its remaining fighters to defend German cities. American bombers still had to contend with flak in France, but air-to-air combat was less of a concern. Between the diminished fighter threat and a shortage of gunners at Kimbolton, Donald Rentschler's crew would be leaving one of their waist gunners behind, flying the June 27 mission as a crew of nine.[2]

The morning's good mood soured when Rentschler's crew learned that *Stump Jumper* was still out of action. While it was being repaired, they would fly in a finicky hulk called *Big Barn Smell*.[3] This was not welcome news. The men knew and loved *Stump Jumper*, which had seen them safely through five months of combat. They were used to its quirks. In contrast, *Big Barn Smell* was a stranger, unknown and untested.

While the pilot and copilot attended their own briefing, the other seven men ran through their pre-flight checks. Donald Rentschler and his best friend, bombardier 2nd Lieutenant George Rogers, prepared their cramped stations in the plane's plexiglass nose, bickering affectionately over which of them was truly the most essential member of the crew.[4]

When they were nearly ready to go, a truck pulled up alongside *Big Barn Smell*. Lieutenant Jamison and his copilot, 2nd Lieutenant Graham Sweet, hopped out, followed by a stranger. The man was tall and broad-shouldered, middle-aged, with the cocksure stance of a star athlete. In later years, the crew would disagree about his attire—Jamison remembered him wearing a flight jacket adorned with a single star; Rogers swore, somewhat implausibly, that he wore a "full dress uniform"—but they all agreed that he alighted among them as a demigod among mortals.[5]

He was Brigadier General Arthur W. Vanaman, the chief of intelligence for the entire Eighth Air Force. Today, he would be flying as an observer on *Big Barn Smell*.[6]

Arthur Vanaman had a long history of distinguished service. A trained engineer, he had volunteered to fly in World War I but never saw combat. During the interwar years, his leadership in engineering and procurement was crucial to the development of American airpower.[7]

In 1937, Vanaman went to Berlin as the U.S. air attaché to Nazi Germany. His job was to observe the development of the Luftwaffe and Germany's aviation industry. In Berlin, Vanaman met the Nazi high command, including Adolf Hitler and Hermann Göring, and formed close relationships with leading figures in German aviation. With their blessing, Vanaman toured aircraft factories and testing facilities. He flew his own personal Messerschmitt.

Vanaman remained in Berlin during the early years of the war but returned to the United States in 1941. In Washington, he became secretary of the Air Staff, working directly for the Air Corps commander, General Henry "Hap" Arnold. Vanaman held several other staff assignments, but he was keen to get into the fight. Finally, in May 1944, just a few weeks before D-Day, he arrived in England to serve under General Jimmy Doolittle as chief of intelligence for the Eighth Air Force.

As chief of intelligence, Vanaman was briefed on the Allies' most closely held secrets. This included Ultra, the critical British code-breaking program run out of Bletchley Park. The British high command had always kept Ultra close to the vest. Briefing General Vanaman was a profound gesture of trust between Allies.[8]

General Vanaman was more interested in gaining the respect of the Eighth Air Force's bomber crews than he was in safeguarding British secrets. Since arriving in England, Vanaman had covertly attended several ordinary mission briefings and was dismayed by what he saw. His intelligence officers were doing their jobs, but airmen frequently grumbled about being sent into combat by men who had never risked their own necks. Perhaps they had a point.

Determined to win them over, Vanaman made a resolution. "I would get enough [missions] to have a medal," he decided. That way, "when I talked to 'Joe Zilch' he could see that I had an air medal."[9]

In the European theater, bomber crewmen were awarded the Air Medal after flying five combat missions. Donald Rentschler had already completed twenty-four. Anyone who saw his blue-and-gold ribbon with its three oak leaf clusters—each representing five missions—knew that he had done his fair share.

Strictly speaking, General Vanaman's plan to fly with his men was against regulations. Officers who had been briefed on Ultra were forbidden to fly over enemy territory lest they fall into the Nazis' hands and reveal their secrets under interrogation.

Vanaman did not let rules stop him. He appealed to his commanding officer, noted maverick General Jimmy Doolittle. Doolittle was in on Ultra as well, but, like Vanaman, he believed that "the effect on morale of my being up there with my boys far outweighed the theoretical possibility of revealing intelligence information."[10] Vanaman pled his case. He would only go on milk runs. General Eisenhower and the rest of the Allied high command would never need to know.

By the time his jeep pulled up next to *Big Barn Smell* on June 27, Vanaman had already ridden along on two combat missions. He needed three more to qualify for his Air Medal.[11]

General Vanaman clambered out of the jeep and introduced himself to Donald Rentschler, George Rogers, and the others. They were more stunned than pleased. Anything that interrupted their routine was unsettling, and this was a whopper. They were already flying an unfamiliar plane, and now they had a general observing their every move. The sooner this mission was over, the better.[12]

Just before they climbed into the bomber, Donald Rentschler handed General Vanaman an escape kit. It was a pouch containing everything an airman needed to survive on the run: a compass, a silk map, emergency rations, benzedrine tablets to overcome fatigue, and a purse full of francs. The 379th Bomb Group's intelligence officer had briefed Vanaman on the basics of escape and evasion that morning, but no one really expected trouble.[13]

Vanaman thanked Rentschler for the kit. Then he hoisted himself through the hatch and crawled into the tiny nose compartment with Rentschler and Rogers. The space was barely large enough for the navigator and the bombardier, let alone an observer, but this was just a quick dash across the English Channel. They could squeeze in for a few hours.

Big Barn Smell took off from Kimbolton at five o'clock in the evening, flying lead position in the high squadron in a formation of fourteen B-17s. All went smoothly until they reached 10,000 feet and donned their oxygen masks. On previous missions, Jamison and Rogers had developed a tradition of singing "Down in the Valley" together over the intercom when they put their masks on. It was a comforting ritual. This time, however, there was no singing. The gunners called over the intercom, clamoring for their song, but Rogers did not reply.

"Maybe the general doesn't like 'Down in the Valley,'" Jamison thought.[14]

The formation straggled into France, only to find their target obscured by clouds. Not wanting to waste the trip, the lead bomber directed the others to drop their bombs on a convenient railway bridge. If they couldn't knock out a V-1 site, at least they could disrupt the German supply line into Normandy.

As they approached the bridge, black bursts of flak rattled the plane. The other B-17s dropped their bombs without difficulty, but something was wrong with *Big Barn Smell*. George Rogers tried to release the bombs on the first pass but failed. He tried again, muttering to himself that their milk run had certainly "clabbered up." Donald Rentschler looked nervously from his friend to General Vanaman, then took off his insulated gloves to help fiddle with the instruments.[15]

Then, disaster. An antiaircraft round hit the right wing of the plane, setting the #4 engine ablaze.

Rentschler couldn't see the fire, but he could hear his crewmates, who "got panicky and started screaming it on intercom."

Clarence Jamison barked at them all to calm down. Panic might be appropriate, but it was not helpful.

Out the right-hand window, Jamison could see a huge plume of flame erupting from the #4 engine, licking along the side of the bomber all the way to the tail. He knew that he had less than a minute before the plane and its 5,000 pounds of bombs blew them all to smithereens.

It was an easy call.

"Bail out!" Jamison rang the emergency jump bell once, twice, and shouted another voice command to his crew: "Bail out! Bail out!"

The copilot, Graham Sweet, was frozen in his seat. He did not respond to Jamison's order, so the pilot leaned over, seized his friend by the jacket, and shoved him toward the escape hatch. As Sweet disappeared, Jamison fought to keep the plane level long enough for the others to jump.

Below, in the crowded nose compartment, Donald Rentschler and George Rogers scrambled to help General Vanaman clip on his parachute. At the opposite end of the plane, the tail gunner, Sal Tomaselli, lost his oxygen mask and passed out. In the middle, the lone waist gunner, Eugene Bruce, was trapped by burning fuel streaming across his escape hatch.[16]

Rentschler and Rogers had a clear path to their own exit. They prompted Vanaman to jump first and then followed him out. Graham Sweet and the top turret gunner, Willie Neal, got out as well. That made five men in the plane and five men plummeting toward the ground.

The jump went badly from the start. George Rogers got caught in the plane's slipstream and slammed against the open bomb bay doors, breaking his jaw. The blow left him barely conscious as he struggled to deploy his parachute.

Donald Rentschler was not as badly injured as Rogers, but he had taken off his gloves in the plane. His fingers froze. As he tumbled through the open air, Rentschler rubbed his hands together, trying to thaw them enough to fumble with his ripcord.

"The ground looked an awfully long way away," he thought, but it was getting closer every second. At last, Rentschler was able to grasp the ripcord, and his parachute bloomed above him.[17]

General Vanaman had trouble as well. He waited too long to open his parachute and came down hard, crashing into a tree and injuring his back. Younger men might bounce back quickly, but Vanaman was slow to get up. Limping away from his crash site, he lay down in some nearby woods and covered himself with leaves in hopes of going unnoticed until dark.

Meanwhile, back aboard *Big Barn Smell*, Clarence Jamison was trying to make his own jump. The bucking, spinning plane tossed him into the air and left him "pinned to the roof of the pilot's compartment by the centrifugal force." Jamison fought to bring the bomber level again, knowing his time was running out. Then, shockingly, a voice called over the intercom.

"Hey! The fire's out!"

Jamison was gobsmacked. He thought he was the only man left aboard. If he had jumped, anyone left in the pilotless plane would have been doomed.

But was it true? Was the fire really out?

It was. The engine was still smoking, and black streaks showed where the flames had melted fuel lines and aileron cables, but *Big Barn Smell* was still in the air.

Incredulous, Jamison ordered the crew to report in. There were still five men aboard. General Vanaman was not among them.

Despite the damage, Jamison was able to wrestle back control of the plane. With mounting dread, he nursed it back to Kimbolton. Under normal circumstances, he would have been relieved to see the control tower—but not today.

"Tower, this is D dog," Jamison called over the radio, keeping his voice calm. "We have an engine out and request permission to land immediately."

An air traffic controller answered back: "D dog, you will have to circle and wait until the group has landed."

Again, Jamison requested permission to land but was denied a second time. He considered his next words carefully. He had to tell the truth, but he couldn't speak plainly over an unsecured channel.

Cautiously, he said, "Tower . . . this is the pilot and I am the only officer left on board."

"D dog, that's too bad."

Jamison waited. He knew they'd work it out eventually.

A few seconds later, his earphones vibrated away from his head.

"WHAT DID YOU SAY?"

"Maybe I should have jumped even after the fire had gone out," Jamison reflected later. "It might have been better than trying to explain why I came back minus one general."[18]

When *Big Barn Smell* landed, higher-ups whisked Jamison off to London for close questioning. His crew backed him up. It really had been a life-or-death emergency.

The squadron's engineering officer agreed. He documented seventeen counts of fire damage to *Big Barn Smell*'s #4 engine, fuel lines, controls, and large sections of skin.

"I don't see why it didn't blow up," the engineer told Jamison. "There isn't one chance in ten thousand they won't blow."[19]

Jamison took comfort in this assessment. He had made the right call, even if the fallout was potentially catastrophic.

Word spread quickly. The Allied high command was already on edge due to the slow rate of progress in Normandy, and news of General Vanaman's loss did not go over well.

"When Van went down, we thought we lost everything," recalled Major General Laurence Kuter, one of the air force's top staff officers and a delegate to the Yalta Conference. "He had all the highly classified stuff. He should have never, ever been there."[20]

It was too late to do anything except hope that Vanaman could somehow evade capture.

Unfortunately, General Vanaman was still not playing by the rules. Basic evasion tactics required airmen to move away from their landing site as quickly as possible and seek help from isolated civilians. They should avoid crowds and never, ever draw unnecessary attention to themselves.

Instead of following this advice, Vanaman hid close to his landing site. When dark fell, he attempted to steal a German Kübelwagen near the village of Lesboeufs.

"I found a bunch of jeeps—German—all covered up with brush," Vanaman recalled. "I was getting the brush off of it, and I felt a rifle in the middle of my back."

His captors were stumped. Their prisoner claimed to be an American brigadier general, but that seemed unlikely. Vanaman, who hid his knowledge of German, overheard a "crusty old sergeant" express his doubts: "He doesn't look like a general to me. He looks like a goddamned farmer that came from the barn."

Eventually, the Germans sent Vanaman to a hospital in Frankfurt. Under constant surveillance and desperate to keep his secrets, the general taped his own mouth shut at night so he would not talk in his sleep. During the day, he actively worked to wipe Ultra from his memory. "A lot of people would be skeptical that that could be done," Vanaman later reflected. But "when I came out of Germany I did not know and remember the code word 'Ultra.' It's funny what a man can do with his mind."[21]

Whether or not General Vanaman truly forgot about Ultra, he did not give it away. The Nazis never tortured him like they did Lucy Hollingdale or Bob Armstrong, who knew so much less and suffered so much more. Ultra remained a secret.

Brigadier General Arthur Vanaman was the highest-ranked American air force officer captured in World War II.[22] He was also the only man from *Big Barn Smell* who was caught.

～

Minutes after the jump, Donald Rentschler landed in a field of unripe wheat near Puisieux, just north of Beaumont-Hamel. He scrambled to hide his telltale parachute, then crouched down low in the grain to consider his options. He could make a break for cover or try to lie low until sunset, which was still at least three hours off. Neither seemed like a good idea.

Luckily, help arrived in the form of four French farmworkers who waded through the wheat and hauled Rentschler to his feet. One of them stripped off his own blue coveralls and boots, while another shoved a hoe into his hand. Then a farmer named Remy Delestré led the hastily disguised navigator to his home in Puisieux. Once safely indoors, Delestré motioned for Rentschler to stay inside while he raced off to Beaumont-Hamel for help.[23]

In half an hour, he returned with Ben Leech.

Donald Rentschler was thrilled to meet the "English gardener from [the] military cemetery," but there was no time to dawdle. Ben explained that the Germans had seen parachutes and were searching the nearby woods and villages for downed airmen. He promised to hide the young American somewhere safe.

The midsummer sun was still high at half past seven, when Ben Leech led Donald Rentschler out of Puisieux, through the tiny hamlet of Serre, and toward Serre Road Cemetery No. 2. They hurried past the headstones, bright with the roses that Ben had coaxed into bloom in spite of everything.

At the back of the cemetery, two snug stone toolhouses were tucked behind the open-air chapels. It was nearly impossible to see them from the road, especially with the back section of the cemetery overgrown as it was. Ben unlocked the southern shed and ushered the young American inside. "He said he would hide me in [the] cemetery while making contacts," Rentschler reported.[24]

That evening, German soldiers searched nearby houses and barns. They tromped through attics and cellars and peered into long-empty livestock stalls. In Puisieux, they tore up Remy Delestré's home but found no trace of an evader.

They never thought to look in the cemetery.

Donald Rentschler spent the next day and night at Serre Road No. 2. On the third day, the toolhouse door opened, and Ben Leech ushered in another airman. Rentschler was desperate for news of his crewmates, particularly his friend George Rogers, but the new arrival wasn't an American. He was Sergeant Kenneth Bulow, an English flight engineer whose Halifax had crashed near Foncquevillers, four miles north. Five of the

Toolhouse at Serre Road Cemetery No. 2. *Photo by author*

seven crew were killed in the crash, and a sixth was captured, but civilians smuggled Bulow past the Germans and into Ben Leech's hands.[25]

If Rentschler and Bulow had crashed in the summer of 1943 instead of 1944, they probably would have stayed only a few days in Beaumont-Hamel before being passed to Arthur Richards or Rosine Witton. But ever since D-Day, transportation across France was nearly impossible. The Germans were using every available train to rush troops and supplies to Normandy, while Resistance saboteurs ripped up tracks and Allied bombers demolished bridges. The old escape lines were finished.

Ben Leech did visit Arthur Richards in July 1944 to deliver a fistful of identity discs and pick up forged papers for his evaders, but they decided that it would be too risky to move the fugitives to Arras with the local Germans so riled up. The airmen's best bet was to hunker down and hope that the ground forces would hurry up and break out of Normandy.[26]

Donald Rentschler and Kenneth Bulow stayed in the toolhouse at Serre Road No. 2 for several days. Arthur Leech, age twelve, brought them food. Then, one night, his older brother Maurice escorted the airmen to "a more comfortable billet." Maurice Leech led Rentschler and Bulow over the fields to the nearby village of Mailly-Maillet and the home of thirty-two-year-old laborer René Muchembled.[27]

René Muchembled was one of the hundreds of French nationals who worked for the Imperial War Graves Commission before the war. Since he was French, Muchembled worked as causal laborer without benefits, and the Commission did not count him as one of their own. Reality on the ground was different. René Muchembled had worked in the cemeteries, forging personal connections with the other War Graves staff that lasted long after the Commission's contracts were dissolved.[28]

René Muchembled welcomed Maurice Leech, Donald Rentschler, and Kenneth Bulow into his home. The next day, he accompanied them to the nearby village of Acheux, where a family of Belgian bricklayers, the Aubrys, offered Rentschler and Bulow shelter in their barn.[29]

Maurice Leech and René Muchembled also gave Donald Rentschler the thing he wanted most: news about his friends.

Immediately after the June 27 jump, at the very moment when Ben Leech was escorting Rentschler to the toolhouse at Serre Road No. 2, Maurice Leech was helping George Rogers, who landed in a field south of Beaumont-Hamel. In addition to his broken jaw, Rogers had broken his foot when he hit the ground. He was fading in and out of consciousness. Maurice Leech and a group of other young men revived Rogers, who was too fuddled to stand, let alone run. They propped the battered bombardier on a bicycle and pushed him to a nearby farmhouse.[30]

After a few rapid relocations to outrun the German searchers, Rogers was delivered to Henri and Henriette Henon of Aveluy, who offered him one of the stranger hiding places on the Somme. Before the war, the Henons had been pioneers in the manufacture of luxury camper-trailers. Their business was on haitus for the duration, but they had a caravan hidden in the woods near Aveluy. George Rogers spent the next two months convalescing in a top-of-the-line camper with a hand-crafted, wood-paneled interior reminiscent of a sleek yacht. Despite numerous searches, the Germans never found him.[31]

Donald Rentschler was relieved to hear that his friend was safe. Graham Sweet and Willie Neal were alive as well, stashed in nearby villages. Maurice Leech and other civilians carried letters between the crew of *Big Barn Smell* so they could reassure one another that they were alright. Rogers's broken bones were healing well. He celebrated his twenty-first birthday in hiding, as did Willie Neal. Graham Sweet, restless, was planning a journey to Spain on foot.[32]

In the skies overhead, the Allied bombing campaign continued unabated. The Luftwaffe may have been weaker than ever, but the sheer number of Allied planes flying over northern France meant that there were more crashes in the summer of 1944 than in 1943. Ben Leech and his neighbors worked full-throttle to rescue the constant influx of new evaders.

It was a tremendous hardship. After five summers of occupation, the civilians of the Somme could barely feed their own children, let alone meet the appetites of healthy young airmen who were accustomed to hot meals and warm beds.

"The hardest was food and clothing for the US airmen who were very big," Maurice Leech remembered.

Marie Leech worked minor miracles to stretch the family's provisions, cutting their portions in half and extending meals with the potatoes, carrots, and cabbages she grew in her garden. She also slaughtered rabbits, which were much more attainable than black-market beef and pork.

"The airmen did not like rabbit," Maurice recalled, so Marie simply stopped telling them what they were eating. "They would eat it without knowing and ask for more and would swear they never ate rabbit."

Everyone in the Leech family pitched in to help the evaders. Marie fed them. Ben arranged shelter and fetched false identity papers from Arthur Richards. Maurice led them from one hideout to the next. The younger Leech children, Beatrice, Roland, and Arthur, carried messages and delivered food to the scattered hiding places because they "could pass more easily through the German surveillance."

Maurice Leech was eager to do more than just courier work. He had been champing at the bit to strike back at the Nazis ever since the massacres of civilian refugees in 1940. Like legions of other young men in France, Maurice supported the invasion by causing chaos behind the German lines. Along with René Muchembled, he snuck out at night on risky missions like pulling up railway tracks and filling German gas tanks with sand. Their group even had a few firearms, which they were trying to learn how to use.

Maurice's work was desperately dangerous, but he relished the chance to strike at the Nazis. "They were the invaders of France for the second time," he explained. "So we got together and became terrorists."[33]

Other War Graves children were also taking up arms. In Nieppe, Stephen Grady and his armed Resistance comrades prepared to hold a bridge against the Nazis once the retreat began. His younger brother, Kleber, made caltrops to scatter on the roads at night and puncture German tires.[34]

Meanwhile, Rosine Witton's neighbor, eighteen-year-old Harry Legg, marched south from Arras with the Communist Francs-Tireurs et Partisans. On June 28, 1944, the day after *Big Barn Smell*'s emergency, Harry was pinned down with two dozen other fighters in a barn near Aizecourt-le-Bas, about twenty miles southeast of Beaumont-Hamel. The Nazis soon overran the position, killing several partisans and capturing the rest. Harry Legg survived the firefight and the executions that followed, but he was deported to Germany on the infamous Train de Loos, the last train of deportees to leave northern France. It departed on September 1 as British troops fought to liberate Lille. Of the 872 deportees, only 284 survived. Harry Legg was not among them.[35]

Dozens of other War Graves youngsters returned home to France as members of the invasion force. Robert Witt, a gardener's son from Authuille, landed on Sword Beach with the 1st East Riding Yeomanry on D-Day and was killed in action the next day. George Hignett, the young gardener from Longueval, was badly wounded in fighting between Caen and Saint-Lô. Overhead, Jerry Eaton of Ypres, Danny Quinn of Poelcapelle, and Hilda Weller's brother Charles flew patrols with the Royal Air Force (RAF). Many others served as well, including gardeners' children whose fathers had died in German hands. Michael Flood's son, Louis, worked in air traffic control for the RAF. Charles M. Baker's son Albert served with the King's Regiment (Liverpool).[36]

At least two War Graves children served with the special forces. Plenty of British subjects spoke French, but the Special Operations Executive (SOE) was particularly interested in people like the War Graves children, who had lived in France all their lives and spoke unaccented Flemish or Ch'ti, the working-class patois of Picardy. They did not need to pretend to be locals.

"An agent's cover story is one of the most vital parts of his armour . . . he must be soaked in every detail of the character he has adopted," reflected SOE recruit Jack Evans, the son of gardener Watkin Evans, who grew up near Abbeville. "It was not necessary for me to go to such pains. All I had to do was be myself."[37]

Jack Evans was twenty years old when he completed the usual SOE training, but his instructors worried that he was "very young for his age." They had doubts about his ability to act independently in the field. Still, Evans was keen and well-liked and had "plenty of guts." He eventually found his niche as a member of No. 62 Commando, also called the Small Scale Raiding Force (SSRF), a group of about fifty commandos trained to carry out amphibious "pinprick" raids. Evans participated in several precise, amphibious missions in France. In 1943, he was sent to North Africa, where he was promoted to captain and commanded a joint Anglo-French special operations party. Jack Evans was captured after parachuting behind enemy lines in the spring of 1943 and spent the rest of the war at Stalag Luft III.[38]

Another War Graves child who became an SOE agent was Elaine Madden, the trilingual War Graves clerk's daughter who escaped via Dunkirk. She parachuted into Belgium in August 1944, a few months after her twenty-first birthday. In addition to gathering information on V-1 and V-2 rockets, Elaine was tasked with minding the fugitive Prince Charles of Belgium as he waited for rescue. Elaine was primarily a courier, but she did learn wireless operations in training, enciphering her messages with a personalized "code poem" that offered a meditation on remembrance:

> Sequestered from this noisy world
> Could I wear out this transitory being
> In peaceful contemplation
> Save the sacred monuments
> Over which the wings of centuries
> Have silently passed by

~

As the Allied invasion advanced farther into France, the Germans around Beaumont-Hamel lashed out at local civilians. In Aveluy, they tore apart the Henon family's home, threatening to shoot them if they did not cooperate. German soldiers also descended on the Aubry house, sending Donald Rentschler and Kenneth Bulow fleeing into the fields, where they hid for days at a time, surviving on chocolate bars from their escape kits and praying that their hosts would not pay the ultimate price for sheltering them.

Both the Henons and the Aubrys survived these raids, but not everyone did.

In mid-July, shortly after René Muchembled helped Maurice Leech move Rentschler and Bulow, Nazis descended on his house in Mailly-Maillet.[39] Accounts differ as to whether Muchembled was betrayed by an informant within the Resistance or tailed by an investigator, but the result was the same. The Germans stormed the house. They found Muchembled at home with his tenant, Charlotte Cauët, and a neighbor, Jules Guéant. They also found a submachine gun.

The Germans grabbed Cauët and Guéant, but Muchembled attempted to flee. He got as far as the hallway before they opened fire. Shot through the neck, René Muchembled bled to death on the floor of his own home.[40]

Muchembled's death sent shock waves through the community. He left behind heartbroken parents, an estranged widow, three young children, and an amateur Resistance network on the edge of panic. It was one thing to know that their work was dangerous and quite another to have one of their friends summarily executed. With Cauët and Guéant in Nazi custody, everyone worried about what they might say.[41]

"Someone in resistance caught nearby who had our names," Donald Rentschler reported. The Aubry family's barn was no longer safe.

If there were few safe houses available before, there were almost none now. The Germans were on high alert, and many potential helpers were badly spooked by René Muchembled's death. This left the evaders caught in a life-or-death shell game, constantly shuffling between ever more precarious hiding places.

With their options dwindling, Donald Rentschler and Kenneth Bulow went back to Ben Leech. This time, instead of taking them to the cemetery, Ben led the two airmen into the Newfoundland Memorial Park, where seventy-four acres of preserved World War I trenches still bristled with screw pickets and rusty strings of barbed wire. The park was a tangle of overgrown scrub and fallen branches, but for once, Ben Leech did not complain about the mess. It was the only place left to hide.

Ben entrusted Rentschler and Bulow to the protection of the bronze Newfoundland caribou with assurances that he would find them real shelter as soon as he could. According to Rentschler's escape and evasion report, Ben even mentioned that "he had contacts [who] could take us out of Arras on RAF plane comes in every 2 weeks."[42]

Rentschler and Bulow spent six nights in the Newfoundland trenches. No RAF rescue materialized, but Ben Leech made other plans. After a few more moves, the airmen ended up back in the toolhouse at Serre Road Cemetery No. 2.

This time, they stayed in the cemetery for a single night. Ben Leech had to keep them moving because he had another group coming in: Major George B. Simler of Johnstown, Pennsylvania, and three members of his B-26 crew, who had crashed near Doullens on July 8.

To make room for these new guests, Maurice Leech moved Donald Rentschler and Kenneth Bulow to a new location. He led them on a ten-mile hike to yet another node in the War Graves network: the home of Irma Demailly Palin.

Irma Palin was married to War Graves gardener Herbert Palin, a former London bus driver who had been interned since 1940. She was also one of the women Rosine Witton visited when she traveled to the villages south of Arras to check on her War Graves friends. In the summer of 1944, Ben Leech sent at least six airmen to Irma.[43]

Madame Palin kept Donald Rentschler and Kenneth Bulow for a few days until another neighbor, Renée Roussel, arrived with her coal-burning truck to drive them to Arras. The truck rattled and belched all the way through the city's southern suburbs, ending up at Arthur Richard's house, just a stone's throw away from Rosine Witton's old café.

Donald Rentschler's path followed a map that only the people on it could see. The invisible road from Serre Road Cemetery No. 2 to René Muchembled's house to the Newfoundland trenches to the threshold of the Coeur de Lion network traced the ties of friendship, family, and shared mission that bound the War Graves community to one another and to the wider French communities in which they lived. Unlike SOE agents who parachuted into occupied areas and attempted to blend in with the locals, the War Graves families already had long-standing relationships with their neighbors, their extended families, and one another. When war came, they did not build from scratch. Instead, they adapted their preexisting community into a resilient Resistance network.

∿

In the last days of August 1944, the Nazis deserted Beaumont-Hamel. There was not much fighting on the Somme this time. British tanks passed Beaumont-Hamel on September 1, then rolled on toward Arras. Everywhere, they were greeted with shouts of "Tommy!" and serenaded with "It's a Long Way to Tipperary."

At Loos prison, the British liberated hundreds of *résistants*, including Berthe Fraser, who was waiting in a solitary cell for her imminent execution. For six months, the Gestapo had tortured her with beatings and near drownings, bullying, and starvation. They stripped her naked in front of assembled German troops and flogged her, but she refused to give up her SOE comrades. Berthe reportedly broke her silence when British soldiers opened her cell, saying, "Thank you, boys. You're just in time."[44]

Northern France erupted in celebration. Donald Rentschler joined in, as did George Rogers, who helped the Henons paint a giant American flag on a sheet and hang it from their house in Aveluy.[45] Farther north, Graham Sweet and Willie Neal were among sixteen evaders being hidden by Josephine Heller, a Hungarian immigrant who coordinated a network of safe houses near Lille. On September 3, as the British routed the last Germans, all sixteen posed for a jubilant photo together. The airmen raised their hands in victory and shouted loud enough to alarm Madame Heller's tiny dog. Someone produced a bottle of champagne.[46]

Within days, the crew of *Big Barn Smell* returned to England. All four of them—Rentschler, Rogers, Sweet, and Neal—filed extensive escape and evasion reports that included written questionnaires and oral interviews detailing their experiences.

Donald Rentschler was interviewed by Captain Dorothy A. Smith, who jotted down the key details in her sprawling, chaotic handwriting. Rentschler told her all about Ben Leech and Serre Road No. 2 and the Newfoundland Park trenches. He spoke of Maurice Leech and the Aubry family and of René Muchembled's bereft parents in Mailly-Mallet. Captain Smith scribbled down every name Rentschler could remember.

Rentschler added more details on his questionnaire. He penciled in short, disjointed notes about George Rogers's broken jaw and Graham Sweet's desire to walk to Spain and the chocolate bars he shared with Kenneth Bulow.

There was one detail that eluded him, though: "A General (name unknown) who was a passenger with us was captured by the Germans."[47]

Willie Neal forgot Arthur Vanaman's name, too. "Observer—Brig. Gen. name unknown," he scribbled. George Rogers called him, "A Brig.

Liberated airmen, including Graham Sweet (middle row, right) and Willie Neal (middle row, third from left). *Photo by Ernest Heller; courtesy of Lona Sweet and Mary and Bruce Hancey*

Gen. 8th AF." It wasn't that they hadn't been introduced. Graham Sweet remembered that the general had been Van Something-or-other.

It just didn't stick in their minds.

Evaders' memories mattered. Their escape and evasion interviews were not just stories. They were official evidence.

Soon after the liberation of France, the British and American intelligence services devoted to escape and evasion, MI9 and MIS-X, set up offices in Paris. Their goal was to investigate the claims of civilians who had helped Allied evaders and to recommend appropriate compensation and medals for people who deserved them. The intelligence officers used many types of evidence to corroborate helpers' stories, but being named in an escape and evasion report was gold-standard proof. The airmen knew the difference between someone who had really done their bit and someone who was just along for the ride.

Most French helpers never received any official acknowledgment. Often, airmen simply did not know the names of civilians who guided them, kept a lookout, or gave up ration coupons to feed them. Donald Rentschler's report was typical. It named five specific helpers, including Ben and Maurice Leech, but made reference to at least a dozen others whose names Rentschler never knew. Most of his helpers, including Marie Leech and the younger children, went unnamed.

Not everyone wanted official recognition. Henriette Henon refused financial compensation from the United States for keeping George Rogers safe in the hidden camper.

"Mme Henon has no claim to present," her American intelligence file notes. "She explained that she was delighted to have helped the boy and outwitted the Boches."[48]

Other French families cherished the little official recognition they received. "We will keep this certificate religiously on behalf of our son, as a token of his bravery and as a memento for his children," wrote René Muchembled's grieving father. Equally welcome were the two American food parcels that arrived in 1948, when the impoverished family was still struggling to feed René's orphaned children.[49]

Ben Leech's American MIS-X file contains several handwritten letters and official reports, along with an exasperated internal memo: "Could someone visit this man, he is English and should at least have a food parcel or something."[50]

In one 1945 letter, Ben reflected on his motivations. He was a patriot, but he was also a father who knew what it was like to wait for his boy to come home from dangerous missions. "The little I did was only my duty as a Britisher and gave it willingly," Ben wrote. "I have been repaid to know that what little service I did render to these men has been greatly appreciated and gave a little joy to their parents."[51]

Finally, Ben's file contains a small, unsigned note, written in a broad hand that resembles Captain Smith's. Perhaps it was dictated by Donald Rentschler or one of the other evaders who hid in the cemetery toolhouse, a message to the man whose name they all remembered:

"Tell Benny—we most certainly have not forgotten him and that we love him dearly."

RETURN TO FRANCE   16

On September 15, 1944, two weeks after the liberation of Arras, the Swedish ship *Drottningholm* arrived in Liverpool carrying hundreds of former civilian internees. Among them were sixty-one members of the War Graves Commission's staff.[1]

They had not come directly from Ilag VIII. Nearly a year earlier, most of the War Graves internees had been transferred from Tost and Kreuzberg back to France. A few joined their interned wives and children at Vittel, but the majority went to Giromagny, near Belfort, about forty miles from the Swiss border. They spent the winter of 1943–1944 making recreational handicrafts, singing in the camp choir, and keeping a rock garden. This last was particularly useful for hiding dirt being excavated by a group of determined tunnelers. "Bucketsfull at a time were discreetly brought out and emptied," recalled Head Gardener Albert Roberts, who told the Germans he was building "a replica of the mountainside."[2]

One gardener did successfully escape from Giromagny though not through the tunnel. Canadian gardener Lewis Fulton Bonnell received a pair of wire cutters from a French electrician who was installing fixtures in the camp and used them to cut gaps in the barbed wire fences surrounding the camp. On November 28, 1943, sixteen men, including Bonnell, made a break for it. With the help of French civilians, fourteen made it across the Swiss border.

"We were wet to the skin, dirty, and hungry, but we did not even think of our physical condition," Bonnell reported. "The first reaction was jubilation."[3]

For most of the War Graves gardeners, liberation would have to wait. After half a year at Giromagny, the group was split in the spring of 1944.

Sixty-three War Graves men were sent to Sweden to be exchanged for German prisoners, while twenty-eight others were sent to another internment camp, Westertimke, in Germany. The Westertimke group—which included Wilfred Legg, Herbert Palin, and at least six gardeners' sons—would endure a fifth winter in dreadful conditions as Nazi Germany collapsed around them. But for the sixty-one War Graves employees repatriated by *Drottningholm* in September 1944, liberation had come at last.

When they stepped off the ship in Liverpool, the men received a welcome letter from Sir Fabian Ware.

"It is a great relief to us to know that you have recovered your freedom and we bid you a warm welcome," Sir Fabian wrote. He expressed "keen sympathy" for the "severe trials you have so patiently and courageously borne" as well as pride that the men "maintained an unbroken spirit."

"But I will not dwell on the past," Sir Fabian concluded. "You will from now onwards wish to look forward to the happier years which, as we all trust and believe, lie surely ahead."[4]

The gardeners were not quite as eager as Sir Fabian to forget about "the past." Commission officers who interviewed the men immediately after they disembarked reported that "there was some evidence that they had been debating whether to complain of neglect by the Commission during their internment." Yet the officers assured the higher-ups that the "warmth of their welcome" erased "any slight feeling they might have had that the Commission had not their interests entirely at heart." The cheerful report also downplayed the physical effects of internment. "Almost without exception," it said, "the men were in an excellent state of health."[5]

This was simply not true. The repatriated gardeners had a host of grievances, and many of them were seriously ill. Some would never be well again.

"I have had to received Medical attention since my Release," wrote gardener Albert Wellings, who reported that trouble with his lungs, stomach, and kidneys made it impossible for him to resume his work in the cemeteries immediately. Arthur Wilson, a gardener from Poix-du-Nord, was so severely underweight that a doctor put him on a medically supervised diet that allowed him to gain more than half a pound per day. When the Commission asked gardener Samuel Chapman whether he was ready to resume work in France, he replied, "I should deem it a favour if I am not recalled yet, as I should like to be fully fit before I return to France, after 4 years in German hands, one is not quite as one was before the invasion."[6]

The gardeners had not forgotten the resolutions they adopted at their meeting at Ilag VIII in October 1940. They were determined to demand both compensation and a full investigation into "the complete disappearance of all our leaders."[7]

Sir Fabian decided to address the issue of the evacuation head-on. On September 9, 1944, just as the men were leaving Sweden, he issued a short, formal statement. It assured all and sundry that the Commission's officers had all submitted detailed reports in 1940, which were "carefully gone into at the time." While the reports recounted "many instances of outstanding conduct," Sir Fabian conceded that "there were a few instances where the response to the emergency may not have been so effective." Even so, there could be no question of actual wrongdoing. Due to the "quite unprecedented demands upon differing temperaments, it was not considered that there was any case in which criticism would be justified." As far as the Commission was concerned, the case was already closed.[8]

The gardeners had more luck getting financial settlements.

Back in the spring of 1944, the Commission had appointed a special subcommittee to devise a financial plan that would head off any discontent among the gardeners. Sir Fabian planted his standard on the high ground. When it came to a settlement, the Commission had to consider "the moral aspect . . . not merely what was the legal view." Sir Herbert Ellissen of the Finance Committee was more practical. "It was important," Ellissen remarked, "for the Commission to be sure they were not giving less than what the men could legally enforce against them."[9]

The committee was led by J. J. Lawson, the Commission's resident Labour member of Parliament. It produced the "Lawson Report," which laid out a plan for paying out ex gratia settlements to all staff who had been stranded in occupied Europe whether they were interned or not.

The exact amount of each settlement was determined by calculating the employee's wages from May 1940 until his repatriation, then deducting any relief payments, wages, or allotments that had to be repaid to the U.K. government, Anciens Combattants, or the Commission itself. If any money was left after these reimbursements, the employee would receive the remainder as a lump sum.

The Lawson Scheme followed Treasury guidelines for compensating interned civil servants, but since it was strictly voluntary, the Commission was free to set its own rates. Rather than calculating the gardeners' settlements based on their actual 1940 wages, the Lawson Scheme set a flat rate of £3.5.0 per week for gardener-caretakers. This was less than the minimum weekly wage—£3.10.0—set by the 1938 Industrial Court decision, let alone the wages that most of the gardeners had achieved with their annual raises. The flat rate for head gardeners was a little higher but still not equal to their 1940 wages.

Under this formula, the final payouts varied widely. The standard settlement for a gardener-caretaker was £728, but the cash-in-hand amount depended on how much he had taken in relief payments. Some unmarried gardeners had drawn only a few pounds in pocket money during their time in the camps, while families trying to survive without their breadwinners often took £500 or more over four and a half years. After the reimbursements, the typical Lawson Scheme payout was around £400 or £450, between two and two and a half years' pay. Some payouts were larger, while a few were much, much smaller. Robert Mullenger, Ben Leech's neighbor in Beaumont-Hamel, received £5.6.10.[10]

The Commission also reserved the right to deny payment altogether. If an investigation found that a gardener had collaborated with the Germans or that his internment was "due to a refusal to comply with instructions given by the Commission," he would receive no money.

The Commission investigated several cases but withheld only a few settlements. Gardener John Thompson of Vlamertinghe was denied a Lawson Scheme settlement because he was arrested by British military authorities as a suspected collaborator. The Commission conceded that investigations by both the British army and the Belgian police "did not yield proof positive of specific acts of collaboration" but decided that retaining Thompson would "not be compatible with the interests of the Commission." They fired him and paid no settlement.[11]

Bernard Parsons, the stonecutter who had helped organize the War Graves men at Ilag VIII, also faced accusations of collaboration for volunteering to work outside the camp. Parsons denied the charge in a sharp letter to the Commission. It was true that he worked briefly at a gravestone manufacturer's shop, but he had explicit permission from the British camp captain to do so in order to make headstones for deceased internees.

"People who kept their morale high by work soon became the object of hatred and suspicion to the inactive elements who had nothing to do all day but brew their Red Cross tea and spread poisonous scandal," Parsons wrote. The Commission verified his account and paid out a full settlement.[12]

Most gardeners did receive Lawson Scheme settlements, but they had to wait a long time for the money. Unlike MI9 and MIS-X, which expedited compensation to returning deportees, the War Graves Commission took more than three years to send the final Lawson Scheme payments.

Some gardeners were able to get partial advances, but the bulk of the settlements were not disbursed until March 1948.[13]

Many gardeners thanked the Commission for the money, but others were dissatisfied. Albert Saville, a gardener from Loos, received the usual £728 less £114.1.7 in relief. Even though he received one of the largest cash payments of any gardener, Saville still felt that the Commission had not done enough.

"It was hard enough to be interned for over 4 years, and now it seems that I have to pay for being interned," he wrote. "It was no fault of mine that the Wife and myself was interned, and up to date the Wife has had no compensation."[14]

The destruction of the gardeners' personnel files makes it difficult to say how many of them were, like Saville, dissatisfied with the Commission's treatment. Some certainly were, though their recourse was limited. In at least one case, a family threatened to shame the Commission in public for what they saw as negligence toward the gardeners.

"I am very loath to call attention in the Press to this undoubted grievance," wrote Walter Weller in June 1944, a few months before his brother, Cyril, was repatriated. Cyril clearly considered his internment a direct consequence of the Commission's actions in 1940. In his letters, he "emphasised the fact that his last instructions from the War Graves Commission were to remain at his post, and this he faithfully complied with, and yet after 4 years' internment and being so long passed back for repatriation, he is still left behind."[15]

Plenty of other gardeners agreed that the Commission bore a share of the blame for their internment. Gardener Herbert Caswell, who had a "disability which precludes cycling," made it well known that he "blames I.W.G.C. Officials for failure to notify evacuation." Some were even threatening to appeal to the court of public opinion. Gardener John W. Oldman, who could not return to work after his internment because of chronic myocarditis, demanded compensation for his ruined health. "I was serving my country by remaining interned," Oldman wrote. The Commission appealed to the Treasury for guidance, noting that "if we definitely reject Oldman's plea it is practically certain to be brought up by him in a more public fashion." That might prove embarrassing. "In view of the disclosures of the conditions in various camps in Germany there will probably be a strong demand that people of this kind should be treated with exceptional generosity."[16]

One gardener who protested the only way he could was William C. Roberts of Morbecque. Roberts reached the United Kingdom safely in

1940, but he was separated from his wife, Virginie, and eighteen-year-old daughter, Paule, during the evacuation. The circumstances of the separation are murky, but Roberts "blamed I.W.G.C. officials for fact that wife and d[aughter] left behind." Both Virginie and Paule were interned. Paule was repatriated in September 1944, but Virginie died at Vittel. Furious with the Commission, Roberts quit and refused to "accept responsibility" for the £10 loan he received when he arrived in England.[17]

According a brief notation, Roberts's outrage was the "subject of much correspondence . . . see note on file." Unfortunately, the War Graves Commission destroyed Roberts's personnel file along with the rest. His protest was routinely and impersonally expunged from its archives.

~

Three weeks after *Drottningholm* docked in Liverpool, the first delegation of War Graves Commission officers returned to France.

This "advance party"—Major William Arnott, Major Andrew Macfarlane, and Captain Frank Grinham—spent months kitting themselves out for the expedition. Northern France was an active military zone, and there was still fighting nearby, so they expected rough conditions. Even so, the Commission officers expected to be able to rely on the army for rations and transport. They had received general list commissions back in 1939, so they were technically army officers even if they had no specific place within the Allied Expeditionary Force. The advance party informed General Eisenhower's headquarters that they planned to arrive in early October and received a prompt reply: the armed forces "do not want the I.W.G.C. personnel at present."[18]

Undeterred, the advance party landed at Gold Beach in Normandy on October 5, 1944, in battledress and good spirits. They had three main objectives: first, to "take early steps" toward reopening a Commission office in France, preferably in Arras; second, to gather information about the current state of the Commission's cemeteries and memorials; and, third, to investigate the resources—food, housing, military protection—available for returning War Graves staff.

Although the advance party was eager to commence their work, they spent the entire month of October kicking their heels as baffled transport officers declined to hand over a car. At the end of the month, the War Office finally sent over two cars and two Commission drivers, one of whom was Bert and Rosine Witton's neighbor, Harold Medlicott. He volunteered to return at once rather than taking more time to recover because he wanted to get back to Marie and the girls as quickly as possible.

Finally equipped with cars and people to operate them, Arnott, Mac-farlane, and Grinham set out to survey the damage.

It was not as bad as it could have been. A few cemeteries were in bad shape, like tiny Thiennes British Cemetery, which was "completely blown away" when a bomb missed the V-1 rocket launch site fifteen meters away, but most were unharmed.[19] There were thousands of broken and missing headstones across the region, superficial damage at the Menin Gate, and a few unfortunate bomb craters, but the Commission had feared much worse.

Some of the most serious damage was at the Australian Monument in Villers-Bretonneux. The memorial had been pummeled by shells and machine-gun fire in the battles of 1940. Afterward, French civilians had taken to scrawling anti-Nazi graffiti on the broad, white walls that listed the names of more than 10,000 missing Australians. At least once, the Nazis rounded up the local youth and made them scrub off the slogans, "some of which were offensive to the Huns." The Commission was not impressed by this repurposing of the monument as an anti-Nazi billboard. One inspector expressed outrage that French locals and British soldiers—"including one giving the rank of Captain!"—had besmirched the monument by carving their own names alongside the names of the dead. He recommended replacing nearly all the panels.[20]

The general condition of the cemeteries was better than the Commission had anticipated, but civilian life in liberated France was in a dreadful state. After more than four years of occupation, food was still ruinously expensive, clothes were impossible to find, and there was no fuel for the coming winter. Much of the consumer economy relied on bartering basic necessities.

"It is difficult adequately to emphasise how great is the lack of all consumer goods," Major Arnott reported. If the Commission wanted to send gardeners back to work, they would need to fully equip the men in England and provide them with food and shelter once they returned to France.

Of course, some gardeners were already in France. On November 10, 1944, the advance party arrived in Beaumont-Hamel. They found Ben Leech right where they had left him four and a half years earlier.

Ben had not spoken with a War Graves officer face-to-face since he left Edward Goad's house on May 17, 1940. Now he told Major Arnott a bit about what had happened to him since.

"Apparently owes his liberty to good offices of Mayor & to lenient German Kommandatur," Arnott reported. It wasn't a satisfying explanation for the unusual freedom of the three gardeners in Beaumont-Hamel, but no one could come up with a better answer.

Ben Leech was more concerned about his immediate needs. Like the other gardeners stranded in France, he was "practically destitute." His work clothes were a patchwork of rags, and he had spent the two months since the liberation "trying to get picked up" by the British army because "he was very short of food." When Major Arnott asked Ben what he needed, Ben said he wanted food. After that, clothing. Once they were fed and clothed, he wanted to get his children out of Beaumont-Hamel.[21]

"Wants two elder boys and daughter to be naturalised British subjects and go to UK," Arnott reported.

When officers inspected Serre Road No. 2, they found the front of the cemetery "neat and tidy." About half of the graves were mown, with roses and ground cover growing in their "clean and cultivated" borders. There was some damage to the stonework, the hedges were diseased, and the grass in the back half of the cemetery was six inches tall, but it was clear that someone had been looking after the place.[22]

Major Arnott, Major Macfarlane, and Captain Grinham thought of themselves as an "advance party," but as they traveled through France, it became clearer and clearer that they were not pioneers. At one cemetery after another, gardeners were already back at work. Some, like Ben Leech, had been free and working all along. Others, like Stephen Grady Sr. and Sidney Wray, had emerged from hiding. Many others were internees who were freed from Saint-Denis when the Allies liberated Paris in August and went directly home to their families instead of being repatriated to the United Kingdom. In all, there were about sixty Commission gardeners on the ground in France before the officers landed in October 1944.

The Commission wanted to get these sixty men back to work as soon as possible but not until they verified that there were no collaborators among them. They directed the advance party to bring the gardeners back under their supervision, "subject to their being 'vetted' by the military and civil security authorities."[23]

Most of the sixty gardeners in France in October 1944 were, like Ben Leech, in desperate straits. They were much sicker, hungrier, and poorer than men who had spent the war working at factories or on private estates in England. At the most basic level, they were "still unable to buy sufficient food in the open market to carry out hard manual labour." In recognition of their need for nourishment, the French government provided ex-internees with double ration coupons for six months after their release, but they still had to find food and pay for it. If the Commission wanted these sixty weary men to care for the cemeteries while their colleagues prepared to return to France, they would at the very least need to ensure they were fed.[24]

The Canadian government had already solved this problem for the Vimy Ridge caretakers. When Major Arnott visited the Canadian Memorial a few days before his trip to Beaumont-Hamel, he found that caretaker George Stubbs had been authorized to "draw rations from a Military Unit" and to wear Canadian army battledress. "On his shoulder is the 'flash'— *Canada*—and on the maple leaf badge on his beret the dates of his internment are shown in gilt figures on a blue background," Arnott reported.[25]

Major Arnott recommended that the War Graves Commission make similar arrangements for its own gardeners. He made inquiries in Arras and concluded that there would be "no difficulty" in requisitioning relatively modest supplies of boots, battledress, and rations from the army if Sir Fabian could get permission.

After some wrangling, the Commission was able to secure army rations for its staff. Beginning in January 1945, Ben Leech and the other working gardeners received bulk rations every two weeks. Unfortunately, their families were not included in the program. Ben's protein-rich army rations—and Red Cross parcels that began arriving in the following months—boosted the Leech family's diet, but the winter of 1944–1945 was still a lean one.

Even with this assistance, the Leech family still lacked basic necessities. Ben wrote to his older sister, Hetty, begging her to send anything she could spare. It was still impossible for Hetty to send ordinary civilian mail from her home in Wales to France, but Ben told her to write personally to Colonel Frank Higginson at the Commission's head office. Hetty implored Higginson to forward a parcel of "clothing + washing soap" to her brother. "He said maybe you could deliver through the office in France," she wrote.[26]

Ben Leech was officially reemployed by the War Graves Commission on January 1, 1945. The advance party had warned the higher-ups that that wages in France were "nearly 3 times as high as they were in 1939-40," but the Commission started the gardeners back to work at their 1940 wage rates.[27] They promised they would reevaluate once things settled down a bit. In the meantime, Ben would carry on as he had all along.

"IT'S HARD FOR ME TO REMEMBER ALL THAT"   **17**

On the day the War Graves officers returned to France, Bob Armstrong was still alive.

He had been sentenced to death on May 3, 1944, about six weeks before D-Day. At the end of the trial, the judge advised Bob and his three codefendants that they had eight days to appeal the ruling. Hope was not lost, but the condemned prisoners were reeling.

When the prisoners returned to Loos, Joseph Cornille's cellmates tried to reassure the distraught teenager. The lawyers would file an appeal. It was sure to succeed. And even if it didn't, the Allied invasion was coming any day to save them all.

Cornille barely heard them. In a stupor, he fixated on details like the electric lights. Prison policy dictated that condemned prisoners' cells must be fully lit around the clock.

"It's because of me you won't be able to sleep," Cornille apologized to his cellmates. "It's my fault."

That night, Cornille lay next to Father Lefebvre, feverish and "tragically pale," clutching the priest's hand and asking, "Do you think they will shoot me?"

Father Lefebvre did his best to comfort the boy but called their conversation "my saddest memory of prison."[1]

Down the hall, Bob Armstrong was living through the same awful, bright night. Perhaps he thought about his old friend Seán MacEoin, who had waited for the hangman at Mountjoy Prison twenty years ago. Now MacEoin was a national hero who represented Currygrane's district in the Dáil Éireann. A death sentence wasn't always the last word.

Over the next week, Bob's case generated a flurry of paperwork: appeals, telegrams, letters to the Irish government.[2]

"Robert condemned to death May 3rd," the Irish representative in Berlin wrote to the foreign secretary in Dublin. "I have taken this up with the German Government, and presume that you will do so too."

Dublin sent back instructions to keep track of Bob's whereabouts and to "employ a reliable lawyer." They noted that Bob's sister, Augusta Lindsay, had promised to "bear cost." Someone mentioned that Bob was "well known to General McKeon Ballinlea," implying that perhaps his old friend might intervene on his behalf.[3]

In the meantime, Bob and his codefendants were deported from Loos to Saint-Gilles prison in Belgium. They left France on May 16, 1944. It was D-Day minus twenty-one and Zeph Cornille's twentieth birthday.

All through the summer of 1944, while Allied forces fought their way across France, Bob Armstrong was shunted from one Nazi prison to another. After a month at Saint-Gilles, he went over the German border to Aachen, then to Cologne, then to Diez prison near Frankfurt. Each move carried him deeper into Germany.

Bob had a particularly terrible time at Diez. One day when the prisoners were returning from the exercise yard, he was brutally attacked by a German guard. The guard, who was "tall and big and blond," threw Bob to the ground and began beating him. Bob's fellow prisoners watched in horror as he was "violently and repeatedly struck on the head."

Bloodied and reeling, Bob struggled back to his cell. The other prisoners did not see him for three or four days. When he finally reappeared in the exercise yard, his "head and neck were continually bleeding through an inadequate bandage."

Bob had been beaten before, but this assault sapped his strength. Over the next few weeks, he "grew rapidly thinner and his condition deteriorated from day to day."[4]

Meanwhile, diplomatic cables continued to ping back and forth between Dublin, Vichy, and Berlin. It is unclear whether the Irish government's intervention actually swayed the Nazis, but something did. On July 20, 1944, a German court commuted Bob Armstrong's sentence from death to eight years' incarceration with heavy labor. At the same time, it reduced Joseph Cornille's sentence from death to four years. Valentine Ployart and Marie Therese Debrabant were left to "the Führer's decision," but neither of them was executed either. If Bob could survive prison, he would be released on November 28, 1951.[5]

Unfortunately, he was already dying by inches.

In early August, Bob "disappeared" from Diez prison. Friends who had witnessed the blond guard's vicious assault and Bob's subsequent decline assumed that he was dead. In fact, Bob had been moved to another prison, Rheinbach, near Bonn. He arrived on August 25, 1944, the day Paris was liberated.

In his Rheinbach intake photograph, Bob Armstrong is shirtless and skeletal. He had always been full-faced and hearty, with broad shoulders and a powerful physique. No longer. In the photo, Bob's face is a jumble of sharp bones and sharper shadows. Dark eyes in deep sockets look out over prominent cheekbones. Lower, his chest is ridged with the clear outlines of clavicles and sternum. His head is shaved.[6]

While Bob was wasting away in German prisons, the Irish government was trying to find him. On September 19, just a few weeks after the photo was taken, they received a tentative offer from German authorities to exchange "condemned Irish prisoners." As far as the Irish government knew, only three people fit that description. They were in touch with two of them, but after so many moves, they had lost track of Bob Armstrong.[7]

Just days before the offer, Bob was transferred yet again, from Rheinbach to Kassel-Wehlheiden prison in central Germany. There, he fell in with a group of Dutch prisoners. Bob did not speak Dutch, but his genius for fellowship was undiminished.

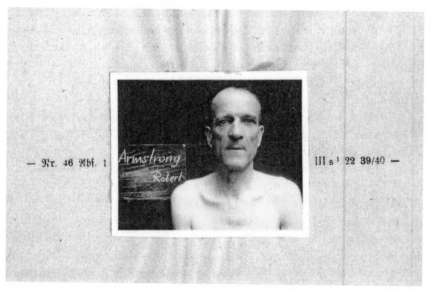

Robert Armstrong intake photo, Rheinbach Prison, August 1944. *Sachsen State Archives, ZC 20.088 11*

"He always kept his courage and good humor," remembered a Dutch prisoner who counted Bob as a friend.[8]

At Kassel, the prisoners worked outdoors, repairing damage done by Allied bombs. The work was strenuous, but as long as the weather stayed warm, many of the men were glad to spend their days outside the prison walls. Some even managed to scavenge potatoes and rutabagas from nearby fields. Bob Armstrong turned fifty on October 7, 1944, two days after the Commission's advance party landed in France.

A few weeks later, the weather turned. Construction work became torture for prisoners who were forced to labor in the biting November wind and freezing sleet. "It became a tough test," wrote the Dutch prisoner, "and Armstrong didn't have enough strength to endure it."

Bob had always had trouble with his legs ever since a German shell had shattered his hip in 1917. In the fall of 1944, when he was starving and exposed to the elements, the old wound tore open again. Witnesses testified that "he had a big boil on his leg, which was very badly treated." The injury spread and festered until "his leg was nothing more than an open sore."

With his strength flowing out through his leg, Bob's health deteriorated still further. "He could hardly move anymore," the Dutch prisoner remembered. "It was necessary to support him while walking." The guards harassed Bob mercilessly. On December 13, one of them knocked him down because he was so weak that he could barely eat his soup.[9]

The day after this final beating, Bob was transferred for the final time, to Waldheim Prison in Saxony. As soon as he arrived, his fellow inmates carried him to the infirmary. Friends from Kassel held out hope that Bob might receive good medical care at Waldheim or "much better than Cassel anyway."

It was too late. Even if the German doctors could have treated Bob's wounds, he was too frail to recover. He died in the Waldheim infirmary a few days after his arrival.

The friends who carried Bob to the infirmary on December 14 guessed that he died "about two days later," though they couldn't be sure. Bob's official death certificate says he lingered longer, dying on the evening of December 18, 1944.

According to the Nazis, Bob died of tuberculosis. His death certificate does not mention his long months of suffering, the brutal assaults, the way the wounds from World War I opened again and ravaged his too-vulnerable body.[10]

Bob Armstrong has no grave. The Nazis sent his body to a crematorium in Döbeln on December 18, 1944, to be incinerated. His ashes were mostly likely dumped in an unmarked pit or pond, mingled with the remains of thousands of others who died in nearby prisons and concentration camps.[11]

~

On the day Bob Armstrong died, December 18, 1944, Rosine Witton sent a postcard to Bert from Holleischen. The brief message was written in German on a Red Cross postcard, penciled in purple block letters rather than in Rosine's own hand.

"Please give this message to my husband," it read. "I received a letter and a message dated August 6 and 4 parcels. I am in good health and hope you are the same. Much love. Rosine."[12]

It was mostly lies, but it was proof of life. That was no small thing in the early months of 1945.

After leaving Holýšov, Rosine's postcard spent the next three months rattling around Europe's rapidly deteriorating postal systems. She had addressed the postcard to Giromagny, the internment camp in France, not knowing that Bert had departed for Sweden months earlier. He was supposed to be repatriated along with the others on SS *Drottningholm*, but there was a "mistake." Sixty-three War Graves men were approved for exchange in September 1944, but only sixty-one were allowed to embark. Bert Witton and John Robertson Young—the last two alphabetically—were left behind in Sweden until the following spring. Rosine's postcard missed Bert in Gothenburg but followed him to London, where the Royal Mail finally delivered it sometime in the spring of 1945.[13]

"He had a terrible shock when he knew I was in a concentration camp," Rosine wrote later.[14]

Around the time Bert received Rosine's postcard, British newspapers were overflowing with gruesome stories about the horrors of Buchenwald, a massive concentration camp liberated by American troops on April 11, 1945, and Bergen-Belsen, liberated by British troops four days later. Bert knew what life was like in a Nazi internment camp. Now the frightening news reports gave him some inkling of how much worse a concentration camp might be. Rosine's brief, censored message left everything to the imagination.

Holleischen was no Buchenwald, but by April 1945, conditions were worse than ever. In addition to the critical lack of food and snow flurries that dusted the spring meadows until the first week of May, Rosine and the other prisoners were now at the mercy of relentless Allied air raids. The Allies sent bombers to obliterate critical infrastructure in Holýšov, but they also sent fighters that strafed the railway station and the factory. Dozens of Czech civilians were killed. So was at least one Jewish prisoner.[15]

"We all dropped to the floor until the bombing was over," remembered Cecilie Klein-Pollack. "When we got up, there was one of our girls dead . . . I didn't see no bleeding, no scratch, no nothing. She looked like she would sleep."[16]

In her secret journal, Marie-Marguerite Michelin recorded a sort of hysterical fatalism about the air raids. "I am not nervous about the bombings," she wrote. "To die right now seems absurd and laughable."[17]

By the last days of April, Metallwerke Holleischen was a roofless ruin, and the Holýšov railway station was in shambles. The camp was hit, too. There was no electricity, no running water, barely any food. At one point, the prisoners went two days without eating, then three. They soon spiraled into "a psychosis of hunger." Madeleine Mallet, age seventeen, remembered finding a jar of glue while shifting rubble at the railway station and promptly eating it. "It was delicious and tasted like nuts."[18]

This was the most dangerous time at Holleischen. The bombs and the escalating starvation crisis were bad enough, but the worst danger was panic. With the factory in ruins and the Americans drawing nearer, the German guards were cornered and desperate. On April 29, guards at the nearby men's camp shot six Italian prisoners, though none of the women at Rosine's camp knew exactly why. Rumors flew. They would all be shot. They would be hanged en masse. They would be forced on a death march. The most persistent rumor was that the SS had orders to leave no witnesses and were planning to set fire to the camp with everyone locked inside.[19]

"Are we going to die by the machine gun or the flamethrower?" wondered Jeanne Bouteille.[20]

A lot depended on "the Rooster." In the early days of May, Emile Fügner called his superiors at Flossenbürg over and over until the telephone lines went dead. Then he attempted to force prisoners to sign a statement saying that he had treated them well. Fügner raged at women who refused to sign, threatening to blow up the entire camp.

He made ominous preparations. Jewish prisoners remembered SS guards priming their barn with barrels of petrol, ready to light a match as soon the order was given. "They were going to burn down our camp," remembered Cecilie Klein-Pollack. "There was everything prepared."[21]

On the morning of May 5, 1945, Holleischen was quiet. The barracks were locked from the outside. There was no work. No food. No water.

Starving prisoners peered through the barred windows as guns fired in the distance.

Then, half an hour before noon, something moved at the edge of the forest. Soldiers in khaki emerged from the trees. Silently, they hurried toward the camp.

"Everything looked like something out of a novel, or like a movie," Marie-Marguerite Michelin wrote in her journal.[22]

The soldiers were members of the Polish Holy Cross Mountains Brigade, an armed unit of the Polish Resistance. Some of the Polish soldiers rushed into the Pičman courtyard. Others broke the locks on the Jewish prisoners' barracks across the road. The SS guards, who were eating lunch, had no time to put any final plan into action. When a single German put up opposition, the Polish soldiers shot him and left his body sprawled in front of the gate.

The battle for the Pičman farm was over before it began. Guards surrendered. Prisoners tumbled out of the barracks. By noon, the camp rang with joyful pandemonium.

As soon as they assessed the situation, the Polish soldiers began distributing bread to the thousand starving women. At first, they attempted to maintain orderly lines, but everyone was impatient. Finally, an exasperated Polish soldier threw bread into the air. "That was the signal for looting." The prisoners stormed the SS quarters, emerging with armfuls of bread and sausages, clothing, and soap.[23]

Cecilie Klein-Pollack did not stay to plunder with the others. Instead, she ran to the potato field. "I was digging feverishly," she remembered. "My sister came brandishing bread, a salami, and she couldn't find me, then it occurred to her to come to the field. I wouldn't budge from those potatoes."[24]

Neus Català also ran to a nearby field. "I bit the grass, the flowers, the earth, I rolled with the little strength I had left with such force that if it hadn't been for some bushes, I would have fallen into a river."[25]

Some survivors attacked the remaining guards. They beat them with their fists and wooden clogs, tearing out the SS women's hair. The Polish soldiers stepped in before anyone died and posted guards to protect the Nazis from their victims.

"You can't imagine our joy, our delirium at seeing our ferocious guards made prisoners," wrote Suzanne Agrapart.[26]

Among the survivors, a heated debate broke out between those who wanted to string the SS up on the spot and those who believed they should be handed over to the fast-approaching Americans. Some of the French communists began singing "*Ça Ira*," the anthem of the French Revolution, with updated lyrics: "Toutes les kapo à la lanterne, toutes les SS on les pendra" ("All the kapos to the lamppost, all the SS, let's hang them").[27]

In the end, the guards were handed over to the American 2nd Infantry Division, who swept through Holýšov on their way to Plzeň. Neus Català was tickled to meet "a boy from Texas" who made a special point of bringing food to the three Spanish women and sending messages to their families. The French women rushed to meet French men from the prisoner-of-war camp, finding comrades and neighbors and a French abbé who gave them general absolution. [28]

The liberated prisoners still needed medical attention and careful feeding, but what they wanted most was to go home.

Rosine Witton left Czechoslovakia in the third week of May and crossed into France on May 20. On the train back to Arras, she carried her blue-and-gray striped concentration camp uniform, which she would preserve carefully for the rest of her life.

Rosine arrived in Arras on May 24, but her journey was not over.

"My Calvary was not finished," she wrote. "A telegram was waiting for me to let me know that my husband was dangerously ill in England."[29]

Bert Witton arrived in London on March 23, 1945, and was immediately admitted to the London Chest Hospital near Victoria Park. On May 5, the same day Holleischen was liberated, doctors operated on his lungs. When Rosine reached Arras three weeks later, Bert was still struggling to recover.

The telegram was the first news Rosine had of her husband since the previous summer. As soon she read it, she was on her way to London. Military officials sent her to Le Bourget airfield near Paris and found her a seat on a flight to England the very next day. It was probably the first time Rosine ever flew in an airplane. She landed at Croydon on May 25, just twenty days after being liberated from Holleischen.[30]

It had been nearly five years since Rosine had seen Bert and nearly two years since they had been in regular communication. Now they were reunited. But it was not the reunion that either of them had imagined.

For Bert, seeing Rosine in her immediate postliberation state must have been as shocking as receiving her postcard. Back in 1943, Bert had worried that Rosine was "a bag of bones," but a year at Ravensbrück and Holleischen had left her hollow-eyed and gaunt, weighing no more than a child. Food would heal some of the damage, but her heart problems, her decalcified spine, and the chronic pain from her wounded leg were just beginning.[31]

For Rosine, the overriding emotion of her reunion with Bert was anguish. He really was dangerously ill. After all they had endured, the joy of liberation was tightly bound with fear.

"Just realize how hard it was for me to see my Husband in Hospital," Rosine wrote.

Bert's doctors explained that "they took his lung out" and found "a very young cancer, two months old." Any cancer diagnosis was serious, but the doctors believed that Bert's prognosis was good. "They never operated a so young cancer," Rosine explained, "so they thought they could save him."[32]

Even with these assurances, Rosine felt bewildered. She was no longer a filthy, starving prisoner at the mercy of SS guards and Allied bombs. Instead, she was a visitor at a clean, modern hospital in England, being stared at by people who had read about concentration camps but had not yet met a survivor. The speed of the transition was overwhelming. And after everything she had already suffered, she could do nothing for Bert except sit at his bedside and bear witness to his decline.

While Rosine watched over Bert, both the American and the British intelligence services were investigating her work for the Comet Line. They checked escape and evasion reports, interviewed witnesses, and reviewed written evidence.

"Mme Witton has done good and serious work for the réseau COMETE and deserves compensation," concluded an American officer.

The Allies owed Rosine Witton a debt they could never repay, but cash was a welcome start. She would eventually receive Bert's Lawson Scheme settlement—£569.6.2—but not for another three years. MI9 was much quicker. In recognition of her service and her immediate needs, they expedited Rosine's first compensation payment. On July 11, 1945, barely two months after being liberated, she received £160, £10 for each month she spent in Nazi custody.[33]

"As Mrs. Witton's plans are so uncertain at the moment I have told her to let me know if she finds herself in need of more money whilst still in England," one British official wrote to Donald Darling, the MI9 agent in charge of verifying helpers' claims. The Americans chimed in with offers of help, wondering if there was anything they could do to help Rosine recover her property in Ronville.[34]

For the moment, Rosine's daily concerns were much more intimate. She spent the summer of 1945 consulting with Bert's doctors and sitting by his side. They celebrated his forty-seventh birthday on June 6, the first anniversary of D-Day.

On her way to and from the hospital, Rosine walked the green and flowering paths of Victoria Park. Each night, she returned to the home of Bert's brother Horace and his family in East Ham, where she ate nourishing food and delighted in her young nieces. Slowly, Rosine was recovering her strength.

Unfortunately, Bert was not.

For a while, Rosine was able to believe that Bert was "slowly improving." The doctors assured her that his cancer had not spread. They gave him blood transfusions, good food, and tender care.

Yet week after week, Bert continued to sink lower. It wasn't the cancer that was killing him. After years of hunger, cold, and stress in the internment camps, his body was simply too weak to recover from the surgery.

Bert Witton died on August 18, 1945.

Outside the hospital, London was celebrating the end of the war. The jubilant city was still littered with confetti from Victory over Japan Day, three days earlier. Millions of people—soldiers, prisoners, displaced persons—were on their way home. Among them were the War Graves gardeners, who were returning to France to be reunited with their families and resume their work.

Brigadier Frank Higginson, Bert's old boss, wrote a condolence letter to Rosine on behalf of the War Graves Commission. "That this blow should have fallen so soon after you had been reunited following a period of anxious separation, must indeed be specially hard for you," he wrote. "I am desired to express, on behalf of the Commission and the staff, the deepest sympathy with you in your great loss."[35]

Bert Witton was not the only gardener who would never return home. In addition to those who died in the internment camps, several gardeners died shortly after being repatriated. Percy Greenwood Johnson, a fifty-three-year-old gardener from Armentières who returned on *Drottning-holm* in September, died just four months later, on January 28, 1945. His twenty-one-year-old son Percy, who was arrested with his father in 1940, also died of an "illness contracted during detention by the Germans."[36]

Frederick Knock, who sent his wife and six small children from Passchendaele to the United Kingdom at Captain Haworth's suggestion, was one of the unlucky gardeners who spent the winter of 1944–1945 at Westertimke. He was repatriated on May 17, 1945, and died within a month. He was fifty years old. Another gardener, Alfred Thomas, who was interned first at Saint-Denis and then at Vittel with his wife, Olivia, and their eleven-year-old daughter, Delia, died on December 28, 1945, age fifty-nine. Others died in 1946, including Omer Briere's friend Bill

Toomer, who had caught the sack of food Jean Briere threw to him on the day the gardeners left Arras. He died on July 31, 1946, a week after his forty-seventh birthday.[37]

These deaths may have been the natural decline of middle-aged men who had lived hard lives. But their last years had been very hard indeed.

Even for gardeners who were not interned by the Nazis, the transition from war to peace was extraordinarily stressful. Thomas A. Beckwith, the South African caretaker of Delville Wood, evacuated to England in 1940 with his wife, Daisy, and their fourteen-year-old daughter, Joyce. When they returned to Longueval in October 1945, Thomas was staggered by the damage to Delville Wood. Just as Ben Leech had reported, hundreds of the largest trees were nothing but stumps. The lawn was rutted, its turf in tatters.

Thomas Beckwith had been wounded and gassed at Delville Wood in 1916 and spent decades caring for the graves of his comrades from the South African Brigade. Now, at age forty-nine, he had to start again.

It was too much. On November 8, 1945, just two weeks after returning to Longueval, Beckwith went to bed feeling ill. In the middle of the night, he "awoke in a rather disturbed frame of mind" and began to dress. "He spoke about going to work," Daisy reported. Suddenly, Beckwith's right side went still. Within a few hours, he was dead of a stroke. He was buried in the communal cemetery across the street from the Delville Wood caretaker's cottage, in sight of the South African cemetery but not part of it. His gravestone is the flat-topped staff variation of the Commission's standard white stone with the epitaph "God's greatest gift—Remembrance."[38]

Several of the pupil gardeners were dead as well, buried in the Commission cemeteries they had just begun learning to tend. Pupil gardener/ Corporal John Harris Jr., whose fifteen-year-old sister, Violette, was killed in an air raid in 1940, died on August 26, 1945, a few weeks after being released from a Japanese prisoner-of-war camp in Thailand. Pupil gardener/Aircraftman 1st Class Alphonsus Egan, who had jumped from the Dunkirk quay onto *St. Helier* with his brothers and sisters in 1940, was lost at sea. Pupil gardener/Private Bernard Gallagher of Ypres is buried under an epitaph reading "In Memory of Buddy—To the world he was just one, To us he was all the world."[39]

The Imperial War Graves Commission kept its policy against repatriating bodies after World War II. This policy applied only to war graves, not civilian dead, which meant that Rosine Witton was able to bring Bert's body home to Arras. She buried him next to her parents at the civil cemetery in Ronville.

On the Thérier-Bécourt family tomb, Auguste and Léontine's names are accompanied by their years of birth and death. Bert's line is longer, with details Rosine wanted to memorialize, like his work and the fact that he did not live to see fifty. In English, she wrote, "Sidney Albert Witton, IWGC, Died 18th August 1945 Age 47."

In time, Rosine would get her house back. She would have friends and adventures and medals for her work on the Comet Line. But she was shattered. For the rest of her long life, Rosine blamed herself for not being able to save the one airman who mattered most. If only they had left a few days earlier in May 1940. If only she had known about the escape networks before July 13 rather than after. If only she had kept sending eggs.

"This is the tragedy of my life," Rosine wrote in 1965. "I am alone since July 1940. So I tell you it's hard for me to remember all that."[40]

"A NICE ADORNMENT WITHOUT **18** BREAD TO EAT"

When Valenciennes was liberated in September 1944, Emmanuel Dossche stormed into the German commandant's abandoned office. The previous November, before the Nazis arrested Bob Armstrong, they had confiscated the memorial plaques from the airmen's graves at Saint-Roch Cemetery. Dossche wanted them back.

With the help of the Valenciennes fire department and a few stray American GIs, Dossche rounded up two dozen shame-faced German prisoners and ordered them to carry the grave offerings back to the cemetery. The Germans shuffled through the streets with their burdens, flanked by helmeted firemen. A watchful crowd gathered along their route.

At Saint-Roch, the World War I headstones needed a wash, but the row of white crosses that Bob had laid out for the airmen was still beautifully kept. Late-season flowers bloomed and the edges were cut so crisply that even Ben Leech could not have complained. One by one, the German prisoners replaced the stolen plaques. Emmanuel Dossche's camera clicked.

"I put everything back in order," Dossche reported in a satisfied letter to the War Graves Commission.[1]

With the cemetery restored, Emmanuel Dossche joined the search for Bob himself. Bob was still alive in September 1944, battered and thin, but still breathing. The Irish government had not had any luck finding him, but his friends on the ground were determined to try.

One of the searchers was Thomas Crowley, the only Irish gardener left in Douai after the arrests of Bob Armstrong and William O'Connor. Crowley never claimed to be a particularly active *résistant* himself, but he helped from time to time. In September 1944—weeks before the Commission's advance party landed in France—Crowley begged a special pass

German prisoners replacing memorial plaques at Saint-Roch Cemetery, Valenciennes, September 1944. *CWGC Archives*

from Allied military authorities to wade into the chaos in search of his friend. The fighting in Belgium was far from over. Civilians could not easily find transportation, food, or lodging in the churning confusion of the active military zone, but Crowley did his best. He tracked Bob as far as Brussels but "could not trace" him any farther.[2]

Bob Armstrong's friends in Valenciennes were on the case as well. They interviewed ex-prisoners and wrote to government officials. Gaston Lepine, the Bureau d'Opérations Aériennes (BOA) captain who "did not hide anything" from Bob, became head of the Valenciennes repatriation office, where he asked returning deportees for any information about the missing. Bit by bit, he began to piece together the story of what happened to Bob.

One person who provided crucial information was Alfred Delporte, the mayor of Montay, who was liberated from Buchenwald in April 1945 weighing only ninety-seven pounds. He told Bob's friends about the awful assault at Diez and how Bob's "condition deteriorated rapidly" before he "disappeared" in August 1944.[3]

Marie-Therese Debrabant returned home around the same time. She had been imprisoned at Waldheim with Valentine Ployart, who died just a few weeks before the liberation. Men and women were separated at Waldheim, so Debrabant did not have firsthand knowledge of Bob's death, but she wrote to other ex-inmates. By the end of May 1945, she had a letter from the unnamed Dutch prisoner who gave the most detailed account of Bob's death.[4]

"As soon as we got to Waldheim, we brought him to the hospital," he wrote. "I myself was one of the people who carried him upstairs." The Dutch prisoner told Debrabant that "all the comrades were very moved by [Bob's] death." Some of the other Dutch prisoners were planning to "make a report on the mistreatment of Mr. Armstrong . . . especially on the negligence of the doctor towards him." "I will also co-sign this," the writer promised.[5]

It would take more than a year for official notice of Bob's death to reach the War Graves Commission, but his friends in Valenciennes had heard enough. They could not save Bob, but they could honor him. Despite their own hardships, people in Valenciennes turned out their pockets without hesitation. By July 1945, they had raised 10,000 francs for a memorial.

"We would be very happy," wrote Emmanuel Dossche, "to bear witness to our sincere gratitude to our valiant Allies, in the person of our friend, who died in the Resistance for the common cause."[6]

Bob's old supervisor, Major Frank Grinham, informed the War Graves Commission about Dossche's proposal. "They wanted the Memorial to be placed in the cemetery he had tended with such care and devotion," Grinham wrote in July 1945. He admitted that he "had never heard of anything like that" but agreed that "erecting a Memorial under what may prove to be unique circumstances, is of some importance."[7]

The Commission had always been wary of mixing civilian memorials with the military cemeteries. War Graves gardeners often received a flat-topped version of the Commission's iconic white headstone, but they were usually buried in civilian cemeteries. Sometimes, when a War Graves plot was located within or adjacent to a civilian cemetery, gardeners were buried in the margin between the two. After Charles Maurice Baker died in Nazi custody in 1941, his wife, Gaby, brought his body home. She buried him at the edge of the War Graves section of Merville Communal Cemetery and reserved a grave for herself just a few feet away, at the edge of the civilian section.[8]

In Bob's case, the Commission was initially unsure whether they could allow an individual memorial plaque at Saint-Roch, but they were tentatively inclined to agree that it would be a good idea. "It adds interest to the Valenciennes Cemetery without detracting from its design + purpose," one official wrote.[9]

Still, they needed precedent. They found it at the Vis-en-Artois memorial, where a plaque commemorated a French worker who was killed during the monument's construction.[10] With a prior example in hand, the Commission gave their blessing for Bob's friends to erect a marble plaque at Saint-Roch, pending approval of the final design and wording.

Emmanuel Dossche's first proposal featured a pair of side-by-side inscriptions in French and English, reading

> To the Memory of
> Robert Armstrong
> Head Gardener
> I.W.G.C. Valenciennes
> Deported by the Germans and
> Died from cruel treatment
> at Waldheim camp (Saxony)
> the 16th December 1944
> Homage from his
> Friends in Valenciennes

The Commission rejected this text because of its "bitter wording." Both "Deported by the Germans" and "Died from cruel treatment" were too accusatory. After some back-and-forth, they approved a version that acknowledged that Bob "Died in Captivity" but said nothing explicit about who captured him or why.[11]

While the Commission debated the wording of Bob's plaque, they were also preparing to defend themselves against accusations that their orders played a part in his death. Higher-ups interviewed Captain Alfred Melles and Jack Day about Bob's last visit to Arras on May 16, 1940. Both witnesses were unequivocal: Bob had explicitly requested permission to withdraw, and Melles had explicitly ordered him back to Valenciennes, in accordance with Brigadier Prower's orders. Melles, for one, was beginning to feel "rather worried that his was the responsibility at that time for sending Armstrong back."

The investigation concluded that Bob "may thus have been prevented from evacuating (assuming he desired to do so) by obeying the orders of an official of the Commission."

Given these facts, the Commission worried that Bob's family might "attack the Commission on this charge." They were already nervous about the pointed questions the Transport and General Workers' Union was asking about the evacuation debacle. Determined not to give Augusta any ammunition, the Commission decided not to tell her that its officers had ordered Bob to remain at his post.

"We have not yet notified his sister in Eire, who is asking for news," read a summary of the investigation's findings, "though a draft letter, leaving out the details, is attached."[12]

Augusta had other sources of news. Bob had told his friends in France that his sister was his next of kin and made sure they had her address. After confirming his death, they sent their condolences and copies of the eyewitness accounts.

Armed with this information, Augusta's letters to the Commission took on an acid tone. "Now we know he was working + we guess he was doing *good* work else he would have been spared such an awful death," she wrote. When her father, James, died at Currygrane in 1946, Augusta attributed his demise, in part, to losing Bob. "The sad news I'm afraid hurried on his end," she wrote. "He was broken-hearted."[13]

James Armstrong's death created a legal and financial mess. Since Bob died without a will, his assets should have gone to James as his legal next of kin. James's own will left his entire estate—£2.14.0 and the farm at Currygrane—to his youngest son, Edward, who lived with him. Since Bob had unexpectedly predeceased James, Edward stood to inherit all of his brother's assets, including insurance payouts, superannuation contributions, and any compensation for his death. Bob's other siblings—Augusta Lindsay, Emmie Megarity, and Fred Armstrong—would get nothing.[14]

Augusta was livid. She argued fiercely that she had a special claim on any money the Commission owed to Bob, in part because they still owed her £108 in monthly allotments. If Bob was still working during the occupation, she argued, the payments should have continued. The Commission countered that Augusta actually owed them £18 for the nine months they had erroneously paid her between May 1940 and March 1941.

To Augusta, the allotment was not just money. It was tangible proof of Bob's promise that he would always take care of her. "He told me on numerous occasions that if ever anything should happen to him, he would see that I was right," she wrote. Their sister Emmie was living what Augusta considered a comfortable life in Northern Ireland; Fred owned a successful garage in Dublin; Edward had the farm at Currygrane. But Augusta and Bob had relied on one another.

"When he was a prisoner of war and in need of money I was the only one he immediately contacted and I sent money to him," Augusta argued. "Records will show how little my brothers and sister bothered about my brother Robert when he was in great need," but with money on the table, "they are all wide awake now."[15]

The Commission agreed with Augusta. Most of Bob's assets would go to Edward as a matter of law, but the Commission controlled £291.14.0 in one of his superannuation accounts. They decided to divide this money among the other siblings and give Augusta a double portion in recognition of her special claim.

The Commission also controlled Bob Armstrong's Lawson Scheme settlement. Lawson payments were entirely ex gratia, so the Commission was free to award each employee or his heirs "either more or less than what would have been legally due." In Bob's case, they decided to award nothing at all.

"Had Armstrong survived it is very probable that he would have received these ex gratia payments," a Commission official conceded. Things might also have been different if he were married. Widows like Rosine Witton and Gaby Baker received their husbands' Lawson Scheme settlements, but Bob Armstrong was divorced and childless. Therefore, the Commission determined that "there is no person to whom they would regard themselves as bound to make any ex gratia payment."

"We know there are no dependents," wrote Frederick C. Sillar, the Commission's assistant secretary of finance. Augusta Lindsay did not count. Sillar acknowledged that Bob supported her financially but argued that a measly £2 each month "indicates a very small degree of dependency if any." Paying a Lawson Scheme settlement to Augusta would be "an improper use of public funds."[16]

This decision did not enrage Bob Armstrong's siblings for one simple reason: they did not know about it. The Commission never informed them about the Lawson Scheme.

The Commission was on firm legal ground when it made a nil award to Bob Armstrong's estate. Things were shakier when both the Irish and the U.K. governments requested reimbursement for Bob's relief payments.

At first, the Commission refused to pay. Technically speaking, they had never explicitly agreed to reimburse relief payments made to Irish citizens.

"It was always understood by the Commission that these relief payments were made not to Commission employees as such, but to British nationals who would otherwise have been in distress," wrote Frederick Sillar.

Sillar conceded that the Commission would probably pay the British Foreign Office if they pressed the issue. After all, the Lawson Scheme funds ultimately derived from British and dominion public funds. But Ireland was different. Sillar saw no reason to reimburse "a Government which does not contribute to the Commission's funds."

Privately, Sillar was petulant about being asked to deal with the Irish government at all. "I do not want to become a sort of debt collector for [Irish president Eamonn] de Valera!"[17]

Eventually, the U.K. Foreign Office requested reimbursement directly from the Irish government. In response, Ireland disavowed Bob altogether. "Robert Armstrong [was] condemned to death by court martial for espionage in favour of England," the Irish high commissioner declared in 1948. By helping Allied airmen and engaging in "other missions: organizing the passage of parachutists, receiving of arms, etc. on behalf of the Allied Forces," Bob had effectively renounced his Irish neutrality. Therefore, "the Irish Government cannot accept responsibility for any payments made to Robert Armstrong." To emphasize this disavowal, the high commissioner sent a counterdemand that the Foreign Office should reimburse Ireland.[18]

At some point, someone calculated what Bob's Lawson Scheme settlement would have been under the standard formula. It came to £795.7.9. If the Commission had reimbursed both governments in full, there would have been £254.2.6 left over for Bob's siblings. They would have received the money in March 1948, just like all the other gardeners' families.

The timing was important. In April 1948, just a few weeks after the settlement checks were issued, the Commission finally approved the details of Bob's memorial plaque. Emmanuel Dossche began planning a dedication ceremony for July 11, 1948.

The Commission did not plan the ceremony, but they did cooperate with Dossche to make it a success. "I am taking preliminary steps to have the site in apple pie order," wrote Major Grinham in mid-May, two months before the unveiling. "It should be lovely and there will be red roses (that were planted by Armstrong) in full flower in the row of Graves nearest to the plaque."[19]

Despite having ample notice, the Commission did not inform Augusta Lindsay about the ceremony. In June, she was surprised to receive an invitation from one of Bob's friends in France who wanted "as many of his family as possible to attend."

Augusta fired off an appalled letter to the Commission on June 21, just three weeks before the dedication.

"I wonder I didn't get any word of this from the Graves Commission, or have you any knowledge of it?" she fumed.

Both time and money were short. Augusta asked the Commission to advance her funds to travel to France with her son, Harry. "Otherwise I am afraid it would be too expensive." Edward Armstrong wrote separately to ask the Commission to "advance me £40 to enable me to go to France for the ceremony."[20]

If the Commission had split a standard Lawson Scheme settlement among Bob's four surviving siblings in March 1948, each of them would have received about £63, enough to cover their travel costs to France.

Augusta Lindsay knew nothing of the Lawson Scheme, but she did know about the double portion from Bob's superannuation account that the Commission had promised her. They sent her an official notice about that money in March 1947 but did not actually send the check until January 1949. Augusta knew that the money was coming to her eventually and hoped that the Commission could advance her travel funds out of what they had already promised her.

The Commission's legal assistant, P. T. Fitzgerald, saw no reason to deny Augusta's request. "When the estate is distributed, she will receive . . . £145.17.3," he wrote on June 23, 1948, two days after Augusta's letter. "It would be quite safe to make an advance in her case and deduct this advance from her share."

Despite this recommendation, the Commission said no.

"I regret it is not possible for the Commission to give you any assistance to visit France," an officer wrote to Augusta on June 30, 1948, eleven days before the unveiling. "You will appreciate that no funds exist for this purpose."[21]

The Commission was happy to participate in a public ceremony, but it was immaterial to them whether Bob's family could attend. Someone used one of Edward's letters as a coaster, leaving the ink smudged with a ring of tea.

Fortunately, Augusta Lindsay and her siblings found help elsewhere. They may have asked for help from Bob's friends in Valenciennes or for an advance from the lawyers handling Edward's probate case. Somehow, Augusta Lindsay, Emmie Megarity, and Edward Armstrong all managed to travel to France in time for the ceremony.

July 11 was cool and drizzly, but the ceremony was everything Emmanuel Dossche had hoped for. The mayor of Valenciennes presided over a phalanx of local dignitaries, representatives from the British and Belgian consulates, and military officers from various Allied nations. There was a procession through the streets and a presentation of medals. In a country of 41 million people, Bob Armstrong was one of the 65,000—less than one-sixth of 1 percent—who was awarded the Médaille de la Résistance. The mayor of Valenciennes pinned the decoration to Edward Armstrong's coat.[22]

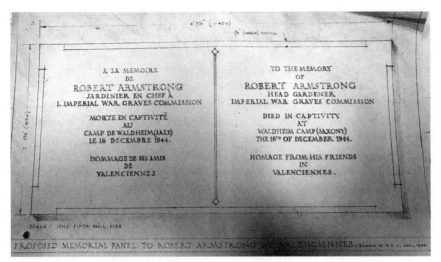

Plan for Robert Armstrong Memorial Plaque. *CWGC Archives*

At Saint-Roch, the crowd gathered at the Cross of Sacrifice, where the memorial plaque was draped with a Union Jack and heaped with wreaths and shamrock. There was an honor guard of gardeners, including Bob's friends Harold Maurice Hill, William O'Connor, and Thomas Crowley. Gaston Lepine gave a speech, as did Major Grinham and several other dignitaries. Emmanuel Dossche did not. He explained that he "was a great friend of Armstrong, and does not wish to do any of the speech making as he fears that emotion would overcome him."[23]

Augusta Lindsay played no official part in the ceremony. She stood by the Cross of Sacrifice in a black coat and a modest, black-trimmed hat, a dark silhouette against the backdrop of bright flags.

"I am very proud of my brother indeed," she wrote, "but at the same time, heartbroken."[24]

~

Of all the War Graves *résistants*, Rosine Witton was the most highly decorated.

After thorough investigations, British intelligence credited her with aiding "at least fifty Allied Service personnel"; the Americans said, "a hundred or more"; the French said, "150 aviateurs." All agreed that Rosine Witton was "one of the principal conveyors of the vast Comet escape line."[25]

An exact count is impossible, but Rosine Witton probably helped about 10 percent of the 750 evaders repatriated by the Comet Line. At least sixteen men stayed at Number 6 or followed Rosine from Arras to

Paris before the July 1943 arrests. The exact number she aided during her time Paris is less clear. Comrades and evaders testified that Rosine made two or three journeys each week, sometimes fetching airmen from the countryside, sometimes guiding them to Bordeaux. Even if she did not maintain this punishing pace for the entire six months between August 1943 and January 1944, Rosine's journeys numbered in the dozens. A conservative estimate of her activities suggests that she aided at least fifty airmen and French fugitives after fleeing Arras.[26]

In recognition of her work with the Comet Line, France awarded Rosine a full slate of Resistance honors. These included the Médaille de la Résistance, the Croix du Combattante Volontaire, and the Croix de Guerre with silver-gilt star. She was made a Chevalier (Knight) and later an Officier of the Legion d'honneur, the highest decoration in France.[27]

"She always acted with remarkable sang-froid and tireless devotion," declared Rosine's Croix de Guerre citation, which was approved by President Charles de Gaulle in 1945.

In the United Kingdom, investigators recommended that Rosine Witton should be made a Member of the Order of the British Empire (MBE). "This award seems to be well earned," concurred Military Secretary General Sir Colevill Wemyss in 1945. Yet, for unknown reasons, Rosine received a slightly lower award, the British Empire Medal, in 1947. The citation praises "Madame Witton's unfailing courage, cooperation and loyalty to the cause she served."[28]

The United States awarded Rosine a Congressional Medal of Freedom with bronze palm. This was a relatively high honor. Most civilians who helped American airmen received certificates of gratitude signed by General Eisenhower, but the Medal of Freedom was reserved for outstanding acts of heroism. The majority of Medal of Freedom recipients—including Lucy Hollingdale and Madeleine Declercq—did not receive the higher honor of a bronze, silver, or gold palm. Rosine was among the few hundred helpers who received a palm of any color.

"Her invincible courage, her ingenuity and daring enabled her to fulfill her perilous mission with outstanding success," reads Rosine's Medal of Freedom citation. "Her loyal contribution to Allied victory merits the recognition and gratitude of the United Nations."[29]

Many of Rosine's friends were also recognized. For her work with the Special Operations Executive (SOE), Berthe Fraser was awarded the George Medal, the second-highest British civilian gallantry award after the George Cross.

"I should like to put on record that it has been a joy and an honour for me to have been able to serve my two homelands to the best of my abilities," Berthe wrote in her final report to SOE. "My motto was and still is—Servir sans ne jambs tracer, souffrir on gardant le sourire—(To serve and never betray, to suffer and keep smiling)."[30]

Arthur Richards won plaudits as well, but the publicity opened old wounds. In 1944, his hometown paper, the *Birmingham Mail*, reprinted a story from *La Voix du Nord* under the headline "'Richards, Coeur de Lion': Birmingham Man as Modern 'Pimpernel'; Resistance Thriller." There were enough identifying details for Arthur's five older children to realize that their father had not, in fact, been killed in World War I. They had questions.[31]

Rosine returned to Arras after Bert's death. She found her café occupied and her finances in disarray. She would eventually receive a Lawson Scheme settlement, but 1948 was a long way away. In the meantime, Rosine turned to the British and Americans for immediate, practical assistance.

"She is a modest type of person and said that she did not want sheltering expenses, although she was considerably out of pocket through her help to evaders," wrote an American officer. "She is, however, still in considerable financial difficulties and now admits that she would be very grateful for help." The Americans sent Rosine another 20,000 francs without a fuss.[32]

In turn, Rosine provided valuable information to British and American investigators. Both she and Berthe Fraser served as contacts who provided reliable evidence and up-to-date contact information for helpers in the Arras area. Several American files contain notes, such as "Madame Fraser and Madame Wilton Terrier are aware and can provide information." Rosine also provided testimony in trials about collaboration, including an ugly 1946 spat when one of the people caught in the Organization civile et militaire (OCM) arrests of 1943 blamed Eugène D'Hallendre for speaking under torture. Rosine was one of the many survivors who rallied around Lucienne D'Hallendre to defend Eugène before a tribunal in Lille.[33]

Rosine eventually recovered her property in Arras, but she decided not to stay. In 1950, she sold up and moved to Wimereux, where she took a job as a stewardess on a cross–English Channel ferry, serving refreshments to travelers on their way to Dover or Boulogne. Few knew that the woman selling them coffee had a string of letters after her name.

By the mid-1960s, the aftereffects of Rosine's ordeal at Holleischen made it difficult for her to work. "I am not in good health," she wrote, citing problems with her spine, heart, liver, stomach, and chronic bronchitis. France awarded her a pension as a disabled *résistante* as well as a standard widow's pension. She eventually moved back to Arras, renting a little house in Ronville. "I like the area," she wrote. "It's near the cemetery, not far from the station."[34]

In 1965, Rosine received word that the U.K. and West German governments had set up a special fund to compensate British victims of Nazi persecution. As a French national, Rosine was not eligible herself, but she applied on Bert's behalf. She was not desperate for the money, but she felt strongly that someone, somewhere, should recognize Bert as a victim of the war. If he had died in the internment camp, he would have been included on the War Graves Commission's Civilian War Dead Roll of Honour 1939–1945. Since he died four months after being repatriated, his name would not "liveth for evermore."

Similarly, Bert did not meet the criteria to qualify as a victim of Nazi persecution. An apologetic civil servant wrote to Rosine to explain why her claim was denied. "For the purposes of this registration, 'Nazi persecution' means illegal detention in a Concentration Camp or comparable place for the purpose of the infliction of deliberate and organized suffering, torture, and death in the furtherance of Nazi ideology." Bert did not qualify because civilian internees did not face the same "systematic, degrading, brutal" dehumanization as the victims of the Nazis' murderous ideology. Instead, their suffering was "incidental to and not the object of the detention."[35]

It was undeniably true that the experiences of civilian internees were not the same as concentration camp victims. But former internees still needed help. Many War Graves internees acquired lifelong disabilities during their internment. Gardener John J. Bowdidge was repatriated from Ilag VIII after "the negligence of young German doctor" ruptured his urinary tract during a procedure, causing permanent incontinence. Even decades later, Bowdidge could "never get a complete night's sleep and I cannot visit friends because of embarrassment." Gardener Alfred Browne wrote that he was "very deprest all the time in the concentration camp" and that he had "never been the man I was before." In an era when depression carried tremendous stigma, this was not a casual admission. Internees were plagued by nightmares, chronic anxiety, and a range of physical ailments that made it difficult for them to work, but they were not eligible for compensation.[36]

Even when War Graves civilians met the criteria for victims of Nazi persecution, they ran into the old problem of nationality. Wilfred Legg filed a claim on behalf of his teenage son Harry, who had been captured fighting with the French partisans. After being deported on the Train de Loos, Harry was held at Sachsenhausen before being transferred to Bremen-Farge, a concentration camp where slave laborers were forced to work in the Nazi submarine pens. A fellow prisoner had seen Harry alive at Sachsenhausen in November 1944, and he was probably among a group of 100 prisoners transferred to Bremen-Farge on February 4, 1945. He died in unspeakable conditions there in the last weeks of the war, age nineteen. Since no surviving witnesses could attest Harry's death, the French government eventually issued a "certificate of disappearance" to his parents.[37]

Harry Legg was undoubtedly a concentration camp victim, but the British Foreign Office denied his father's compensation claim because Harry was a dual national. He would have been eligible if he had claimed his full British citizenship during the six months before his twenty-first birthday. Harry did not live that long.

"I am sorry to have to send a disappointing reply," an apologetic official wrote to Wilfred Legg. "I return the copy of the certificate of disappearance of your son."[38]

Only a handful of War Graves civilians' compensation claims were approved.

George Horn, the gardener from Albert who had assisted Eliane Meplaux, was eligible because he was arrested as a *résistant*, not interned as a civilian. In 1942, Horn was deported to Bochum prison near Essen, where his imprisonment featured "more kicks than food" and interminable months of isolation. "I was in solitary confinement which is very hard to bear," Horn testified, "and the Guards were very brutal." To support his claim, Horn enclosed two photos of himself, one from before his arrest and the other after his liberation, seventy pounds lighter. The Foreign Office approved a payment of £1,018.10.0, but Horn died before receiving the money.[39]

The Foreign Office also approved a claim filed by Bob Armstrong's sister, Emmie Megarity, who lived in Northern Ireland. They noted Bob's Irish citizenship, but it did not prove an insurmountable barrier. The four Armstrong siblings split £1,000.[40]

The largest Nazi persecution settlement paid to any member of the War Graves community went to Lucy Hollingdale—and not a moment too soon.

For more than a decade after the war, Lucy fought unsuccessfully for a war widow's pension. The French refused to grant her a pension on the grounds that Harry had asthma, so "the Gestapo were responsible for only 50% of his death—whatever that means." The British refused to give her the pension due to an ex-serviceman's widow because she did not live in the United Kingdom. Even the Royal Air Force (RAF) Escaping Society initially declined to help, deciding that Lucy's case "does not come directly within the scope of the Society's aims and objects."[41]

By the mid-1950s, Lucy Hollingdale was destitute and living on public assistance in Lille.

"I have been advised by the French Government that I shall receive the Medal of Liberated France," she wrote in 1954. She already had a British Empire Medal and an American Congressional Medal of Freedom. "I shall then have three medals in addition to the Campaign Medal—four in all—a nice adornment without bread to eat."[42]

By circuitous routes, Lucy's case crossed the desk of Air Chief Marshal Sir Basil Embry, the commander in chief of Allied Air Forces Central Europe.

"The whole matter is quite disgraceful," Sir Basil proclaimed.

He swung into action, personally sending Lucy a food parcel, dispatching lawyers to sort out her pension claims, and raking both the RAF Escaping Society and the British Legion over the coals. Thanks to Sir Basil's continued agitation, France finally awarded Lucy a war widow's pension in 1958. In 1966, she received two compensation awards from the U.K. Nazi persecution funds—one for her own suffering and one for Harry's—totaling £2,649.12.6. The money allowed her to live more comfortably until her death in 1984.[43]

Paradoxes of nationality had dogged members of the War Graves community since the beginning. Gardeners were cut off from social programs because they lived abroad. Their children fell through every bureaucratic crack. Harry Legg died too young; Lucy Hollingdale lived in the wrong place. The War Graves civilians were interned because of their nationality, which meant they could not receive compensation.

Strict definitions of citizenship rarely redounded to the War Graves community's benefit. One particularly baroque case involved Elaine Madden, the trilingual SOE agent who escaped via Dunkirk in disguise and parachuted back into Belgium in 1944. Despite being a bona fide SOE agent, Madden was never able to obtain a British pension for her war service. She was born British under Belgian law, but the British government considered her Australian. Australia refused to recognize her because she never resided in Australia.

"I've been British all my life but now I'm a foreigner in England as well," Elaine Madden told her biographer, Sue Elliott, late in her life. She died impoverished, lonely, and estranged from the country she had served.[44]

In 2013, eighteen months after her death, Elaine Madden's name was inscribed on a memorial to the seventy-five female SOE agents who flew out of RAF Tempsford. The Prince of Wales, now King Charles III, unveiled the monument with the usual speeches and applause. It was always easier to honor someone who was safely dead.

Rosine Witton lived a long life. She kept in touch with some of her airmen and received many heartfelt thanks. Charlie Saville, the young RAF sergeant captured in Paris when his host was shot, was "incapable of saying in cold writing just how your hospitality, and comforting shelter meant, just when everything seemed so hopeless in enemy territory alone."[45]

Rosine maintained an avid interest in the minutiae of the airmen's lives, often gossiping about the state of their marriages and asking about their houses, vacations, and jobs. She was particularly delighted by news about their children and frequently ended her chatty letters to Alfie Martin with "a big kiss" for his two daughters.

Sometimes, Rosine dwelled on regrets. She was particularly stuck on Gordon Crowther's broken ankle, telling the story over and over in many letters. "We had to take his plaster off too soon, as it was too dangerous to keep him any longer at my house in Arras," she wrote. "I can still picture him, he was so courageous I tell you, I was so sorry for him and I admired him; I thought a lot of him since I convoyed him to Paris in that condition."[46]

In 1967, Alfie Martin invited Rosine to Canada as a guest of the Canadian branch of the RAF Escaping Society, of which he was president. The trip lasted three weeks and included a joyful reunion with Doug Hoehn, who made the trip from his home in Chicago. The airmen treated Rosine and several other French helpers to a tour of Niagara Falls, a day at Expo 67 in Montreal, and a ceremony at the Canadian Parliament Buildings in Ottawa.

Sometime between laying a wreath at the War Memorial and attending a banquet at Confederation Hall, Rosine lost her British Empire Medal.[47] The mishap merited an item in the *Ottawa Journal*, but Rosine did not seem to care. She never mentioned it in any of the gushing letters she sent to Alfie Martin after she returned home. "I still feel dreamy about the beautiful country that is Canada," she wrote. "I am very often picturing you in your nice home . . . to see you all so happy is a comfort to me."

Rosine was interested in Doug Hoehn's life as well, but he would say only that he "never married." In fact, Hoehn attended the 1967 reunion without his longtime partner, Millard Mack. A few years later, Hoehn and Mack bought a house in Sarasota, Florida, where Doug worked as a teacher and Millard directed the Golden Apple Children's Theatre.[48] He was not an assiduous correspondent, but he did reminisce with Alfie Martin about their stay at Rosine's house: "I will never forget her," Hoehn wrote. "The time she was getting ready to take us to Paris + she asked me to shave her—the time the gendarme made an unexpected call."

Both Martin and Hoehn sent gifts to Rosine until she took up Bert's old line: "Please don't send any more parcel it's too kind of you; I only want to hear from time to time from the airmen I helped." That sort of protest had never stopped Rosine, and it did not stop her airmen. "Really you have all done so much for me," Rosine wrote. "It was a great comfort to have had your sincere affection as when one is alone what you miss more is that; I never had so many presents since I lost my husband."[49]

Rosine also stayed in touch with her fellow *résistants*. Berthe Fraser died in 1956 and Arthur Richards in 1957, but Rosine remained close with Lucienne D'Hallendre for decades. Sometimes, when an airman wrote to one of them in English, Rosine would translate the letters into French for Lucienne. When Rosine went to visit Jean-François Nothomb after the war, she wrote to assure Lucienne that "our dear Franco" was feeling "better, but still not very strong"[50] and passed along his address so that Lucienne could ask for details about what happened to Eugène. "You have heard of our misfortunes from Madame Witton," Lucienne wrote to Franco. "The world is uglier than it was before."[51]

Rosine and the D'Hallendres were united by grief, but they were also some of the only people who understood the absurdities of their shared experience.

"The Germans devastated her house, making all her provisions disappear," Edgard D'Hallendre wrote after interviewing Rosine in 1983, "eggs, ham, and above all, she says forty years later, the 33 pots of currant jelly."[52]

Other than speaking to Edgard for his unpublished memoir, Rosine did not grant many interviews. She did speak to André Coilliot, a local historian and collector who included bits of her story in his chronological account of life in Arras under the occupation. In her old age, Rosine entrusted the blue-and-gray striped uniform she wore at Holleischen to Coilliot. Years later, he sold his collection to a small museum in Auchonvillers, just down the road from Beaumont-Hamel, where Rosine's uniform remains on display.[53]

Rosine Witton's name appears only fleetingly in the Commonwealth War Graves Commission's archives. Like so many other War Graves wives, she surfaces briefly as "Mrs. S. A. Witton" and then slips quietly back into oblivion. She probably corresponded with the Commission on many matters—Bert's employment, his last illness, and perhaps even her own experiences—but the Commission discarded Bert's personnel file along with the others. He was dead, but not war dead, so they had no duty to remember him.

Rosine Thérier Witton died at age eighty-eight on July 28, 1995.

"She lived intensely, courageously, resisted, loved faithfully, struggled all her life," her funeral bulletin declared. Rosine's cortege included representatives from the Pas-de-Calais Union des Combattants Volontaires de la Résistance, a veteran's organization of which she was vice president, and the Union Fraternelle Franco-Britannique, an Arras social club dedicated to Anglo-French friendship, along with dozens of friends, neighbors, and comrades.

The following year, fifty people, including Alfie Martin, attended a ceremony in Rosine's honor at the Imperial War Museum in London. The gathering celebrated the museum's acceptance of Rosine's medals and important papers—Bert's letters, the pencil drawings of airplanes, her certificates and citations from grateful nations—into its collections.[54]

Rosine is buried in the Thérier family tomb in Arras with Bert and her parents. Affixed beside her name are miniatures of her most cherished French medals: the Légion d'Honneur, the Croix de Guerre, and the Médaille de la Résistance.

Well-tended French graves are often decorated with ceramic wreaths or artificial flower arrangements, but Rosine's is bare. The only offering is a memorial plaque from her comrades in OCM and the BOA, slowly fading in the sun.

Grave of Rosine Witton and Bert Witton, Arras Communal Cemetery. *Photo by author*

Grave of Rosine Witton and Bert Witton, Arras Communal Cemetery. *Photo by author*

~

For Ben Leech, the years after World War II were, in some ways, more difficult than the aftermath of World War I. It was awfully difficult to start again, again.

Like most of the other gardeners, Ben received a Lawson Scheme settlement in 1948, but that did not help his family in the lean, shabby years of 1945, 1946, and 1947. They got by on army rations and produce from Marie's garden, but the family was poorer than Ben had ever been growing up in Manchester. Much of his personnel file from this period is mired in long-running pleas for British clothing coupons so that Marie and the children could replace the rags they had been wearing for years.

Ben Leech was not impressed by the Lawson Scheme. He had abided by every provision of his contract, obeyed every order, fulfilled every duty. He believed he was entitled to his full wages and benefits, not a lower flat rate. True, there had been no War Graves officer to oversee his work during the occupation, but Ben had kept meticulous records and gone to extraordinary lengths to forward them to the Commission.

"Sir, I cannot think that my particular and perhaps unique case has been put before the Vice Chairman of the Staff Committee in a favorable manner," Ben protested when he was informed of his Lawson Scheme settlement, "or I would, I know, have been treated better."[55]

Ben had many specific objections. He wanted his accumulated leave, his scheduled raises, and the interest his settlement money was earning as it sat in the bank, undisbursed, year after year. He also found an outright error in the Commission's calculations. They said that Ben had received £203.6.0 in relief payments when in fact he had received only £189.0.0. He had receipts.

Privately, the Commission's officers ridiculed Ben for his persnickety insistence on getting what was owed to him. "I have had a visit from Ben LEACH who is not satisfied about his 40-45 account," wrote finance officer Charles Abbot. Ben had visited the Arras office to reiterate his expectation that the Commission would "pay him in full for the War years."

"Of course, we have no proof as to the amount of time he actually put in," Abbot wrote, "but, as you know, he is an honest type although a nuisance at times with his demands for his 'rights.'"[56]

A year passed, then another and another, but no Lawson Scheme settlement materialized. By 1948, Ben Leech's questions grew more pointed. When, exactly, had the Commission reimbursed Anciens Combattants for his wartime wages? In pounds or francs? At what exchange rate?

The Commission ignored Ben's questions, so he wrote directly to Anciens Combattants to obtain "a complete statement of accounts from both sides."

The official response from Anciens Combattants finally caught the Commission's attention, not because of its contents but because it existed at all. Major William Arnott, now the senior administrative officer in France, wrote Ben a scathing disciplinary letter that lambasted him for writing to the French government without explicit permission.

"You have incurred the Commission's grave displeasure," Arnott fumed. "Under no circumstance should a member of the staff correspond with any person or Authority, British or foreign, on any matter concerned with the work or policy of the Commission without the authority of the Commission."

This was an extraordinary thing to tell a man who had spent years corresponding with the Swiss consulate, the American embassy, and the International Red Cross on Commission business, but Arnott did not see the irony. Instead, he made vague claims that Ben's inquiry "might well have had a harmful effect on relations with the higher French authorities." In consequence, "a note . . . has been made in your official record." If the impertinence was repeated, there would be "serious disciplinary consequences."[57]

In the end, after all the deductions, disputes, and corrections, Ben Leech received a Lawson Scheme settlement of £84.5.9 in 1948. As far as the War Graves Commission was concerned, his case was closed.

Ben continued to raise objections until 1952, when the Commission sent him a firm and final letter.

"In the end you came out on the right side with £84 in your pocket," wrote a frustrated financial officer, "and I do not think you really have grounds for complaint."[58]

Meanwhile, in Paris, American military intelligence was also trying to verify Ben Leech's claim that he had helped Allied airmen. His neighbors had doubts. In 1946, Robert Lenglet, the mayor of Beaumont-Hamel, told French authorities that Ben Leech "took credit for acts committed by others in the rescue of allied paratroopers" and that he "did not do anything to justify an award." The French forwarded this accusation to the Americans.[59]

Ben bristled. "I have never tried to take all the credit for myself," he wrote to an American intelligence officer the following year. "[I] have given names of all the persons who assisted at the risk of their lives."

The Americans at MIS-X conducted a thorough investigation. In their records, they found half a dozen verified helpers who explicitly named Ben Leech as a comrade, including Arthur Richards, who gave specific details about Ben's work. They also found escape and evasion reports by Donald Rentschler and George Simler's crew, all of whom confirmed Ben's story. Some airmen who did not mention Ben in their initial reports did remember him when MIS-X asked them directly. "Lt. [George] Rogers has been contacted and has submitted a full report in which he pays high tribute to you for all the excellent work that you have done," an American officer told Ben.[60]

"His claim does not seem exaggerated," one MIS-X officer wrote after reviewing the evidence. "He says his son Maurice did more than he did. What a declaration."

In the end, the U.S. government recognized both Ben and Maurice Leech as "Grade 5" helpers. This was the most common tier of recognition for civilians who aided evaders. It entitled them to official recognition and a certificate of gratitude signed by General Eisenhower, but not to any medals or financial compensation. Some of Ben's neighbors remained unconvinced.

Life went on. The older Leech children went to the United Kingdom to work or marry. The youngest, Arthur, remained in Beaumont-Hamel and began working for the Commission as a casual laborer. Supervisors considered him a "big strapping bright lad" who was a dab hand with a motor mower, but, "unfortunately, his knowledge of english is practically NIL." Ben and Marie packed the boy off to England for language practice so that he could qualify for a permanent job as a gardener-caretaker. [61]

Even as Arthur Leech prepared for a career as a War Graves gardener, the old labor disputes were making life difficult for the wage staff in France and Belgium. When Ben returned to work in 1945, the Commission paid him 1940 wages, which were wholly inadequate to postwar realities. Prices in France were still astronomical. The Commission attempted to investigate the cost of living, but this was easier said than done. One qualitative inflation index submitted to the Commission by a Treasury official in 1945 seemed drawn from a holiday weekend rather than the daily life of a gardener. Its fifteen items included half a dozen magazines, newspapers, and "literary revues" along with a bottle of champagne, a bunch of lilies, "lunch on train," and a copy of *Gone with the Wind*.[62]

Even practical price indices did not fully capture the gardeners' expenses. When gardener Wilfred Wilshaw submitted a sample weekly budget to the Commission in 1945, it showed that his household spent 933 francs on mundane items like rent, firewood, food, and taxes. This was fifty-three francs more than his weekly pay of 880, which made it impossible for him to pay expenses related to his wartime suffering. "During my internment I lost most of my teeth," Wilshaw explained. As a former internee, he got a discount on an "ordinary set" of dentures—5,000 francs instead of 7,000—but that was still nearly six weeks' wages.[63]

The Commission did agree to give the gardeners a temporary allowance while they debated a new wage scale, but it was not enough. The frustrated wage staff revived their union and insisted on having a representative from the Transport and General Workers' Union sit in on relevant Commission meetings. This raised some hackles among the commissioners. Sir John J. Shute, a commissioner and Conservative member of Parliament, declared himself "very averse" to letting the Union "butt in on our decision."

"Who are their employers, are we, or is the aforesaid Union?" Shute grumbled. "If the men are not satisfied they can resign and find work elsewhere."[64]

The gardeners' union stood firm. They brought actions before the Industrial Court in 1946 and again in 1950, both of which were embarrassing to the Commission but did force them to lurch toward acceptance of less patriarchal labor relations. At the same time, other forces were reshaping the Commission's workforce, including the global distribution of World War II cemeteries and strengthening anti-imperial movements across the empire. The Commission began hiring more local gardeners rather than insisting on sending British ex-servicemen abroad. It was cheaper, but it was also politically expedient. As ever, part of the Commission's mission was to bind the colonies and commonwealths closer to Britain, which meant adapting to changing times. In 1960, they dropped the old "Imperial" name and became the Commonwealth War Graves Commission.

Many of the World War I veterans retired from the Commission staff in the late 1940s, but Ben Leech held on for a few more years. His obstinate complaints did not prevent his supervisors from promoting him to head gardener grade "C" in 1948 and grade "B" in 1952. At last, he was officially in charge of four cemeteries around Beaumont-Hamel though not Serre Road No. 2.

Ben's final performance review in 1955 rated him as "very active, fairly efficient" and his character as "mixed, generally good-hearted." Across the bottom, Major Arnott wrote, "Mr. Leech is of the rough diamond type."

Ben Leech worked as long as he could. Commission policy dictated that gardeners should retire at age sixty but allowed them to remain until age sixty-five if they were in good health. Ben turned sixty-five on November 3, 1954. In a show of beneficence, the Commission allowed him to remain on staff until February 28, 1955, "when your reckonable service will have reached a total of 30 years." In fact, Ben had begun working for the Commission on July 27, 1920, which made thirty-four years and seven months, but his nine years as a blacksmith were discounted by half because he was technically a "temporary" worker during that period.[65]

Some retired War Graves gardeners stayed in France with their in-laws and grandchildren, but Ben returned to Manchester. He had not lived there since 1916, but he still had family in the area, including his daughter Beatrice and her family.

The move may have been promoted by grim economics. The Leech family had never recovered financially from the war, which wiped out their savings and hit them with many expenses that a belated £84.5.9 could not cover. Ben's foreign labor permit expired when he retired, so he could not work legally in France. His Commission pension—one-third of his weekly wage—was not enough to live on. In England, he might be able to find a job, though the prospect of finding housing was dim. Ben appealed to the Manchester Housing Department, which reviewed his unusual case and agreed to add him to the wait list for council housing without the usual two-year residency requirement. Even so, the estimated wait for a vacancy in public housing was five years or more.

Ben was too old for the War Graves Commission but too poor to stop working. Unfortunately, no one was eager to hire a sixty-five-year-old man with arthritis and no fixed address. Ben applied for many jobs in England without luck. He even explored the possibility of staying in France but could not make it work. His options were dwindling to nothing.

Finally, in May 1955, three months after being retired by the Commission, Ben Leech marched into the headquarters of the American Third Air Force in Ruislip, near London, intent on doing "a light bit of blackmail." He bluffed his way into an audience with an American colonel and slapped a paper down on the desk. It was his certificate of thanks, signed by General Eisenhower, expressing the "gratitude and appreciation of the American people for gallant service in assisting the escape of Allied soldiers from the enemy." Ben asked whether the U.S. Air Force was actually grateful or not. No doubt startled, the American colonel agreed that they were and "showed his appreciation" by making sure that they found a job for Ben.

By the end of the month, Ben Leech was working in a warehouse on the U.S. Air Force base at Burtonwood, west of Manchester. Five days a week, he packed and shipped clothing to American air bases around the world.

"I have made numbers of friends," he wrote, "and have lost my old christian name I was known by in Commission (OLD BEN) now it's POP."

Ben did not find the work overly taxing, but he still could not afford stable housing. He lived in lodgings near the air base while Marie remained in Beaumont-Hamel with Arthur. "My housing problem seems as far off as ever," Ben wrote in 1957, after two years of separation.[66]

Before they could be reunited, Marie developed breast cancer. Ben hurried back to France and brought her to Manchester for treatment. "The operation was successful," he wrote, though he regretted not having a home for Marie to convalesce in. Instead, she stayed with Beatrice for several months. Ben visited on weekends. When Marie was well enough to travel, Arthur escorted her back to France.

As he neared seventy, Ben Leech moved from place to place, finding shelter with relatives or in lodgings he could afford. Eventually, his application reached the top of the Manchester council housing list. The brick duplex on a corner lot in Denton was modest, but there was enough room for Ben, Marie, and their son Maurice. It had a sunny garden and was just down the street from fields and woods, though Ben could no longer roam the countryside on foot or bicycle. His arthritis made walking more than ten yards painful.

"I'm sure you will overcome it in your usual phlegmatic way," wrote a friend at the Commission who kept in touch.[67]

In his last years, Ben received Christmas cards from the RAF Escaping Society, but he did not travel to participate in reunions as Rosine Witton did. The Americans had given him a job, but Ben still felt let down by the lack of recognition for his efforts during the war.

"Our greatest disappointment was never to have received acknowledgement from the Air Force (only a diploma in 1945)," Maurice wrote. "But later nothing else."[68]

Marie Leech died on March 7, 1963, six years after her cancer diagnosis. Ben lived another two years, dying on December 1, 1965, at age seventy-six. He left no will and no estate. His body was cremated. The War Graves Commission sent a brief note of condolence to Maurice and closed out Ben's pension account with a check for 10s 11p.

Years later, a journalist from The Times interviewed Arthur Leech during a visit to Beaumont-Hamel. Arthur was still keeping the cemeteries, a job and a tribute to the beloved dead, as it had always been. Over glasses of watered Pernod, Arthur told the journalist about how Ben "emerged from the Somme unscathed" and stayed "to care for his old pals." He recalled that Ben used to say, "They're my friends. They're still alive to me—the battle goes on."[69]

Ben Leech dedicated his life to caring for the war dead, whose loss was fraught with meaning both for himself and for the nation that stridently insisted that it would never forget a single name. Yet Ben Leech—the living person—could not be transformed into a silent, passive symbol. He was too poor, too stubborn, too insistent on his "rights." He worked for an organization whose purpose was to memorialize the war dead, not to take care of the people who survived.

Ben Leech did both.

ACKNOWLEDGMENTS

This book could not have been written without the help of many people who generously shared their time, their expertise, and their friendship with me. I can only send them all my most heartfelt thanks and apologies for any mistakes or omissions.

My first thanks go to the families of War Graves gardeners and airmen who answered e-mails from a stranger and shared their stories, memories, artifacts, and family papers. In particular, thanks to Marcel Hayler; Andre and Karen Hayler; Angus and Garry Moir; Doug Armstrong; David Richards; Julie and Sheila Martin; Jane Evans; Mike Simler; Terry, Scot, and Hunter Jamison; Willie Wemheuer; Paul Chapman; Elizabeth Haworth; Rhydian Evans; Robert Flood; David and Virginie Holton; Lynda Higgs; Alan Kirouac; Pete Boettcher; Lona Sweet and Mary and Bruce Hancey; Chuck Tomaselli; Carl and Jean Follin and Glenda Neal; Ginny Faucette; Jackie Davies; Shelagh Clunes; David Healey; Laif Clark; Suzanne Gwilliam; and Graham Flevill.

Many archivists in many archives supported this project. Special thanks go to Andrew Fetherston and Michael Greet at the Commonwealth War Graves Commission and to George Hay.

Another special thanks to Sherri Ottis, who was the first historian to encourage me in this project.

Special thanks and many apologies go to my friends in France, whose generosity and patience were unparalleled, in particular, Claire Crétel-Diest and Hélène Priego at the Musée de la Résistance in Bondues and Frédéric Turner, Grégory Célerse, Avril Williams, René Lesage, and the late André Coilliot, who generously answered my letters. Thanks also to the Association des Déportés et Familles de Disparus du Camp de Concentration de Flossenbürg & Kommandos.

At a time when travel was not possible, several researchers helped provide access to records I would otherwise have been unable to see. Thanks especially to Sabina von Thuemmler, who not only helped me access records but also translated several fragile, blurry court documents from German to English. Thanks also to Anne Morddel, Stewart Mitchell, Paul Nixon, Leslie Turner, and Alexandra Churchill.

At the United States National Archives and Records Administration, thanks to Suzanne Zoumbaris. Thanks also to Kyle Hovious at the University of Tennessee, Knoxville; Cheryl Boone Perez at Saint Mary's University of Minnesota; the staff of the University Archives at the University of Illinois; and the staff of the Air Force Historical Research Agency in Maxwell, Alabama.

My enthusiasm for this project has been buoyed throughout by the many people interested in the history of the Imperial War Graves Commission who have connected with me via social media. Thanks especially to Paul Reed, Poppy Mercier, Tim Bell, Ben Mayne, Tim Godden, Hanna Smyth, Sarah Ashbridge, Genevra Charsley, Alex Nelepovitz, Simon Bendry, Andrew Thornton, and the Great War Group.

Thanks also to the many historians who generously responded to my queries, including Sue Elliott, Isadore Ryan, Despina Stratigakos, Oliver Clutton-Brock, Michael LeBlanc, D. B. Cherry, Carl Barwise, and Jan Valeš.

This book would not have existed without the support of my Book-Squad pals, who offered friendship and encouragement as well as sensible advice. Thanks to Megan Kate Nelson, Sara Georgini, Liz Covart, Kevin Levin, Joe Adelman, Kate Grandjean, Karin Wulf, Chris Parsons, and Reed Gochberg and to my other writing group, who deserve more credit: Claire, Alina, Kristina, Caroline, Nancy, Trish, Jess, Rebecca, and Jo.

This book is infinitely better than it would have been without the careful reading and insightful comments of Kay Ben-Avram.

It would not exist at all without Amanda Jain, who believed in it right away, and Jake Bonar, who made it possible.

My final thanks go to my family. To Mark DeAngelis and Meg Galante-DeAngelis, my first battlefield guides, who introduced me to cemeteries and to all of history. To my siblings, Ben, Graham, Wheeler, and Brighid, who understand, and to Maureen, Emily, Ellen, and Vinnie, who know what they've gotten themselves into. To Mali and Sam, for being themselves. And most especially to my wife, Fiona, who made it all possible in ways both concrete and ineffable, with every sort of support there is, and who will finally get to hear about something else for once.

NOTES

Abbreviations in the Notes

AD-Nord: Archives départmentales du Nord
AD-PdC: Archives départmentales du Pas de Calais
AD-Somme: Archives départmentales de la Somme
CWGC: Commonwealth War Graves Commission Archives, Maidenhead, UK
CWGC Rolled Records: An uncatalogued roll of oversize records in the CWGC Archives containing brief notes on members of staff in occupied Europe
IWM: Imperial War Museum
LAC: Library and Archives Canada
MOD UK: United Kingdom Ministry of Defence
MRB: Musée de la Résistance, Bondues
NARA: National Archives and Records Administration, United States
TNA: The National Archives, United Kingdom
Vincennes/Caen: Service historique de la Défense Archives, France

Prologue

1. Beaumont-Hamel had a population of 547 in 1911. In 1921, the population was 103. The population did recover a bit, reaching 279 in 1936, but in 2019, it was 208. Of the 7,128 people buried at Serre Road No. 2, 2,193 are identified. See "Cemetery Details: Serre Road Cemetery No. 2," https://www.CWGC.org.

2. A note on terminology: The words "toolhouse" and a "toolshed" are often used interchangeably. In documents of the Imperial War Graves Commission, a "toolhouse" is generally a permanent structure, often made of stone, while a "toolshed" is generally a temporary structure, often metal. Ben Leech called the structure at Serre Road No. 2 a "toolhouse," so I will follow his lead.

3. Commonwealth War Graves Commission, https://www.cwgc.org/who-we-are/our-story, 23 May 2023.

4. Michèle Barrett, "Subalterns at War," *Interventions* 9, no. 3 (2007): 451–74; "The Unremembered: Britain's Forgotten War Heroes," presented by David Lammy, November 2019; CWGC Non-Commemoration Report (2021), https://www.cwgc.org/non-commemoration-report.

5. Previous work on the Imperial War Graves Commission's wage staff and their families include Sue Elliott and James Fox's excellent book about the community in Ypres, *The Children Who Fought Hitler: A British Outpost in Europe* (London: John Murray, 2009); Stephen Grady's memoir *Gardens of Stone: My Boyhood in the French Resistance* (London: Hodder & Stoughton, 2013); and a chapter about Robert Armstrong in Ronan McGreevy, *Wherever the Firing Line Extends: Ireland and the Western Front* (Stroud: The History Press, 2016).

Chapter 1

1. Charles Abbott to John Day, August 26, 1947, Benjamin Morris Leech personnel file P653, Commonwealth War Graves Commission Archives, Maidenhead, UK. Subsequent references to Ben Leech's personnel file will be abbreviated as BML P653, CWGC.

2. Ben Leech's daily gardening log, May 17, 1940, BML, CWGC. Subsequent quotations in this section are from Ben Leech's gardening log, May–August 1940, unless otherwise specified.

3. Maurice Leech to Sherri Ottis, August 1997, courtesy of Sherri Ottis.

4. Michael Watkins, "The Somme's Undying Echoes," *The Times* (London), June 27, 1986, 14.

5. Lawson Report, June 7, 1944, CWGC/1/1/7/B/82.

6. Benjamin Morris Leech service record, Manchester Regiment #27354, TNA; Roy E. Bailey, Timothy J. Hatton, and Kris Inwood, "Health, Height, and the Household at the Turn of the 20th Century," *Economic History Review*, 69, no. 1 (2014): 35–53.

7. In 1899, the compulsory age for attending school was raised from eleven to twelve. This rose again to fourteen in 1918. While not everyone obeyed the law, census records from 1901 and 1911 show that children in the Leech family stayed in school past the compulsory age. Ben's siblings were consistently listed as students at age thirteen but workers at age fifteen. Ben Leech was definitely still attending school at eleven, as shown in the 1901 census.

8. Ben Leech to IWGC, December 17, 1947, BML P653, CWGC.

9. 1911 UK Census; Benjamin Morris Leech service record, Manchester Regiment #27354, TNA.

10. Michael Stedman, *Manchester Pals: A History of the Two Manchester Brigades* (Barnsley: Leo Cooper, 1994).

11. "The Recruiting Campaign; Lord Derby's Plan of Working; The Scheme in Full Operation," *The Times*, November 3, 1915, 39.

12. Benjamin Morris Leech service record, Manchester Regiment #27354, TNA.

13. Thanks to Paul Nixon for contextual research regrading William Brown Leech and Harry Leech with sources including First World War Medal Index Card, British War & Victory Medal Roll, Soldiers' Effects Register, Dependents' Pension Records, and Commonwealth War Graves Commission Casualty registers.

14. Benjamin Morris Leech service record, Manchester Regiment #27354, TNA.

15. For the Somme Offensive of 1916, see Martin Middlebrook, *The First Day on the Somme* (London: Allen Lane, 1971); Lyn MacDonald, *Somme* (London: Michael Joseph, 1983); Peter Hart, *The Somme: The Darkest Hour on the Western Front* (New York: Pegasus, 2013); Gary Sheffield, *The Somme: A New History* (London: Cassell, 2015); and Hugh Sebag-Montefiore, *Somme: Into the Breach* (Cambridge, MA: Harvard University Press, 2016).

16. According to Ben Leech's service record, he was posted to the 18th Manchesters on May 27, 1916, but the battalion's war diary records only one draft of men arriving from its reserves after that time: forty-eight men who arrived on June 21, 1916. War Diary, 18th Battalion Manchester Regiment (3rd City Battalion), WO 95/2339/3, TNA.

17. Journal of Kenneth Callan Macardle, Private Papers of KC Macardle, Documents 12292, IWM.

18. Sheffield, *The Somme*; Newfoundland Memorial Park Museum, Beaumont-Hamel.

19. K. C. Macardle, IWM.

20. War Diary, 18th Battalion Manchester Regiment, TNA, WO 95/2339/3; Stedman, *Manchester Pals*.

21. The 18th Manchesters were definitely not at full strength on July 1, 1916, as they had suffered small numbers of casualties from bombardments, trench raids, and accidents throughout the preceding months. On June 29, less than forty-eight hours before the attack, twenty-three men were wounded by a grenade that exploded in their camp behind the lines in Étinehem. These men may or may not have recovered enough to take part in the attack on July 1. The battalion received numerous small drafts from the reserve battalion (25th Manchesters), but they were not at full strength on July 1. The war diary does not give an exact strength for July 1, but an estimate of 800 is not particularly pessimistic. The war diary reports six officers wounded on July 1 and 170 other ranks killed, wounded, or missing, a casualty rate of approximately 22 percent.

22. War Diary, 18th Battalion Manchester Regiment, TNA, WO 95/2339/3.

23. War Diary, 18th Battalion Manchester Regiment, TNA, WO 95/2339/3; Stedman, *Manchester Pals*.

24. Many of these casualties were men from a ragtag draft of 440 replacements from twenty-eight different battalions that was folded into the 18th Manchesters in the middle of the month. War Diary, 18th Battalion Manchester Regiment,

TNA, WO 95/2339/3. Stedman puts the casualty total at 1,332 in *The Manchester Pals*, p. 53. I count 1,003 other ranks and thirty-two officers in the War Diary of the 18th Battalion Manchester Regiment, TNA. Whatever the exact number, the point is the same: the battalion's casualty figures far exceed 100 percent in the month of July 1916.

25. Benjamin Morris Leech service record, Manchester Regiment #27354, TNA. By this time, the 18th Battalion Manchester Regiment had been disbanded and its men parceled out to a number of units. Ben remained in France, possibly with a pioneer battalion.

26. With thanks to Paul Nixon. CWGC casualty records for William Brown Leech (32810, 4th and 1st Battalions Manchester Regiment) died January 9, 1917, buried at Amara War Cemetery, Iraq, and Harry Leech (originally 49705, Manchester Regiment, then 31283, 2nd Battalion East Lancashire Regiment), died April 24, 1918, buried at Crucifix Corner Cemetery, Villers-Bretonneux, Somme, France.

27. Ben Leech, 27354, Dependent's Pension, roll 48079_118^0557 LEE-LEE, UK World War I Pension Ledgers and Index Cards, 1914–1923, Western Front Association.

28. BML P653, CWGC. A note in Ben Leech's service record indicates that he was "severely reprimanded" on January 15, 1920, the day before he was demobilized. Unfortunately, the quality of the microfilm reproduction makes it difficult to say what, exactly, his offense was, and the National Archives (UK) does not allow researcher access to the original records.

29. For the history of British military burials, see David Crane, *Empires of the Dead: How One Man's Vision Led to the Creation of WWI's War Graves* (London: William Collins, 2013); Robert Sackville-West, *The Searchers: The Quest for the Lost of the First World War* (New York: Bloomsbury, 2021); Thomas Laqueur, *The Work of the Dead: A Cultural History of Mortal Remains* (Princeton, NJ: Princeton University Press, 2015); and Philip Longworth, *The Unending Vigil: A History of the Commonwealth War Graves Commission* (London: Constable, 1967).

30. New research by Waterloo Uncovered, a historical and archaeological team exploring the Waterloo battlefield, has established the use of bones in the production of beet sugar at nearby factories (see https://www.waterloouncovered .com): chief executive officer Mark Evans and archaeological directors Tony Pollard, Stuart Eve, and Dominique Bosquet with research by Robin Schäfer and Bernard Wilkin. See also Paul O'Keefe, *Waterloo: The Aftermath* (New York: The Overlook Press, 2017).

31. J. David Hacker, "A Census-Based Count of the Civil War Dead," *Civil War History* 57, no. 4 (December 2011): 307–48.

32. United States National Cemetery Administration, "History and Development of the NCA," https://www.cem.va.gov; Drew Gilpin Faust, *This Republic of Suffering: Death and the American Civil War* (New York: Vintage Books, 2008).

33. Other countries' military burial traditions developed in their own contexts. During the Franco-Prussian War (1870–1871), France drew on its long tradition of ossuary burials, turning anonymous mass graves into national reliquaries. The Prussian army used identification tags and established some military cemeteries but did not promise completeness. After World War I, the care of German graves fell to a private charity, the Volksbund Deutsche Kriegsgräberfürsorge. Lorenzo Zambernardi, *Life, Death, and the Western Way of War* (Oxford: Oxford University Press, 2022).

34. Lord Derby letter to "unscarred" men, widely reprinted in the autumn of 1915.

35. Crane, *Empires of the Dead*.

36. Fabian Ware, *The Worker and His Country* (London: E. Arnold, 1912).

37. Crane, *Empires of the Dead*, 78.

38. Numbers fluctuated; these are from the 1931 count and cited in subsequent annual reports. The percentages changed slightly between 1921 and 1931 but not meaningfully; Royal Charter of the Imperial War Graves Commission, 1917.

39. CWGC/6/1/1: Staff Committee Meeting Minutes, 1927–1937, 92.

40. The work of Dr. Michèle Barrett brought the story of the East African porters to global attention, in particular with the broadcast of "The Unremembered: Britain's Forgotten War Heroes," a documentary presented by David Lammy in November 2019. Dr. Barrett's work led to the Commonwealth War Graves Commission establishing a special committee that issued a report, "The Report of the Special Committee to Review Historical Inequalities in Commemoration," also known as "The Non-Commemoration Report," in 2021. See Michèle Barrett, "Subalterns at War," *Interventions* 9, no. 3 (2007): 451–74, and CWGC Non-Commemoration Report (2021), https://www.cwgc.org/non-commemoration-report.

41. Adrian Gregory, *The Silence of Memory: Armistice Day, 1919–1946* (New York: Bloomsbury, 2014); Laqueur, *The Work of the Dead*, 470.

42. Ruth Jervis to IWGC, December 1, 1918, CWGC Archives, CWGC/1/1/7/B/42: Exhumation in France and Belgium; see also Richard van Emden, *The Quick and the Dead: Fallen Soldiers and Their Families in the Great War* (New York: Bloomsbury, 2011); Viscount Wolmer, member of Parliament quoted in Crane, *Empires of the Dead*, 158; and Veronica Cusack, *The Invisible Soldier: Captain W.A.P. Durie, His Life and Afterlife* (New York: Penguin Random House, 2013).

43. Petition to the Prince of Wales from Lady Florence Cecil, wife of the Bishop of Exeter, 1919, CWGC/1/1/5/14.

44. Sackville-West, *The Searchers*.

45. There is some discrepancy between records as to whether Harry Leech was nineteen or twenty when he died. The family gravestone in Gorton Cemetery, Manchester, says nineteen, but birth and census records indicate that he was twenty.

46. War Diary, 2nd Battalion East Lancashire Regiment, WO 95/1729/2, TNA.

47. Harry Leech, 31283, 2nd Battalion East Lancashire Regiment, UK Army Register of Soldiers' Effects, 1901–1929.

48. Ann Leech gravestone, 1930, Gorton Cemetery, Manchester, UK.

49. Rudyard Kipling, quoted in Longworth, *The Unending Vigil.*

50. CWGC/6/1/1: Staff Committee Meeting Minutes, 1927–1937.

51. BML P653, CWGC. With thanks to Andrew Fetherston.

52. CWGC/2/1: Eleventh Annual Report of the IWGC, 1929-30.

53. With thanks to Alan Kirouac, Paul Chapman, Jackie Davies, and Marcel, Andre, and Karen Hayler. See also Albert Census, 1926, AD-Somme; service records of Albert Douglas Chapman (36060, Canadian Army Service Corps) and Lewis Fulton Bonnell (1251003, 78th Battery Canadian Field Artillery), Library and Archives Canada, and Paul Chapman, *Cameos of the Western Front: In the Shadow of Hell, Ypres Sector, 1914–18* (Barnsley: Leo Cooper, 2008).

54. Yvonne Caron birth record, Tatinghem, PdC, France, September 13, 1907. With thanks to Anne Morddel. Marie Caron lived in the same boarding-house as Edwin Carr (a War Graves mechanic) and his wife, Marie, so she may have met Ben Leech through them. Saint-Omer Census 1921, AD-PdC.

55. Maurice Leech birth record, Saint-Omer, PdC, France, June 16, 1921; marriage record for Benjamin Leech and Marie Caron, Saint-Omer, PdC, France, September 2, 1922. AD-PdC. With thanks to Anne Morddel. Back in Manchester, Agnes Groves married someone else. Young Benjamin Leech Groves lived a short life and died a terrible death. In 1921, Ben Groves boarded with Egbert and Selina Jackson in Ardwick. In 1928, the eleven-year-old's body was found floating in an industrial canal not far from the Railway Street home where his father grew up. The coroner ruled his death an accidental drowning. See marriage record for Agnes Groves and John Mangan, Gorton, Manchester, October 14, 1922; 1921 Census of England and Wales; Death registration for Ben L. Groves, Ashton, Lancashire, Vol. 8d, p. 740, May 13–14, 1928. With thanks to Leslie Turner.

56. IWGC annual reports 1920–1940; CWGC/1/2/D/7/9 Re-Opening of Commission's Work in France and Belgium, 1944.

57. BML P653, CWGC.

58. The population of Beaumont-Hamel was 222 in 1926 and 271 in 1931; see Beaumont-Hamel Census, AD-Somme.

59. By 1928, much of the Zone Rouge had been cleared, but 526 acres around Thiepval, the village next to Beaumont-Hamel, remained unrehabilitated. See Hugh Clout, *After the Ruins: Restoring the Countryside of Northern France after the Great War* (Exeter: University of Exeter Press, 1996), 265; CWGC/6/1/1: Minutes of the Staff Committee Meetings, 1927–1937.

60. Benjamin Morris Leech contract, July 1, 1928, BML P653, CWGC.

Chapter 2

1. Rosine Witton to Alfie Martin, May 9, 1966. Courtesy of Sheila and Julie Martin; Rosine Witton, "French Helper" file, NARA, RG 0498, UD 193.

2. See chapter 18.

3. Various sources call Rosine's store a café, a *café-tabac*, and a tobacconist. It was probably a small shop with a few tables that sold tobacco, newspapers, sundries, and alcohol. It may also have offered light fare, though Bert's letters suggest that Rosine's cooking was a running joke. André Coilliot, *1940–1944, 4 Longues Années d'Occupation: Le Récit des Événements Vécus dans la Region d'Arras*, 3 vols. (privately printed at Beaurains, 1985–1986); Frédéric Turner, *Les Oublies de 39-45: Les Britanniques Internés a Tost, Kreuzberg, Giromagny et Westertimke* (Arras: Editions JAFT, 2013); Rosine Witton, "French Helper" file, NARA, RG 0498, UD 193.

4. One of the quarries, Carrière Wellington, is now a museum that offers tours of the tunnels. The museum is located about 300 meters from Rosine Witton's house at Number 6 Route de Bapaume, now rue Fernand Lobbedez.

5. According to census records from the 1870s to the 1930s, Rosine's extended family members were mostly laborers, craftspeople, and shopkeepers in Arras and Saint-Laurent-Blangy. AD-PdC.

6. *Wall Street Journal*, October 19, 1914. By the spring of 1917, only 1,000 civilians were still living in the ruins of Arras. See Alex Dowdall, *Communities under Fire: Urban Life at the Western Front, 1914–1918* (Oxford: Oxford University Press, 2020).

7. *Refugies de Pas de Calais*, December 29, 1915, and February 9, 1916, in the collection of the AD-PdC.

8. Gaston Alexis Becourt, solder de 2e classe, 128th Infantry Regiment, son of Leontine Becourt's brother Amies, died October 31, 1916, Berny-en-Santerre, Somme, database of Morts pour la France de la Première Guerre Mondiale, Mémoire des hommes, Ministère de la défense de France, https://www.memoire deshommes.sga.defense.gouv.fr.

9. Photographs by French official photographers in the Destruction on the Western Front, 1914–1918 collection at the Imperial War Museum, London, including "Ruined street at Ronville (Faubourg-d'Amiens, Arras), 30 June 1917" (Q 78358), and "The Road from Ronville (Arras) to Beaurains, 30 June 1917" (Q 61254); Harold Grover letter to Reginald Haworth, June 22, 1966, CWGC/1/2/I/20: Letters and Accounts by Retired Employees of the Commission (Reminiscences); *Le Bellfroi d'Arras*, April 29, 1920.

10. The struggle to restore basic infrastructure to Ronville was a long-running subject in the newspaper *Le Bellfroi d'Arras* through the 1920s; Hugh Clout, *After the Ruins: Restoring the Countryside of Northern France after the Great War* (Exeter: University of Exeter Press, 1996).

11. *Le Lion d'Arras*, August 21, 1919, and October 30, 1919; Matthew Tomlinson, *Rebuilding Albert: Reconstruction and Remembrance on the Western Front, 1914–1932* (PhD thesis, University of York, 2005).

12. Clout, *After the Ruins*, 151.

13. Tomlinson, *Rebuilding Albert*, 145; interview with Marcel Hayler, December 12, 2019; Sue Elliott and James Fox, *The Children Who Fought Hitler: A British Outpost in Europe* (London: John Murray, 2009).

14. Albert Roberts (September 18, 1966) and Margaret Grinham (August 12, 1965) to Reginald Haworth, CWGC/1/2/I/20: Letters and Accounts by Retired Employees of the Commission (Reminiscences).

15. Elliott and Fox. *The Children Who Fought Hitler*.

16. "Spent Childhood Near War Graves in France," *Manchester Guardian*, February 3, 1940. Joseph Hillier lived in Achicourt from the ages of two to ten (1922–1930).

17. Auguste Thérier Sr. and Jr. both worked for Le Service de Reconstitution des Régions Libérées (SRRL). Arras census, 1921, in the collection of the AD-PdC.

18. Harold Grover to Reginald Haworth, June 22, 1966, CWGC/1/2/I/20: Letters and Accounts by Retired Employees of the Commission (Reminiscences).

19. Technically, Number 6 was in the suburb of Achicourt but only because Route de Bapaume was the boundary line, with even-numbered houses in Achicourt and odd-numbered houses in Arras. The distinction did not matter much in everyday life, and people who lived on Route de Bapaume frequently gave their address as "Arras" even if they lived on the even-numbered side of the street.

20. Mary Dewhurst Lewis. *The Boundaries of the Republic: Migrant Rights and the Limits of Universalism in France, 1918–1940* (Stanford, CA: Stanford University Press, 2007); Patrick Weil and Catherine Porter, *How to Be French: Nationality in the Making since 1789* (Durham, NC: Duke University Press, 2008).

21. Census records of Thiepval, Beaumont-Hamel, Montauban, Courcelette, Pozières, Guillemont, Longueval, Contalmaison, and other villages, 1911–1931, in the collection of the AD-Somme.

22. Many published works say that John Fraser was Scottish, but he was born in London (St. Pancras) on September 11, 1896. His father, George James Fraser, was also born in London, and his mother, Beatrice Mary Heal, was from Essex. His grandparents on both sides were also from southern England. The confusion likely stems from assumptions made by the Special Operations Executive based on his surname and repeated by others since.

23. Ben Leech, April 27, 1946, "French Helper" file, NARA, RG 0498, UD 193.

24. CWGC/6/1/1: Staff Committee Meeting Minutes, 1927–1937, 105.

25. Sir Frederic Kenyon, September 19, 1918, Frank Higginson personnel file P 315, CWGC/1/1/13/32; Higginson was born in Carlisle (UK) and moved to New York as a young architect. He lived in Canada for only a few months in 1914 but served with the Canadians (14th Infantry Battalion CEF [Royal Montreal Regiment]).

26. CWGC/6/1/1: Staff Committee Meeting Minutes, 1927–1937, 71.

27. Olivia Smith, "The Women Gardeners of the First World War," CWGC blog, https://www.cwgc.org/our-work/blog/the-women-gardeners-of-the-first -world-war.

28. The absence of women from the commission was a contentious issue. Mourning mothers and widows held a particular moral significance in postwar British remembrance culture, and their exclusion was one of the many objections raised against the War Graves Commission by its critics in Parliament. "It is extremely unfortunate that there is not a single woman upon that Commission," Viscount Wolmer told the House in 1920. The influential garden designer Gertrude Jekyll consulted with the architects on planting schemes for the cemeteries, but she was not a member of the staff. See David Crane, *Empires of the Dead* (Glasgow: William Collins, 2013), 161, and CWGC Staff Cards.

29. Report to the Finance Committee, October 21, 1919. in Finance Committee meeting of October 29, 1919, CWGC/4/2/9.

30. Guoqi Xu, *Strangers on the Western Front: Chinese Workers in the Great War* (Cambridge, MA: Harvard University Press, 2011).

31. CWGC/4/2/19: Notes of the 19th IWGC Finance Committee Meeting, April 14, 1920. With thanks to Andrew Fetherston, former chief archivist of the Commonwealth War Graves Commission (CWGC), presentation of research on Chinese Labour Corps Headstones, 2022. In many cases, these headstones have since been replaced a second time with stones that do bear transliterated names, but the original names carved by the Chinese stone carvers have mostly been lost.

32. "Gratuity for Kurnatowski, Retired Cemetery Gardener," FO 371/135139, TNA; CWGC/6/1/1: Minutes of Staff Committee Meetings 1–27 (1927–1937).

33. Achicourt census, 1931, AD-PdC.

34. Arras and Achicourt census records, 1926, 1931, 1936, AD-PdC.

35. Marriage Record for Rosine Thérier and Sidney Albert Witton, October 8, 1932, Achicourt, Pas-de-Calais

36. John A. Tully, *Silvertown: The Lost Story of a Strike That Shook London and Helped Launch the Modern Labor Movement* (New York: Monthly Review Press, 2014); Graham Hill and Howard Bloch, *The Silvertown Explosion: London 1917* (Stroud: Tempus Publishing, 2003); Albert Sydney Witton (aka Sidney Albert Witton), Royal Air Force service file, AIR 79/743/81893, TNA. The factory that the Witton family worked in was the India Rubber, Gutta Percha, and Telegraph Works.

37. Unless otherwise specified, quotations in the following section are drawn from CWGC/6/1/1: Minutes of Staff Committee Meetings 1–27 (1927–1937).

38. In 1909, Belgium passed liberal nationalization laws that allowed children born in Belgium to claim Belgian citizenship, but these laws were repealed by a strict *jus sanguines* law passed in 1922. Thus, some Belgian-born War Graves children born before 1922 may have been Belgian citizens. Marie-Claire Foblets and Zeynep Yanasmayan, *Country Report: Belgium* (Florence: EUDO Citizenship Observatory, 2010); Cyril Chapman, "My Life," submitted by the Doddridge

Centre, Northampton, to "WW2 People's War: An Archive of World War Two Memories Written by the Public, Gathered by the BBC," BBC.

39. For a comprehensive account of the Memorial School in Ypres and interviews with many of its former students, see Elliott and Fox, *The Children Who Fought Hitler*.

40. My analysis of the War Graves Commission's labor history owes a debt to Fobazi Ettarh, who coined the term "vocational awe" in "Vocational Awe and Librarianship: The Lies We Tell Ourselves," In the Library with a Lead Pipe, January 10, 2018, https://www.inthelibrarywiththeleadpipe.org/2018/vocational-awe.

41. CWGC/1/1/3/28: General Strike.

42. "Establishment: War Graves Commission: Wage and Employment Questions regarding Men Employed as Gardeners in France and Belgium," T 162/867/7, TNA.

43. Peter Moir Service Record, Gordon Highlanders, 2874076, MOD UK. With thanks to Angus Moir and Garry Moir.

44. W. Parker, dated May 3, 1939, T 162/867/7, TNA.

45. Frederick Sillar to I. Wild, April 11, 1940, T 162/867/7, TNA.

46. CWGC/1/1/4/28: Interdepartmental Correspondence Economies (1938).

47. Minutes of the Meetings of the Imperial War Graves Commission: 215th Meeting, May 1938 (CWGC/2/2/1/215); 218th Meeting, September 1938 (CWGC/2/2/1/218).

48. Brigadier Prower's wage scale began at £800, rising £50 per year to £1,000, with a £200 per year special allowance. Frank Higginson's salary for the same position was £1,200. See Higginson, P 315, CWGC/1/1/13/32.

49. According to his staff card in the CWGC archives, Bert Witton earned £143 per year (£2.15.0 per week) after being promoted from laborer to gardener-caretaker in 1936; £3.10.0 was the minimum for gardener-caretakers with three years' experience according to the Industrial Court decision. It is possible that the commission discounted Bert's prior experience and paid him the new gardener wage of £3.7.0, in which case the raise was 22 percent.

Chapter 3

1. John Mervyn Prower service record, British Columbia Militia, Canada, Certificates of Military Instruction, 1867–1932, RG9 II-K-6; Volume: 59, LAC; John Mervyn Prower service record, Canadian Expeditionary Force, RG 150, LAC.

2. War Diary of the 8th Canadian Infantry Battalion, R611-78-4-E, RG9-III-C-3, LAC. Prower also served as a staff officer at 2nd Brigade headquarters before being promoted to Lieutenant Colonel in August 1916 and given command of the 8th Battalion; letter from H.C. Osborne to IWGC, February 15, 1938, CWGC/1/1/7/B/73.

3. Prower CEF service record, LAC.

4. CWGC/2/2/1/215: Minutes of IWGC Meeting No. 215, May 18, 1938.

5. CWGC/1/1/7/B/77: Sir Fabian Ware to Oscar Gill, September 20, 1939.

6. CWGC/1/1/7/B/73: Fabian Ware to H. C. Osborn, January 1940.

7. CWGC/1/1/7/B/73: Prower to Ware, October 12, 1939; Ware to Prower, February 13, 1940.

8. CWGC/1/1/7/B/73: Ware to Prower, January 19, 1940; Prower to Ware, January 26, 1940.

9. Letters from Colonel E. A. W. Courtney (December 28, 1918) and Major General Lovick B. Friend (January 5, 1920) describing Haworth's war work in Reginald Haworth personnel file, P 144 CWGC/1/1/13/29.

10. Mr. Walton, Hesketh Golf Club, Southport, November 5, 1930, in Reginald Haworth personnel file, P144 CWGC/1/1/13/29.

11. CWGC/1/1/7/B/73: Prower to Ware, April 18, 1939; Ware's report, September 28, 1939.

12. CWGC/1/1/7/B/73: Ware to Prower, June 19, 1939.

13. The caps were shipped to France in December 1939, but it is unclear whether they were ever distributed. See Ben Leech's account of the children of Albert wearing Commission hats in 1940, chapter 5. CWGC/1/1/7/B/73; CWGC/2/2/1/232: Minutes of the 232nd meeting of the Commission; William Arnott to Chettle, September 1944, CWGC/1/2/A/505: Re-Opening of Commission's Work, France and Belgium; CWGC/1/1/7/78: Greensill's Account.

14. Allan Allport, *Britain at Bay: The Epic Story of the Second World War, 1938–1941* (New York: Knopf, 2020); Hugh Sebag-Montefiore, *Dunkirk: Fight to the Last Man* (Cambridge, MA: Harvard University Press, 2006).

15. CWGC/1/1/7/B/73: Prower to Ware, October 12, 1939.

16. CWGC/1/1/7/B/73: Prower to Ware, January 12, 1940.

17. Reginald Haworth to Sir Fabian Ware, September 28, 1939, CWGC/1/1/7/B/77.

18. CWGC 1/1/7/B/79: Report on the Withdrawal of Staff from France and Belgium.

19. CWGC/1/1/7/B/77: Withdrawal of Staff from France and Belgium.

20. Letters between Sir Fabian Ware and Ambassador Clive, 1939, CWGC/1/1/7/B/75.

21. CWGC/1/1/7/B/74: France: Evacuation of Personnel.

22. Brigadier Prower wrote this on May 25, 1940, in a letter requesting that the policy be changed. The quotation is from the opening of the letter, which summarizes Commission policy prior to May 25, 1940.

23. Marcel Hayler, interview and unpublished memoir, December 12, 2019. With thanks to Marcel, Andre, and Karen Hayler.

24. Peter had previously served in a machine gun company, so he was assigned to the 4th Battalion, which was a specialist machine gun unit. With thanks to Stewart Mitchell.

25. War Diary Entry, November 23, 1939, War Diary of the Deputy Assistant Director Graves Registration and Enquiries, October 1939–April 1940, WO 167/1370, TNA; C. K. Phillips personnel file, T 48, CWGC/1/1/13/64.

26. CWGC/1/2/I/14.

27. War Diary Entry, November 11, 1939, War Diary of the Deputy Assistant Director Graves Registration and Enquiries, October 1939–April 1940, WO 167/1370, TNA.

28. CWGC/1/1/7/B/73: Ware to Prower, October 11, 1939; CWGC/1/2/I/14, December 8, 1939.

29. CWGC/1/1/7/B/73: Ware telegram addressed to Colonel Chettle, undated but from context probably October 1939; Prower to Ware, January 26, 1940.

30. Per Prower's order of October 31, 1939, the letters were kept by the horticultural officers and by Traveling Superintendent Gardeners Bird, Richardson, and Prynn. CWGC/1/1/7/B/74.

31. Haworth Circular, May 18, 1940, CWGC/1/1/7/B/76.

Chapter 4

1. This account of Bob Armstrong's visit to the War Graves Commission office in Arras on May 16, 1940, is reconstructed from the reports filed by TSG R. Bird (May 26, 1940) and Captain Alfred Melles (May 29, 1940) in CWGC/1/1/7/B/78 as well as Jack Day's statement dated July 2, 1945, in RA P624 CWGC. Many of the accounts in this chapter come from reports written by the IWGC officers after they returned to England in late May and early June 1940 and were used by the Commission to write its June 8 report. Accounts by Bird, Melles, Burkey, Arnott, Greensill, Phillips, Haworth, and Prower are used extensively in this chapter, and all can be found in CWGC/1/1/7/B/78: Withdrawal of Staff from France and Belgium.

2. RA P624 CWGC.

3. Bob Armstrong's ex-wife was named Claire Maricq. Various records have different dates for their divorce, but Bob recorded it as 1932 on his intake papers at Rheinbach Prison in 1944. Robert Armstrong, personnel file, Rheinbach Prison, 1944, collection 13471, NS-Archive of the Ministry of State Security, ZC 20.088, file 11, Sachsen State Archive, Dresden. With thanks to Sabina von Thuemmler. On May 16, Bob met with James Rodger, a Scottish neighbor who lived in his neighborhood in Valenciennes, before going to Arras. Rodger escaped Valenciennes and wrote to the IWGC asking for news of Bob. RA P624 CWGC.

4. CWGC/1/1/7/B/78: R. Bird's Account.

5. CWGC/1/1/7/B/78: S. Burkey's Account says they left Albert at 7:45 p.m.

6. Sue Elliott and James Fox, *The Children Who Fought Hitler: A British Outpost in Europe* (London: John Murray, 2009).

7. CWGC/1/1/7/B/78: Haworth's Account; Elliott and Fox, *The Children Who Fought Hitler*.

8. CWGC/1/1/7/B/78: Greensill's Account.

9. Elliott and Fox, *The Children Who Fought Hitler*.

10. Cyril Chapman, "My Life," submitted by the Doddridge Centre, Northampton, to "WW2 People's War: An Archive of World War Two Memories Written by the Public, Gathered by the BBC," BBC; Paul Chapman, *Cameos of the Western Front: In the Shadow of Hell, Ypres Sector, 1914–18* (Barnsley: Leo Cooper, 2008). With thanks to Paul Chapman.

11. Cyril Chapman, "My Life," BBC.

12. CWGC/1/1/7/B/78: Price's Account.

13. André Coilliot, *1940–1944, 4 Longues Années d'Occupation: Le Récit des Événements Vécus dans la Region d'Arras*, vol. 1 (privately printed at Beaurains, 1985–1986); Testimony of 2nd Lt. Tony Younger, Royal Engineers in Sebag-Montefiore, Dunkirk; CWGC/1/1/7/B/78: Gothwaite's Account.

14. Day's Account, RA P624 CWGC.

15. CWGC/1/1/7/B/78: Greensill's Account.

16. CWGC/1/1/7/B/77: phone memo, May 20, 1940.

17. For a full account of the Dawson and Wilkins families, including interviews, see Elliott and Fox, *The Children Who Fought Hitler.*

18. Charles Abbot to Reginald Haworth, June 30, 1965, CWGC/1/2/I/20.

19. Prower to Ware, undated, but the context indicates that this was written in early June 1940, likely in response to a telegram from Ware dated June 6, 1940. CWGC/1/1/7/B/76: Evacuation.

20. With thanks to Andrew Thornton.

21. Allan Allport, *Britain at Bay: The Epic Story of the Second World War, 1938–1941* (New York: Knopf, 2020); Tim Saunders, *Arras Counter-Attack 1940* (Barnsley: Pen & Sword Military, 2018).

22. Marcel Hayler, interview and unpublished memoir, December 12, 2019. With thanks to Marcel, Andre, and Karen Hayler.

23. "Aliens Rules Offenses," *Portsmouth Evening News*, March 31, 1943.

24. Chapman, "My Life," BBC.

25. Sue Elliott, *I Heard My Country Calling: Elaine Madden, the Unsung Heroine of the SOE* (Stroud: The History Press, 2015).

26. Prower to Ware, May 25, 1940, CWGC/1/1/7/B/78.

27. MacDougall was able to escape to the United Kingdom on June 17, 1940. See list dated June 17, 1940, CWGC/1/1/7/B/77; Prower report, June 7, 1940, CWGC/1/1/7/B/76: Evacuation; Ware to Prower, June 5, 1940, CWGC/1/1/7/B/77.

28. Prower received letters from Haines, Keed, Kirkwood, Morton, and Gifford, all of whom were later interned. CWGC/1/1/7/B/77.

29. Sir Fabian Ware to Duff Cooper, June 10, 1940, CWGC/1/1/7/B/79: Report on the Withdrawal of Staff from France and Belgium.

30. Duff Cooper to Fabian Ware, June 13, 1940.

31. Sir John Kennedy to Sir Fabian Ware, June 11, 1940; Sir George Macdonogh to Sir Fabian Ware, June 12, 1940. I cannot read the third signature, but it is with the others and dated June 13, 1940. CWGC/1/1/7/B/79.

32. William Hogan testimony, 1942, CWGC/1/2/D/7/10: Aliens and Refugees Register; Walter Coller will proved, Oxford, April 14, 1948, Coller declared dead "on or since the month of May 1940."

33. CWGC Rolled Records.

34. Maynard Pursglove's death certificate lists his causes of death as pneumonia and "disseminated sclerosis," June 8, 1940, Brenchley, Kent; "The Late Mr. Pursglove," *Kent and Sussex Courier*, June 14, 1940; CWGC Staff Card.

35. CWGC Rolled Records.

36. Similarly, no effort was ever made to investigate the fates of the Commission's many temporary employees, though several were interned, and at least one was shot by the Nazis. William Hogan testimony, 1942, CWGC/1/2/D/7/10: Aliens and Refugees Register; CWGC/1/1/7/B/77.

37. CWGC/1/1/7/B/78: Bird's Account.

38. CWGC/1/1/7/B/76: Ware to Prower, June 6, 1940; Sir George Macdonogh to Sir Fabian Ware, June 12, 1940, CWGC/1/1/7/B/79.

39. "The fact remains that during the more very critical hours [Prower] was not in command at Wimereux as he should have been." Sir Fabian Ware, June 11, 1940, CWGC/1/1/7/B/77.

40. There is a mention of "R.G. Armstrong" in Grinham's report regarding evacuees from Boulogne, but this is Robert George Armstrong (P727), who joined the Commission as a probationary gardener in 1936, not Robert Armstrong (P624), the head gardener from Valenciennes.

41. IWGC to Augusta Lindsay, May 27, 1940, RA P624 CWGC.

Chapter 5

1. Ben Leech gardening log, May 17, 1940, BML P653 CWGC.

2. Frederick Martin, June 4, 1940, Frederick Martin personnel file, P 415, CWGC/1/1/13/113.

3. Tim Lynch, *Dunkirk 1940: Whereabouts Unknown: How Untrained Troops of the Labour Divisions Were Sacrificed to Save an Army* (Stroud: The History Press, 2010). The 1st Tyneside Scottish were on their way to Bapaume by way of Doullens, Hedauville, and Pusieux. This route would have taken them directly past Sucrerie Cemetery. Private Papers of C H Baggs, Documents.2922, IWM.

4. CWGC/1/1/7/B/78: Burkey's Account.

5. Edward Goad to Sir Fabian Ware, September 28, 1941, CWGC/1/1/7/B/77.

6. Edward Goad to Sir Fabian Ware, September 28, 1941, CWGC/1/1/7/B/77; Goad's Account in CWGC/1/1/7/B/78.

7. Edward Goad to Sir Fabian Ware, September 28, 1941, CWGC/1/1/7/B/77; CWGC Rolled Records.

8. O'Neill says this happened on "Friday May 18," which is a mistake because Friday was the 17th and Saturday was the 18th. It is clear from context that he means Friday the 17th. Michael O'Neill Testimony, April 1942,

CWGC/1/2/D/7/10: Aliens and Refugees Register. CWGC Rolled Records say that Clark died at Vittel on February 27, 1944.

9. Officers' families also evacuated with unusual success. Only one officer's family—Captain William Arnott's wife, Andrée, and their daughters, eighteen-year-old Leslie and fifteen-year-old Genevieve—were left behind. Early in the evacuation, Arnott went to assist Captain Haworth's group and was not able to return to his own family. All the other officers' families reached England safely. CWGC Rolled Records; William Arnott personnel file, P 538, CWGC/1/1/13/100.

10. CWGC/1/1/7/B/78: S. Burkey's Account.

11. CWGC/1/1/7/B/77: Withdrawal of Staff from France and Belgium. With thanks to Angus Moir and Garry Moir.

12. BML P653 CWGC.

13. BML P653 CWGC; André Coilliot, *1940–1944, 4 Longues Années d'Occupation: Le Récit des Événements Vécus dans la Region d'Arras*, vol. 1 (privately printed at Beaurains, 1985–1986).

14. Coilliot, *1940–1944, 4 Longues Années d'Occupation*, vol. 1.

15. N. Dombrowski Risser, *France under Fire: German Invasion, Civilian Flight and Family Survival during World War II* (Cambridge: Cambridge University Press, 2012); Raffael Scheck, "'They Are Just Savages': German Massacres of Black Soldiers from the French Army in 1940," *Journal of Modern History* 77, no. 2 (June 2005): 325–44; Sean Longden, *Dunkirk: The Men They Left Behind* (London: Constable, 2009).

16. Because he was buried on the southern end of this battlefield, Peter Moir was probably with B or D Company, under command of the 143rd Brigade and supporting the 1/7 and 1/8 Warwicks.

17. In census records, the Pronier name is spelled Pronnier, but I have used Pronier because that is what is in most published sources, both in English and in French. Private Papers of C H Baggs, Documents.2922, IWM; Coilliot, *1940–1944, 4 Longues Années d'Occupation*, vol. 1.

18. Coilliot, *1940–1944, 4 Longues Années d'Occupation*, vol. 1, 49–64.

19 Anatole Lefebvre in Coilliot, *1940–1944, 4 Longues Années d'Occupation*, vol. 1, 63–64.

20. Coilliot interviewed gardener Jack Peet about events in Gavrelle. Coilliot, *1940–1944, 4 Longues Années d'Occupation*, vol. 1, 16.

21. Testimony of Alfred Wells, Percy Hammerton, and Albert Roberts, CWGC/1/2/D/7/12.

22. William Hogan testimony, 1942, CWGC/1/2/D/7/10: Aliens and Refugees Register.

23. Stephen Grady, *Gardens of Stone: My Boyhood in the French Resistance* (London: Hodder & Stoughton, 2013), 68–69.

24. Photographs of Hitler's June 1940 "Frontfahrt" by his photographer, Heinrich Hoffmann, exist in a number of archives, including negatives in the

U.S. National Archives and Records Administration, RG 242: Foreign Records Seized (242-HLB 4965-5074). The photos of Hitler passing the Gare d'Arras are on roll 5036.

25. Bob Carruthers, *Hitler's Propaganda Pilgrimage: Rare Photographs from Wartime Archives* (Barnsley: Pen & Sword Military, 2015).

26. Musée de l'Armistice 14-18, Compiègne.

27. *Daily Mirror*, June 3, 1940; *Liverpool Echo*, June 1, 1940; *Edmonton Journal*, June 1, 1940. Allward's quotes were reprinted in many newspapers on June 1, including the *Windsor Star* (Ontario), the *Vancouver Sun*, and the *Edmonton Journal*; *New York Times*, June 5, 1940, 5; Carruthers, *Hitler's Propaganda Pilgrimage*.

28. Kirrily Freeman, *Bronzes to Bullets: Vichy and the Destruction of French Public Statuary, 1941–1944* (Stanford, CA: Stanford University Press, 2009); Bertram M. Gordon, *War Tourism: Second World War France from Defeat and Occupation to the Creation of Heritage* (Ithaca, NY: Cornell University Press, 2018).

29. Despina Stratigakos, "The Invasion of Memory: Hitler's Attempt to Rewrite the History of World War I," *Architect: The Journal of the American Institute of Architects*, November 6, 2019. With thanks to Professor Stratigakos for her generosity in discussing and sharing the Haßdenkmäler order with me.

30. Haßdenkmäler order of August 12, 1940. With thanks to Despina Stratigakos.

31. The monument was certainly disfigured before September 4, 1940, when George Gregson mentions its partial destruction in his journal as an event that galvanized the people of Lille against the occupation.

32. Matthew Fraser, *Monumental Fury: The History of Iconoclasm and the Future of Our Past* (Lanham, MD: Prometheus, 2022); Freeman, *Bronzes to Bullets*.

33. Ben Leech gardening log, July 14, 1940, BML P653 CWGC.

34. David Crane, *Empires of the Dead* (Glasgow: William Collins, 2013), 160; Philip Longworth, *The Unending Vigil: A History of the Commonwealth War Graves Commission* (Barnsley: Pen & Sword Military, 2003), 159.

Chapter 6

1. The indispensable resource for this chapter is Frédéric Turner's *Les Oublies de 39-45: Les Britanniques Internés a Tost, Kreuzberg, Giromagny et Westertimke* (Arras: Editions JAFT, 2013), which provides an alphabetical list of British prisoners and testimony from survivors and descendants. Turner's own father, grandfather, and uncle were interned with the IWGC staff. With many thanks to Frédéric Turner for discussion, friendship, and help connecting with other descendants of internees. This chapter also relies on individual internee cards in WO 416, a series of German prisoner of war records now held at the U.K. National Archives (TNA). There are approximately 150 WO 416 records related to IWGC personnel.

2. Albert Grounds testimony CWGC/1/2/D/7/12.

3. Bernard Parsons Journal, July 28, 1940, Private Papers of B. A. Parsons, Documents.6526, IWM.

4. Arthur Richards, "French Helper" file, NARA, RG 0498, UD 193; Jack Evans, "A Prisoner of War's Escape from the Germans," *The Spokesman-Review* (Spokane, WA), May 24, 1953; Jean-Claude Fichaux, "La prison d'Arras sous l'Occupation: Des prisonniers témoignent," Criminocorpus, *Varia*, May 30, 2012, https://doi.org/10.4000/criminocorpus.1834.

5. Frédéric Turner, *Les Oublies de 39-45*.

6. Jane Evans, *Charles Maurice Baker*, family history book, courtesy of Jane Evans.

7. Frédéric Turner, *Les Oublies de 39-45*.

8. "Cemetries all correct gave Petrol and oil to baker at Habeturne, to run his mixing machine, to supply us with bread." Ben Leech, gardening log, May 27, 1940, BML P653 CWGC.

9. According to the U.K. Foreign and Oversees Registers of British subjects, Holton worked for the 42nd Broad Gauge Co., Railway Operations, Royal Engineers when he married Maria Sauty. A younger son died of burns as a toddler, so in 1940, the Holton family consisted of Charlie, Maria, their five surviving children, and Noëlla's two-year-old daughter, Ghiselaine. Charles Henry Holton personnel file, P 633, CWGC/1/1/13/39.

10. Frédéric Turner, *Les Oublies de 39-45*, 285.

11. Frédéric Turner, *Les Oublies de 39-45*, 141.

12. Ilag Tost Report, FO 916/524, TNA.

13. Alain Fernagut, "John et Marthe Wood, Un Couple Houplinois," *La Voix du Nord*, May 8, 2011.

14. Evans, "A Prisoner of War's Escape from the Germans."

15. Albert Grounds testimony CWGC/1/2/D/7/12.

16. Greenwood was injured badly enough that the Nazis released him on September 8, 1940, rather than sending him on to the next camp. Nazi Persecution Claim: William Greenwood, TNA, FO 950/4567.

17. Bernard Parsons Journal, Private Papers of B. A. Parsons, Documents.6526, IWM; Evans, "A Prisoner of War's Escape from the Germans."

18. Wodehouse, *Performing Flea* (London: H. Jenkins, 1953); Wodehouse to William Townend, February 24, 1945, in *P. G. Wodehouse: A Life in Letters*, ed. Sophie Ratcliffe (London: Cornerstone, 2013), 358.

19. Ben Leech gardening log, BML P653 CWGC.

20. CWGC/1/1/7/B/80: Missing Staff; CWGC Rolled Records.

21. The United States initially put Marcelle Lattreux on the list for consideration for a Medal of Freedom but removed her once it was clear that she had helped a Canadian civilian, not an American serviceman. Marcelle Lattreux "French Helper" file, NARA, RG 0498, UD 193.

22. Nazi Persecution Claim, George Horn, FO 950/2239, TNA.

23. The War Graves Commission employed two gardeners named S. C. Humphreys. The practice of referring using initials rather than full names in records led to much confusion between Sidney Charles Humphreys and Stephen Charles

Humphreys. The commission's "Missing Staff" records say that the gardener at Beaumont-Hamel was Sidney, and a note in the "Aliens and Refugees" file lists Sidney as returning safely to England. I am slightly inclined to think that the gardener in Beaumont-Hamel was Stephen rather than Sidney because Stephen's prewar address was Bienvillers-au-Bois, about seven miles from Beaumont-Hamel, while Sidney C. Humphreys lived near Béthune, forty miles away. In his 1943 report to the mayor of Beaumont-Hamel, S. C. Humphreys mentions working at the Newfoundland Park before the war, which would make more sense if he lived relatively nearby. Then again, Humphreys did not receive a Lawson Scheme settlement, which points toward Sidney (who was a temporary employee in 1940 and taken onto the permanent staff only in 1946 and thus easily excluded from the Lawson Scheme). In any case, there is enough confusion between Sidney versus Stephen that I will stick to "S. C. Humphreys," which is the name signed on the 1943 report to the mayor of Beaumont-Hamel.

24. Maurice Leech to Sherri Ottis, 1997. Courtesy of Sherri Ottis.

25. Gardener William Mercer of Bouzincourt was also left at liberty for reasons unknown. CWGC Rolled Records.

26. CWGC Rolled Records.

27. Sue Elliott and James Fox, *The Children Who Fought Hitler: A British Outpost in Europe* (London: John Murray, 2009).

28. There were no hard-and-fast rules when it came to the internment of women and children. For the story of a British-born woman and her daughters who were paroled, see Jeanne Gask, *Nell and the Girls: The True Story of a British Girl and Her Family in Occupied France 1940–1944* (Newcastle upon Tyne: Myrmidon Books, 2015).

29. Nazi Persecution Claim, Gabrielle Plockyn for CM Baker (deceased), FO 950/2369, TNA; according to the CWGC Rolled Records, Mary Weller died at Besançon in 1943 and Virginie Roberts at Vittel in March 1944. For a discussion of French-born British women held in Avesnes-sur-Helpe, see Frédéric Turner, *Les Oublies de 39-45.* Turner's aunt was interned in Avesnes-sur-Helpe along with several members of the War Graves community.

30. Matthew Stibbe and Kim Wünschmann, "Internment Practices during the First and Second World Wars," in *Internment Refugee Camps, Historical and Contemporary Perspectives*, ed. Gabriele Anderl, Linda Erker, and Christoph Reinprecht (New York: Transcript Publishing, 2023), 29–47.

31. John Howard, *Concentration Camps on the Homefront: Japanese Americans in the House of Jim Crow* (Chicago: University of Chicago Press, 2009); Yoshinori H. T. Hamel, "Americans' Misuse of 'Internment,'" *Seattle Journal of Social Justice* 14, issue 3 (Spring 2016), article 12.

32. Petition from Jewish Prisoners, 1942, HO 215/169, TNA; Simon Parkin, *The Island of Extraordinary Captives: A Painter, a Poet, an Heiress, and a Spy in a World War II British Internment Camp* (New York: Scribner, 2022).

33. Bernard Parsons Journal, July 28, August 3, and September 11, 1940, Private Papers of B. A. Parsons, Documents.6526, IWM.

34. Ilag Tost Report, FO 916/524, TNA; Frédéric Turner, *Les Oublies de 39-45*; Elliott and Fox, *The Children Who Fought Hitler.*

35. Sidney Albert Witton Prisoner Card, WO 416/398/1, TNA.

36. Along with current employees, Parsons included a handful of retired gardeners and temporary employees like Ernest Marsh and Eric Clulow. CWGC/1/2/D/7/12.

37. Bernard Parsons Journal, October 17, 1940, Private Papers of B. A. Parsons, Documents.6526, IWM.

38. Bernard Parsons Journal, October 26, 1940, Private Papers of B. A. Parsons, Documents.6526, IWM.

Chapter 7

1. Previous work on Robert Armstrong includes Isadore Ryan, *No Way Out: The Irish in Wartime France, 1939–1945* (Cork: Mercier Press, 2017), and Ronan McGreevy, *Wherever the Firing Line Extends: Ireland and the Western Front* (Stroud: The History Press, 2016), and *Great Hatred: The Assassination of Field Marshal Sir Henry Wilson* (London: Faber & Faber, 2022).

2. In 1915, eighteen-year-old Private James Henry Armstrong of the 2nd Irish Guards was court-martialed for striking a sergeant. He also fathered an illegitimate child born to Mary Ann Terry in Liphook, Hampshire, where the 2nd Irish Guards were training.

3. Sean Connolly and his brother Lewis were from the townland called France outside Ballinalee, directly adjacent to Currygrane. Sean was killed in the Selton Hill Massacre, March 11, 1921. Sean Connolly pension file, letter dated December 3, 1923, file W3D78A, Military Service Pensions (1916–1923), Military Archives, Óglaigh na hÉireann (Defence Forces Ireland), Ireland.

4. McGreevy, *Great Hatred.*

5. RA P624 CWGC; McGreevy, *Wherever the Firing Line Extends.*

6. Ryan, *No Way Out*, 63.

7. Harold Maurice Hill was arrested and released twice, as discussed elsewhere in this book. Canadian William Turnbull remained interned for the duration, as did Hill's son, Maurice.

8. Colonel Chettle to Foreign Office, February 4, 1941, RA P624 CWGC.

9. Augusta Lindsay to IWGC, received February 3, 1941; James Armstrong to IWGC, February 1, 1941, RA P624 CWGC.

10. Lawson Report, June 7, 1944, CWGC/1/1/7/B/82.

11. Bernard Parsons Journal, October 17, 1940, Private Papers of B.A. Parsons, Documents.6526, IWM.

12. Much of the explicit discussion of these legal decisions is preserved in files from early 1944, when the IWGC was planning financial settlements for interned staff (see chapter 16). Commission Meeting, March 8, 1944, CWGC ½/D/7/12.

13. CWGC/4/2/300: Minutes of the 300th Finance Committee Meeting, February 16, 1944.

14. In 1944, this was converted into a grant, which ruffled some feathers among men who had refused the money on the understanding that it was a loan. CWGC/1/2/H/1 Concession Rates of Pay to TSGs and Wages Staff Evacuated from France and Belgium.

15. Hugh Gabriel to IWGC, July 31, 1941, CWGC/1/2/H/1 Concession Rates of Pay to TSGs and Wages Staff Evacuated from France and Belgium.

16. Sidney Stock to IWGC, August 3, 1941, CWGC/1/2/H/1 Concession Rates of Pay to TSGs and Wages Staff Evacuated from France and Belgium.

17. CWGC/4/2/286: Minutes of the 286th Finance Committee Meeting; CWGC/2/2/1/235: Minutes of the 235th Meeting of the Commission, January 8, 1941.

18. Samuel E. Chapman personnel file P 451, CWGC/1/1/13/104.

19. Chettle to Foreign Office, February 4, 1941, and penciled notes from telephone conversation, RA P624 CWGC.

20. Ryan, *No Way Out*.

21. Colonel Chettle to Augusta Lindsay, February 12, 1941, RA P624 CWGC.

22. Augusta Lindsay to IWGC, February 11, 1947, RA P624 CWGC. Augusta does not mention the exact amount that she sent to Bob, but she mentions multiple cables and directs the IWGC to get receipts directly from the Irish Department of External Affairs.

23. Samuel E. Chapman personnel file P 451, CWGC/1/1/13/104.

24. Edwin Hinbest to IWGC, February 26, 1941, Charles P. Hinbest personnel file, P 527, CWGC/1/1/13/105.

25. Alice Hinbest to IWGC, February 12, 1941, March 6, 1942, Charles P. Hinbest personnel file, P 527, CWGC/1/1/13/105.

26. Arthur L. Kirkwood personnel file, P 48, CWGC/1/1/13/110.

27. Alfred Arthur Wilson personnel file, P 51, CWGC/1/1/13/120.

28. CWGC/1/2/D/7/11: Arrangements for the Repatriation of the Commission's Staff.

29. Alfred G. Wells personnel file, P 511, CWGC/1/1/13/119.

30. CWGC Rolled Records.

31. IWGC to Walter Layland, July 9, 1942, A. L. Layland personnel file, P 45, CWGC/1/1/13/112. The Commission did eventually pay Layland his full wages because the American diplomats in Marseille vouched for him, but they were reluctant to advance him money against that payment.

32. CWGC/1/2/D/7/11: Arrangements for the Repatriation of the Commission's Staff.

33. Samuel E. Chapman personnel file P 451, CWGC/1/1/13/104.

34. CWGC/2/2/1/234: Minutes of the 240th Meeting of the Commission, April 10, 1940; CWGC/2/2/1/240: Minutes of the 240th Meeting of the Commission, January 15, 1942.

35. Alfred Arthur Wilson personnel file, P 51, CWGC/1/1/13/120; Alfred G. Wells personnel file, P 511, CWGC/1/1/13/119.

36. Frederick Martin personnel file, P 415, CWGC/1/1/13/113.

37. Eugene Dennis to Major John White, June 20, 1946, Robert Armstrong "French Helper" file, NARA, RG 0498, UD 193.

38. Robert Armstrong, GR 16P 17321, Vincennes.

39. McGreevy, *Great Hatred*.

40. Catherine J Killean (sometimes Kathleen Killean or Kate Duffy Killean), file 34D2296 and MSP34REF44897, Military Service Pensions (1916–1923), Military Archives, Óglaigh na hÉireann (Defence Forces Ireland), Ireland.

41. Stewart Mitchell, *St. Valery and Its Aftermath: The Gordon Highlanders Captured in France in 1940* (Barnsley: Pen & Sword Military, 2017).

42. Ben Leech gardening log, July 10, 1940, BML P653 CWGC; George Hignett MI9 interview, February 24, 1941, WO/373/60/624, TNA. With thanks to Stewart Mitchell.

43. Hignett's companion in his evasion was Private John Edgar. George Hignett MI9 interview, February 24, 1941, WO/373/60/624, TNA. With thanks to Stewart Mitchell.

44. Nazi Persecution Claim, E. R. Megarity for Robert Armstrong (deceased), FO 950/3602, TNA.

45. Guy Vérines, *Mes Souvenirs Du Réseau Saint-Jacques* (Panazol: Lavauzelle, 1990).

46. Ryan, *No Way Out*; David Murphy, "'Paddy fait de la résistance.' Les Irlandais dans la Résistance française et la section F du SOE, 1940–1945," *Revue historique des armées* 253 (2008): 86–98. Janie McCarthy lived at 64 rue Sainte-Anne, which is just a few blocks from the 8 Place Vendome building, where both O'Kelly's wine business and the Duclos family firm were headquartered.

47. Réseau Saint-Jacques, Listes des agents du sous-réseau Vérines, French National Archives, Archives of the Second World War History Committee, Buckmaster Networks IV, 72AJ/80; Gaston Lepine testimony in Nazi Persecution Claim, E. R. Megarity for Robert Armstrong (deceased), FO 950/3602, TNA.

48. This note was in the possession of Emmanuel Dossche. In his testimony, Dossche notes that Bob entrusted him with documents before his arrest in 1943, but it is not clear if this was one of those documents (it is undated). It is not clear how Dainton, Croydon, and Uden would have sent a message from the prisoner-of-war camp, though it may have been transmitted before they were captured or after they were liberated (after Bob Armstrong's death). Nazi Persecution Claim, E. R. Megarity for Robert Armstrong (deceased), FO 950/3602, TNA.

Chapter 8

1. In the 1970s and 1980s, a local historian named André Coilliot interviewed many local *résistants* and survivors of World War II in the Arras region, including Rosine Witton. He published his work in 1985–1986 in a three-volume series that collates his many interviews and extensive private collections into a chronological

narrative of the Nazi occupation in Arras. Coilliot includes vignettes based on the recollections that Rosine Witton shared with him, though he tends to paraphrase rather than quote. André Coilliot, *1940–1944, 4 Longues Années d'Occupation: Le Récit des Événements Vécus dans la Region d'Arras*, vol. 1 (privately printed at Beaurains, 1985–1986), 131.

2. Information about Eugène D'Hallendre via the Musée de la Résistance, Bondues, Nord, which holds the D'Hallendre family papers. In particular, *Eugène D'Hallendre: Cheminot*, an unpublished work by Edgard D'Hallendre, son of Eugène D'Hallendre, narrates some of the events related here. With many thanks to the museum, Claire Crétel-Diest, Hélène Priego, and Grégory Célerse.

3. F. F. E. Yeo-Thomas, "Seahorse Report," April 28, 1943, HS 9/1458, TNA.

4. The four safe houses were run by Rosine Witton (Ronville), Emile and Madeleine Didier (Ronville), Valentine Ployart (La Madeleine), and Albert Bricout (Sars-Poteries).

5. Halik Kochanski, *Resistance: The Underground War against Hitler, 1939–1945* (New York: Norton, 2022); Richard Vinen, *The Unfree French: Life under the Occupation* (New Haven, CT: Yale University Press, 2006); Olivier Wieviorka, *The French Resistance* (Cambridge, MA: Harvard University Press, 2016).

6. M. R. D. Foot, *SOE in France: An Account of the Work of the British Special Operations Executive in France, 1940–1945* (London: HMSO, 1966); Kate Vigurs, *Mission France: The True History of the Women of SOE* (New Haven, CT: Yale University Press, 2021).

7. Arthur Richards, "French Helper" file, NARA, RG 0498, UD 193; Arthur Kirkwood letter to IWGC, September 4, 1944, Arthur Kirkwood personnel file #48, Commonwealth War Graves Commission Archives, Maidenhead, UK; René Lesage, *100 figures de la Résistants dans le Pas de Calais* (Editions Les Echos du Pas-de-Calais, 2013).

8. Report by Berthe Fraser, December 7, 1944, in Michael Trotobas SOE personnel file, HS9/1487/1, TNA; Papers concerning Berthe Fraser, GM, IWM, London, Documents.1768, IWM.

9. For the British-American Civilian Emergency Services (BACES), see the Papers of Paul B. Anderson at the University of Illinois Archives, 15/35/54, particularly Box 39, correspondence with Gertrude Hamilton and Reports of the British-American Civilian Emergency Services; "Témoignage de Madame FRASER," Testimony of Berthe Fraser, collected by Edouard Perroy, June 28, 1947, French National Archives, Archives of the Second World War History Committee, Buckmaster Networks IV, 72AJ/35-72AJ/89.

10. Bert Witton to Rosine Witton, July 24, 1942, Private Papers of Madame R. Witton, Documents.7565, IWM.

11. Témoignage de Madame FRASER.

12. Eliane Meplaux testified that she kept four British soldiers at her house from June 11, 1940, until August 6, 1940. Eliane Meplaux, "French Helper" file, NARA, RG 0498, UD 193; Michel Poiteau, "French Helper" file, NARA, RG

0498, UD 193; "Témoignage de Madame FRASER"; Marcel Roussel, "French Helper" file, NARA, RG 0498, UD 193; Nazi Persecution Claim: Mr. George William Horn, 1965, FO 950/2239, TNA.

13. Helen Fry, *MI9: A History of the Secret Service for Escape and Evasion in World War Two* (New Haven, CT: Yale University Press, 2020); Oliver Clutton-Brock, *RAF Evaders: The Complete Story of RAF Escapees and Their Escape Lines, Western Europe, 1940–1945* (London: Grubb Street Publishing, 2009); Sherri Ottis, *Silent Heroes: Downed Airmen and the French Underground* (Lexington: University Press of Kentucky, 2001); Airey Neave, *Saturday at M.I.9* (London: Hodder & Stoughton, 1969); Herman Bodson, *Downed Allied Airmen and Evasion of Capture: The Role of Local Resistance Networks in World War II* (Jefferson, NC: McFarland, 2005).

14. Coilliot, *1940–1944, 4 Longues Années d'Occupation*, vol. 1, 119.

15. With thanks to David Richards, descendant of Arthur Richards, for family history and records; Arras census, 1921, 1926, 1931, 1936, AD-PdC, Arras, France; Arthur Clarke Richards, Royal Warwickshire Regiment, "Burnt Documents" (Microfilm Copies); National Archives Microfilm Publication WO363; National Archives of the UK (TNA), Kew, Surrey, England; Arthur Richards, "French Helper" file, NARA, RG 0498, UD 193.

16. The three soldiers who spent Christmas 1940 with Arthur Richards were John Carroll, 2883238; John Macaulay, 3245405; and Michael Donnelly, 2883908. The designer who worked with Arthur Richards to create false identity documents was Marcel Maurice. Arthur Richards, "French Helper" file, NARA, RG 0498, UD 193.

17. René Lesage, *100 Figures de la Résistance dans le Pas-de-Calais* (Paris: Editions Les Echos du Pas-de-Calais, 2013).

18. Arthur Richards, "French Helper" file, NARA, RG 0498, UD 193; Benjamin Morris Leech, "French Helper" file, NARA, RG 0498, UD 193; letter from Maurice Leech to Sherri Ottis, August 1997, courtesy of Sherri Ottis; Edgard D'Hallendre, *Eugène D'Hallendre*, MRB.

19. Rosine Witton had no children. Berthe Fraser's only son, Emile, drowned in a beach accident in 1934, age twenty; Jean-Jacques Duthoy, *Zoé, 1892–1954* (Prague: Koniasch Latin Press, 1995). With thanks to Frédéric Turner.

20. Coilliot, *1940–1944, 4 Longues Années d'Occupation*, vol. 1, 131

21. Coilliot, *1940–1944, 4 Longues Années d'Occupation*, vol. 1, 131.

22. Edgard D'Hallendre, *Eugène D'Hallendre*, MRB.

23. Stephen Grady, *Gardens of Stone: My Boyhood in the French Resistance* (London: Hodder & Stoughton, 2013).

24. Hilda Weller, "French Helper" file, NARA, RG 0498, UD 193; Jacques Dartevelle, "French Helper" file, NARA, RG 0498, UD 193; Bernard Zyglowicz E&E 1600.

25. Edgard D'Hallendre, *Eugène D'Hallendre*, MRB.

26. Military Sentence, Military Tribunal Lille [Armstrong, Cornille, Debrabant, Maillard, Ployart], May 10, 1944, collections 13471, ZC 20.088-11, Sachsen State Archives, Dresden.

27. Ben Leech gardening log, BML P653 CWGC.

28. Grady, *Gardens of Stone*, 82.

29. Marcel Roussell names the evaders helped by Lewis Bonnell as John Mac-Cormick and Douglas Hem. Marcel Roussel, "French Helper" file, NARA, RG 0498, UD 193. With thanks to Jackie Davies, a relative of Lewis Fulton Bonnell.

30. CWGC/1/1/7/B/80: Missing Staff; Nazi Persecution Claim, George Horn, FO 950/2239, TNA.

31. Eliane Meplaux, "French Helper" file, NARA, RG 0498, UD 193.

32. Adele Zoé Caron Evans, GR 16P 107562, Vincennes; Duthoy, *Zoé, 1892–1954*. With thanks to René Lesage.

33. *Résistants* frequently referred to any German police as the "gestapo," but there were several overlapping agencies at work in Pas-de-Calais. First were the various French police forces, which often collaborated with the Germans. The Feldgendarmerie, the German military police, were responsible for many arrests of *résistants* but usually at the behest of other investigative bodies. The Geheime Feldpolizei (GFP), the secret police who worked for German military intelligence, had an office in Arras and actively worked to trap *résistants*. The actual Gestapo—the secret state police—were still establishing a foothold in northern France in 1941. Their headquarters were in La Madeleine, not far from Eugène D'Hallendre's house. It was a very small office with only a handful of officers tasked with surveilling millions of residents, including the active trade unions and communists in the mining districts. Given the Gestapo's limited resources in the region in 1941, it is quite likely that Arthur Richards was arrested by the GFP. See Grégory Célerse, *La Traque des résistants nordistes, 1940–1944* (Marcq-en-Barœul: Les Lumières de Lille Éditions, 2011).

34. Arthur Richards, "French Helper" file, NARA, RG 0498, UD 193.

35. Bert Witton to Rosine Witton, December 7, 1941, Private Papers of Madame R. Witton, Documents.7565, IWM.

36. Aimee Lievre, "French Helper" file, NARA, RG 0498, UD 193; Grady, *Gardens of Stone*, 105.

37. Details of Berthe Fraser's arrest and trial (June 4, 1942) can be found in a copy of the sentencing document in the personnel file of Jules Gosse, imprisoned at Diez. Gosse, Fraser, and Copin were tried together, along with Marcel Roussel, Lewis Bonnell's neighbor. Caen 25 P 5 677. With thanks to Grégory Célerse and to Sabina von Thuemmler for translation from German.

38. Laurent Thiery, *Le Répression allemande dans le Nord de la France 1940–1944* (Villeneuve d'Ascq: Presses Universitaires di Septentrion, 2013).

39. Coilliot, *1940–1944, 4 Longues Années d'Occupation*, vol. 1, 131.

40. Alfie Martin, *Bale Out! Escaping Occupied France with the Resistance* (Newtownards: Colourpoint Books, 2005), 55.

41. Bert Witton to Rosine Witton, December 23, 1941, Private Papers of Madame R. Witton, Documents.7565, IWM.

42. Nazi Persecution Claim, Rosine Leontine Witton for Sidney Albert Witton (deceased), FO 950/3423, TNA.

Chapter 9

1. Letter from Bert Witton to Rosine Witton, June 25, 1943, Private Papers of Madame R. Witton, Documents.7565, IWM. All quotations from Bert's letters (1941–1943) are from Rosine Witton's papers at the IWM. In all, approximately fifty of Bert's letters and postcards survive, all of them dated between August 13, 1941, and August 25, 1943.

2. See Red Cross Report, December 3, 1942, Ilag Tost Report FO 916/524, TNA; WO 416.

3. Roberts testimony, CWGC/1/2/D/7/12; *The Tost Times*, June 1, 1941; Ilag Tost Report, December 3, 1942, FO 916/524, TNA; Sue Elliott and James Fox, *The Children Who Fought Hitler: A British Outpost in Europe* (London: John Murray, 2009).

4. Filip Marcinowski and Tadeusz Nasierowski, "The Extermination of People with Disabilities in Occupied Poland: The Beginning of Genocide," in *Mass Murder of People with Disabilities in the Holocaust*, ed. Brigitte Bailer and Juliane Wetzel (Stockholm: International Holocaust Remembrance Alliance and Metropol Verlag, 2019), 135–50.

5. Marcinowski and Nasierowski, "The Extermination of People with Disabilities in Occupied Poland," 145; Paul Weindling, "The Need to Name: The Victims of Nazi 'Euthanasia' of the Mentally and Physically Disabled and Ill, 1939–1945," in Bailer and Wetzel, *Mass Murder of People with Disabilities in the Holocaust*, 49–85; Lawrence A. Zeidman, *Brain Science under the Swastika: Ethical Violations, Resistance, and Victimization of Neuroscientists in Nazi Europe* (Oxford: Oxford University Press, 2020).

6. Account of the deportations from Tost from Yad Vashem: transport from Gleiwitz, Gleiwitz (Oppeln), Silesia (Upper), Germany, to unstated place on June 15, 1942, https://deportation.yadvashem.org.

7. Sebastian Rosenbaum, Bogusław Tracz, and Dariusz Węgryzyn, *Tiurma-łagier Tost: Historia obozu NKWD w Toszku w 1945 roku* (Gmina Toszek: Ministra Kultury i Dziedzictwa Narodowego, 2017); Sybille Krägel and Siegfried Petschel, *Bild-Dokumentation TOST: Gefängnislager des sowjetischen NKWD in Oberschlesien* (N.p.: Walter Bode, 1998); Keith Lowe, *Savage Continent: Europe in the Aftermath of World War II* (New York: St. Martin's Press, 2012).

8. Bernard Parsons Journal, Private Papers of B. A. Parsons, Documents.6526, IWM; Douglas F. S. Filliter, UK Consul-General in Hamburg (1934–1937) and Naples (1937–1940), Ilag Tost Report, December 3, 1942, FO 916/524, TNA.

9. The wards were 72 by 20 feet, or 1,440 square feet (133.8 square meters). The size of parking spaces varies, but standard parking spaces in the United States and United Kingdom are generally 124 to 164 square feet (11.5 to 15.2 square meters).

10. George Gregson, January 5 and March 8, 1941, *Diary of George Gregson* (Hertfordshire: Holywell House Publishing, n.d.).

11. Nazi Persecution Claim, Reginald Robert Seeley, FO 950/3611, TNA.

12. Ilag Tost Report, FO 916/524, TNA.

13. Bernard Parsons Journal, October 15 and 22, 1940, Private Papers of B. A. Parsons, Documents.6526, IWM.

14. Frédéric Turner, *Les Oublies de 39-45: Les Britanniques Internés a Tost, Kreuzberg, Giromagny et Westertimke* (Arras: Editions JAFT, 2013), 143.

15. Alfred G. Wells diary as quoted in Elliott and Fox, *The Children Who Fought Hitler*; Private Papers of WC Duncan, Documents.7955, IWM.

16. CWGC/1/2/D/7/12.

17. Bernard Parsons Journal, August 26, 1940, Private Papers of B. A. Parsons, Documents.6526, IWM. This particular quote is about an inspector at Huy, but Parsons also writes about cutting open the cakes at Tost on November 11, 1940.

18. A Red Cross report (September 10, 1941) said that around 600 cans were opened at Tost on an ordinary day and 2,000 to 3,000 on Saturday mornings. Ilag Tost Report, September 10, 1941, and February 9, 1943, FO 916/524, TNA.

19. Bert Witton to Rosine Witton, August 13, 1941; October 31, 1941; and June 13, 1943, Private Papers of Madame R. Witton, Documents.7565, IWM.

20. G. B. Leyton, "Effects of Slow Starvation," *The Lancet*, July 20, 1946, 73–79.

21. Henry Sherbourne's leg was amputated in 1922 after an accident, not as a consequence of his war service. He was interned with the others for several months but eventually released because of his disability. CWGC Rolled Records; B. A. Parsons diary.

22. Ilag Tost Report, December 3, 1942, FO 916/524, TNA.

23. Bernard Parsons Journal, January 5 and 6, 1941, Private Papers of B. A. Parsons, Documents.6526, IWM.

24. Charles Henry Holton personnel file, P 633, CWGC/1/1/13/39.

25. Charles Henry Holton personnel file, P 633, CWGC/1/1/13/39. "A man who slept near me is dead," wrote William Roys, an internee who kept a diary. "His name was Holton, a good man. It is very sad to die so far from his wife and his children." In Turner, *Les Oublies de 39-45*.

26. Charles Henry Holton personnel file, P 633, CWGC/1/1/13/39.

27. Alfred Haines to Annie Twelftree, May 28, 1941, in CHH P633 CWGC.

28. Jane Evans, *Charles Maurice Baker*, family history book, courtesy of Jane Evans; CWGC Rolled Records; Death Record for Stanley Hawkins, December 1, 1941, Lamsdorf, UK, Foreign and Overseas Registers of British Subjects, 1628–1969.

29. William Robert Meller, CWGC Rolled Records; CWGC Staff Card CWGC/6/4/1/1/229. Some former War Graves employees also died as internees but were not included in Commission investigations because they were not current staff. For example, James Edwards of Andricq worked as a Commission gardener from 1922 until he resigned on December 31, 1938. He was interned at Ilag VIII (#444) and died on July 5, 1942. James Edwards staff card at CWGC; James Edwards, WO 416/109/236; Sundry claims for "personal prejudice." Code 217 file 37 (papers 1316 to end), 1947, FO 950/192 (1316 to end), TNA.

30. Ilag Tost Report, February 1943, FO 916/524, TNA.

31. George Gregson, December 21, 1941, *Diary of George Gregson.*

32. Wilfred Legg, WO 416/220/436, Bernard Parsons Journal, December 21–23, 1940, Private Papers of B. A. Parsons, Documents.6526, IWM.

33. Bert Witton to Rosine Witton, September 28, 1942 Private Papers of Madame R. Witton, Documents.7565, IWM.

34. Jane Evans, *Charles Maurice Baker,* family history book, courtesy of Jane Evans.

35. Bert Witton to Rosine Witton, May 30, 1943, Private Papers of Madame R. Witton, Documents.7565, IWM.

36. Aircraftman Alexander William Cook, 990 Squadron RAF, died on September 26, 1941. He was the son of Bert's older sister, Rose Cook. Sergeant Arthur Witton, Rifle Brigade, 6916587, was a prisoner of war in Italy. He was the son of Bert's older brother, James Witton. Private William John Graham Witton, RAOC clerk, 7649629, was captured on February 15, 1942, in Singapore. He was the son of Bert's older brother, Bill. In May 1943, Bert Witton wrote about "young Billy Witton one of Bill's boys," whose parents had not yet heard from him. Bill Witton's home, 62 Coolfin Road, was destroyed by bombing. *Daily Mirror,* July 6, 1944.

37. Bert Witton to Rosine Witton, May 5, 1943, Private Papers of Madame R. Witton, Documents.7565, IWM.

38. Bert to Rosine Witton, July 24, August 9, and October 26, 1942, and May 5 and 30, 1943, Private Papers of Madame R. Witton, Documents.7565, IWM.

Chapter 10

1. Ben Leech, gardening log, January 24, 1941, BML P653 CWGC.

2. Ben Leech, gardening log, BML P653 CWGC.

3. Matthew Tomlinson, *Rebuilding Albert: Reconstruction and Remembrance on the Western Front, 1914–1932* (PhD thesis, University of York, 2005), 169.

4. Correspondence of Gertrude Hamilton and the Records of the British American Civilian Emergency Service in the Paul B. Anderson Papers (1909–1988), 15/35/54, University of Illinois Archives, Champaign.

5. Ben Leech to IWGC, September 20, 1942, BML P653 CWGC.

6. Berthe Shreeve was the wife of Leopold Ernest Shreeve, the son of Leopold George Shreeve. Her husband was an assistant gardener but left the Commission in 1940 to join the Royal Engineers. See CWGC/1/2/D/7/12. Michael O'Neill also reported helping wives: he "directly or indirectly passed information to gardeners' wives as to procedure to obtain assistance and relief money through American Consuls." Michael O'Neill Testimony, April 1942, CWGC/1/2/D/7/10: Aliens and Refugees Register.

7. Bert Witton to Rosine Witton, January 26, 1943.

8. According to the mayor's office of Beaumont-Hamel, Etienne Duban was the mayor during this period, and Ben's agricultural work was for "M. Dubon."

However, he also sometimes refers to Monsieur Lenglet as the mayor and makes many references to the "deputy mayor" in a way that makes it difficult to tell if he is referring to Duban or Lenglet. It makes little difference to the point here—Ben was working for the village officials to earn his bread—but which specific official is not always crystal clear.

9. H. S. C. Hawkins personnel file, T 189, CWGC/1/2/H/3.

10. Ben Leech to American Vice Consul, June 7, 1941, BML P653 CWGC.

11. Ben Leech gardening log, March 20, 1941; letter to the American Vice Consul Paris, June 7, 1941, BML P653 CWGC.

12. Ben Leech to Fabian Ware, September 20, 1942, BML P653 CWGC.

13. BML P653 CWGC.

14. CWGC Rolled Records.

15. Among the idiosyncratic cases were H. C. Mills, who was allowed to remain in Dernancourt with his dying wife during the first round of arrests and turned sixty before anyone revisited his case, and W. A. Mercier, who worked in nearby Bouzincourt until he was interned in 1943. Another group worth mentioning were British civilians who worked as gardeners despite having no prior affiliation with the War Graves Commission. John Barnes, who kept the Cabaret Rouge teahouse in Souchez, was "ordered to work at British War Cemetery Cabaret Rouge." Despite being well over sixty, Barnes was interned briefly at Ilag VIII Tost. He was released and worked in the cemetery for more than a year but was arrested again in November 1942 and interned for the remainder of the war.

16. Stephen Grady, *Gardens of Stone: My Boyhood in the French Resistance* (London: Hodder & Stoughton, 2013), 94.

17. CWGC Rolled Records.

18. Ben Leech to IWGC, September 20, 1942, BML P653 CWGC.

19. Ben Leech to IWGC, December 31, 1942, CWGC/1/1/10/A/15: Delville Wood.

20. Foreign Office, April 23, 1943, CWGC/1/1/10/A/15: Delville Wood.

21. S. C. Humphreys to Robert Lenglet, January 29, 1943, CWGC/1/1/10/A/15: Delville Wood.

22. Michael Stedman, *Manchester Pals: A History of the Two Manchester Brigades* (Barnsley: Leo Cooper, 1994); Donald Rentschler, escape and evasion report, E&E 1512, NARA; Arthur Richards "French Helper" file, NARA, RG 0498, UD 193.

Chapter 11

1. Sergeant James Allison McConnell, RNZAF NZ414646; Sergeant Selwyn Clarence Smith, RNZAF NZ41952; Sergeant Douglas Noel Tonkin, RNZAF NZ413285; Sergeant Arthur Quinn, RAFVR 1095594; Sergeant Vallance Albert Oliver Dimock , RNZAF NZ412317; Richard Worrall, *The Italian Blitz 1940–43: Bomber Command's War against Mussolini's Cities, Docks and Factories* (Oxford: Osprey Publishing, 2020).

2. Testimony of Gaston Lepine, in Nazi Persecution Claim, E. R. Megarity for Robert Armstrong (deceased), FO 950/3602, TNA.

3. M. H. Ellison, office of the High Commissioner of Ireland to the Foreign Office, 11 June 1948, RA P624 CWGC; Testimony of Charles Deketelaere, in Nazi Persecution Claim, E. R. Megarity for Robert Armstrong (deceased), FO 950/3602, TNA.

4. Testimony of Emmanuel Dossche, in Nazi Persecution Claim, E. R. Megarity for Robert Armstrong (deceased), FO 950/3602, TNA.

5. Andrew Arthy, "An Ever-Increasing Might: The 9 October 1942 Bombing Raid on Lille," Air War Publications, 2020, https://airwarpublications.com/pro duct/an-ever-increasing-might; Wesley Frank Craven and James Lea Cate, eds., *The Army Air Forces in World War II. Volume 2: Europe—Torch to Pointblank (August 1942 to December 1943)* (Chicago: University of Chicago Press, 1949), 220.

6. The other three were Second Lieutenant Grady Roper, Second Lieutenant William Gise, and Technical Sergeant Erwin Wissenback. Daniel Carville, "France-Crashes 39-45," https://francecrashes39-45.net; escape and evasion reports (hereafter E&E): Roper (E&E 27), Gise (E&E 15), Wissenback (E&E 11), NARA.

7. Arthur B. Cox, E&E 47.

8. Arthur Bogle Cox, *Escape through Enemy Territory* (Knoxville, TN: McCormack Company, 1988), copy at the University of Tennessee, Knoxville. With thanks to Kyle Hovious.

9. Victoria Bajeux "French Helper" file, NARA, RG 0498, UD 193.

10. Cox, *Escape through Enemy Territory*.

11. Marie Therese Debrabant, September 14, 1945, "French Helper" file, NARA, RG 0498, UD 193.

12. Marie Therese Debrabant "French Helper" file, NARA, RG 0498, UD 193.

13. Private Papers of Madame R. Witton, Documents.7565, IWM.

14. Photographs courtesy of the Musée de la Résistance, Bondues, Nord. With thanks to Hélène Priego and Claire Crétel-Diest and to Brighid DeAngelis for historical clothing consultation.

15. Arthur B. Cox, E&E 47.

16. For more on the Pat O'Leary Line, see Peter Janes, *Conscript Heroes* (N.p.: Paul Mould Publishing, 2004), and the associated website at https://www.con script-heroes.com; see also Oliver Clutton-Brock, *RAF Evaders: The Comprehensive Story of Thousands of Escapers and Their Escape Lines, Western Europe, 1940–1945* (London: Grub Street Publishing, 2009).

17. Testimony of Annelies Schmidt, quoted in Donald L. Miller, *Masters of the Air: America's Bomber Boys Who Fought the Air War against Nazi Germany* (New York: Simon and Schuster, 2007); Police President of Hamburg on Firestorm (August 1943) via German History in Documents and Images (GHDI), https://ghdi.ghi-dc.org; Richard Overy, *The Bombers and the Bombed: Allied Air War over Europe, 1940–1945* (New York: Penguin, 2015).

18. Many of the details of this mission are still classified. Available records list it as part of Operation Archdeacon, presumably resupplying the Archdeacon network in the Ardennes, as well as Operations Playbill, Caracal, and Mouflon. Emmanuel Debruyne and Adeline Remy, "Le réseaux belges et leurs finances," in *La Clandestinité en Belgique et en Zone Interdite (1940–1944)*, ed. Robert Vandenbussche (Lille: Publications de l'Institut de recherches historiques du Septentrion, 2009), 113–58; Robert Body, *Runways to Freedom* (N.p.: Robert Body, 2016); Hugh Verity, *We Landed by Moonlight: The Secret RAF Landings in France 1940–1944* (Manchester: Crécy Publishing, 2000).

19. Dossche may have been mistaken, though he did provide specific details of the recovery and burial of the bodies in three distinct groups. MI6 records related to this mission remain classified, so it is not possible to corroborate or refute his testimony. Nor is it possible to detail the precise circumstances of the crash or to determine whether Bob Armstrong, Gaston Lepine, or any other local BOA operatives were involved in its mission. Emmanuel Dossche to IWGC, July 23, 1945, RA P624 CWGC.

20. Emmanuel Dossche to IWGC, July 23, 1945, RA P624 CWGC.

Chapter 12

1. Joseph Wemheuer, escape and evasion report (E&E) 36.

2. Wemheuer biographical information from U.S. federal censuses of 1920, 1930, and 1940; Joseph Wemheuer enlistment records; marriage records from the State of Idaho (1942); and author's correspondence with St. Mary's University of Minnesota. With thanks to Willie Wemheuer.

3. Donald L. Miller, *Masters of the Air: America's Bomber Boys Who Fought the Air War against Nazi Germany* (New York: Simon and Schuster, 2007).

4. Interview with Laurence Kuter by Hugh Ahmann and Tom Sturm, September 30–October 3, 1974, Naples, Florida, United States Air Force Oral History Program, K239.0512-810 (transcript page 274, PDF page 1,069). The May 13 raid on Méaulte was an inflection point for the Eighth Air Force. So far, no B-17 crews had completed twenty-five missions, but that would change the next day, when *Hell's Angels*, a bomber in the 303rd, became the first. At the same time, long-awaited replacements had finally arrived from the United States. Four new bomb groups became operational on May 13 and 14, bolstering the ragged remnants of the veteran groups. The 100-bomber mission on May 13 was followed by a 200-bomber mission the next day, the first time the Eighth Air Force had fielded so many planes.

5. Kit C. Carter and Robert Mueller, *US Army Air Forces in World War II: Combat Chronology, 1941–1945* (Washington, DC: Center for Air Force History, 1991). 91st Bomb Group Records, RG 18: Records of the Army Air Forces, World War II Combat Operations Report, 1941–6, ARC ID 596339, Box 320, NARA.

6. Wemheuer, E&E 36.

7. The number of evaders is not exact because every government and agency had different definitions and counts. Oliver Clutton-Brock's definitive review of various estimates gives a figure of approximately 5,800, including 1,000 British soldiers and sailors. Most estimates range between 4,000 and 6,000. Airey Neave says 1,000 Dunkirk evaders, 3,000 airmen exfiltrated, and 500 to 600 still in hiding at liberation, The collection of Escape and Evasion reports in the U.S. National Archives contains 2,953 E&E reports, some of which are from other theaters of the war and some of which are from paratroopers and other soldiers who were trapped behind enemy lines. See also Joseph E. Tucker, "French Resistance Aid to Allied Airmen," *The French Review* 21, no. 1 (October 1947): 29–34.

8. A significant number of the evaders did not return to combat duty. The Allied air forces were reluctant to let evaders fly over enemy territory a second time lest they give away the escape lines, though some (particularly RAF fighter pilots) did return to combat. The U.S. Army Air Forces generally reassigned evaders to train new airmen in evasion techniques or return to the United States for goodwill tours. Given the resources invested in their training, the return of a combat pilot was indeed a boon to the Allied air forces, but it should be noted that most evaders were gunners, radio operators, navigators, or bombardiers, not pilots.

9. Airey Neave, *Saturday at M.I.9* (London: Hodder & Stoughton, 1969).

10. Oliver Clutton-Brock, *RAF Evaders: The Complete Story of RAF Escapees and Their Escape Lines, Western Europe, 1940–1945* (London: Grubb Street Publishing, 2009), 207; Helen Fry, *MI9: A History of the Secret Service for Escape and Evasion in World War Two* (New Haven, CT: Yale University Press, 2020).

11. Jacques Le Grelle in Rémy, *Réseau Comète: La Ligne de Démarcation*, vol. 2 (Paris: Librairie Académique Perrin, 1967), 554.

12. Letter from Maurice Wilson to Rosine Witton, February 3, 1943, Private Papers of Madame R. Witton, Documents.7565, IWM.

13. See MRB and http://ecole.nav.traditions.free.fr/cdo_autres_cesar.htm.

14. Maurice Marcel Cesar was one of the fifteen French commandos who took part in the Dieppe raid. MRB; André Coilliot, *1940–1944, 4 Longues Années d'Occupation: Le Récit des Événements Vécus dans la Region d'Arras*, vol. 1 (privately printed at Beaurains, 1985–1986), 269.

15. Wemheuer, E&E 36.

16. Herman Bodson, *Downed Allied Airmen and Evasion of Capture: The Role of Local Resistance Networks in World War II* (Jefferson, NC: McFarland, 2005), 40.

17. André Dewavrin and Jean-Louis Crémieux-Brilhac, *Mémoires Du Chef Des Services Secrets de La France Libre* (Paris: Jacob, 2000).

18. Grégory Célerse, *La Traque des résistants nordistes 1940–1944* (Marcq-en-Barœul: Les Lumières De Lille Editions, 2011), 115; Edgard D'Hallendre, *Eugène D'Hallendre: Cheminot*, MRB.

19. Alfie Martin, *Bale Out! Escaping Occupied France with the Resistance* (Newtownards: Colourpoint Books, 2005), 53.

20. Rosine Witton to Alfie Martin, February 11, 1966, courtesy of Julie and Sheila Martin. Somehow, Gordon Crowther made it across the Pyrenees on a half-healed ankle and arrived safely in England.

21. D'Hallendre, *Eugène D'Hallendre*, MRB.

22. Private Papers of Madame R. Witton, Documents.7565, IWM; MRB.

23. Others include Clarence Motherall and William Dumsday (both RCAF), who stayed for several weeks with the Grady family in Nieppe before being passed to Madeleine Declercq in Bapaume, and half a dozen airmen aided by Ben Leech and Irma Palin (see chapter 15).

24. Nazi Persecution Claim, E. R. Megarity for Robert Armstrong (deceased), FO 950/3602, TNA. Brian Desmond Barker, S/P.G. 1298, WO 208/3314, TNA; Private Papers of Madame R. Witton, Documents.7565, IWM.

25. Original prints of these photos exist in the collection of the Musée de la Résistance, Bondues, and the private collection of Sheila and Julie Martin. Both copies appear to have near-contemporaneous inscriptions on the back, which suggests that both Rosine Witton and Eugène D'Hallendre may have kept copies. Douglas Hoehn, E&E 38.

26. Gordon Johnston and Emma Robertson, *BBC World Service: Overseas Broadcasting, 1932–2018* (London: Palgrave Macmillan, 2019).

27. Doug Hoehn to Alfie Martin, March 7, 1967, courtesy of Sheila and Julie Martin.

28. Bert Witton to Rosine Witton, April 5, 1943, Private Papers of Madame R. Witton, Documents.7565, IWM.

29. Hoehn remembers the man as a gendarme, while Martin says he was Gestapo. Hoehn's account is preferred because it was filed within a month of the incident rather than many decades later, and he actually saw the man, which Martin may not have. Besides, many people frequently used "Gestapo" to mean any police in occupied France. Hoehn, E&E 38; Martin, *Bale Out!*

30. Coilliot, *1940–1944, 4 Longues Années d'Occupation*, vol. 1, 269.

31. Wemheuer, E&E 36.

32. Hoehn, E&E 38.

33. Individual Deceased Personnel Files: Austin W. Borlen, O-733596; Kenneth Brooks, 395311335; Ralph Olbert, 38068892; Harold Pierce, O-791494; Earl Tharp, 37449902, NARA.

34. Report by Berthe Fraser, December 7, 1944, in Michael Trotobas SOE personnel file, HS9/1487/1, TNA; Stewart Kent and Nick Nicholas, *Agent Michael Trotobas and SOE in Northern France* (Barnsley: Pen & Sword Military, 2015).

35. M. R. D. Foot, *SOE in France: An Account of the British Special Operations Executive in France, 1940–1944* (London: Routledge, 1966). Hugh Verity says that the two women were Madame M. Guyot aka "Mlle Virolle" and Mlle Pichard; Hugh Verity, *We Landed by Moonlight: Secret RAF Landings in France, 1940–1944*, rev. 2nd ed. (Manchester: Crécy Publishing, 2000), 216. Berthe Fraser called them "Kate de Villars" and "Micheline, sister of Michel (Pig) of the Paris office."

Report by Berthe Fraser, December 7, 1944, in Michael Trotobas SOE personnel file, HS9/1487/1, TNA.

36. For more on Harry Legg and the FTP, see chapter 15. Report by Berthe Fraser, December 7, 1944, in Michael Trotobas SOE personnel file, HS9/1487/1, TNA; F. F. E. Yeo-Thomas personnel file, HS 9/1458, TNA; Grady, *Gardens of Stone*; Papers concerning Berthe Fraser, GM, IWM, London, Documents.1768, IWM.

37. Bert Witton to Rosine Witton, April 5, 1943, Private Papers of Madame R. Witton, Documents.7565, IWM.

38. Bert Witton to Rosine Witton, January 26, April 5, June 24, June 27, August 11, and August 20, 1943, Private Papers of Madame R. Witton, Documents.7565, IWM.

39. See Eugène D'Hallendre's expense reports from MRB. There is some confusion about this evader, whose full name was John Arthur Ayliff Morgans David. Some of D'Hallendre's records have him as "David Ayliff"; Clutton-Brock, *RAF Evaders*; Dennis Hornsey describes Rosine Witton using forged ration tickets in *The Pilot Walked Home* (London: Collins, 1946).

40. Bert Witton to Rosine Witton, July 18, 1943, Private Papers of Madame R. Witton, Documents.7565, IWM.

41. "Note de frais d'Eugène D'Hallendre, 2017.1.75–78," D'Hallendre Family Papers, Musée de la Résistance, Bondues.

42. Hornsey, *The Pilot Walked Home*, 88.

43. Martin, *Bale Out!*; Wemheuer, E&E 36.

44. Wemheuer's companions were Sergeant W. L. Canter (RAF), Captain Elmer McTaggart (U.S. Army Air Forces), and Sergeant R. E. Walls (U.S. Army Air Forces). Wemheuer, E&E 36; Clutton-Brock, *RAF Evaders*, 414.

45. Martin, *Bale Out!*

46. Bert Witton to Rosine Witton, June 25 and July 19, 1943, Private Papers of Madame R. Witton, Documents.7565, IWM.

47. Sherri Ottis, *Silent Heroes: Downed Airmen and the French Resistance* (Lexington, University Press of Kentucky, 2001); Fry, *MI9*.

48. Michel A. Marx, *The Hidden River: A Memoir of Resistance, Recovery, and Renewal* (Bloomington, IN: AuthorHouse, 2012).

49. Célerse, *La Traque des résistants nordistes 1940–1944*, 110; testimony of Guy Mollet and others, OCM, French National Archives, Archives of the Second World War History Committee.

50. D'Hallendre, *Eugène D'Hallendre*, MRB; Célerse, *La Traque des résistants nordistes 1940–1944*, 111.

51. D'Hallendre, *Eugène D'Hallendre*, MRB.

52. Edgar D'Hallendre calls her Madame "Bendicot," but this seems to be a mishearing of an English name that was unfamiliar to him. In his notes from an interview with Rosine Witton (1983), he spells the name as both "Bendicot" and "Bellicott." Handwritten notes on scratch paper in D'Hallendre Family Papers, MRB.

53. This incident is related from Rosine Witton's perspective in Edgard D'Hallendre, *Eugène D'Hallendre*, MRB, and in primary sources in the NARA "French Helper" files for Lillian Medlicott, Henriette Balesi, Huguette Lobbedez, and Arthur Richards.

54. While some of the evaders appear to have believed that Madeleine Declercq was William Bailey's wife, she was actually his sister-in-law. Bailey's wife, Sylvie Goedgezelschap, was born in Uccle, Belgium, in 1890 to Pierre and Marie Goedgezelschap. Her sister, Marie Madeleine Goedgezelschap, was born in Seneffe, Belgium, in 1900. In 1921, William Bailey was a lodger living with the Goedgezelschap family in Achiet-le-Grand, near Bapaume. William and Sylvie's son, Frantz Georges Bailey, was born in Achiet-le-Grand on October 30, 1922. Frantz George (called George by the IWGC) became a pupil gardener in 1937. Madeleine Goedgezelschap lived with her sister's family in Bapaume in 1931. From her NARA file, it appears that she was probably living elsewhere in Bapaume in 1943 but had custody of the Bailey house while William, Sylvie, and George were interned at Saint-Denis and Vittel. Since Percy Eely and Madeleine Declerq were not married, she is not listed in CWGC files. Resseguie (E&E 228), Greene (E&E 386), and Erickson (E&E 387) all call her "Madame Eley." Madeleine Goedgezelschap Declercq's name is sometimes spelled Declerq or De Clerck. Census and vital records of Achiet-le-Grand and Bapaume, AD-PdC; Madeleine Declerq "French Helper" file, NARA, RG 0498, UD 193.

55. Bert Witton to Rosine Witton, July 28, 1943, Private Papers of Madame R. Witton, Documents.7565, IWM.

56. Edgard D'Hallendre, *Eugène D'Hallendre*, MRB; Emile and Madeleine Didier "French Helper" file, NARA, RG 0498, UD 193; Emile Didier Resistance Dossier, GR 16P 184597, Vincennes.

57. One of the reasons Rosine Witton is not often recognized as an important person in histories of the Comet Line goes back to a foundational source, Rémy's *Réseau Comète*. In this two-volume work, published in 1967 and 1968, the *résistant* Rémy interviewed Comet Line operatives and published their stories. However, he did not quite capture Rosine's part of the Comet Line, even though he does include Dennis Hornsey's story and interviews with Albert Bricout, who worked closely with Eugène D'Hallendre. Rosine Witton does appear fleetingly in Rémy's work, particularly in interviews with Jacques Le Grelle, who explicitly names her more than once, but Rémy does not integrate her into the narrative. He treats "Rolande" and the person he calls "Rosa" in Dennis Hornsey's account as separate people. Rémy also mentions Eugène D'Hallendre and Marcelle Douard, but he misspells both of their names, indicating that he was not very familiar with them. The segmented nature of Resistance work meant that many people working for a common cause did not know details about one another, and it seems that Rémy largely missed the OCM group within the Comet Line, except for brief, individual glimpses. Rémy, *Réseau Comète*, vol. 2.

58. Testimony of Marcelle Douard, collected by F. Perroy and R. Galliard, March 5, 1946, Archives du Comité d'histoire de la Deuxième Guerre mondiale—

Résistance intérieure: Mouvements, réseaux, partis politiques et syndicats, Ligne Comète, 72AJ/45; Hornsey, *The Pilot Walked Home.*

59. Nazi Persecution Claim, Rosine Leontine Witton for Sidney Albert Witton (deceased), FO 950/3423, TNA; Rosine Witton testimony against Raymond Hermand before a tribunal in Lille, 1946, Musée de la Résistance, Bondues, 2017.1.103.

60. Marcel and Berthe Roger "French Helper" file, NARA, RG 0498, UD 193; Coilliot, *1940–1944, 4 Longues Années d'Occupation,* vol. 1; Neave, *Saturday at M.I.9*; Rémy, *Réseau Comète,* vol. 2.

61. Hornsey, *The Pilot Walked Home,* chapter 12.

62. Private Papers of Madame R. Witton, Documents.7565, IWM.

63. Roy F. Claytor, E&E 120; McElroy, E&E 203. Claytor describes a joint mission by Rosine Witton and Marcelle Douard. Witton and Douard are often difficult to tell apart in E&Es because both were short, slight, and dark haired. Clayton says, "Cowherd and I met the Chief of the organization and a lady (35 years old, English husband now P/W, spoke fluent English) in an amusement park. At 2300 hours this woman took us on to a train, I saw a small woman lead Major Cole on to the train. We rode to Bordeaux where we met a French man [Max Roger] and a Belgian [Franco]." Some evaders who knew Rosine Witton's name did not include it in their escape and evasion reports. For an example, see George Gineikis, E&E 257. Gineikis traveled with Dennis Hornsey and features prominently in Hornsey's account of his trip with Rosine Witton, which was written in or before 1946. Yet Gineikis's escape and evasion report does not mention his helpers in Paris.

64. Bert Witton to Rosine Witton, August 11 and 25, 1943, Private Papers of Madame R. Witton, Documents.7565, IWM.

Chapter 13

1. Lucy Hollingdale to Mrs. Sutton, March 21, 1954, Private Papers of LME Hollingdale, Documents.1545, IWM.

2. For papers and correspondence related to Lucy Hollingdale, see Private Papers of LME Hollingdale, Documents.1545, IWM, and Lucille Hollingdale "French Helper" file, NARA, RG 0498, UD 193. Both NARA and the IWM record her name as Lucille, including on exhibit text in the IWM's Second World War galleries (2022), but her birth name was Lucienne, and she went by Lucy. Lucienne Marie Eleonore Gantier, born to Louis Gantier and Catherine Joly, February 18, 1895, Blendecques, Pas-de-Calais; married Henry William Charles Hollingdale, September 3, 1921, Blendecques; died January 28, 1984, Calais, Pas-de-Calais. See vital records in the collection of the AD-PdC.

3. Lucy Hollingdale to Major John White, undated but stamped "received," September 5, 1946; Lucy Hollingdale to William Middledorf, May 22, 1946, Lucy Hollingdale "French Helper" file, NARA, RG 0498, UD 193.

4. Lucy Hollingdale to Major John White, Lucy Hollingdale "French Helper" file, NARA, RG 0498, UD 193.

5. Lucy Hollingdale, December 17, 1970, Documents.1545, IWM.

6. Lucy Hollingdale to William Middledorf, May 22, 1946, Lucy Hollingdale "French Helper" file, NARA, RG 0498, UD 193.

7. Lucy Hollingdale to Mrs. Sutton, March 21, 1954, Private Papers of LME Hollingdale, Documents.1545, IWM.

8. Lucy Hollingdale to Major John White, Lucy Hollingdale "French Helper" file, NARA, RG 0498, UD 193.

9. Lucy Hollingdale made all of these accusations at various times in surviving correspondence, but it is not possible for her to know exactly what happened. Emile and Madeleine Didier died in concentration camps, Jack and Marthe Wood were searched many times but never deported, and the French woman from Douai appears to have been Emilie Nisse, who was arrested a week after Lucy. In all likelihood, the Germans' evidence came from many different sources during the widespread crackdown on OCM in the summer of 1943.

10. Lucy Hollingdale to Major John White, Lucy Hollingdale "French Helper" file, NARA, RG 0498, UD 193.

11. Marcel Maillard, GR 16P 384688; William O'Connor, GR 16P 448836; Isadore Ryan, *No Way Out: The Irish in Wartime France, 1939–1945* (Cork: Mercier Press, 2017). With thanks to Anne Morddel and Isadore Ryan.

12. IWGC summary of a statement by Alfred Arthur Wilson, RA P624 CWGC.

13. Report by Frank Grinham, RA P624 CWGC.

14. Grégory Célerse, *La Traque des résistants nordistes 1940–1944* (Marcq-en-Barœul: *Les Lumières De Lille Editions,* 2011).

15. Citation for Medal of Freedom with Bronze Palm (posthumous), Valentine Defeller Ployart "French Helper" file, NARA, RG 0498, UD 193.

16. Military Sentence, Military Tribunal Lille [Armstrong, Cornille, Debrabant, Maillard, Ployart], May 10, 1944, collections 13471, ZC 20.088-11, Sachsen State Archives, Dresden. With thanks to Sabina von Thuemmler for translation.

17. Debrabant believed that D'Hallendre and Lisfranc talked, but, just as with Lucy Hollingdale, it was impossible for her to know for sure. The Gestapo had dismantled the entire network. The U.S. officials say that Roger Le Neveau "could easily have given away the whole show to the Gestapo." Marie Therese Debrabant "French Helper" file, NARA, RG 0498, UD 193. Unfortunately, Joseph Cornille's NARA file is missing. It is listed in the index, but it is not in the box where it should be.

18. Testimony of Emmanuel Dossche, in Nazi Persecution Claim, E. R. Megarity for Robert Armstrong (deceased), FO 950/3602, TNA.

19. Testimony of Emmanuel Dossche and Gaston Lepine, in Nazi Persecution Claim, E. R. Megarity for Robert Armstrong (deceased), FO 950/3602, TNA; Testimony of Thomas Crowley and Report by Frank Grinham, RA P624 CWGC.

20. Thanks to Grégory Célerse and the residents of 18 and 20 rue Francois de Badts.

21. Robert Lefebvre, *Cellule 16: Journal d'un detenu Politique de Loos* (Cambrai : Editions Boduelle, 1944). Lefebvre was arrested on December 14, 1943, and interrogated by Kurt Kohl during the week of December 14–21, 1943. This was either immediately after Bob's interrogation or overlapping with it. His memoir, *Cellule 16*, was one of the earliest published accounts from a detainee in northern France. It was published in Cambrai in late 1944, within three months of the liberation of Loos prison. Lefebvre was released from Loos on June 6, 1944, and wrote his account very soon after returning home, when he still remembered many details. Although Lefebvre seems not to have met Bob Armstrong, his description of Joseph Cornille's trial and his codefendants is correct in many small details that are corroborated by the trial records.

22. Alfred Delporte was arrested on November 29, 1943. Alfred Delporte "French Helper" file, NARA, RG 0498, UD 193.

23. Alfred Delporte "French Helper" file, NARA, RG 0498, UD 193.

24. Célerse, *La Traque des résistants nordistes 1940–1944*, 105.

25. Marie Therese Debrabant mentioned being shown a photo of Cox during her interrogation. Marie Therese Debrabant "French Helper" file, NARA, RG 0498, UD 193.

26. Lefebvre, *Cellule 16*.

27. SOE communication dated 3 January 1944, Michael Trotobas personnel file, HS9/1487/1, TNA; Papers Concerning Berthe Fraser, GM, IWM, London, Documents.1768, IWM.

28. MRB exhibits and papers of Eugène D'Hallendre, MRB.

29. Emile and Madeleine Didier "French Helper" file, NARA, RG 0498, UD 193; Emile Didier Resistance Dossier, GR 16P 184597, Vincennes; Henri Artisson BCRA Dossier, GR 28 P 11 / 08 DOSSIER 22274, Vincennes.

30. Célerse, *La Traque des résistants nordistes 1940–1944*, 126–31.

31. Lefebvre, *Cellule 16*, 177.

32. A copy of the sentencing document, which summarizes the proceedings against Robert Armstrong and his codefendants, is held in the Sachsen State Archives in Dresden. With many thanks to Sabina von Thuemmler for research assistance and translation of a very challenging document from German into English. Military Sentence, Military Tribunal Lille [Armstrong, Cornille, Debrabant, Maillard, Ployart], May 10, 1944, collections 13471, ZC 20.088-11, Sachsen State Archives, Dresden. Hereafter abbreviated Armstrong Sentence, 1944.

33. Léonie Maton was born on April 28, 1871, in Ohain, Nord. She gave birth to her daughter Marie on October 17, 1892, and married François Theodore Longatte in Trélon on October 7, 1899. She died on April 10, 1943, in Douai. See birth, marriage, and death records in the collection of the AD-Nord.

34. Dr. Kurt Kalberlah was an expert in international law with a PhD from the University of Jena. He was generally considered moderate, even liberal, among Nazi jurists for his tentative acknowledgment that a soldier might, in theory, have the right to disobey an unlawful order. More relevant to Bob Armstrong's

case, Kalberlah argued in his academic work that "it is self-evident that prisoners of war are subject to the due process of law." See Andreas Topp, *Militär und Kriegsvölkerrecht: Rechtsnorm, Fachdiskurs und Kriegspraxis in Deutschland 1899–1940* (Berlin: Walter de Gruyter, 2008), 380. With thanks to Sabina von Thuemmler for research into Kalberlah's student files at the University of Jena.

35. Lefebvre, *Cellule 16*, 166. Joseph Cornille's lawyer argued that his client was only tangentially involved with "Arthur's" evasion and that the arrest, which happened a full year after the alleged crime, was based on hearsay rather than fact. Dr. Kalberlah listened but "refused to take it into account."

Chapter 14

1. Rosine Witton's account of these events is told in an unpublished memoir, *Eugène D'Hallendre: Cheminot* (ca. 1983–1985), by Edgard D'Hallendre, son of Eugène D'Hallendre, which is held in the collection of the Musée de la Résistance, Bondues. Quotations from her conversations with Nothomb, Grampin, and Madame Roger are related by D'Hallendre and translated by the author. Notes from an interview that Edgard D'Hallendre conducted with Rosine Witton around 1983 are also in the D'Hallendre family papers at the MRB. With many thanks to the MRB, Claire Crétel-Diest, Hélène Priego, and Grégory Célerse.

2. Rosine Witton, "French Helper" file, NARA, RG 0498, UD 193.

3. Airey Neave, *Saturday at M.I.9* (London: Hodder & Stoughton, 1969).

4. Letters from Rosine Witton to Alfie Martin, March 21, 1983, and to Mr. Wright, June 1, 1967, courtesy of Sheila and Julie Martin.

5. Testimony of Rosine Witton, 1946, 2017.1.103, D'Hallendre family papers, Musée de la Résistance, Bondues.

6. There are many Resistance memoirs that discuss Fresnes prison. Two that relate experiences that were probably similar to Rosine Witton's in some ways are by Jacqueline Pery d'Alincourt, who was deported on the same transport as Rosine, and Virginia d'Albert-Lake, who worked for the Comet Line and was arrested a few months later. François Berriot, *Chronicles of Resistance and Deportation: Jacqueline Pery d'Alincourt and Her World*, trans. Theodore P. Fraser and Daniel J. Chisholm (Auburn, ME: Androscoggin Press, 2021); Virginia d'Albert-Lake and Judy Barrett Litoff, *An American Heroine in the French Resistance: The Diary and Memoir of Virginia d'Albert-Lake* (New York: Fordham University Press, 2006).

7. Edgard D'Hallendre, *Eugène D'Hallendre: Cheminot*, MRB.

8. The 417 women on this transport are sometimes referred to as "35000s" in reference to the prisoner numbers they were assigned at Ravensbrück. In addition to Rosine Witton and Marcelle Douard, other Comet Line operatives in the group included Lucienne Laurentie and Louise Lenoir.

9. Accounts of this journey are reconstructed from memoirs, biographies, and interviews with deportees. Some of these, like Catherine Roux's *Triangle Rouge* (Lyon: M. Audin Et Cie, 1946) and Jeanne Bouteille's *Infernal Rebus* (Moulins:

Crépin-Leblond, 1946), were published in the immediate aftermath of the war, while others were testimony collected from survivors like Andrée Paté and Yvonne Bridoux, who continued their anti-fascist work into the twenty-first century. The main eyewitness sources that inform this chapter are Roux, *Triangle Rouge*; Bouteille-Garagnon, *Infernal Rebus*; Neus Català, *Testimoni d'una supervivent* (Barcelona: El Periódico, Edicions Primera Plana, 2007); and Teresa Noce, *Rivoluzionaria professionale: Autobiografia di una Partigiana Comunista* (Rome: Red Star Press, 2016). Primary sources are Jacqueline Pery d'Alincourt, published in François Berriot's *Chronicles of Resistance and Deportation: Jacqueline Pery d'Alincourt and Her World* (Kennebunk, ME: Androscoggin Press, 2021), translated by Theodore P. Fraser and Daniel J. Chisholm III; Suzanne Agrapart, published in Jean-Pierre Harbulot, *Une famille de déportes* (Nancy: PU NANCY, 1983); Yvonne Abbas, interview with Laurence Mauriacourt, October 2007, published on YouTube by *Journal l'Humanité*; Yvonne Bridoux Chatelaine via the Association des Déportés et Familles de Disparus du Camp de Concentration de Flossenbürg & Kommandos, https://asso-flossenburg.com; Andree Paté, Marie "Betty" Desbat, and Marie-Marguerite Micheline, in Jan Valeš and Libor Schröpfer, *Pobočný koncentrační tábor Holýšov 1944–1945—Francouzské Deníky* (Prague: Nakladatelství Klika, 2017); Cecilie Klein-Pollack, oral history in the collection of the United States Holocaust Memorial Museum, Accession Number 1990.383.1, RG Number RG-50.030.0107; and Ruth Friedman Cohen, oral history in the collection of the United States Holocaust Memorial Museum, Accession Number 2011.209, RG Number RG-50.106.0190.

10. Berriot, *Chronicles of Resistance and Deportation.*

11. For a history of Ravensbrück, see Sarah Helm, *Ravensbrück: Life and Death in Hitler's Concentration Camp for Women* (New York: Anchor Books, 2015).

12. d'Alincourt in Berriot, 88.

13. d'Alincourt in Berriot, 58.

14. Yvonne Abbas, interview with Laurence Mauriaucourt, October 2007, *Journal d'Humanité.*

15. d'Albert-Lake and Litoff, *An American Heroine in the French Resistance.*

16. Helm, *Ravensbrück.*

17. Members of this transport are recognizable by their Holleischen prisoner numbers, which ranged from 50676 to 50822. With thanks to Jan Valeš.

18. d'Alincourt in Berriot.

19. Roux, *Triangle Rouge.*

20. For histories of KZ-Außenlager Holleischen, see Valeš and Schröpfer, *Pobočný koncentrační tábor Holýšov 1944–1945*, and Carl Barwise, "Holleischen Concentration Camp," *After the Battle*, No. 162.

21. Roux, *Triangle Rouge*; Yvonne Bridoux Chatelain.

22. The British soldiers who held Pegasus Bridge on D-Day were from Company D 2nd Ox and Bucks Light Infantry, which was the company Harry Hollingdale served with in World War I.

23. At some camps, the red triangle also held a letter (F for French prisoners), but Rosine's surviving uniform does not have a letter in the triangle. Bouteille, *Infernal Rebus*; Roux, *Triangle Rouge*; Valeš and Schröpfer, *Pobočný koncentrační tábor Holýšov 1944–1945*. With thanks to Avril Williams.

24. Harbulot, *Une famille de déportes*, 76.

25. Marie-Marguerite Michelin in Valeš and Schröpfer, *Pobočný koncentrační tábor Holýšov 1944–1945*, recounting what was told to her by a prisoner who arrived at Holleischen earlier than she did.

26. Teresa Noce was imprisoned at Holleischen under a pseudonym, Jeanette Pinelli. Noce, *Rivoluzionaria professionale*, 289.

27. Bouteille, *Infernal Rebus*, 210.

28. Rosine Witton to French Ministry of Defense, January 11, 1954, GR 16P 567216, Vincennes.

29. Valeš and Schröpfer, *Pobočný koncentrační tábor Holýšov 1944–1945*, 278.

30. Roux, *Triangle Rouge*; Bouteille, *Infernal Rebus*, 229.

31. Possibly Natalie Bialek. Catherine Roux does not give a full name for "Natacha," but there are no other Natalies or Natachas on Valeš's camp roster. For examples of badges and rosettes made at Holleischen, see Anne-Marie Pavillard, "Les archives de l'Association des anciennes déportées et internées de la Résistance (ADIR) à la BDIC," Histoire@Politique, *Politique, culture, société*, no. 5, May–August 2008, "Femmes en résistance à Ravensbruck."

32. Noce, *Rivoluzionaria professionale*, 299.

33. Andrée Paté in Valeš and Schröpfer, *Pobočný koncentrační tábor Holýšov 1944–1945*.

34. Roux, *Triangle Rouge*.

35. Neus Català, *Testimoni d'una supervivent*, 92. Many of the Holleischen prisoners believed that the Nazis adulterated their food or inoculations with a poison that sterilized them. Whether or not that was true, many French prisoners blamed their lifelong struggles with infertility and amenorrhea on Nazi medical experiments. See Yvonne Abbas interview and Marie Desbat and Andree Paté in Valeš and Schröpfer, *Pobočný koncentrační tábor Holýšov 1944–1945*, 267, 279.

36. Geoffrey P. Megargee, *The United States Holocaust Memorial Museum Encyclopedia of Camps and Ghettos, 1933–1945: Volume I. Early Camps, Youth Camps, and Concentration Camps and Subcamps under the SS-Business Administration Main Office (WVHA)* (Bloomington: Indiana University Press, 2011); Valeš and Schröpfer, *Pobočný koncentrační tábor Holýšov 1944–1945*; Barwise, "Holleischen Concentration Camp."

37. Megargee, *The United States Holocaust Memorial Museum Encyclopedia of Camps and Ghettos, 1933–1945*, 615; Valeš and Schröpfer, *Pobočný koncentrační tábor Holýšov 1944–1945*, 125; Bouteille, *Infernal Rebus*, 233.

38. Of all the sub-camps of Ravensbrück, Holleischen was one of the farthest from the main camp. Flossenbürg was much closer and took over the administration of Holleischen on September 1, 1944.

39. d'Albert-Lake, *An American Heroine*; Helm, *Ravensbrück*.

40. Many of the French women who were still alive at Ravensbrück were extracted by the Swedish Red Cross in March and April 1945. Madeleine Didier was not, possibly because she had already died or possibly because she was an NN prisoner. Emile and Madeleine Didier "French Helper" file, NARA, RG 0498, UD 193.

41. Ten of the eleven official deaths are from 1945; one has no specific date. There are a number of deaths recounted in prisoner testimony that are not included in that number. These include the Polish woman killed in the explosion, the Jewish woman killed in a bombing in late April or early May 1945, and the two Jewish sisters who may have been beaten to death some time in March or April 1945. The official toll also excludes the three French women transported to Flossenbürg for execution in April 1945. There may have been other deaths in 1944, but prisoner testimony indicates that the true number of deaths among Holleischen prisoners probably did not exceed twenty. See Valeš and Schröpfer, *Pobočný koncentrační tábor Holýšov 1944–1945*.

42. Transport from Romainville to Ravensbrück, April 18, 1944, Fondation pour la Memoire de la Deportation Database, ed. Yves Lescure, http://www.bddm.org.

43. Rosine Witton to French Ministry of Defense, January 11, 1954, GR 16P 567216, Vincennes.

44. Bouteille, *Infernal Rebus*. Catherine Roux mentions a "disemboweled Polish" prisoner in her roll of the dead in *Triangle Rouge*. The death of a Polish woman in an explosion is also noted by J. Hourcabie in Valeš and Schröpfer, *Pobočný koncentrační tábor Holýšov 1944–1945*, 255. The Polish woman's name is not recorded in any of the French sources. Death records from Holleischen do not have an obvious match, though there are a few possibilities. A Belorussian prisoner named M. Dziemieczyk was buried in the Holýšov cemetery, but no details of the date or cause of death are recorded. It is possible that the French prisoners were imprecise in calling the dead woman "Polish." However, M. Dziemieczyk was born in 1924, so she would have been very young to have multiple children. Another possibility is that the dead woman may have been Anna Josipenko, a Polish woman who died of unrecorded causes on January 23, 1945. This date does not match Rosine Witton's testimony, but it is possible that details were garbled in her memory. If the Polish woman really did die in October 1944 as Rosine remembered, this suggests that the death records for Holleischen—which do not include any deaths before January 1945—may be incomplete.

45. Noce, *Rivoluzionaria professionale*, 292.

46. Rosine Witton to French Ministry of Defense, January 11, 1954, GR 16P 567216, Vincennes.

47. Barwise, "Holleischen Concentration Camp," 34.

48. Bouteille, *Infernal Rebus*, 224; Roux, *Triangle Rouge*.

49. Bouteille, *Infernal Rebus*, 246; Noce, *Rivoluzionaria professionale*.

50. Harbulot, *Une famille de déportes*, 77; Andree Paté and Marie-Marguerite Michelin in Valeš and Schröpfer, *Pobočný koncentrační tábor Holýšov 1944–1945*. Marie-Marguerite Puiseux married Jean Michelin, whose father, André, codirected the Michelin tire company with his brother, Edouard, and also published the first Michelin Guide.

51. Cecilie Klein-Pollack, oral history in the collection of the United States Holocaust Memorial Museum, Accession Number 1990.383.1, RG Number RG-50.030.0107; Ruth Friedman Cohen, oral history in the collection of the United States Holocaust Memorial Museum, Accession Number 2011.209, RG Number RG-50.106.0190.

52. Noce, *Rivoluzionaria professionale*, 295.

53. Ruth René Friedman (later Cohen) was born on April 26, 1930, in Mukacevo, a town that was variously part of Czechoslovakia, Hungary, and Ukraine. Her parents were Berta and Herman Friedman. Valeš and Schröpfer have her birth date as 1927, but her birth certificate (1930) is in the collection of the USHMM, Friedman Family Papers, Accession Number 2009.348.2, suggesting that she was passing for older than she was. Ruth Cohen Oral History, Accession Number 2011.209, RG Number RG-50.106.0190, Track 1 at 4:45.

54. Harbulot, *Une famille de déportes*, 77; Paté in Valeš and Schröpfer, *Pobočný koncentrační tábor Holýšov 1944–1945*.

55. Cecilie Klein-Pollack, USHMM Oral History, Accession Number 1990.383.1, RG Number RG-50.030.0107; 45:00.

56. Bouteille, *Infernal Rebus*, 267.

57. Marie-Marguerite Michelin journal, April 27, 1945, in Valeš and Schröpfer, *Pobočný koncentrační tábor Holýšov 1944–1945*, 232; Valeš and Schröpfer, *Pobočný koncentrační tábor Holýšov 1944–1945*, 71.

58. Michelin writes that both Solange Hartmann and Rosine Witton were Protestants. I have not found much evidence of Rosine's religious faith. Marcelle Douard and Lucienne Laurentie were committed Catholics whose religious activities are frequently mentioned by Michelin and other witnesses, but no one ever mentions Rosine in the same breath. Even if Rosine was not herself a Protestant, she would have been more familiar with Protestant traditions than most of the French prisoners because of her marriage to Bert.

Chapter 15

1. 379th Bomb Group Records, NARA, RG 18: Records of the Army Air Forces, World War II Combat Operations Report, 1941-6, ARC ID 596339, Box 1523, NARA. The primary target for this mission was a V-1 rocket site at St-Martin-l'Hortier, but cloud cover forced the attack to divert to a "target of opportunity," in this case, a bridge near Hazebrouck. The group's recent missions included May 24: Berlin; June 18: Hamburg; June 21: Ruhrland; and June 24: Bremen.

2. "Flying Rentschler Brothers Home on Visit," *South Bend Tribune*, April 6, 1945; "Missing Airman Safe in England," *South Bend Tribune*, September 8, 1944; Donald A. Rentschler Escape & Evasion Report 1512, September 5, 1944; Donald A. Rentschler WWII Draft Card; Federal Censuses of 1920, 1930, 1940. The nine men who flew this mission in *Big Barn Smell* were 1st Lieutenant Clarence Jamison, pilot; 2nd Lieutenant Graham Sweet, copilot; 2nd Lieutenant Donald Rentschler, navigator; 2nd Lieutenant George Rogers, bombardier; Technical Sergeant Knapp Vallas, radio operator; Staff Sergeant Willie Neal, engineer/top turret gunner; Staff Sergeant Salvatore Tomaselli, tail gunner; Staff Sergeant Henry Swanson, ball turret gunner; and Staff Sergeant Eugene Bruce, waist gunner.

3. *Stump Jumper* was never wholly fit to fly again. It was eventually reassigned to Operation Aphrodite, an ill-fated program that used old B-17s stuffed with bombs as remote-controlled missiles. A pilot and copilot would take off and then bail out while the plane was guided to its target remotely. The program was not very successful and is remembered mostly for killing Lieutenant Joseph P. Kennedy Jr., the elder brother of President John F. Kennedy. *Stump Jumper* was one of the last planes used in Operation Aphrodite, flying its final (unsuccessful) mission against the Oldenberg power station on January 1, 1945. B-17 42-30237; see American Air Museum in Britain, part of the Imperial War Museum, americanairmuseum. com/archive/aircraft/42-30237.

4. Clarence Jamison, "Come Ride with Me," unpublished memoir courtesy of Terry, Scot, and Hunter Jamison.

5. George Rogers told this story to the U.S. Army in 1961. It was published by the Information Division, US COMZEUR, Release #61-185, Orleans, France, July 28, 1961. With thanks to Pete Boettcher.

6. A version of General Vanaman's story was published in Thomas Parrish's *The Ultra Americans: The U.S. Role in Breaking the Nazi Codes* (New York: Stein & Day, 1985), based in large part on Parrish's interview with Major General John W. Huston. Huston was a decorated Air Force general, a history professor at the U.S. Naval Academy, and chief of the Office of Air Force History. According to Parrish, Huston was the navigator on Vanaman's fateful mission, but this is not true. A thorough review of the primary sources, including the 379th Bomb Group Combat Operations Reports at the U.S. National Archives and Records Administration, the escape and evasion reports filed by Donald Rentschler and the rest of the crew in 1944, and their subsequent memoirs, shows that Huston was not a member of the crew that flew with General Vanaman on June 27, 1944. It is not clear where the error originated. Parrish's version includes many errors, from the name of the plane (*Nightjar n-Nan* instead of the correct *Big Barn Smell*) to the time of the mission (morning instead of the correct evening) to the total number of men aboard (twelve instead of the correct ten). It is possible that Huston flew on one of General Vanaman's previous observation missions and that either he or Parrish conflated the two. See 379th Bomb Group Records, NARA, RG 18: Records of the Army Air Forces, World War II Combat Operations Report,

1941–1946, ARC ID 596339, Box 1523, NARA; escape and evasion reports (E&E) 1512 (Rentschler), E&E 1563 (Sweet), E&E 1564 (Rogers), E&E 1865 (Neal). RG 498 UD133-4, NARA.

7. Arthur W. Vanaman, official Air Force biography, https://www.af.mil /About-Us/Biographies/Display/Article/105308/major-general-arthur-w-vana man; interview with Arthur W. Vanaman conducted by Hugh N. Ahmann, February 10–12, 1976, Air Force Oral History Interview #K239.0512-855, Maxwell Air Force Base, Alabama. Subsequent references to this interview are abbreviated as Vanaman interview.

8. Parrish, *The Ultra Americans*.

9. Vanaman interview, 411.

10. James Doolittle and Carroll V. Glines, *I Could Never Be So Lucky Again* (New York: Bantam Books, 1991), 318, 373.

11. Vanaman interview, 435.

12. Jamison, "Come Ride with Me."

13. Captain John J. O'Connell Report, Clarence Jamison Report, June 27, 1944, S-2, 379th Bomb Group Records, RG 18: Records of the Army Air Forces, World War II Combat Operations Report, 1941–1946, ARC ID 596339, Box 1523, NARA.

14. Jamison, "Come Ride with Me."

15. The lead pilot, Clifford Blue, reported, "There were no encounters with enemy aircraft . . . there was occasional flak but none close to us." Rentschler's crew remembered it differently, but Blue's report shows what a fluke the whole thing was. Report by Lieutenant Clifford Blue, 379th Bomb Group Records, RG 18: Records of the Army Air Forces, World War II Combat Operations Report, 1941–1946, ARC ID 596339, Box 1523, NARA; George Rogers, Release #61-185; Donald Rentschler E&E 1512.

16. Vanaman interview, 412; Jamison, "Come Ride with Me"; Report by Technical Sergeant Knapp Vallas, June 27, 1944, 379th Bomb Group Records, RG 18: Records of the Army Air Forces, World War II Combat Operations Report, 1941–1946, ARC ID 596339, Box 1523, NARA.

17. Rentschler E&E 1512; "Flying Rentschler Brothers Home on Visit," *South Bend Tribune*, April 6, 1945.

18. Jamison, "Come Ride with Me."

19. "The fire came back once or twice," testified the radio operator, twenty-two-year-old Sergeant Knapp Vallas. "We didn't know whether it would continue to burn." Report by Technical Sergeant Knapp Vallas, June 27, 1944, and Report by Captain Howard W. Silver, 524th Squadron Engineering Officer, report dated June 29, 1944, 379th Bomb Group Records, RG 18: Records of the Army Air Forces, World War II Combat Operations Report, 1941–1946, ARC ID 596339, Box 1523, NARA; Jamison, "Come Ride with Me."

20. Donald L. Miller, *Masters of the Air: America's Bomber Boys Who Fought the Air War against Nazi Germany* (New York: Simon and Schuster, 2007), 393.

21. Vanaman interview, 414–19.

22. Vanaman interview, 417; Miller, *Masters of the Air*, 393. When he recovered from his injuries, Vanaman was transferred to Stalag Luft III. He remained a prisoner until April 1945, when SS-Brigadeführer Walter Schellenberg, one of Hitler's most senior intelligence officers, sent him to Switzerland in a last-ditch effort to deliver Germany to the Americans instead of the Russians. See Reinhard R. Doerries, *Hitler's Intelligence Chief: Walter Schellenberg* (Cleveland, OH: Enigma Books, 2009).

23. Ben Leech "French Helper" file, NARA, RG 0498, UD 193; Rentschler E&E 1512.

24. Rentschler E&E 1512.

25. Katie Daubs, "The RCAF Helmet That Sparked a 70-Year Mystery," *Toronto Star*, November 9, 2015.

26. "July 1944—The following identity discs were handed to me by Mr. Ben Leech, Gardener I.W.G.C. Beaumont Hamel, but could not transfer them because the roads were barred by the gestapo: 116379 F/Lt Pilot Ewart V. Forwell RAF, 412891 F/Sgt N.J. Helen RNZAF, 126292 F/O Arthur Roberts RCAF, 100664 W/O James Kelly, RCAF, 19886 PO Leslie Richard Lauzon, RCAF, 200327 Sgt. Chris Christoff, RCAF." Arthur Richards "French Helper" file, NARA, RG 0498, UD 193.

27. Ben Leech "French Helper" file, NARA, RG 0498, UD 193.

28. 1936 Mailly-Maillet census, AD-Somme.

29. Leon Aubry "French Helper" file, NARA, RG 0498, UD 193; Acheux census 1926. AD-Somme.

30. Ben Leech "French Helper" file, NARA, RG 0498, UD 193; George Rogers Release #61-185.

31. Rogers's injuries treated by Dr. Gilbert Duquesnes from Albert; George Rogers Release #61-185.

32. E&E 1563 (Sweet), 1865 (Neal).

33. Maurice Leech to Sherri Ottis, 1997, courtesy of Sherri Ottis.

34. Stephen Grady, *Gardens of Stone: My Boyhood in the French Resistance* (London: Hodder & Stoughton, 2013).

35. MRB. With thanks to Grégory Célerse.

36. With thanks to Robert Flood, Jane Evans, and Stewart Mitchell. See also Sue Elliott and James Fox, *The Children Who Fought Hitler: A British Outpost in Europe* (London: John Murray, 2009).

37. Jack Evans and Ernest Dudley, *Confessions of a Special Agent: Wartime Service in the Small Scale Raiding Force and SOE* (Barnsley: Frontline Books, 2018). With thanks to Rhydian Evans.

38. Brian Lett, in *The Small Scale Raiding Force* (Barnsley: Pen & Sword Military, 2013), expressed some skepticism about Jack Evans but after considering the evidence concluded that he was, in fact, "a real person" who "was truly a member of SSRF and SOE." However, Lett found Jack Evans's memoir *Confessions*

of a Secret Agent (London: Robert Hale, 1957) too riddled with inaccuracies and implausible timelines to be reliable. One of Lett's unanswered questions was the matter of Evans's age. In *Confessions*, Evans claimed he was sixteen when he joined SOE and that he was pulled off an SOE mission at the last moment because he was underage. In fact, Evans was born in 1921 and joined SOE in 1941 at age twenty. A birth date of May 11, 1921, for Jack Etienne Olive Evans is confirmed in his SOE personnel file (TNA, HS 9/489/3), his prisoner-of-war card (TNA, WO 416/114/211), and the vital records of Boismont, Somme. In the War Graves Commission's 1940 evacuation files, Jack Evans's age is noted as eighteen, though he turned nineteen on May 11. Lett was also unsure whether Evans was dead, but the Boismont records record his death on April 2, 1981, in Labastide-Beauvoir, Haute-Garonne.

39. Some accounts say René Muchembled was killed on July 10, others say July 16.

40. René Muchembled "French Helper" file, NARA, RG 0498, UD 193.

41. Jules Guéant died at Buchenwald on March 20, 1945, Arolsen Archives.

42. Rentschler E&E 1512.

43. Herbert Palin staff card, CWGC Archives. The six were Rentschler, Bulow, Simler, Meche, Blight, and Moser. Ben Leech and Irma Palin "French Helper" files, NARA, RG 0498, UD 193.

44. Papers concerning Berthe Fraser, GM, IWM, London, Documents.1768, IWM.

45. With thanks to Pete Boettcher.

46. Anne Jacobson Robertson, *The Road Home* (1996), telling the story of Chuck Carlson, who is holding the little dog in the photo. This self-published book includes an image of the handwritten, dated menu for the celebratory dinner given by the Hellers on September 3, 1944. It includes champagne and is signed by the airmen in the photo. With thanks to Lona Sweet, Mary Hancey, and Bruce Hancey.

47. Rentschler E&E 1512.

48. Henriette Henon "French Helper" file, NARA, RG 0498, UD 193.

49. Paul Muchembled to U.S. Army, February 24, 1948, René Muchembled "French Helper" file NARA, RG 0498, UD 193.

50. Memo dated September 8, 1945, Ben Leech "French Helper" file, NARA, RG 0498, UD 193.

51. Ben Leech to Major John White, May 21, 1945, Ben Leech "French Helper" file, NARA, RG 0498, UD 193.

Chapter 16

1. An earlier cohort arrived August 10, mostly men from Vittel and Giromagny.

2. Albert Roberts to Reginald Haworth, November 18, 1966, CWGC/1/2/I/20.

3. Jack Evans, "A Prisoner of War's Escape from the Germans," *The Spokesman-Review* (Spokane, WA), May 24, 1953. With thanks to Jackie Davies.

4. Fabian Ware, dated July 1944 but actually delivered to returnees in August and September, CWGC/1/1/7/B/82

5. 262nd Commission Meeting, October 18, 1944; CWGC/1/2/D/7/11: Arrangements for the Repatriation of the Commission's Staff.

6. Albert Wellings FO 950/2702, TNA; Alfred Arthur Wilson personnel file, P 51, CWGC/1/1/13/120; Samuel E. Chapman personnel file P 451, CWGC/1/1/13/104.

7. Bernard Parsons journal, October 26, 1940, Private Papers of B. A. Parsons, Documents.6526, IWM; Arthur Kirkwood to IWGC, September 18, 1944, Arthur Kirkwood personnel file, P 48, CWGC/1/1/3/110.

8. CWGC/1/1/7/B/77: Withdrawal of Staff from France and Belgium.

9. CWGC/1/2/D/7/12: Treatment of Interned Staff—Lawson Report.

10. CWGC/1/1/7/B/83: Treatment of Staff Ex France and Belgium Detained Abroad.

11. CWGC/1/2/D/7/12: Treatment of Interned Staff—Lawson Report; CWGC/4/2/319: Minutes of the Finance Committee Meeting 319, December 12, 1945; CWGC/1/1/7/B/80: Missing Staff.

12. CWGC/1/2/D/1/6: Collaboration with the Enemy—Allegations against Staff France and Belgium.

13. CWGC/1/17/B/83: Treatment of Staff Ex France and Belgium Detained Abroad.

14. Albert Saville to IWGC, March 10, 1947, CWGC/1/1/7/B/83.

15. Walter Weller to IWGC, June 28, 1944, CWGC/1/1/7/B/80.

16. CWGC/1/1/7/B/83; John W. Oldman to IWGC, April 2, 1945, and Frederick Sillar to C. H. Willcox, Treasury, April 21, 1945, T 164/349, TNA.

17. Virginie Roberts died at Vittel on March 23, 1944. CWGC/1/2/D/7/11: Arrangements for the Repatriation of the Commission's Staff.

18. Brigadier T. J. B. Bosvile, Supreme Headquarters Allied Expeditionary Force to Sir Fabian Ware, September 6, 1944, CWGC 1/2/A/505: Re-Opening of Commission's Work France and Belgium.

19. Albert Roberts to Philip Longworth, November 18, 1966, CWGC/1/2/I/20.

20. Report by George Greensill, May 23, 1945, CWGC/1/1/10/A/4: Villers-Bretonneux Australian Memorial.

21. Report by William Arnott, November 8, 1944; Haworth letter to Wardley, November 29, 1944; BML P653 CWGC.

22. Serre Road No. 2 Condition Report, February 20, 1945, CWGC/7/4/2/18826-1.

23. Minutes of a Meeting Held in the Vice Chairman's Room, September 29, 1944, CWGC 1/2/A/505: Re-Opening of Commission's Work France and Belgium.

24. CWGC 1/2/A/505: Re-Opening of Commission's Work France and Belgium.

25. Report by William Arnott, November 8, 1944, CWGC 1/2/A/505: Re-Opening of Commission's Work France and Belgium.

26. Harriet Lawson to Frank Higginson, dated February 7, 1945, BML P653 CWGC.

27. Report by Andrew Macfarlane, December 27, 1944, CWGC 1/2/A/505: Re-Opening of Commission's Work France and Belgium.

Chapter 17

1. Robert Lefebvre, *Cellule 16: Journal d'un detenu Politique de Loos* (Cambrai : Editions Boduelle, 1944), 165–67.

2. Marie Therese Debrabant mentions her lawyers' fees in a letter to U.S. intelligence Captain Tucker, dated September 14, 1945, Marie Therese Debrabant "French Helper" files, NARA, RG 0498, UD 193. Lefebvre says that Joseph Cornille's family hired a lawyer for him. The Irish Legation communications indicate that Bob Armstrong had a lawyer named Delcourt. It is quite likely that Valentine Ployart also filed an appeal.

3. Diplomatic Cables Vichy to Dublin, 131755, TNA, dated May 9, 1944; Isadore Ryan, *No Way Out: The Irish in Wartime France, 1939–1945* (Cork: Mercier Press, 2017); Ronan McGreevy, *Wherever the Firing Line Extends: Ireland and the Western Front* (Stroud: The History Press, 2016).

4. Alfred Delporte to IWGC, February 13, 1946, RA P624 CWGC.

5. Commutation dated July 12, 1944, Robert Armstrong file, collection 13471, NS-Archive of the Ministry of State Security, ZC 20.088, file 11, Sachsen State Archive, Dresden.

6. Robert Armstrong, personnel file, Rheinbach Prison, 1944, collection 13471, NS-Archive of the Ministry of State Security, ZC 20.088, file 11, Sachsen State Archive, Dresden.

7. The other two Irish prisoners were an artist-turned-wireless-operator named Robert Vernon and a dauntless translator named Mary Cummins. Ryan, *No Way Out.*

8. From the Unnamed Dutch prisoner to Madame Debrabant. Unfortunately, the signature is transcribed as "illegible." Although signed by the Dutch prisoner, it also purports to represent the views of Victor Pecquer, a *résistant* from Douai who also knew Bob Armstrong at Kassel.

9. Dutch Prisoner ("signature illegible" in copies) to Marie Therese Debrabant, May 31, 1945, copied in RA P624 CWGC and Robert Armstrong "French Helper" file, NARA, RG 0498, UD 193.

10. The Germans attempted to forward Bob's death certificate to his family at "Curryjrane, Eije Wortshistown" but without success. Logistics and diplomacy were collapsing. None of the three condemned Irish prisoners was ever ex-

changed, and only one of them survived. Robert Armstrong personnel file, 1944, collection 13471, NS-Archive of the Ministry of State Security, ZC 20.088, file 11, Sachsen State Archive, Dresden; Ryan, *No Way Out*, 135.

11. The notation on Robert Armstrong's death record reads, "18.12.44 nach Döbeln zur Einäscherung überführt." Robert Armstrong personnel file, 1944, collection 13471, NS-Archive of the Ministry of State Security, ZC 20.088, file 11, Sachsen State Archive, Dresden; Ryan, *No Way Out*, 135.

12. Rosine Witton to Bert Witton, December 18, 1944, Private Papers of Madame R. Witton, Documents.7565, IWM.

13. IWGC memo dated November 9, 1944, CWGC/1/1/7/B/80; Rosine mentions in Bert's FO 950 Nazi Persecution Claim that he was left behind in Sweden alphabetically. He reached the United Kingdom on March 23, 1945, so he probably received the postcard between the end of March and the middle of May.

14. Nazi Persecution Claim, Rosine Leontine Witton for Sidney Albert Witton (deceased), FO 950/3423, TNA.

15. Jeanne Bouteille, *Infernal Rebus* (Moulins: Crépin-Leblond, 1946), 294.

16. Cecilie Klein-Pollack, USHMM Oral History, Accession Number 1990.383.1, RG Number RG-50.030.0107, 46:00.

17. Jan Valeš and Libor Schröpfer, *Pobočný koncentrační tábor Holýšov 1944–1945—Francouzské Deníky* (Prague: Klika, 2017), 232–235.

18. Valeš and Schröpfer, *Pobočný koncentrační tábor Holýšov 1944–1945*, 263.

19. Valeš and Schröpfer, *Pobočný koncentrační tábor Holýšov 1944–1945*, 224–78.

20. Bouteille, *Infernal Rebus*, 294.

21. Cecilie Klein-Pollack, USHMM Oral History.

22. Valeš and Schröpfer, *Pobočný koncentrační tábor Holýšov 1944–1945*, 239.

23. Valeš and Schröpfer, *Pobočný koncentrační tábor Holýšov 1944–1945*, 240.

24. Cecilie Klein-Pollack, USHMM Oral History.

25. Neus Català, *Testimoni d'una supervivent* (Barcelona: El Periódico, Edicions Primera Plana, 2007), 105.

26. Suzanne Agrapart, May 9, 1945, in Jean-Pierre Harbulot, *Une famille de déportes* (Nancy: PU NANCY, 1983), 104.

27. Teresa Noce, *Rivoluzionaria professionale: Autobiografia di una Partigiana Comunista* (Rome: Red Star Press, 2016), 302. Andrée Paté was among those strongly in favor of immediate execution, but Teresa Noce tried to "curb that chaos." Later, Noce regretted standing in the way of her younger comrades' fury. "Only much later did I realize that they were right. It would have been better to do justice in the moment, rather than wait for the Allies and the courts. There would be fewer camouflaged billionaire Nazi criminals around today."

28. Català, *Testimoni d'una supervivent*, 104.

29. Rosine Witton to Mr. Wright, June 1, 1967, courtesy of Julie and Sheila Martin.

30. "I understand that Madame Witton's departure to UK from Paris was rather hurried and the usual procedure with a returned deportee was not gone through." Rosine Witton "French Helper" file, NARA, RG 0498, UD 193.

31. Women liberated from Holleischen who mention their weight typically weighed forty kilograms (eighty-eight pounds) or less; Nazi Persecution Claim, Rosine Leontine Witton for Sidney Albert Witton (deceased), FO 950/3423, TNA.

32. Nazi Persecution Claim, Rosine Leontine Witton for Sidney Albert Witton (deceased), FO 950/3423, TNA.

33. Rosine Witton "French Helper" file, NARA, RG 0498, UD 193.

34. MK Mowat, ATS to Donald Darling, IS9 in Paris (copied to Major White), July 26, 1945, Rosine Witton "French Helper" file, NARA, RG 0498, UD 193.

35. Frank Higginson to Rosine Witton, August 11, 1945, Private Papers of Madame R. Witton, Documents.7565, IWM.

36. Jeanne Johnson widow of Percy Greenwood Johnson, Sundry Claims for Personal Prejudice, Code 217, File 37 (1316 to end), FO 950/192, TNA.

37. Percy Johnson Jr. was born in Coulogne, Pas-de-Calais, on May 12, 1920, and died in Armentières on December 10, 1941. Jeanne Johnson widow of Percy Greenwood Johnson, Sundry Claims for Personal Prejudice, Code 217, File 37 (1316 to end), FO 950/192. Frederick Knock died June 12, 1945. A. J. Poole, interned at Saint-Denis, died September 22, 1946. William Toomer died July 31, 1946. CWGC/1/17/B/83: Treatment of Staff Ex France and Belgium Detained Abroad.

38. William Arnott to IWGC, November 13, 1945, CWGC/1/1/10/A/15, Thomas Beckwith headstone, Longueval.

39. Corporal John Harris (Pupil Gardener CWGC/1/1/13/26), Intelligence Corps 15 Field Security Sec., 1470402, died August 16, 1945, age twenty-six, buried at Kanchanaburi War Cemetery; Aircraftman 1st Class Alphonsus Thomas Egan (Pupil Gardener CWGC/6/4/1/2/1976), Royal Air Force, 1264688, died July 5, 1941, age twenty-two, commemorated on the Runnymede Memorial; Private Bernard Gallagher (Pupil Gardener CWGC/6/4/1/2/2370), Sherwood Foresters, 4981523, died October 30, 1941, age nineteen, buried at Newark-upon-Trent Cemetery.

40. Rosine Witton to Foreign Office, June 28, 1965, Nazi Persecution Claim, Rosine Leontine Witton for Sidney Albert Witton (deceased), FO 950/3423, TNA.

Chapter 18

1. RA P624 CWGC.

2. Marcel Maillard GR P16 384688, Vincennes; RA P624 CWGC.

3. Alfred Delporte to IWGC, February 13, 1946, RA P624 CWGC.

4. Valentine Ployart died on April 2, 1945. The letter from the "illegible" Dutch prisoner, dated May 31, 1945, is reproduced in both RA P624 CWGC and Robert Armstrong's French helper file at NARA.

5. Dutch Prisoner to Marie Therese Debrabant, May 31, 1945, copied in RA P624 CWGC, and Robert Armstrong "French Helper" file, NARA, RG 0498, UD 193.

6. Emmanuel Dossche to IWGC, May 19, 1947, RA P624 CWGC.

7. Frank Grinham to Colonel Chettle, September 16, 1945, RA P624 CWGC.

8. Several of the gardeners who died at Ilag VIII Tost were moved to the Commission's cemeteries in Kraków after the war. Charlie Holton's gravestone bears the crest of the Imperial War Graves Commission and an inscription chosen by Maria and the children: "A notre cher époux et père regretté: Nous ne t'oublierons jamais" ("To our dear spouse and lamented father: We will never forget you"). Charles Henry Holton personnel file, P 633, CWGC/1/1/13/39; Jane Evans, *Charles Maurice Baker*, family history book, courtesy of Jane Evans.

9. July 23, 1946, RA P624 CWGC.

10. Memorial plaque for Felix Fremery, Vis-en Artois Memorial, 1932. With thanks to Poppy Mercier.

11. EJ King to Greensill, September 26, 1947, RA P624 CWGC.

12. Summary of Bob Armstrong case, July 2, 1945, RA P624 CWGC.

13. Augusta Lindsay to IWGC, January 16, 1946, and August 8, 1946, RA P24 CWGC.

14. Edward Armstrong to IWGC, September 21, 1948, RA P24 CWGC.

15. Augusta Lindsay to IWGC, February 11, 1947, RA P24 CWGC.

16. CWGC/4/2/300: Minutes of the 300th Finance Committee Meeting, February 16, 1944; Frederick Sillar memo, March 21, 1947, in RA P24 CWGC.

17. Ireland claimed £257.10 in reimbursement for relief payments to Bob Armstrong, and the United Kingdom claimed £283.15.0. Frederick Sillar, March 21, 1947, and March 31, 1947; Foreign Office to IWGC, January 3, 1949.

18. Office of the High Commissioner for Ireland to Foreign Office, June 11, 1948, RA P24 CWGC.

19. Frank Grinham to IWGC, May 15, 1948, RA P24 CWGC.

20. Augusta Lindsay to IWGC, June 21, 1948, RA P24 CWGC.

21. Edward Armstrong's case was slightly different, but Fitzgerald suggested that the Commission could award him an ex gratia payment to attend the dedication. Patrick Fitzgerald memo, June 23, 1948, RA P24 CWGC.

22. Database of Resistance Medal Recipients, Mémoire des hommes, Ministère de la défense de France, https://www.memoiredeshommes.sga.defense.gouv.fr. Other recipients included Rosine Witton, Valentine Ployart, Marie Therese Debrabant, Berthe Fraser, Emile Didier, Madeleine Didier, Edgar D'Hallendre, and John Wood.

23. Summary of Plan for Unveiling Ceremony, May 15, 1948, RA P24 CWGC.

24. Augusta Lindsay to IWGC, November 18, 1946, RA P24 CWGC.

25. Rosine Witton Recommendation for M.B.E. (Civil), August 19, 1945, WO 208/5452 TNA; Rosine Witton Citation for Medal of Freedom With Bronze Palm, "French Helper" file, NARA, RG 0498, UD 193.

26. The majority of men Rosine helped were in the August 1943–January 1944 period, and most of them either did not know her name or did not specify it in their reports. Two separate sources (Marcelle Douard and Dennis Hornsey) say that Rosine made the Paris-to-Bordeaux trip three times per week. We should not assume that she made the trip with maximum consistency and efficiency every single week during the twenty-week period she was active on the Paris-to-Bordeaux run, so the total number of evaders is probably substantially lower than twenty weeks × three trips × two evaders per trip = 120 evaders. On the other hand, Rosine was also supervising Marcelle Douard during this period, and they often made the trip together, each escorting two evaders. She also made trips to bring evaders to Paris and guided French evaders like Raymond Hermand, whose names do not usually appear in lists of Allied evaders. If her internal trips around France and French fugitives are included, it is possible that Rosine Witton guided 100 or more evaders on some part of their journey. The true number is likely lower than 100 but higher than fifty (including the sixteen in Arras and excluding any indirect assistance she provided in 1940). Testimony of Marcelle Douard, collected by F. Perroy and R. Galliard, March 5, 1946, Archives du Comité d'histoire de la Deuxième Guerre mondiale—Résistance intérieure: Mouvements, réseaux, partis politiques et syndicats, Ligne Comète, 72AJ/45; Dennis Hornsey, *The Pilot Walked Home* (London: Collins, 1946).

27. Several sources say that Rosine Witton was awarded the Croix de Guerre with bronze palm, but the citation in her IWM papers is for the silver-gilt star.

28. Private Papers of Madame R. Witton, Documents.7565, IWM; *London Gazette*, July 1, 1947; WO 208/5452 TNA; Rosine Witton Recommendation for M.B.E. (Civil), August 19, 1945, WO 208/5452 TNA.

29. Rosine Witton Citation for Medal of Freedom with Bronze Palm, "French Helper" file, NARA, RG 0498, UD 193; Private Papers of Madame R. Witton, Documents.7565, IWM; *Federal Register* 26, issues 126–144 (1961): 6434.

30. *London Gazette*, July 23, 1946; Report by Berthe Fraser, December 7, 1944, in Michael Trotobas SOE personnel file, HS9/1487/1, TNA.

31. "'Richards, Coeur de Lion': Birmingham Man as Modern 'Pimpernel'; Resistance Thriller," *Birmingham Mail*, October 2, 1944, reprinted from *La Voix du Nord*. With thanks to David Richards and family.

32. Rosine Witton "French Helper" file, NARA, RG 0498, UD 193.

33. Marcel Arrondel "French Helper" file, NARA, RG 0498, UD 193; Musée de la Résistance, Bondues, file 20.17.1, Rosine's testimony 2017.1.103.

34. Rosine moved back to Arras in the late 1960s. In 1968, she rented a "little house" at 12 Rue Grassin-Baledans in Ronville. Number 6 Route de Bapaume became a pharmacy as early as the 1950s and is still a pharmacy as of this writing. It is called "Pharmacie Wellington" after the nearby Carrière Wellington. Nazi

Persecution Claim, Rosine Leontine Witton for Sidney Albert Witton (deceased), FO 950/3423, TNA; Rosine Witton to Alfie Martin, June 18, 1969. Courtesy of Julie and Sheila Martin.

35. Nazi Persecution Claim, Rosine Leontine Witton for Sidney Albert Witton (deceased), FO 950/3423, TNA.

36. Nazi Persecution Claims, J. J. Bowdidge (FO 950/2659), Anthony Browne (FO 950/2738), TNA. With thanks to Frédéric Turner.

37. Train de Loos exhibit, MRB; Nazi Persecution Claim, Wilfred Charles Legg for Harry Legg (deceased), FO 950/4362, TNA.

38. Wilfred Charles Legg for Harry Legg (deceased), FO 950/4362, TNA.

39. Nazi Persecution Claim, George Horn, FO 950/2239, TNA.

40. Nazi Persecution Claim, E. R. Megarity for Robert Armstrong (deceased), FO 950/3602, TNA.

41. Royal Air Force Escaping Society to J. H. Garrett, May 31, 1954, Private Papers of LME Hollingdale, Documents.1545, IWM.

42. Sir Basil Embry, November 4, 1954, and Royal Air Force Escaping Society, May 31, 1954; Lucy Hollingdale to Mrs. Sutton, March 21, 1954, Private Papers of LME Hollingdale, Documents.1545, IWM.

43. Nazi Persecution Claim, Lucienne Hollingdale, FO 950/3107, TNA.

44. Sue Elliott, *I Heard My Country Calling: Elaine Madden, the Unsung Heroine of the SOE* (Stroud: The History Press, 2015).

45. Both Alfie Martin and another of Rosine's evaders, Dennis Hornsey, wrote short books about their experiences. Hornsey inscribed a copy of his 1946 memoir, *The Pilot Walked Home*, to Rosine: "To 'Madamoiselle'—Mrs. Witton—a souvenir of her heroic work in the 'Underground'—with the grateful thanks of the author." Private Papers of Madame R. Witton, Documents.7565, IWM; Charles Saville to Rosine Witton, March 3, 1946, 2017.1.162, Musée de la Résistance, Bondues.

46. Rosine Witton to Alfie Martin, February 11, 1966, and December 27, 1966. Courtesy of Julie and Sheila Martin.

47. "Cherished Medal Lost," *Ottawa Journal*, September 27, 1967, 3.

48. Douglas Hoehn to Alfie Martin, November 27, 1970; Douglas Hoehn obituary (died December 23, 2002); Millard Mack obituary (died March 12, 2013); property records of Sarasota, Florida; coverage of the Golden Apple Children's Theatre in the *Sarasota Herald Tribune*, 1970s.

49. Rosine Witton to Alfie Martin, November 3, 1967. Courtesy of Julie and Sheila Martin.

50. Rosine Witton to Lucienne D'Hallendre, August 11, 1946, 2017.1.163, Musée de la Résistance, Bondues.

51. Lucienne D'Hallendre to Jean-François Nothomb, January 24, 1946, 2017.1.91, Musée de la Résistance, Bondues.

52. Edgar D'Hallendre, *Eugène D'Hallendre: Cheminot*, MRB.

53. Avril Williams Guest House and Tea Rooms, "Ocean Villas," Auchonvillers, Somme.

54. Private Papers of Madame R. Witton, Documents.7565, IWM; Alfie Martin, *Bale Out! Escaping Occupied France with the Resistance* (Newtownards: Colourpoint Books, 2005).

55. Ben Leech to William Arnott, March 8, 1948, BML P653 CWGC.

56. Charles Abbott to John Day, August 26, 1947, BML P653 CWGC.

57. William Arnott to Ben Leech, September 8, 1948, BML P653 CWGC.

58. IWGC to Ben Leech, August 21, 1952, BML P653 CWGC.

59. Robert Lenglet, August 26, 1946, Ben Leech "French Helper" file, NARA, RG 0498, UD 193.

60. Undated, but from context, this is probably around May 1945.

61. William Arnott to AK Pallot, February 27, 1950, BML P653 CWGC.

62. CWGC/4/2/314: 314th Finance Committee Meeting, June 13, 1945.

63. CWGC/4/2/318: 318th Finance Committee Meeting, November 28, 1945.

64. Sir John J. Shute to Frederick Sillar, August 3, 1945, in notes of the 316th Finance Committee Meeting, August 15, 1945, CWGC/4/2/316.

65. IWGC to Ben Leech, June 2, 1954, BML P653 CWGC.

66. Ben Leech letter to Pollock, August 1957, BML P653 CWGC.

67. Pollock to Ben Leech, August 20, 1957, BML P653 CWGC.

68. Maurice Leech to Sherri Ottis, August 1997. Courtesy of Sherri Ottis.

69. Michael Watkins, "The Somme's Undying Echoes," *The Times* (London), June 27, 1986, 14.

INDEX